The Alternative View

A way back for the Liberal Democrats

THE
ALTERNATIVE
VIEW

A way back for
the Liberal Democrats

Lembit Öpik & Ed Joyce

Q
Queensferry
PUBLISHERS

Q
Queensferry
PUBLISHERS

Published by Queensferry Publishing Limited
Copyright © Lembit Öpik and Ed Joyce 2012
All rights Reserved.

No part of this publication may be reproduced, stored in a retrieval system, or transmitted, in any form or by any means, without the prior permission in writing of the publisher, nor be otherwise circulated in any form of binding or cover other than that in which it is published and without a similar condition including this condition being imposed on the subsequent purchaser.

Typeset by Elaine Sharples
Cover design by Steve Caplin
Photograph by Merily McGivern
Printed in Great Britain.

Queensferry Publishing Limited
145 – 157
St John Street
London
EC1V 4PW
www.queensferrypublishing.co.uk
www.alternative-view.com

ISBN 978-1-908570-01-7

*Dedicated to
every political activist
who has served the cause
of community politics*

For Endel Öpik & David Hamer

The Alternative View

A way back for the Liberal Democrats

Foreword		ix
Introduction		1
Part One		**9**
Stepping up (A brief history of the liberal movement)		
Chapter 1	Empathy and optimism (1689-1992)	11
Chapter 2	Breakthrough (1992-2008)	29
Chapter 3	One more heave (2008-2010)	55
Chapter 4	A year to deliver (2010-2011)	79
Part Two		**93**
Falling down (Liberal Democrats in coalition)		
Chapter 5	A night to remember (6 May 2011)	95
Chapter 6	Paradise lost (Alternative Vote referendum)	105
Chapter 7	Orange Bookends (Analysis of leading group)	125
Chapter 8	Muscular liberalism (Analysis of concept)	159
Chapter 9	The hollow men (Party issues)	177
Part Three		**193**
Moving on (Practical steps towards recovery)		
Chapter 10	Focus on community politics (Rebuilding the foundations)	195
Chapter 11	Focus on narrative (A Liberal worldview)	217

Chapter 12	Focus on image (Campaigning like Lib Dems)	229
Chapter 13	Focus on policy (Liberal Democrat agenda)	247
Chapter 14	Focus on leadership (Analysis of ruling team)	275
Chapter 15	Succession scenarios (Transition planning)	313
Chapter 16	Clegg's defence (In his own words)	341
Chapter 17	The way back (Steps towards recovery)	355

References 369

Appendices 393

Index 423

Foreword

In 2004, I wrote for *The Orange Book* which was aimed at reclaiming liberalism and attempted to carry its values into power. The Orange Book group became very influential, and many of its members were elevated to ministerial positions, including the Cabinet, after the formation of the coalition between the Conservatives and Lib Dems in 2010. The Orange Book also contained a number of different ideas. Over time, those who gravitated towards 'muscular liberalism' gained control and many of the values I myself wrote about were lost. Yet the urge to provide a truly liberal narrative remains. This book, co-authored by Lembit Öpik and Councillor Ed Joyce, is consistent with that aim.

As for Lembit Öpik, even the very name is complex. In one whirlwind of a human you have somebody so full of energy and contradictions, a showman but very private. Annoying, but at times brilliant. He once said to me the only things you regret in life are the things you don't do: well, he can't have many regrets then! Near-death adventures, a love life in the tabloids, a political risk-taker and a regular on shows that take him on rides through green rooms, coach trips and bush tucker trials.

But there is another side to Lembit. Loyalty and friendship don't make for TV show laughs, but his fierce support to protect Charles Kennedy – and me – during tough times shows a rare quality in a politician. He stood by his liberal values then as he does today. Behind the chat-show personality is a serious political figure and a really decent guy – for me, simply a friend. So set aside any preconceptions – read on and get to know the other side of him better, through The Alternative View.

Mark Oaten

Mark Oaten was the Liberal Democrat Member of Parliament for Winchester from 1997 to 2010. In 2004, he contributed a chapter to *The Orange Book*: 'Tough liberalism: a liberal approach to cutting crime.' He stood as a candidate for the Lib Dem leadership in 2006. In 2007, he authored *'Coalition: The politics and personalities of coalition government from 1850,'* Harriman House Publishing.

Introduction

Ultimate Survival

A summit attempt on the highest peaks takes years of planning, preparation and persistence. Then there's the financial cost, which can rise to millions – and usually has to be covered by a large and disparate group of expedition supporters. They raise cash, knowing all the time that their contributions will not take them anywhere near the mountain, let alone to its summit.

Success is also dependent on factors outside the expedition's control, such as weather, illness and luck. However, it is also intimately related to the quality of decision-making and the intuitions of the expedition leader and his deputies.

It's tough to lead in such a thin, cold atmosphere. Few people ever experience that kind of environment and even fewer are genuinely prepared for it. The weather can turn in moments. Illness can incapacitate in minutes. The team is at the mercy of even small mistakes. Individual errors can quickly propagate catastrophic difficulties for the entire party.

The harsh reality is that, at altitude, even a single careless step by just one climber can jeopardise the whole endeavour. Prospects of reaching the summit and returning safely hinge on quick, informed assessments at all times; for example, the severity of an injury has to be assessed very quickly, the risks of carrying on calculated objectively. An unfolding drama needs dispassionate

The Alternative View

analysis before it spirals into a crisis. In extremis, the decision must be made about whether pushing on exposes the party to unacceptable jeopardy.

Selflessness is key. Nobody should be permitted to continue up on the basis of sentiment. This especially applies to the leader and senior team members: they must be particularly mindful of that intoxicating state which hypoxia and ambition incubate at altitude, the nearest cousin of which at sea level is hubris. Then there's that insidious affliction known as 'summit fever' which ferments privately – and is inflamed by the mere act of 'being there'. This phenomenon has infamously prevented obstinate expedition members from stepping aside for other candidates more suited to continuing an ascent – occasionally with fatal results.

Crisis reveals a team's true character. It exposes whether the mission is a collective initiative to ensure that a summit is reached. Sometimes the analysis uncovers a less noble dynamic, where individual ambition dominates regardless of consequences. Those wedded to personal – rather than collective – success are more likely to precipitate disaster than those who subjugate personal goals to the collective interest of the party. This can determine the ultimate survival of the whole expedition.

It is not always easy to do the right thing when you are so near to achieving a goal which it has taken years, or even a lifetime, to plan for. It is a test. Those who have lived through high-altitude dilemmas also know that mountaineering offers an instructive and visceral allegory for other spheres of human experience, such as disaster relief, war and politics.

From *Helpless with Altitude*
(Reproduced with permission)

Introduction

Mountaineering for politicians

There's a man called Reinhold Messner. He's probably the greatest mountaineer who ever lived. He was the first man ever to scale the 14 highest mountains of the world – those with peaks exceeding 8,000 metres – and he did many of these alone. On 20 August 1980, he also achieved the first solo ascent of Everest – without oxygen.[1] He's one of a kind.

Everybody else needs a team.

So it is with politics. Very occasionally, one or two independent-minded British politicians, like Martin Bell or Richard Taylor, make it into Parliament on the basis of a single campaign or cause. They make their mark and move on. These people represent a vital strand in politics. However, as with virtually all solo ascents to power, they cannot scale a very high peak – and rarely remain at the summit for very long. *For that you need a team.* That's where political parties come in.

Parties do not exist for the personal convenience of individuals but for the collective benefit of a group with a shared narrative and philosophy. The extent to which this group seeks to serve others varies, in large part determined by the world view, or 'narrative,' of the party in question. However, there is an accepted, if informal, law of political physics. In political parties, if you don't run for it together you won't run anything much at all.

Stepping up

It took 20 years for the Liberal Democrats to find the surefootedness to scale the summit of government... and just one year to lose it. The sudden and dramatic reversal in the fortunes of the 'third party' in so short a time was no shock to independent observers. But it was a great shock to Liberal Democrat activists and members.

For over half a century, the Liberal Democrats – and previously the Liberal party – had patiently soldiered on, building camp after camp, in a stoic team effort to negotiate the steep inclines which lay between it and power. Sometimes they suffered reversals at the hands of some political avalanche or other which carried them back down again. On other occasions, they appeared to make great progress only to be overwhelmed by a freak change in political weather, making further progress temporarily impossible. At no time did this stoic clan give up.

At about this time a small band of parliamentarians inside the Liberal Democrats got together and wrote a book. The front depicted a woman on a step ladder painting the book's cover orange: it was called... *The Orange Book*. The subtitle announced that the book was all about 'reclaiming liberalism'.[2] Two years later, they wrote another book. Four MPs wrote for both books. All four ended up serving on the Cabinet at some point. This time the front showed a man overpainting Prime Minister Tony Blair's face with that same orange hue. This volume was entitled *Britain After Blair*.[3] It was the final act in establishing the Orange Bookers as a well defined and exclusive 'caucus' within the Liberal Democrats.

Two years later, the Orange Bookers were running the party.

And then it happened. In 2010, a small band of Liberal Democrats finally reached the political summit of government. This victory was bought at the cost of teaming up with another rival expedition. Tories and Liberal Democrats knew that they could not escape the mathematical reality of a hung Parliament. Both conceded that neither could make it alone. An unlikely partnership between two ideological adversaries was brokered. This was the price of power.

The Lib Dem team, from the ground up, celebrated. Most members had no chance of serving in government themselves – and never would. But they enjoyed their achievement 'by proxy' and felt pride that, somehow, the movement had finally come in from the political cold to enter government, after almost a century in the wilderness of opposition.

Introduction

Falling down

As sometimes happens at the heady altitude of real authority, the political weather seemed to change quickly, apparently catching the Liberal Democrat contingent off guard. As the winds of public disenchantment rose to a howl, activists, who had spent decades building the staging camps for the ascent to office, looked up in horror to see an avalanche bury years of painstaking investment. Hope of electoral reform – at least in the short term – was also lost in the turmoil.

The prospect of fairer votes – the one summit that truly *had* to be conquered in the eyes of the Liberal Democrat membership – had been key to convincing sceptical members to support the coalition between Conservatives and Lib Dems. This consent had not been a foregone conclusion: the inconclusive outcome of the 2010 general election had offered, at least theoretically, various arrangements in the eyes of those who doubted the wisdom of an alliance with their political arch-rivals. Furthermore, the electoral reform on offer – Alternative Vote or 'AV' – was not the party's preferred option. Lib Dems were wedded to the Single Transferable Vote (STV) system.

Across a period of negotiation, the consensus gravitated towards the view that some change was better than none, and far more attractive than the existing first past the post (FPTP) system which, for decades, had hindered the Liberals – and then the Liberal Democrats – from making significant progress at the polls. That old system overtly favoured Conservatives and Labour. Thus, a referendum on reform was a necessary condition to seal the Conservative-Liberal Democrat coalition.

The decisive defeat in the AV referendum rang a death knell for electoral reform for British general elections in the medium term. Within days of this defeat, rank-and-file activists began to talk openly of their concerns about the great reversals in the party's performance. Others questioned the value of supporting a

Conservative-led Government. The debacle made public a – till then – privately conducted, and unstructured, debate about the price of being in the Cabinet, with some even calling for the leader, Nick Clegg, to consider his position.

Candidates who had lost their seats added their voices to constitutional enthusiasts who had also seen their hopes dashed by the harsh realities of the ballot box. A palpable loss of morale added to a lost sense of direction. Yet the objectors were also without direction. Within the party, there was a need for reassurance from the leadership. May 2011 left others feeling as if the movement was touching the void of oblivion once again.

Moving on

The alternative view evaluates the key factors which influenced the movement's transition from opposition to government. We assess events which recently shaped the party's fortunes following that shift, including questions about what the Orange Bookers stand for as a unit: what their narrative truly is. And we offer a pathway to recovery – a way back to electoral success.

We assert that Lib Dems do not need to profoundly review the political structures to recover their position. This is not where the failure lies. The alternative view is that the challenge indeed resides within the leadership, that they are responsible for ensuring a robust and easily accessible narrative that underpins everything the party does. We argue that the large-scale loss of seats at a local level endangers the campaigning strength of the entire movement. Without a local base, the capacity to conduct community politics becomes gravely weakened. The viability of the party as a strong national force is compromised, reducing its ability to gain – or even hold – parliamentary seats; this is a core consideration because the leadership in 2011 reasserted a key measure of its electoral success to be the doubling of the party's MPs compared to the 2005 result.

They had also specifically marked the next general election after

Introduction

May 2010 as the time by which they would achieve this. The leadership had therefore committed itself to a very clear numerical goal: winning a total of at least 124 seats in or before 2015 – the most likely date for the next general election.

The alternative view offers a route map to recovery to halt the contraction of the party, across challenging years for the organisation and its grassroots supporters. We outline the pressures which could precipitate its fracture into rival factions – and what might prevent this from occurring.

Underlying this analysis is the proposition that action must be taken to establish a clear narrative, a focus on a collective world vision rather than on personal interests or individual ambitions. Otherwise, decline and fragmentation are inevitable.

All our observations arise directly from our research. They are rational action steps, and some of these have difficult implications for the leadership which follow consequentially from our analysis; however, this was not our primary purpose. The alternative view's primary concern is the advancement of the core values of a movement which thousands of activists have spent many years promoting.

If the leadership of the party – the Orange Bookers – do not acknowledge and act upon these demonstrable home truths it will lead either to the temporary reversal of the movement's electoral fortunes or to the removal of the current leadership. We explain why, in any event, the leadership is likely to change through one of five scenarios before 2015 – which itself is the very longest time for which Nick Clegg will continue as leader. We suggest that the leader is in the best position to steer the movement towards a managed, rather than a chaotic, transition, and that he should take that opportunity, which diminishes as an option from 2014 onwards.

In May 2011, the movement lost 25 years' worth of local government progress in just one night. The alternative view's purpose is to reverse this, and help safeguard a narrative which is bigger than any individual exponent – at any level – in the party. We believe that the interests of citizens are best served by the collective advancement of a traditional liberal vision.

The purpose of the alternative view is to contribute to the re-establishment and furtherance of a liberal narrative – as defined by the rank and file – for the political security of the party and for the long-term benefit of the country. We explain why the heart of that recovery must be the theory and practice of community politics.

If our assessment is correct, the political necessity for the leadership seems clear. They must now alter course and generate a consistent, resonant liberal agenda which attracts back the party's lost support; and it needs to happen at a local level. Essentially, as their campaigning focus – and political vision – becomes the subject of scrutiny, the Orange Book leadership faces a choice: reclaim liberalism, or leave it to those who can.

Part 1

Stepping Up

*When Labour sang 'the only way is up' I
remember thinking, 'Really?
Try being a Lib Dem.'*

Councillor Peter Maughan,
Liberal Democrat parliamentary candidate,
1992, 1997, 2001 & 2005[1]

Chapter 1

Empathy and Optimism (1689 to 1992)

This is a late parrot.
Margaret Thatcher, 12 October 1990

To understand where the Liberal Democrats are now, it is necessary to understand why the Liberal Democrats 'are' at all. There are many learned works on the subject, and here we dwell on the past only as much as is necessary to provide a relevant perspective on matters which matter to challenges facing liberalism today.

A few centuries ago something very terrible happened to the working public. Back then, a large number of open fields were enclosed under a series of acts. As part of this 'land grab,' existing rights of local people to work the land were effectively removed. This included the right to graze animals and cut hay.[2] The iconic writer and social commentator George Orwell summarised the change in these acerbic terms:

> Stop to consider how the so-called owners of the land got hold of it. They simply seized it by force, afterwards hiring lawyers to provide them with title-deeds. In the case of the enclosure of

the common lands, which was going on from about 1600 to 1850, the land-grabbers did not even have the excuse of being foreign conquerors; they were quite frankly taking the heritage of their own countrymen, upon no sort of pretext except that they had the power to do so.[3]

An anonymous poem from the era puts the point succinctly:

The law doth punish man or woman
That steals the goose from off the common,
But lets the greater felon loose
That steals the common from the goose.

As the land was taken away, one seed germinated: a small movement in reaction to the land grab. It was nurtured and cultivated by virtue of two endearing and noble human characteristics: empathy and optimism. A group of educated and philanthropic individuals observed what had gone on and felt an intuitive sense of common cause with the plight of their fellow citizens. They felt encouraged about the prospect of developing a political agenda which protected the interests of all people, without persecuting or disadvantaging individuals, groups or communities in the process. These were the beginnings of modern liberalism.

The instincts that drive liberalism also find roots in the struggle between the monarchy and Parliament. This struggle sent ripples through the minds of those absorbed by questions relating to the power of the ordinary person to influence decisions which affected them but were made from high above and far away. One person who was inspired to consider these matters back in the 1600s was a son of Puritan parents, John Locke. He was the first to observe the human condition in ways which reasonably closely resemble the movement today. It is for this reason that Locke is rightly known as the 'father of liberalism'.[4]

Empathy and Optimism

Although philosophy doesn't always seem terribly relevant to our daily lives, in Locke's case it mattered – a lot. A difference of views between Mr Locke and a contemporary thinker by the name of Hobbes lies at the heart of the matter. Hobbes depressingly observed that life in the state of nature was 'solitary, poor, nasty, brutish, and short.'[5] Curiously, he then went on to use this to argue the case for the absolute power of the monarch.[6]

By contrast, Locke viewed the state of nature very differently, and in tones rather more optimistic and, it can be said, more empathic to those who did not happen to enjoy the benefit of a royal connection or title:

> To properly understand political power and trace its origins, we must consider the state that all people are in naturally. That is a state of perfect freedom of acting and disposing of their own possessions and persons as they think fit within the bounds of the law of nature. People in this state do not have to ask permission to act or depend on the will of others to arrange matters on their behalf. The natural state is also one of equality in which all power and jurisdiction is reciprocal and no one has more than another.[7]

These words must have been refreshing to people weary of the oppression of their day-to-day existence, who had long harboured a faint dream of a little more freedom – a little more hope – in their troubled lives.

Sometimes, miracles do happen. As far as ordinary people were concerned the English Revolution of 1688, which overthrew King James II and finally ceded power to Parliament, was a great change in the order of politics. The establishment of a constitutional monarchy effectively removed political power from the monarch and put Parliament in control.[8] This permanently limited the powers of monarchs, who, on occasion, were prone to dictatorial rule. It also opened the door to the eventual practice of blaming MPs for much that was wrong in the lives of citizens with little regard for whether or not these accusations were justified – a feature of political life which has haunted Members of Parliament ever since.

For citizens, there was more good news. The subsequent Bill of Rights in 1689 gave Parliament all tax-raising powers and strengthened freedom of speech. It even gave the elected government the exclusive right to maintain a standing army in peacetime.[9] This was a welcome relief to a population which had regularly endured the slings and arrows of warmongering barons, who pursued their territorial and material ambitions ruthlessly and with scant regard for the population caught up in the fray. The Bill also laid the basis for modern parliamentary democracy. It was strengthened further by reform acts which extended suffrage – the vote – throughout the 19th century. Thus, two centuries after the first stirrings of modern liberalism, some of John Locke's ideas were becoming enshrined in the fabric of British political structures. Eventually, suffrage was extended even more broadly, but progress was achingly slow in the eyes of reformists hungry to achieve greater equality for citizens of the country, regardless of their financial or social standing.

In fact, to say that all of this took time is to greatly *understate* the length of the process. There was a lot to put right after many centuries of feudal rule, made worse by the concentration of land and power. In a sense, this process is still going on. After all, the widening of freedoms for the public at large has been a key dynamic of politics over the whole period from the 1830s – when further significant reforms were made – to the present day.

It is vital to grasp the importance of the question of land ownership – the 'land grab' – throughout this entire process. This 'enclosure' caused a crisis amongst the poor and disenfranchised. Until then, the less wealthy at least enjoyed the benefit of small plots of land, which provided a guaranteed opportunity to, for example, grow their own food and perhaps even generate small quantities of tradable produce.

Then, with the advent of new farming techniques, the powerful used their power to take the land into their own hands. Land was de facto confiscated by the upper echelons of society, leaving the least empowered with no underlying land-based support mechanism. It was this which led directly to the Poor Laws, themselves the progenitor of the Welfare State. Despite the romanticism associated with it, the harsh reality is that the latter was at least in part a logical development from more rudimentary support structures introduced as compensation for the emphatic redistribution of land to the most wealthy. It was, after all, expedient to avoid a revolution, and some kind of replacement for the land was therefore in the interests of the empowered. After all, there remained an imperative to ensure that the least wealthy continued to be capable of tending to the basic systems necessary to keep the upper classes in comfort. This was key to ensuring that the industrial base of the British Empire worked effectively at home and abroad.

Antipathy towards the 'land grab' attitude has been at the heart of the motivations for liberals through the ages to seek more egalitarian solutions to the inequalities of society than their traditional Conservative opponents. A look at manifesto documents from 1959 indicates how little had changed in this regard right up to around 2008 – only the terminology had altered, and not much at that:

> We must have more Liberals in Parliament and Local Government for the sake of honest, aboveboard politics. We must have Liberals to raise these Liberal issues. The Conservative Party is clearly identified in the minds of the electors with employers and big business, and they cannot deal objectively or fairly with the problems continually arising

between employer and employee. The Labour Party is in the hands of the Trade Union Leaders. The return of a Socialist Government inevitably means that management is put on the defensive, for it does not know what is going to hit it next. The return of a Conservative Government means that the Trade Unions feel justified in going on to the offensive. The whole nation is the loser from this crazy line up of power politics, and those who lose most in the struggle are those who live on fixed incomes, such as old age pensioners and a host of others who are solicited at Election time but are forgotten after the result is declared. A Liberal vote is a protest against the British political system being divided up between two powerful Party machines, one largely financed by the employers and the other by the Trade Unions.[10]

In 1964 sentiments specifically relating to land were emphasised:

Liberals will... abolish the present unfair system of rating and replace it with a scheme based on site value rating. This would encourage development and better use of land, lower the burden of rates on the householder and ensure that the community shares in any rise in land values.[11]

This historical context is important today because the inequitable distribution of land, property and – crucially – opportunity continues to represent the difference between conservative-minded rulers and liberal-minded ones. The significance of fairness, tolerance and redistribution continues to lie at the heart of mainstream liberal thinking, with 'The Land' remaining the nearest thing to an anthem for the Party in the 21st century: 'why should we be beggars with a ballot in our hand?'[12] remains a clarion cry at Liberal Democrat events, and at the traditional social gathering on the last evening of their federal conferences (see Appendix 1).

For the avoidance of doubt, it is important to recognise that the ownership of land is not an end in itself. Rather, it encapsulates the inequalities in the distribution of wealth – the driver at the heart of the ethical dispute which split the Tories and Liberals of yore. The extent to which this is still the dividing line is a key element in the analysis of where the Lib Dems stand now, a significant and enduring counterpoint to the outlook of Conservatives and Labour.

Liberals versus Conservatives

Back in the very early days, in the midst of all this change, the Liberal Party was formally established in 1859. If liberals then are similar to liberals now, they were doubtless spurred on by an unshakable conviction that writing leaflets, knocking on doors and making earnest speeches would sort out British society within, say, four or five years. Liberals have thought in this way ever since.

This warmth of spirit and philosophical largesse puts liberals in direct conflict with those primarily motivated by self-interest as well as by concerns about the wellbeing of the relatively wealthy and empowered in society. This category of people gravitated long ago to a movement which has led directly to the existence of the modern-day Conservative Party. At the heart of British politics lies the age-old struggle between two movements which, as collectives, have different core purposes: the alternative view suggests that one was founded on the ideal of improving the lot of all people, while the other existed primarily to protect the interests of its own social grouping.

Following the enfranchisement of the general worker, a political pressure grew for meaningful political concern for the interests of the industrial force which kept Britain going. This was the key dynamic behind the creation of the fully-fledged welfare state. Lloyd George and Winston Churchill, labelled the 'Terrible Twins,'[13] produced a powerfully argued case for a new welfare state in the 'People's Budget' in 1909. This used the ideas of Henry George to use land taxes to pay for financial benefits to the whole population, paid equally: a means-tested guaranteed income for those aged over 70[14], paid for by a tax on high incomes[15] and land[16] – including that which had changed hands as a result of the enclosures, or 'land grab'.

With a typically unsurprising flourish of self-interest, the Conservatives argued that funds should be supplied by a tariff on imports, which – naturally – would have benefited landowners. They used their majority in the House of Lords to block the budget. They were then able to remove land taxes from the budget. Thus, although the Liberal welfare reforms were introduced, they were ultimately funded by income tax, a much less radical arrangement than might otherwise have been the case.

The architects of the welfare state were unquestionably motivated by a liberal-minded intent. Still, the likes of Beverage and Bevan identified with a need to provide it precisely because of an ongoing and debilitating vacuum – precisely because of the uneven distribution of land and therefore wealth. The vacuum had only partially been filled by the state's arrangements for the support of citizens in need at the time. However, it is worth noting that even the establishment of the welfare state was stiffly opposed by the Conservative Party. This obstinacy has frequently resurfaced in the intervening years, particularly during the era of Conservative Prime Minister Margaret Thatcher. It is consistently reflected in the anti-Tory suspicions of many in the working base. It was summarised by a Labour supporter in summer 2011 in Peckham during a local by-election, who exclaimed to the unsuspecting Liberal Democrat canvasser:

> the Tories still think that if you can't make it on your own you're either a burden which has to be managed as cheaply as possible, or an indolent ['so and so' – this is a euphemism] scrounging off the hardworking poor rich people.[17]

A tacit scepticism towards welfare benefits has characterised a contemporary Conservative prime minister, David Cameron. In April 2011 he questioned the legitimacy of providing disability payments to heavy drinkers and the obese.[18] In July 2008, two years before he would become prime minister, the Tory leader rejected the concept of 'moral neutrality'. Cameron went on to say

> We talk about people being 'at risk of obesity' instead of talking about people who eat too much and take too little exercise... We talk about people being at risk of poverty, or social exclusion: it's as if these things — obesity, alcohol abuse, drug addiction — are purely external events like a plague or bad weather. Of course, circumstances — where you are born, your neighbourhood, your school and the choices your parents make — have a huge impact. But social problems are often the consequence of the choices people make.[19]

In another article, in the tabloid *The Sun* on the same day, the headline read: 'David Cameron Blasts Druggies,' adding:

> Tory chief David Cameron visits an estate – and declares drug addicts, obese people, and the poor often have no one to blame but themselves.[20]

The Conservative love of absolutist rather than relativist or morally neutral values has been a recurring theme. As we shall see, it even gave birth to a new definition: 'muscular liberalism,' which we will examine in greater detail later.

In the years before and after the 2010 general election there was little sign of any real change in the character of these Conservative pronouncements. For example, in October 2011, Home Secretary Theresa May continued the general theme in regard to reversing legislation – this time relating to citizen's rights. The Tory-supporting *Sun* proudly and enthusiastically reported:

> May: Scrap the Human Rights Act. Home Secretary calls for hated laws to be axed... Theresa May risked angering the Lib Dems by calling for the hated Human Rights Act to be axed last night. Mrs May said she would 'personally' like to see it go because of the problems it has caused. Her comments will endear her to many infuriated by foreign terrorists, killers and rapists who use the law to avoid deportation.[21]

While liberals would tend to take a diametrically opposite view, Cameron's and May's comments were not surprising. They reflected a typically Conservative outlook on personal responsibility and human rights, and their words resonated with conservative-minded voters. However, their observations also highlighted stark differences between liberal and conservative thinking. It was entirely consistent with the Tories' Darwinist outlook on society: if you can't make it on your own, you are a problem which, ideally, can be dealt with in some fashion that requires the minimum of intervention or investment from the state. And if you experience social or health problems, there is a fair chance that these are, in fact, your own fault.

It has been suggested that benefits have been used by previous Tory administrations for expedient political ends – at variance with a liberal view that the state ought to empower individuals to make the most of their abilities and circumstances by genuinely nurturing their capacity to help themselves. For example, there is a school of thought that points to a murky genesis for the allowance made available for those unable to work due to incapacity. Disability Living Allowance (DLA) was established in the days of Margaret Thatcher's highly polarising administration. It was regarded by some as an attempt to divert large numbers of people who would otherwise have been included in the already high unemployment statistics onto another list, to keep the jobless totals at an artificially lower level.

Empathy and Optimism

As recently as 28 July 2011, Declan Gaffney, part of the 'Left Foot Forward' group and a writer for the *Guardian* newspaper, commented:

> It is well known that sickness and disability benefits were extensively used in the 1980s and 90s by the UK and other governments to encourage some unemployed workers – especially older male industrial workers – to leave the labour market.[22]

A large number of informal websites in 2011 took a similar view, and hold that Thatcher's administration used DLA in this way. If so, the fact that the Tories now lament the inevitable consequences of the DLA system would be a classic example of political turkeys coming home to roost.

Given the difference that we observe towards values, outlook on human empowerment and policies, it is hardly surprising that there have been so many skirmishes across the ages between the two historic adversaries, liberalism and conservatism. Occasionally, efforts have been made by liberals to reason with Tories. At local and less often national levels, liberal-minded organisations have sought to work with more conservative ones. There is a built-in tension in these arrangements, because traditional liberals and conservatives approach social, political and economic issues from a different starting point in terms of how these competing value systems wish to structure human society.

In many cases, the tensions arise from a profoundly different viewpoint regarding human nature. For example, Tories seek to tackle poverty by incentivising wealthy entrepreneurs with tax cuts, prompting them to work harder, expand their businesses and thus create jobs for the poor. This has been a recurring Conservative mantra, and one which deeply influences their policies on matters such as taxation. Liberals tackle poverty by redistributing the value of natural resources such as land and ensuring that the inequalities which enslave the poor are addressed through state-managed redistribution of wealth. This difference of view lay at the heart of resurgent calls from many Conservative MPs, in 2011, for a reduction in the 50% top rate of tax paid by the wealthiest members of society. This angered many in the Liberal Democrats for exactly the same reason that it angered their political forefathers across three centuries. It symbolised an ideological dispute which was older than any of its protagonists.

From a party management perspective, conservative elements have occasionally tried to laugh the Liberals out of existence. At those times, they portrayed Liberals as not a serious movement... or at the very least one which they need not take seriously. On 12 October 1990 Thatcher famously made a speech at the Tory Party Conference in which she ridiculed the new 'Bird of Freedom' logo introduced by the newly reconstituted Liberal Democrats at the time. The Liberal movement was struggling with very low poll ratings and Thatcher took the opportunity to undermine the fledgling Lib Dem party's credibility as a major force in British politics. Her weapon of choice was a sketch from the cult alternative comedy series *Monty Python*, which she paraphrased to the delight of the Tory delegates:

> I will say only this of the Liberal Democrat symbol, and of the party it symbolises: this is an ex-parrot. It is not merely stunned, it has ceased to be, expired and gone to meet its maker. It is a parrot no more. It has run down the curtain and joined the choir invisible. This is a late parrot.[23]

The audience laughed their heads off with glee, and her words entered public parlance for years. Incidentally, it is ironic to note that John Cleese himself, the architect of the *Monty Python* sketch which Thatcher had so effectively plagiarised, was himself a Liberal

Democrat and appeared in a number of events and broadcasts to promote the liberal cause.[24]

Promoting the irrelevance of the Liberal movement through jocular speeches was a relatively light example of the Conservative outlook on the third party. Electoral evidence, which we shall analyse in later sections, indicates that Tory animosity towards Liberals went far deeper. The evidence indicates that the active desire to overwhelm liberalism would be ongoing even while the Conservatives governed Britain with their Liberal Democrat partners.

At times when the Conservatives have governed as a majority party, the divergence between Liberal and Conservative approaches has been starkly displayed in the enactment of policy. In the 1980s liberals, and indeed much of society, watched helplessly as Conservatives went about rearranging the cultural, economic and social furniture to suit the wealthier, the more able and the powerful in Britain – frequently at the cost of the poorest and the least empowered. Many felt that the Tories' dogmatic admiration for privatisation was a case in point. For example, Pat Thane, Leverhulme Professor of Contemporary British History at the University of London, submitted the following evidence to the House of Commons Health Committee's inquiry into the provision of social care in October 2009. Referring to policies implemented during the period of Thatcher's rule, she wrote:

> Local authorities found it increasingly difficult to provide affordable care with the funding available to them. The number of private sector residential homes grew from 18,800 in 1975 to 119,900 in 1990. Until 1980 voluntary sector homes received public funding from local authorities in addition to means-tested payments by the residents themselves. From 1980, means-tested board-and-lodging supplementary benefit allowances became available for residents of all independent-sector homes, which encouraged the expansion of the private sector.

> By the late 1980s, services were increasingly targeted on the most disabled to cut costs, and by 1990 it was becoming difficult for older and disabled people to access help with tasks such as shopping and cleaning... There was evidence of much unmet need.[25]

Liberals feared that the longer the rightwing rulers remained in power, the more the country would diverge from the liberal ideals of empowering and caring for the most vulnerable. Liberals empathised with the oppressed masses while remaining emphatically optimistic that things *would* be turned around in due course – that brighter times *would* come – as long as the liberal home fires were kept burning. It is this unfathomable resilience against adversity which has provided the liberal movement with the stamina to survive as a functioning entity. This is all the more creditable across a century which, for the most part, served the liberal cause with a diet of spoiling tactics cooked up by its competitors and served up on an electoral system which primarily benefited Conservatives and Labour at the cost of the liberal movement's fortunes. An indication of the expedience of the resistance to electoral change amongst the Tory movement is found in the 1970s. Conservatives did in fact win more *votes* than Labour in the first general election of February 1974, but Labour won more *seats*.[26] However, the Tories concluded that first past the post was still a preferable arrangement for the party – they were willing to wait till this system again favoured them in a future election. It did so handsomely in 1979 – and in the three elections after that too – providing them with more than half the seats for less than half the votes in four consecutive elections, enabling them to govern the country alone for 18 years.[27]

Liberals versus Labour

The other great hindrance to liberalism was Labour's progress as a party in the 20th century. As the Left organised itself into a credible mass-membership organisation with intimate trade union links the Liberals watched on, apparently impotent to act to stem this challenge to a part of their support base. The movement paid the price electorally, declining dramatically from 1923 onwards to a tiny fraction of its size during the halcyon days of Lloyd George's radical and reforming Liberal government in the early years of the 20th century. The party's lowest ebb occurred between 1951 and 1964 and again from 1970 to 1974. Across those two lean periods the party mustered a compliment of only six MPs.[28] The old joke that the Liberal Parliamentary Party could fit into a single London taxi was not true – unless one of them sat next to the driver in the space usually reserved for luggage.

Ironically, the existence of Labour assisted the Tories greatly. Labour and Liberal candidates split the left-leaning vote, providing a continuous fillip to the Conservatives' electoral performance by default. In 17 out of the 18 elections held since 1945, the 'Liberal plus Labour' number of votes exceeded those secured by the Conservatives. Out of all the postwar elections, only in 1955 did the Tories outpoll the 'Labour plus Liberal' vote, and even then only by the tiniest of margins: 0.5%.[29]

The assumption here is, of course, that most Labour voters in these elections would have preferred to vote Liberal rather than Conservative. It is very likely that this is a view also taken by the Tories, who formally opposed the concept of a reform to the electoral system. If it reunified the left-leaning vote, it would compromise the electoral fortunes of the Conservatives – potentially permanently. Electoral ballots held under systems where votes are transferred have tended to suggest that the Tories read the situation correctly. For instance, we can see this dynamic in the election of a Liberal Democrat mayor in Bedford in May 2011, carried out under a proportional representation system. Even on an evening where the party had suffered heavy losses across the land, the transfer of votes in Bedford showed that the great majority of left-leaning voters chose the Lib Dem Dave Hodgson – and not the Conservative – as their 'second preference'.[30] Hodgson was a highly popular individual and clearly this was sufficient to overcome the general resistance to voting Liberal Democrat on a difficult night for the party.

Given the evidence of the 20th century, it was peculiar that the Labour movement itself had never seemed willing to enthusiastically back a change that could have consigned the Right to opposition for the long term. This could have vastly improved Labour's patchy record of winning enough seats to govern the country, though they would, on the whole, probably have had to share power in a coalition. There is no certainty that the Liberals would necessarily have agreed to play at partnership with Labour throughout this period with any consistency – if, indeed, they had even won enough seats to be able to form a partnership. The Liberals tended to back electoral reform, which they believed to be right for society, even though this reduced the chances of the liberal movement ever governing alone again, as it had in the radical days of the early 20th century. At only six MPs, they had rather less to lose. Nevertheless, the Conservatives and Labour were very happy to sustain an electoral system which kept Liberals very much on the sidelines. It is fair to say that, on the particular question of electoral reform, for Liberals the road to hell was paved with *other parties'* bad intentions.

Labour informally conspired with Conservatives to maintain an electoral system which favoured them both at the cost of the Liberal Democrats for decades. The alternative view nevertheless holds that there is a more natural association between traditional liberals and traditional Labour supporters. This is not immediately obvious, nor an intuitive conclusion.

A comparison of the core reasons for which the two movements exist points to it. Both parties are concerned about the plight of the disempowered. Both are committed to attempting to increase the strength of the ordinary citizen in regard to the 'ruling classes,' though definitions of what this means vary in nuance. Both actively seek to protect the least advantaged from the ravages of poverty. This is a difference in emphasis from the Conservative ethos which seeks success for individuals and the country through personal ambition. To quote from the Conservative community mission statement:

> We believe in enterprise and aspiration... Personal ambition should be set as high as is humanly possible, with no barriers put in its way by the state.[31]

At a Westminster parliamentary level, Labour's efforts to give voice to the voiceless nevertheless sought to exclude Liberals from national government – with only an incomplete and asymmetric alliance between the two as an act of expedience in the late 1970s. This grudging standoffishness between Labour and Liberals effectively helped the Tories stay in office far more often than would otherwise have been the case.

Seeds for a breakthrough

In the 1990s Labour embarked on a journey which took its leadership towards a more right-leaning agenda. Tony Blair's New Labour aligned his party more closely to the Conservative image, and thus made it easier for disenchanted Tory voters to make a smaller jump from Conservative to New Labour in order to oust a very unpopular Tory administration. While this shift to the right had harmed his popularity amongst more traditional Labour members, Blair's electoral success insulated him from any actionable challenge by his membership.

A debate ensued regarding the relative positioning of the Liberal Democrats at this time. There was consideration of whether the Liberal party had, thanks to the 'Toryfication' of Labour under Blair, become the most leftwing of the three by default. The argument was, in large part, irrelevant to the electorate. Faced with a choice between Labour, Conservative and Liberal Democrat candidates, the public could tell the difference for themselves, and, if they were indeed to do so, were more than capable of voting for non-Tory candidates.

Despite Labour's rightward shift, Labour and Liberal Democrat parties would be prepared to align themselves informally against the Conservatives for one great push against the Tories. This was only possible because of the relatively good interaction between the two party leaders Blair and Ashdown, plus a sense that, in different ways, both of these parties shared an empathy for the public despair at the Conservative Government.

Summary

In 1997 a rift that had lasted for a century would briefly be healed, as two parties limbered up to a common conservative enemy – one that the liberal movement had been competing with for even longer than Labour had existed. A unique confluence of circumstances would lay the way for dramatic events leading to a great breakthrough for the Liberal Democrats in May 1997.

For the party, this would be a watershed election. But they still had to make it through 1990, and some precarious years in which the liberal movement came dangerously close to acting out the mocking parody of Thatcher's dead parrot.

Chapter 2

Breakthrough (1992 to 2008)

In all of this the interests of the party have to come first. That is where my personal, political and constitutional duty lies.

Charles Kennedy, 7 January 2006

In keeping with the general travails of the liberal movement, its most recent journey towards power has been an arduous one. This long march has exacted a painful toll on those who have patiently kept faith with faltering progress. Liberalism's unheralded ambassadors have waged a local war of hope along the streets of Britain come sun, rain, sleet and snow. Armed only with leaflets and information about electors generated by inkjet printer cartridges, their paperwork had a habit of running when dampened by drizzle, so that patiently acquired data would fade into smudges staining the canvassers' fingers at the end of the night. But they just got on with it, regardless of personal gain.

Yet the suffering was not reserved for the foot-soldiers alone. From the most humble local activist – whose reward for a year of effort was little more than a plastic cup of medium white wine out of a box after the last local party meeting before Christmas – to those at the very top of the party, hardship was never far away. At least one leader, who delivered the best consistent general election growth since Lloyd George, was repaid with a coup by his own colleagues, forcing his sudden resignation.

By and large, the life and progression of the movement were not bought at the cost of any dilution in its ideology. British liberals in the latter part of the 20th century held on firmly and proudly to the values and policy aspirations which the movement had cherished for longer than anyone could remember. However, its failure to expand in a parliamentary sense reflected the Liberals' tendency to organise their thinking and statements in a 'worthy' fashion which resonated with the party faithful – but not in a form which energised the British electorate. As a result, the Tory and Labour parties, with simpler propositions and a willingness to take a more pragmatic approach to their presentation of ideas, tended to win out.

Even a brief and dramatic alliance between two parties, the Liberals and the SDP, in the 1980s, caused little more than a short-lived uplift in the fortunes of the liberal movement. This colourful turn of events created only a brief spike in their poll ratings, before the political order settled back to roughly the same levels as before. Others have written in detail of these events and we need not duplicate their contributions here.

During recent decades, Tory and Labour strategists enjoyed the 'double whammy' of a press which generally preferred to divide itself in a binary, rather than tripartite, fashion according to traditional left-right party lines. After all, the electoral system overtly favoured the larger two parties. It was a lot more straightforward for the media to reflect this, rather than to make the extra effort to try to 'triangulate' their coverage. After all, the three corners of a triangle are more complicated to draw in words on a newspaper page than a straight line between left and right.

Breakthrough

In this period of limbo, unless members of the centre party provoked some kind of creative, amusing or salacious story, there was only a fleeting chance of attention by the media. This was hardly surprising. Labour's relatively radical agenda in its formative years in the early 20th century had attracted former liberal supporters who had become unimpressed with the Liberal party for various reasons. This was partly the Liberals' own fault, since they had drifted into the domain of being an 'establishment' party.

A worthy but lacklustre 'marketing' approach and an inability to appeal to the mass public turned out to be nearly fatal to the continued existence of the Liberals in those long dark years between the late 1940s and the early 1970s. This malaise persisted with only occasional flashes of brightness, all of which turned out to be disappointing false dawns.

The most recent period of nemesis for liberalism came in 1989-1990. In those wilderness years, the movement's support virtually disappeared, with levels of public backing so febrile that they could hardly be measured by pollsters. Only the plucky resolve of a small, but dedicated, band of liberal-minded stalwarts sustained the party through this period of financial and political uncertainty – as its very future hung in the balance.

Even in 1990, at this point of lowest ebb, a trickle of idealistic and optimistic new members signed up. They did so for various eclectic and diverse reasons. Many exhausted activists were retiring from the front line, leaving politics altogether or paying their dues and remaining silent about their affiliation, as if to admit that to be in the party was to invite patronising ridicule. The derision stirred up by the foes of liberalism – especially the Conservatives, who briefly made it fashionable to aspire to great wealth and a 'greed is good' mindset – meant that there was almost a stigma to being a Liberal Democrat. Backers were virtually made to feel that admitting this political leaning was a weakness in one's judgement – perhaps an indication of the need for some kind of personal counselling.

As the party barely registered on the British political radar, this ignominious position created a somewhat unexpected and intriguing renaissance in political thinking within the organisation's policymaking processes. Those keeping the liberal home fires burning exercised the freedom to speak both idealistically and boldly of their agenda. There was no pressure to conform, because the party did not find itself constrained with an overbearing mass of conformists set on converging the movement's thoughts and actions towards what might loosely be called the mainstream. There was no pull back to the moderate centre by peer group pressure, because the peer group survived only as a result of its insuppressibly positive dreams of liberalism. This phenomenon displayed itself in the party's 1992 manifesto, which was loaded with worthy ideas and great solutions which few people read.[1]

1992

Given the state of the party in 1990, the continued existence of the movement is a tribute to optimism. A dedicated rump fought hard to save the Lib Dems from extinction. Meetings of Liberal Democrats discussed the future more than the present. New members were almost immediately given official posts in the party, almost as a sign of gratitude that they bothered to turn up at all.

The 1992 general election result was not an impressive highpoint. After it, party leader Paddy Ashdown debriefed the Federal Executive, the committee with responsibility for the governance of the organisation: he said that the party held roughly the same number of seats as it had held before the election. This was, to an extent, spin. It had, in fact, declined by two seats, in grim contrast to the hopes that the membership had harboured prior to polling day.[2] Yet it could have been a great deal worse. If the election had been held in 1990, the party could have been virtually wiped out. Ashdown had presided over a decline, but also a recovery, all within the space of five years.

Breakthrough

Amongst the 20 seats which the party had won, a notable victory had been achieved over Conservative Party Chairman Chris Patten by Liberal Democrat Don Foster. It was a moment of celebration in a night of disappointments. Yet the absence of substantial progress was not caused by any divergence from the party's socially liberal and economically left-leaning, redistributive agenda. Liberal Democrats had not succeeded in connecting with the electorate in a way which persuaded them to back the party. Why not?

Internal discussions at the time concluded that fighting on a manifesto featuring constitutional reform had been a poor strategy. Despite general approval for the leader, Paddy Ashdown, who was regarded as a strong force for the movement – as well as a bit of a 'lad' – the public simply did not share the party's enthusiasm for conversations about electoral reform and constitutional discourse on how Britain would be run under a Liberal Democrat administration. Frankly, they thought that it was boring. At a time when people were having their houses repossessed, a change to the voting system did not seem like a very high priority. This was typical of the party's good intent. But their offering did not relate to people's deeper concerns about their economic circumstances, as the country limped slowly out of deep recession.

The Lib Dem campaign had failed to acknowledge that the ordinary person in the street was about as engaged with constitutional reform as they were with the average surface temperature of Mars. An agenda which failed to excite the public on its policy propositions did not damn the political agenda long held by the Lib Dems. It merely suggested that, as presented, the public didn't really give two hoots about it at that time. This would be an error which returned to haunt the Liberal Democrats again in 2011.

In addition to the flaws in policy emphasis, 1992 also saw a fallback in support because of a tactical error. The party blundered by making positioning statements which indicated a willingness between Lib Dem leader Ashdown and Labour leader Neil Kinnock to work together in a coalition, should the electoral mathematics give no party an overall majority. The association with a shaky Labour campaign was not helped by an infamous rally in Sheffield in the last week of campaigning. Neil Kinnock performed in what might be called an 'exuberant' fashion in front of thousands of Labour activists and the national press. His style fell short of reassuring floating voters that he was the right man for the job of Prime Minister.

Electors were dissuaded by the prospect of a Labour government and a 'Lib-Lab' pact and grudgingly re-elected a Conservative government, which surprised everyone, including the Tory leader John Major, who had done just about everything except book a removal van for. He had even taken to the streets with, quite literally, a handheld megaphone and a soapbox, to address the public 'in the good old-fashioned way'. Nobody had expected it to work, least of all him. To quote Major's opening words as Prime Minister at his first Cabinet Meeting in 1990 after taking over from Margaret Thatcher: 'Well, who would have thought it?'[3] Major's phrase, from two years before his preposterously unlikely victory in the 1992 general election, summed up the stunned sense of disbelief felt by many who had not backed the Tories on that fateful day, as they watched Major meekly – and almost apologetically – return to Number 10 to run the country for another five years.

The fact that errors made in the last week of campaigning at the top level by Labour harmed the performance of the Lib Dems is a salutary lesson in becoming associated with statements which owe their genesis to the aspirations of other party leaders. The miscalculation made a weary public run for political safety, muttering collectively 'we don't like the Conservatives much, but, from what we've seen, we will like Labour even less; and, since the Lib Dem leader could do a deal with Labour, we'd better vote Tory again after all.' The election was not so much won by John Major as lost by the opposition parties, working in a careless electoral coalition to give them a marginal victory and keep Major in as Prime Minister.[4] Thus Liberal Democrats in 1992 made no forward progress, though again it must be said that the prevention of a meltdown was itself a bit of a triumph.

In those dark times, local heroes of the party forged their anonymous place in the history of the movement, by keeping calm and carrying on. It was to be another five years before the first truly dramatic breakthrough finally arrived. And, once again, it is better to take a realistic, rather than a romantic, view of the party's performance in that and subsequent elections.

The 'one more heave' strategy would be played out again. But it would soon transpire that no amount of heaving by the Liberal Democrats could on its own match the rewards accrued when the public decided that enough was enough, causing it to rail against another five years of Conservatism. A lot of that wasn't due to the Liberal Democrats. It was precipitated by the Tories themselves.

1997

Much has been written about the causes of the result of the 1997 general election. Some of it has attempted to fit facts round dogma – for example, to prove that the Liberal Democrat national campaign was responsible for the success. Local campaigning was tremendously important. But some of the claims are flavoured with hubris and under-emphasise a few simple truths which lay behind many of the Liberal Democrat victories. Three factors enabled the Lib Dems to do so well.

Firstly, the policy positions and image of the Lib Dems and the party's leadership were generally credible and popular. This was a necessary – but not sufficient – condition for progress. Manifestos on their own are read by few, and only headline policy positions tend to permeate the public consciousness. The second condition was that the Conservative vote was very soft. Electors were looking for anyone else to vote for apart from the incumbent government. The rout of the Tories inevitably meant that leading opposition parties would do well in seats where they represented the most likely victor against the incumbent Conservative Member of Parliament.

The third condition was entirely practical. Lib Dems did well where they had strong local representation on the ground. Local councillors and activists and their involvement in local community politics were vital components for progress. Without this, the party simply would not have had the momentum to present themselves as the best people to beat the Tories. As it was, in 1997 the Liberal Democrats had become the second largest party of local government, behind Labour and ahead of the Conservatives. As we will see, this was a crucial element in the party's success. Indeed, it could be said that the result in the general election was really only a reflection of the leadership's *greatest* triumph, namely the accumulation of over 5,000 local authority councillors in 1996, the biggest number in the party's history.[5]

In an election where the number of Tory MPs more than halved from 336 to 165,[6] there were rich pickings for Labour and the Lib Dems. They were the new homes for disillusioned former Conservative voters. After the untimely death of Labour leader John Smith, new supremo Tony Blair had repositioned Labour to appear more 'acceptable' to Tories. He gained considerably from the rightwing exodus. Lib Dems, who had not represented as difficult a switch on account of their perceived 'centre ground' positioning, did very well too.

Nor did Labour lose its traditional voters, however much they grumbled about the apparent 'Blairite' lurch to the right. These supporters had no other party than Labour to vote for. It resulted in a very substantial majority for Blair's rebranded movement, with the number of seats rocketing from 271 five years previously to 418 seats in 1997.[7]

It was in this context that the Lib Dems finally doubled their parliamentary representation, winning a total of 46 seats, a net gain of 26 MPs. This was heralded as a triumph, and represented the best performance that it had achieved since its formation as the Liberal Democrats about two decades previously.[8]

It would be naïve to claim – or to privately believe – that the Lib Dems could have doubled their seats without the anti-Tory mood, however attractive the Lib Dem manifesto, the party broadcasts or the leader. While the third party did ride the wave of anti-Tory discontentment competently, the tidal electoral forces which carried them so far up the estuary of electoral success were only partly within their control. As we shall see when we consider the 2005 election, it is possible for the leadership to surf this tide against other parties to an extent; but the mood of the country is an ever-present consideration, whether leaders like it or not.

A relatively large number of Lib Dem candidates were propelled onto the green benches of the Commons because they looked like the people most likely to oust a Tory on a seat-by-seat basis and had good grassroots support in the form of activists and councillors. Ashdown's manifesto didn't frighten Tories; Lib Dems were elected as a replacement for the right wing's busted flush, just as Labour candidates beat Tories in exactly the same manner. 1997 was also living proof of the importance of the local government base, where local strength for the Lib Dems led to the gaining of new Parliamentary seats.

2001

Four years later, the Conservatives remained weak. They had done a good job of fighting amongst themselves for the intervening time, without addressing the underlying reasons why they had been so roundly rejected in 1997. Lib Dems were hopeful of further gains at their expense. They had done well in the previous election, but were still hungry for more influence in Parliament. As long as they had the capacity to consolidate without the pressure of a Tory resurgence, there was the prospect of a good result. Labour still appeared strong, so the prospects of gains from them were lower. Nevertheless, Lib Dems could offer a comfortable home for Labour electors who had become disappointed with their own government's performance. The charismatic and hugely popular Scottish Liberal Democrat MP Charles Kennedy had taken over as Lib Dem leader on 9 August 1999, following Paddy Ashdown's sudden retirement from the role after 11 years in the job. Kennedy's formidable challenge was to build on Ashdown's legacy of progress. The party had not held so many seats since 1929, and to improve on that would be quite a tall order.

The election was delayed slightly by an outbreak of the cursed farm animal disease foot and mouth. Amid confusion over the best way to deal with the outbreak, it was decided to hold the election a month later, during which time very little happened to alter the result. As much of the countryside languished in a poorly-enforced kind of quarantine, electors continued to do the same to the Conservative Party. On election night, 7 June 2001, the Right made no progress, creeping up from 165 seats to 166.[9] It was, by any measure, a pathetic 'recovery' and immediately caused their likeable, underrated and honourable leader William Hague to step down from the leadership immediately after the results had been announced.

Meanwhile, there was further growth for the Lib Dems. The detail within the figures gives a clearer picture of the dynamics of that election. The Lib Dems had actually gained eight seats, seven from the Conservatives and one from Labour.[10] They had also lost two to the Conservatives, leading to a net increase of six. Thus the gains had been achieved almost exclusively at the cost of the Tories, just as had happened in 1997. This was a worse result than many had predicted for the Conservative Party and illustrated how dependent Lib Dem gains were upon Tory weakness. Kennedy had succeeded in building on Ashdown's achievements. He had expanded the party's Parliamentary representation in the Commons in his first general election as leader.

The number of MPs that a party holds is regularly used as a key measure of a party leader's efficacy. This is a deception. What the figures do not reveal, but analysis of the facts behind them does, is the intimate relationship between local government base and parliamentary success. The Lib Dem successes in general elections rose and fell like a cork on the sea of council seats held by the party. Although down from their peak in 1996, Liberal Democrats still held over 4,300 council seats – a great legion of activists across the land, helping the movement to forge ahead.[11] As we will consider later, the number of Liberal Democrat MPs is in a sense the measure of the party's strength on the ground, where the real campaigning power resides. Although less glamorous in the eyes of the media, the true badge of honour for Liberal Democrat leaders is how many councillors the party holds under their tenure. This is the foundation of the party's electoral success, and a more important driver than any other single factor.

It must be said that in 2001 the population were heavily influenced in their voting decisions by the continuing disarray in the Conservative movement. The Right had been unable to break the image of being the 'Nasty Party'. By contrast, in 2001 Labour had shown impressive resilience, losing only a minimal number of seats. Nevertheless, it was the Lib Dems who were regarded as having the right to feel most pleased with the outcome of the evening.

A strong local government base and a focus on community politics, coupled with a generally benign image of the Lib Dems thanks to the popularity of Kennedy as a likeable and down-to-earth leader, had made the most of the opportunity to secure growth. Again and again in the history of the movement these same three factors were at play in the fortunes of the third party: Tory weakness, a popular party image and leader, and strong local community political activity.

2005

Despite the previous, and unofficial, collective efforts of Labour and Lib Dem leaders to oust the Tories in 1997, by the run-up to the 2005 general election this informal working relationship had been long forgotten. Unlike retired party leader Paddy Ashdown, who had been sufficiently keen on links with Labour to have made a speech about it in Chard on 9 May 1992,[12] new leader Charles Kennedy did not seek to promote a close relationship with Prime Minister Blair. Indeed, Kennedy had stood alone amongst the three main party leaders in 2003 when he opposed the military Anglo-American action in Iraq in that year. Publicly, at least, there had been no effort at building a warm political interaction between the two parties, or between himself and Blair as individuals.

Enduring Tory and Labour howls and barracking – the behaviour which characterises the most harrowing moments in the House of Commons – Kennedy repeatedly put the case for opposing the war. On the day of the Parliamentary vote, Kennedy summed up his position, in response to an intervention by a Tory MP.

> Our consistent line is that we do not believe that a case for war has been established under these procedures in the absence of a second UN Security Council resolution. That is our position.[13]

Prime Minister Blair repeatedly attacked Kennedy and the Lib Dem position in the strongest terms: 'Ah yes, of course, the Liberal Democrat. Unified as ever in opportunism and error.'[14] Despite enormous pressure on him inside Parliament and through the media, Kennedy stuck to his position.

His resolve was underlined by Kennedy's participation in a huge march through London which physically illustrated to the party – and the country – that Kennedy was not for turning. On 15 February 2003, Kennedy addressed over a million fellow demonstrators:

> I join with you today because I have yet to be persuaded as to the case for war against Iraq. The information has been inconclusive and misleading. The arguments have been inconsistent and contradictory. The real aims – what would follow a war – have never been properly explained. No wonder people are suspicious and scared. I say this as someone who is not personally a pacifist – although I respect sincerely pacifist beliefs. As someone who is not anti-American – but is deeply worried by the Bush administration. And as someone who has no illusions about Saddam Hussein's brutal dictatorship and appalling regime. But I return to the United Nations. If great powers ignore it, then great damage will be done to world order and the best hope of international justice. Without a second UN resolution, there is no way that the Liberal Democrats could or should support war.[15]

Kennedy stood alone amongst the three main party leaders in attending and speaking at the march, in opposition to military action. The party's participation in the demonstration had been the subject of internal debate, but after Kennedy's performance it became obvious, even to the internal sceptics, that this had been the right thing to do.

Holding the line was not easy. The press made some effort to suggest that, since Lib Dems later supported the troops in the theatre of conflict, it meant that they were now also supporting the war politically. At a young person's *Question Time* event, the Liberal Democrat representative had to defend the party against the accusation of being flaky on the issue.[16] This was happening all over the country. Any ambiguity in Parliament by a Lib Dem spokesperson on the issue was taken as a sign of confusion. However, the leadership held firm and over time it became accepted that the party had opposed the war and that it continued to do so.

Kennedy reaped the returns for his solidity in the 2005 general election. Lib Dems had been successful at differentiating themselves from both Labour and Conservatives on individual policy issues such as the war. Ironically, the fact that Lib Dems had been accused of 'opportunism' in opposing the military intervention ultimately served the party well in the eyes of a fair-minded and angry electorate who had felt betrayed by claims made to justify the war. Lib Dems were perceived as having taken a principled position and this was rewarded at the ballot box.

The overall result was pleasing for Lib Dems; but the internal details of the results were not. Overall, Liberal Democrats had made 11 net gains (the actual numerical increase appears as 10 compared to the 52 achieved in 2001, but boundary changes meant that the notional increase was 11). Thus, Kennedy had again presided over impressive progress. Labour was left with 35.2%, a record low for a British party securing an overall majority. The Tories were not far behind on 32.4% and the Lib Dems had risen to 22%.[17] Thus Kennedy had also closed the percentage gap in votes between the parties to the smallest for 18 years.

Hidden within the overall results was a flashing warning light, signalling a looming problem. On election night, the Lib Dems had made three gains from the Conservatives, but five seats had been lost to them – a net loss of two to the Tories. This was disguised by the fact that the Lib Dems also gained 12 seats from Labour and one from the Welsh Nationalists with no further losses to either party.[18] The Tories were on the move and, as well as taking a bite out of Labour's parliamentary representation, they were eating up Lib Dem seats along the way. Without a coping strategy to address this, it was clear that there could be even greater problems next time around.

What could be learned from Kennedy's performance? Most impressive of all was his double success in two elections. His tenure had led to an increase of six seats in 2001 followed by a further increase of 11 seats in 2005. Amazing as it may seem, no Liberal or Liberal Democrat leader had achieved such a numerical growth in two consecutive elections since 1906! In percentage terms, such growth in the parliamentary party across two consecutive elections had not been exceeded since 1966 – when the starting point had been merely six MPs, not 46.[19]

Many people made the 2005 result happen for the Lib Dems, including a professional and dedicated campaigning team. An element of leadership is taking blame – or credit – for results which happen under the leader's watch. Kennedy had every right to feel entitled to expect major plaudits for what had been built during his time from an already high base. Kennedy had also shown the way to create a distinctive platform. He had shown that differentiation is a necessary (though not sufficient) condition for Lib Dem advancement. He had developed a principled position, in line with liberal values, on a subject of genuine concern to the electorate. The stand against war had won out against the incumbent Labour government. It illustrated that a determined leadership could do well against political competitors by acting strategically and consistently in ways that the public related to. Had he caved in to his rivals he would probably not have achieved these gains.

Once again, a popular party image and leadership, coupled with a strong on-the-ground capacity to deliver the message of the party at a local community level, had delivered progress. It had been vital for Lib Dems to separate their image from the other two major parties on an issue that electors cared about. The third factor – the state of the other parties – was beyond the direct control of the Lib Dems but, by taking a strong position on a totemic issue, it had been possible for the third party leader to 'wag the other two dogs'.

However, the spectre of losses to the Tories was hidden in the numbers. Unchecked, Conservatives could cause great losses to Liberal Democrats in future. The only defence would be to replace lost votes from elsewhere – in other words, Labour – or prevent the votes leaking away to the Tories in the first place. Without one or both of these strategies, a reversal in the party's fortunes at elections seemed certain.

Apart from the usual sprinkling of individual surprise gains and defeats around the country, results reflect national swings. The greatest protection of all would be to gain seats en masse. It was achievable by building the party on the strongest foundation of all: community politics. This would be the best insurance for the next general election – if it was done.

The Kennedy Coup

The party had clearly enjoyed considerable parliamentary successes with Kennedy at the helm. This made what happened next all the more bemusing for those looking on from a casual distance.

After the departure of leader Paddy Ashdown, whose own leadership approach had been forceful as well as somewhat authoritarian, Charles Kennedy's leadership was defining the party in a different light. Ashdown's had been an era of white-knuckle, rollercoaster political brinkmanship. His extramarital affair had actually raised the party's popularity, as well as earning him the affectionate nickname 'Paddy Pantsdown'. By contrast, 'Chatshow Charlie' brought in a period of calmer consolidation, coupled to a very human, celebrity personality. His *laissez-faire* attitude enabled more liberal names and faces to make an impact on the national scene. 'Let a thousand flowers bloom' was a favourite Kennedy catchphrase – and he meant what he said. Where Ashdown's furrow would pop with veins of testosterone when challenged, Charles's face would warm to a smirk and his victory would be won through a witty retort rather than a tense stand-off.

Some establishment insiders regarded Kennedy's leadership as relatively anarchic. The alternative view believes that his collegiate approach was in no way harmful to the evolution of the Lib Dems. Kennedy's relaxed style enabled a great deal of initiative to blossom amongst the more senior members of the Parliamentary party. He also proved extremely popular with the general public and the membership throughout his reign.

Yet, in keeping with the tenets of a Greek tragedy, Kennedy's own largesse would prove to be his downfall. He had ploughed the fields of opportunity for his fellow Liberal Democrats and left the land fallow for a more sinister crop – grown from seeds of ambition which, until then, had been kept in the dark by the strong, opinionated leadership style of his predecessor, a style which railed against direct criticism or challenge. Now, with a more benign supremo, young pretenders to the throne felt more bold. A self-selected and overtly exclusive caucus decided to work together to create a new power base, to sow the political fields with a harvest that they themselves might one day reap. Out of this grew an erratically written document known as *The Orange Book*. It was to play a central part in the next phase of the party's existence.

As 2006 came to an end, a number of Parliamentarians launched a coup against Charles Kennedy's continuing leadership. The primary argument offered for this move was Kennedy's struggle with alcohol. Despite very little support for this overthrow amongst the greater party rank and file and the public, during a remorseless campaign against him Kennedy faced ever more public challenges to his authority as leader.

The alternative view believes that there was little consideration of the fact that Kennedy enjoyed immense public support. He had been accused by colleagues of suffering from a drinking problem, and, as time went on, it became clear that Kennedy did indeed have a struggle with alcohol. No doubt his drinking was an issue in his professional life but, by any measure, Kennedy had also been a tremendous asset to the party's fortunes, as witnessed by a series of spectacular election successes and his impressive personal popularity ratings. In the 2005 general election Kennedy had enjoyed spectacular popularity ratings.

The Alternative View

A tearful Sarah Teather MP, who had been supported by Kennedy in her by-election victory for the Parliamentary seat of Brent East on 18 September 2003, appeared on television. She had jointly headed up – with Ed Davey MP – a list of 25 MPs who had signed a letter saying that they would not be willing to work under Kennedy if he continued as leader.[20] 19 of the signatories were Liberal Democrat frontbenchers. One member of this group was recently elected MP Nick Clegg, who had held the seat of Sheffield Hallam following the retirement of outgoing Liberal Democrat MP Richard Allan. Another was Chris Huhne MP, another newcomer in the 2005 elections. It also included David Laws, who, together with Paul Marshall, had conceived and created *The Orange Book* – a bright orange work, the cover of which implied that the 'yellow' hue which had for decades been used as the 'party colour' should now be superseded by a new 'orange' shade of political thought which varied markedly from the movement's more traditional positioning. In total, 10 of the 25 signatories to the letter calling on Kennedy to stand down would be contributors to either *The Orange Book* or its soon-to-be-published sequel, *Britain After Blair* – which was the same orange colour as the first book. Clearly, these two volumes were meant to be seen as two halves of a whole. Ironically, Kennedy had written a foreword to *The Orange Book*, though in no way could he have been considered an 'Orange Booker' himself (see Appendix 2).

One third of those MPs not associated with either the existing *Orange Book* or *Britain After Blair* had signed the letter, compared to over half of *Orange Book/Britain After Blair* contributors – an interesting, but not in itself compelling, statistic. More notable is that leadership aspirants Huhne and Clegg had both signed the letter calling for Kennedy to stand down. One of the letter's two lead signatories – Ed Davey – had also written for *The Orange Book*. The other lead signatory, Teather, would write for *Britain After Blair*. All four of these MPs would go on to serve as ministers after 2010.

Breakthrough

By 6 January the pressure on Kennedy had grown, with just over half of Lib Dem MPs now saying that they thought he should leave. In another twist, Kennedy now admitted his problems with alcohol and offered the party a leadership election. He stated that he would himself stand as a candidate, so that the membership, not MPs, would be able to decide whether to endorse his leadership – which he made clear he hoped that they would.

Despite this candidness, Kennedy's admission about alcohol was not treated as a catalyst for compassion and support by his detractors. The alternative view believes that Kennedy's position offered the party an honest, empathic lead in de-stigmatising the discussion of alcoholism in the country at large. Without any Machiavellian intent Kennedy had again created the basis for a principled and genuine connection with millions of people. Those with direct or indirect experience of alcohol-related issues could well have been sympathetic to the leadership – and the party – for helping to remove the taboo from this common and, in many cases, treatable affliction. Public opinion at the time was split.

An informal poll conducted by the BBC shortly after Kennedy announced his struggle with alcohol indicated that public opinion was deeply divided on whether he should resign. Over 14,000 people participated in this poll.[21] It is notoriously easy to make statistics prove what one wants them to prove. It is instructive to note that, initially, public opposition to Kennedy's position on the Iraq war was as pronounced as the slight majority believing that he should resign in January 2006,[22] suggesting that, for the public at least, these matters were not necessarily as set in stone as they seemed to the MPs who were calling upon him to stand down.

None of this made any difference to those who led the charge against him. They continued to call for his departure. There was no change of heart whatever amongst his opponents. More MPs now sided with the original group who had signed the letter and the pressure became irresistible.

7 January 2006 was a chilly, grey day. It is called 'pathetic fallacy' when the weather reflects the mood. That afternoon, the weather very much echoed the tenor of an announcement that the Liberal Democrat leader felt he could no longer avoid. Standing on the steps of the Liberal Democrat party headquarters in Cowley Street before a throng of journalists, cameras and photographers, Charles Kennedy announced that he was standing down with immediate effect.

> In all of this the interests of the party have to come first. That is where my personal, political and constitutional duty lies.[23]

Those who had shunned the manner of Kennedy's ejection had not been sufficiently organised or powerful to challenge the pragmatic orchestration of his demise. Arguments pointing out the value of taking a sympathetic and more forgiving line to Kennedy's honest admission of a drink problem had fallen on deaf ears. Kennedy's occasionally exasperating, but always generous and empathic, tenure had been terminated and that was that. The pressure from so many colleagues was impossible for Kennedy to resist, and he left with dignified humility, to the great distress of those who had tried and failed to defend his tenure.

Many members did not support what had been done – nor the vetoing of what many perceived as their right to choose whether to keep Kennedy as their leader through an election. This view was reflected in much commentary from party activists. After Kennedy's resignation, Councillor Paul Whitehead stated on the BBC website:

> I'm not convinced that Charles needed to go and regret that party members didn't get a chance to endorse him.[24]

This is typical of many views expressed at the time. However, the

Breakthrough

absence of any spontaneous and coordinated campaign in response to those seeking to oust Kennedy meant that MPs had successfully removed a leader elected not by parliamentarians but by members. The alternative view is that, given Kennedy's own willingness to appeal to the membership, stymieing this ballot compromised the constitutional rights of party members who had been disenfranchised by the actions of a small number of MPs who, as far as electing a leader was concerned, constitutionally had the status of members – just like everyone else. The argument that they had to 'put up' with Kennedy in a way which the membership did not isn't a consideration reflected in the wording of the party's constitution.[25]

Kennedy's resignation left open a vacancy which was immediately seized upon by those who had ambitions of leadership. This included members of the Orange Book caucus, who perhaps saw the prospect of advancement as kingmakers. Simon Hughes still represented a more traditional liberal philosophy and outlook. Although he would write a section for the second Orange Book volume – *Britain After Blair* – he did not really fit the same mould as the majority of those involved in the project. His candidature may have stirred mainstream Orange Bookers into action partly out of concern that his alternative appeal could play well with members, not least because he had stood apart from the vanguard which had forced Kennedy out.

Once the vacancy existed, Clegg, who had been an MP for eight months, is said to have stepped into the backstage with great speed, announcing his support for Menzies Campbell's campaign for the leadership. It is rumoured that he had secured support for his own future bid as the price for this support, though this has never been formally confirmed by Clegg himself. While interesting to the narrative of this work, it is not central to it and we leave it for others to confirm or deny whether this was the case, should they one day wish to do so.

In a move which surprised many, Chris Huhne offered himself as one of the candidates for the leadership election. Formerly an MEP, Huhne had in fact been an MP for less than one year – joining Parliament on the same day as Clegg, when Huhne took over from David Chidgey. He joined a line-up of leadership candidates comprising Mark Oaten, Simon Hughes and Menzies – or 'Ming' – Campbell. Oaten and Huhne had both contributed to the original *Orange Book*. Hughes had not.

Oaten withdrew from the contest following media interest in his personal life. Hughes did not withdraw, but again endured scrutiny for much of the campaign regarding his sexuality.

Shortly after 3pm on 2 March 2006, in a stuffy and packed conference room in Local Government Association offices in Smith Square just half a mile from Parliament, it was revealed that Ming Campbell had won, with parliamentary newcomer Chris Huhne coming second. Everyone pledged their support for the new dynasty, as Hughes showed grace in his third place. Huhne had marked the territory as a certain candidate for the next leadership election, whenever that would be.

Ming's dynasty

During the leadership election, an impressive by-election gain in Dumfermline and West Fife on 9 February 2006 propelled Willie Rennie into the Commons.[26] This occurred during the leadership election, but provided a brief boost to the spirits of the party. It seemed like a good omen prior to the election of a new leadership.

Thus, spirits were high as Ming Campbell marked his tenure with a turning point in leadership style. His approach was in stark contrast to that of Kennedy or Ashdown. Despite his unquestioned stature as Shadow Foreign Secretary Campbell was unable to make a similar impact in the leader's role. His performance was not regarded as outstanding in the Commons, nor across the country. Campbell was a competent contributor on television debates, but he lacked 'connection' in the sense that Kennedy had truly related to the wider public. In the *New Statesman* of 29 May 2006, political columnist Kevin Maguire claimed to have overheard Nick Clegg at Bournemouth Station criticising Campbell in a phone conversation. Maguire's article said of Clegg that he described Campbell as

> hesitant and disorganised, commits avoidable errors and lacks momentum but – this was the loyal bit – is capable of recovering.

This was reported only months after Clegg had backed Campbell for the leadership.[27]

After 20 months in post, Ming Campbell came to the view that his position as leader was not tenable. On Monday 15 October 2007, Campbell fled silently to Scotland, leaving the party's ruling Federal Executive meeting in a committee room in the Houses of Parliament to come to terms with the shock news. Confusion reigned, as television crews sought interviews with surprised Liberal Democrats who had been unaware of the resignation of their boss. The BBC reported Campbell's comments: he admitted that his leadership was 'getting in the way of further progress by the party.'[28]

Campbell's departure prompted a brief resurgence of criticism by those who had always felt that Charles Kennedy's flawed character was nevertheless greatly to be preferred over the style of leadership which had replaced it. This also raised suspicions that some support for the coup against Kennedy had been motivated not so much by Campbell's capabilities but rather by his putative supporters' own ambitions thereafter. Certainly, there never appeared to be any great grief over Campbell's departure amongst those who had stood so enthusiastically behind his campaign less than two years earlier.

What matters here for our study is the recognition that

individuals closely associated with *The Orange Book*, who manifestly harboured leadership ambitions of their own, were greatly aided in their own rise by the departure of two leaders within the space of two years. To those who had never wished to see the departure of Kennedy, it seemed inevitable that individuals associated with Kennedy's resignation would now take the opportunity to attempt to acquire the leadership.

With Campbell's demise, the Orange Book hopefuls did indeed step forward. In a bad-tempered and personal campaign between parliamentary newcomers Chris Huhne and Nick Clegg, insults flew between the two opposing teams. The spectre of negative campaigning, implicitly introduced against Kennedy, now returned to explicitly haunt its progenitors.

On 18 December 2007, Huhne lost to the man his campaign had labelled 'Calamity Clegg,'[29] but only by the smallest of margins. Just 511 votes had stood between him and victory. In terms of the campaign style, a change had occurred within the Liberal Democrats which seemed to infer that personal ambition was an acceptable motive for personal jibes the like of which had not been seen in the party in living memory.

After this bitter leadership election, negative briefing appeared to become more frequent. It is questionable whether it was in keeping with the party's constitution:

> The Liberal Democrats exist to build and safeguard a fair, free and open society, in which we seek to balance the fundamental values of liberty, equality and community, and in which no-one shall be enslaved by poverty, ignorance or conformity.[30]

Briefing the press anonymously about fellow Liberal Democrats appeared to fail the test of defending against conformity and, potentially, ignorance. We will return to the question of negative campaigning – a practice firmly established as an internal mechanism by 2008 and *which had been demonstrably used by Orange Bookers against each other in the leadership election of 2007* – later.

The membership and activist base of the party continued to adhere to its traditional ethos of backing the elected leader. Meanwhile Clegg set about filling the key roles of the high command with 'his own people.' This is nothing unusual. It is a natural part of the leadership process to install trusted individuals in this way. Clegg was no exception. However, the alternative view is that, in this particular case, the new Orange Book order introduced with it a willingness to campaign in more aggressive ways at high levels within the party.

Summary

Clegg had a weighty responsibility. He had inherited from Charles Kennedy's 2005 general election result the largest liberal grouping in Westminster for over 70 years. It was his responsibility to build on that. His targets were clear. In the years ahead Clegg would reaffirm a self-imposed growth goal for the party: a doubling of MPs across two elections and, later, a growth target for local councillors too.

By the end of 2008, the only thing missing for Clegg was a significant profile amongst the public. While the party membership knew who led the Lib Dems, few others did. This was neither surprising nor alarming. Anonymity in the early days of being a Liberal Democrat leader was not uncommon. It would take just two years for 'Cleggmania' to achieve its brief and dazzling zenith.

Chapter 3

One More Heave

It is five days since I accepted the position of Deputy Prime Minister.
Nick Clegg, 16 May 2010

From 2008 Liberal Democrats focused their attention on preparing for a great opportunity at the ballot boxes. 6 May 2010 would be Clegg's first test as leader at a general election.

Performance indicators

Although there is always polling data available for the parties, it's no substitute for the real thing. And for the Lib Dems, the real thing had not all been honey and roses. True, in the 2008 local elections Lib Dems experienced small growth, from an already high base of over 4,400 council seats (4,420 to 4,467 to be precise). However, the Conservatives had done even better, gaining almost 300 seats as Labour took a tumble.[1] Advantage: Cameron.

12 months later, Lib Dems achieved something of a coup when they sailed in a full 3% ahead of Labour, attaining 25% of the vote.[2] It was quite a night for the party – and only the second time they'd done so well in share of vote. The party went wild with delight – as much as political observers ever go wild. Spokespeople across the

land sat in regional radio studios and battered Labour's already low morale with the figures.

The Lib Dem surge at the polls had translated not into a surge in seats but into a public relations exercise; the media were still happy to take the Lib Dem line. On Friday 5 June 2009, under the title 'UK's Labour Party suffers big losses in local polls,' news outlet Reuters announced to the world:

> Based on provisional results, the BBC calculated Labour's projected share of the national vote had fallen to 23 percent, behind the Conservatives on 38 percent and the Liberal Democrats on 28 percent.[3]

In perhaps one of the least informative comments of the day, the BBC reported Labour Olympics Minister Tessa Jowell saying, 'These are very bad results' – an observation which was one step away from saying nothing at all.[4] While the scale of the defeat for Labour had been overestimated by the BBC, the original impression stuck and Labour *felt* as if they had come a very poor third.

The Lib Dem share of poll had an intoxicating effect on some elements of the party. In a carefree conversation in the Westminster Arms public house across the square from Parliament a few days later, a particularly upbeat Liberal Democrat staff member suggested to party pals that Lib Dems now had a theoretical chance of beating Labour at the general election. 'Well, it is *theoretically* possible, I suppose,' mused a wily veteran Liberal Democrat of many years' standing to his chirpy chum.

> Then again, so is alien abduction and the Loch Ness Monster. Though I've met people who claim to have seen those two; I'd have to say yours comes a valiant third.[5]

However, the most important news of those local elections was not the Lib Dem poll rating. It was that Tories had won the share of poll once again – as they had in every round of local elections since 2006.[6] They also held about half of all the council seats.[7] This was a colossal base of councillors around the country. It would serve them well in the general election.

There were other straws in the wind. In the European Elections, which had been held on the same day as the local elections, Liberal Democrats declined by one seat. This was due to the reduced UK quota of seats caused by the expansion of the European Union.[8] Existing EU countries lost 'quota' to new members. But that wasn't the main thing: vote share also declined, from 14.9% to 13.7%.[9] Reporting of the decline had been partially obscured by Labour's drubbing in the local elections. The Orange Book leadership successfully accentuated the positives and continued to talk up the potential for the party to forge ahead.

The fightback starts – er... here?

Meanwhile, one of the most ineffective 'fightbacks' in history was not taking shape in the party. Some left-leaning and libertarian members outside the Orange Book circle were beginning to notice the extent to which this grouping had taken hold of key positions. There was some discomfort with the 'tone' of the leader's grouping, which seemed at ease with a right-leaning economic agenda. Non-Orange Bookers found their doubts hard to define – so they didn't define them. The dissenters' rebellion consisted of a series of lethargic negatives: they didn't coalesce into an active grouping; they didn't debate these issues with any gusto; they didn't get together to work out where it was all going wrong; in fact, they didn't do anything much except have a sort of odd feeling about it in the same way that people at dinner say 'does this taste a bit funny to you?' and carry on eating.

In fairness, there was a lot to be lethargic about. Conference policymaking seemed to be 'business as usual'. Delegates passed motions to reaffirm their opposition to no platform – the censorship of controversial speakers (see Appendix 3). They reasserted their commitment to opposing student tuition fees.[10] Orange Bookers didn't resist these policies. So what *was* there to worry about? As far as most people in the party could see, *The Orange Book* was still just a book – or, indeed, two books, *The Orange Book* and *Britain After Blair*. After all, those scowling askance at the Orange Bookers found no clear narrative to 'grab hold of'. If they were 'rightwing,' why was Simon Hughes a contributor? If they were authoritarian, why was Oaten there?

In fact, this grouping was being protected in a most curious way – by an unusual 'guilty secret'. It was that the Orange Bookers *themselves* did not feel that they shared a particular philosophy. It was a blindingly obvious omission for a group which had fed so many key players into the high command of the party. Yet the Orange Book's main shield was its very opacity of thought when it came to a narrative or 'worldview'. The edifice of the Orange Book may have been constructed out of personal expedience, not timeless principles, but few people realised this – not least because David Laws, the architect of the books, was an erudite and deeply insightful thinker, who had not shied away from marching to the beat of his own comprehensive philosophical tune. When a libertarian issue was at stake, the odds were that if the authoritarians said 'aye' he would say 'no'. His voting record in Parliament showed this in abundance. Yet something had prevented the Orange Book from coalescing around a similarly pin-sharp narrative for the group – something which will become very clear presently.

Occasional skirmishes did arise. In the run-up to the general election of 2010, traditional elements of the Lib Dems remained concerned about the party's stance on, for example, the use of the free market to supply public services, and 'Public-Private

Initiatives'. Internal discussions in the parliamentary party debated the merits of partial privatisation of the Royal Mail. These debates never amounted to a challenge against the leadership, and were not really reported outside the meetings. The opponents of the privatisation almost universally lived outside the Orange Book circle. Yet criticisms were still aimed at particular policies as opposed to the Orange Book caucus as a whole. The concern about the apparent willingness of Orange Bookers to swap public monopolies for private ones was argued on individual examples, rather than as indicative of a rift. Those who did not like the state carrying risk and private firms carrying profit occasionally voiced their opinions, but discussions never amounted to a strategic challenge to where the party was drifting strategically.

The Orange Book takeover continued. Left-leaning and libertarian elements seemed on the wane. In contrast to outgoing president Simon Hughes, new president Ros Scott – the first to be elected since Clegg's rise to the leadership – was not identified, internally or externally, with a leftwing or libertarian tendency. Clegg's Chief of Staff, Danny Alexander, faithfully echoed his leader's approach and outlook. There was no effective or organised counterpoint to this new order at any level.

High hopes

Phrases like 'this isn't the party I joined' and general griping are always to be heard from nostalgic activists who populate the ranks of the 'awkward squad'. But by 2010, even the curmudgeons were optimistic. The party embraced a bullish prognosis of its prospects, with confidence that this election could be a further leap forward, adding to progress made in 1997, 2001 and 2005 at a cost to one or both of the other major parties. The Lib Dems had long felt robbed of representation in the Commons. Perhaps at last – under Clegg – they would get it.

In January 2008, Clegg confirmed that he still held to his promise of doubling the number of seats in two elections – namely by 2015 at the latest. Referring to an internal review of party structures, he said

> the Party Reform Commission is critical in ensuring that we make the best electoral impact over the coming years. I am determined that this root-and-branch review should take us towards meeting my commitment of at least doubling our number of seats within two elections.[11]

This was a bold commitment. Liberal Democrats had not gained more than 26 seats in any general election since the formation of the party.

Clegg's commitment to 'double the number of seats' – meaning a total of 124 Lib Dem MPs or more – was a stupendous ambition. The last time anything like that had happened to the Liberals was in 1923, when they'd gained 96 seats.[12] Even this occurred thanks to the disappearance of the short-lived National Liberals and also a loss of momentum by the Conservatives. The two factors had provided Liberals with the political opportunity for huge growth through gobbling up the leftovers of another party. In the run-up to 2010, without the opportunity for political cannibalism and faced with the spectre of a strengthened Tory party, gaining large numbers of Lib Dem seats would be far more challenging.

For Clegg to have any serious hope of achieving his Parliamentary target, he needed to make advances in 2010. 100% growth could only realistically be achieved with positive increases in two consecutive elections. Otherwise Clegg's sky-high 2015 target would become a castle in the air. Nobody had even equalled Charles Kennedy's sparkling results across two elections in the previous century.

And then there was David Cameron. This was his big chance to become Prime Minister. The Tories were working very hard to gain seats, with 'Dangerous Dave' appearing in everything from charity events to men's magazines, such as the upmarket *GQ*, which slapped a slick picture of him on the cover with the title 'Mr Ambition'.[13] Elsewhere, a struggling Labour Party would fight like a wounded animal to minimise its losses.

But were the three parties equally prepared for the contest? Let's see.

Labour's malaise

Something which stood to assist Clegg's ambitious goal was the parlous condition of Labour's fortunes. They were on a 'sticky wicket,' with little momentum and few new ideas. Their leader, Gordon Brown, was being portrayed as the *bête noire* of British politics. His poor image was further reinforced by a media which had decided that Gordon Brown had to go.

Brown was persistently portrayed as the reason that it had all gone wrong. His tenure as Chancellor was presented as having little merit. There was a degree of hubris in this. Tory Shadow Chancellor Osborne had previously offered highly contradictory views on bank deregulation, as we shall presently see. But none of that seemed to matter – Labour was condemned as the architect of a political environment in which the banks collapsed.

By early 2010, the press were damning Brown as a hopeless prime minister, incapable of campaigning, debating or taking Labour into government for a fourth term. Some who knew Brown regarded this as unfair. He was no showman. But a number of associates saw him as a thoughtful, intelligent and decent person. His lack of public appeal was as much a reflection of the wilful misrepresentation of his character as it was a statement of his limitations in the field of public relations – traits he would never conquer. By March 2010, Brown might as well have gone on a long holiday: it would have made little difference to his treatment in the media. This was doubtless galling for him but, by that point, it was far beyond his control.

Conservative immunity

Meanwhile, the Conservatives had a different problem. Despite the unpopularity of the Labour administration, the Tories appeared to lack the momentum to overcome a general resistance amongst electors to vote for them again. For many, Conservatives still carried the indelible marks of failure from the years of Thatcherism. Their inability to fully address the doubts of a large proportion of the public sector workforce was hardly surprising: what the Conservatives had done to the United Kingdom in the 1980s and 1990s had ricocheted like a 'magic bullet' through the memories of a large proportion of voters ever since. They feared that the worst excesses of Thatcherism would be played out once again.

Cameron did not calm these fears. Quite the opposite. He personally associated himself with the infamous woman. Presenting his frail and increasingly confused predecessor with a lifetime achievement award at the Guildhall on 31 January 2008, Cameron claimed:

> As one of the towering figures of the past 50 years, Baroness Thatcher modernised and transformed our country and once again gave Britain a powerful voice in world affairs.

He didn't stop there. Cameron went on to describe Thatcher as

> the greatest peacetime prime minister of the 20th century and one of the great prime ministers of all time,

adding,

> She rescued our country from economic disaster – but she did much more. She rescued our people from despair – the belief that nothing could change for the better and that the best politicians could do was manage decline gracefully.

Cameron also claimed to believe that the 'whole country – and every political party, whether they acknowledge it or not – owes Margaret Thatcher a debt of gratitude.'[14]

Cameron's words were a world apart from those that had been shouted in the streets of London about her by people who had vociferously demonstrated over the Poll Tax, the miners' strike, unemployment, health service cuts and so much else. A whole generation of activists had known that the reply to the shouted words 'Maggie! Maggie! Maggie!' was 'Out! Out! Out!' Yet here was a 21st-century Tory leader talking up their nemesis. Thatcher had – in the eyes of the Left and many liberals – brought a blight upon the country and a legacy of social deprivation which still undermined many communities. It is an interesting – and rarely cited – fact that the Thatcher administration was even responsible for the introduction of the discredited expenses system for British MPs.[15] This itself caused incalculable harm to the reputation of Parliament many years later.

It is possible that Cameron's determination to praise someone who had eventually been forced out of office – by a *coup d'état* from within the Tory party itself – cost him votes. Cameron's party poll ratings remained buoyant, though it is interesting to ponder the extent to which his fulsome praise of one of the most unpopular British premiers in history actually affected support for the Conservatives in the run-up to the 2010 election.

Perhaps even more remarkably, the Conservatives appeared to evade the consequences of another – potentially greater – policy blunder which could have totally scuppered their economic credibility. Until the global economic downturn in 2007, the Conservatives had been calling for further *deregulation* of the banks, not an increase in control over them.

Shortly before the global financial crash, the Conservative-leaning *Sunday Telegraph* proudly published an article on work completed by Tory grandee John Redwood. His report advocated large reductions in expenditure, predicated on a tremendous plan to deregulate everything from private businesses to financial services. The newspaper explained:

> The Conservatives have drawn up a radical programme of cuts in red tape and regulation aimed at saving British businesses £14 billion a year, *The Sunday Telegraph* has learnt. The proposals, to be endorsed by David Cameron, would achieve savings by scrapping huge amounts of legislation imposed on businesses by both Whitehall and Brussels, including rules on working hours and employee protection and restrictions on financial services.

The paper went on to reveal Redwood's belief that:

> A vast range of regulations on the financial services industry should either be abolished or watered down, including money-laundering restrictions affecting banks and building societies. Mr Redwood's group also sees 'no need to continue' to regulate mortgage provision, saying it is the lender, not the client, who takes the risk.[16]

This directly contradicted what the Conservatives said shortly after the markets crashed. This evident U-turn in thinking immediately before and after the economic crisis barely registered in the public's view or the media's coverage. Had Redwood's report been enacted prior to the economic downturn, the financial crisis could well have hit Redwood's even more financially deregulated Britain even harder than it did under Labour.

Labour energetically – and repeatedly – tried to activate public sentiment on this matter. For instance, the Chief Secretary to the Treasury, Yvette Cooper MP, quoted George Osborne's *own words* at him in a Commons debate on 18 March 2009 – well after the financial crisis had begun:

The idea that the Conservatives would have proposed stronger financial regulation here at home is even more of a joke. Here is what the shadow Chancellor said just before the credit crunch started: 'Regulation... inhibits enterprise. For example, speak to any business in financial services—from the largest investment bank to the smallest independent financial adviser—and the threat of future regulation from Whitehall and Brussels is now their number one concern.'[17]

The Tory strategy to deal with such attacks was, on the face of it, very cheeky. He did not attempt to defend his comments – or even to put them into some sort of mitigating context. Osborne baldly retorted:

the Chief Secretary... was quoting what people were saying just before the credit crunch. Let me quote what the present Secretary of State for Children, Schools and Families said in October 2006. He said 'I favour... market forces and competition policy to promote efficiency through open and competitive markets.'[18]

The future Conservative Chancellor made no effort to justify his own U-turn – even though, having supported *deregulation*, he now condemned Labour for *not regulating enough*.

His reply was muddled in another way: was he praising a Labour Minister for agreeing with Osborne's support for deregulation? Or he was he saying that, prior to the crash, the Labour Secretary of State for Children, Schools and Families (who also just *happened* to be Yvette Cooper's husband) had made the same misjudgements about deregulation as Osborne *himself*? Either way, in any rational sense, it did not help Osborne's defence: if a lack of regulation was to blame, Osborne's own words damned him by indicating that he would have deregulated further, making the crisis worse by allowing the country to sink into even greater over-borrowing – and subsequent catastrophe. This illogical doublespeak was studiously ignored. It did not fit the narrative being portrayed by the Tory party – or by the media on the party's behalf.

Attempts by Labour to highlight these contradictions in Tory thinking made little impact. Conservatives carried on blaming the administration and winning over public opinion. By accident or design, this apparently shameless approach achieved its end. Whatever Labour did or said, they could not shed the mantle of economic failure from their shoulders, any more than a man in quicksand can thrash his way out of it. The Tories appeared to enjoy a degree of political immunity from any economic attack, even in the Commons – and even when the evidence clearly exposed the 'deregulate-regulate' oscillations of an illogical Conservative economic policy.

The Conservatives may not have been winning the spirited admiration of the British public. But a following wind was providing a consistent degree of advantage to them – one which had, long ago, become an ill wind for Labour.

Lib Dem growing pains

While Labour and Conservative forces limbered up for the gathering electoral storm, Lib Dems had their own issues. The organisation's fortunes as a whole now orbited around Nick Clegg and his Orange Book caucus. Many felt that Vince Cable's brief and spectacular tenure as acting leader after Ming Campbell's sudden resignation had been an object lesson in effective leadership. His crowning glory had come on the floor of the Commons on 28 November 2007. On that day in Prime Minister's Questions, Cable scored a famous victory against Gordon Brown to the considerable amusement of the Commons when, referring to a popular fictional comedy character know to all British people at the time, he made the memorable observation:

> The House has noticed the Prime Minister's remarkable transformation in the last few weeks from Stalin to Mr Bean, creating chaos out of order rather than order out of chaos.

It brought the House down.[19]

After Cable's spectacular success as acting leader, it was now Nick Clegg's weekly duty to hold his own in the ring with two other party leaders – and in the British media. The extent to which he could do this would be a factor in the general election. Clegg added to the unease with a series of minor errors. In a fairly straightforward interview with veteran journalist Piers Morgan, Clegg dropped the ball when Morgan seduced him into carelessly implying – certainly incorrectly – that, down the years, he had made love to 29 women.[20] This caused a ripple of amusement in the press, who delighted in playing up Clegg's gaffe in Morgan's cheeky interrogation. It was not an isolated incident.

Nevertheless, the party rallied round Clegg. Even those not close to him, and who had to an extent suffered ostracism by the Orange Book clique, spoke up for him in the collective interest. With allies all around him, he was well placed to conduct a productive campaign.

Leader debates

The initial stages of the election went brilliantly for the party in general – and for Clegg in particular. On 15 April 2010, in the first of three 'leaders' debates' – themselves historic, as these had never happened in a UK general election before – Clegg stole the show.[21] His performance led to the highest poll ratings for the Lib Dems in almost 30 years. More than half of those who had watched him (51%) gave Clegg victory in the three-way tussle, leaving Conservatives in panic (at 29%) and Labour morose (at 19%).[22]

After this bravura first performance, Clegg did not sustain the advantage. By the time of the second debate, David Cameron's advisers had evidently carried out a meticulous analysis of Clegg's achievement and general approach. This enabled Cameron to emulate the best aspects of Clegg's performance. Clegg remained competent in debate number two. However, and understandably, he basically repeated the style of performance which had worked so well in the first programme.[23] The public reflected their verdict in the order of merit. The same YouGov pollsters gave Clegg 32%, Cameron 36% and Brown 29%.[24]

The third debate – on the economy – should have been the Liberal Democrats' strongest suit, thanks to Liberal Democrat Shadow Chancellor Vince Cable's wholly accurate prognosis of the economic crisis *before* it happened, as well as its causes. Cable had also outlined a credible game plan for recovery. Clegg did not seem to make the most of this advantage. Again, Cameron came out fighting with stature and solutions, as well as again emulating the best stylistic aspects of Clegg's presentation in the first and second debates.[25] Clegg wasn't bad, but it wasn't good enough to win. The YouGov poll immediately following that third debate put Cameron on 41%, outstripping both Clegg on 32% and Brown on 25%, at this crucial time in the election.[26]

A vast number of polls were conducted during the three debates. An overall poll of polls concluded that Cameron had scored victory in the third debate. The hapless outgoing Prime Minister, Gordon Brown, came third again, as he had done in all three.[27] Thus it seems that while Clegg was generally accepted as the winner of the first debate his lead was lost to Cameron by the third.

The alternative view suggests that the loss of momentum in Clegg's support between the first and third debates was caused by two factors. In debates two and three, Cameron 'out-Clegged' Clegg – for example, by looking into the camera and directly connecting with the studio audience. First time round, Clegg had uniquely built a strong rapport with questioners, and Cameron emulated this. Secondly, Cameron's answers appeared solution-based, particularly on the economy, while he sought to portray Clegg's prospectus as one of 'uncertainty' for the country. A look at the closing statements in the third debate gives a good summary of the comparative positions which Cameron and Clegg took. Cameron sounded reassuring and calm, while Clegg's main thrust focused on 'doing things differently... real change' and an exhortation to 'follow your instincts'. Policy assurances on taxes and class sizes were mentioned too, but only very briefly.

Given the demonstrated contradictions in the Tory position on deregulation – especially with regard to Osborne – it was in a sense surprising that Cameron was able to win the third leaders' debate, which was focused on this very subject. At this time, Liberal Democrat Vince Cable had been lauded by the media and public as a supreme authority on the economy. One may have expected Clegg to use his colleague's stature and insights as firepower to dismantle the Tory position, using the Tory support for deregulation before the crash. He could also have promoted Cable's status as a chancellor-in-waiting. Since the television debate was live, there would have been no opportunity for a cynical editor to misrepresent the broadcast. The opportunity was not taken, and a crucial victory was handed to Cameron just days before polling day.

Though the Lib Dem leader had performed competently the final impression was steadiness, versus Cameron's reassuring gravitas. As opinion polls tracked a swing back to the Conservatives away from the Liberal Democrats, it was clear to those who dared to face the truth that the brief period of 'Cleggmania' had waxed and waned. Despite this, Liberal Democrats did what the liberal movement traditionally did – work like mad and hope for the best. After all, it wasn't about opinion polls but votes in ballot boxes.

Results

Election day, 6 May 2011, was still laden with optimism for the Liberal Democrats. There had been a tremendous amount of media attention towards the party, thanks to the remarkable support that Clegg had garnered in the early stages of the campaign. Lib Dem investment in target seats had also been considerable and it was felt that this might provide a bridgehead of new seats for the party. Coupled with this, the Conservatives did not appear to have achieved a powerful momentum, even in the face of an accident-prone and exhausted Labour campaign.

And then it was election night. As the polls closed, nobody knew for sure what the result would be, but everyone knew that it was not going to be a landslide for any party. Soon enough, the figures started to come in, and as fast as they did, visions of a Cleggmania-inspired national revolution began to fade. The breakthrough which had been mooted by pundits – and dreamt of by Liberal Democrats – had not materialised. Lib Dem poll ratings did go up versus 2005 – but by only 1% to 23%.[28] This was a great disappointment to those who had once again dared to believe that this would be another landmark election of progress, as 1997 had been, when the movement had more than doubled its MPs.

In fact, it was all rather more disappointing than that. May 2010 witnessed the first decline in the party's parliamentary representation since 1992. Labour's weakness had benefited the Conservatives, just as local election results in the run-up to 2010 had hinted that it would. Yet the unavoidable reality was that the Orange Book leadership had been unable to stem the flow of votes away from the Lib Dems to the Tories.

The reduction of numbers from 62 to 57 was directly related to the Conservative resurgence. This echoed events in 1979, the last time the Conservatives had come to power following a British general election, which also coincided with a decline in seats for the third party.[29]

There was disappointment in those target seats not held or gained. Amongst the 30 seats not held by the party, and considered by the BBC as the most viable targets for the Liberal Democrats,[30] the party gained only one out of 13 from Labour (Norwich South) and three out of 17 from the Conservatives (Eastbourne, Wells and Solihull).[31] One of these – Solihull – was effectively a 'hold'; it was classed as a 'gain' due to boundary changes making the seat notionally Conservative.[32] Hardworking local Liberal Democrat MP Lorely Burt had committed half a decade to ensuring that her tenure would continue. Wells was also something of a special case. It was gained thanks to the superhuman efforts of gifted Lib Dem candidate Tessa Munt. She had dedicated years to leafleting, canvassing and winning the hearts and minds of the local people.

Statistically, another problem was concealed in the details. Altogether, Liberal Democrats gained five seats from Labour and three from the Conservatives. But they also lost one seat to Labour... and no less than 12 seats to the Conservatives – roughly one-fifth of the existing Lib Dem complement of seats had been snatched by Tory candidates. The Lib Dem net decline, from 62 MPs to 57, was largely a result of Tory *gains* against *sitting* Liberal Democrat MPs. The very movement against which liberalism had fought since the 1800s had again exacted a painful toll.

The 2010 general election resulted in more lost seats for Liberalism than at any general election since 1970 – and the second biggest drop in absolute numbers since 1945.[33] The underlying dynamic across Britain unquestionably demonstrated that the national campaign had not been able to deliver a sufficient upswing in the vote to drive the party forward against a Tory revival.

The figures also revealed another worrying close call. All major parties have marginal seats. In 2010 Liberal Democrats had the highest proportion of seats held by fewer than 1,500 votes.[34] At least seven more seats would not have been won by Lib Dems if a *total* of 4,600 votes had been cast altogether against Lib Dems for their main rivals in those seven seats. So it could have been much worse. But it was bad enough.

Worst of all – from the leadership's perspective – was that Clegg's commitment to double the number of seats by 2015 now lay in tatters. Far from growing towards that goal, the 2010 result left him further away. He now needed gains of 67 seats in a *single* general election – close to the leap in 1923 following the collapse of the National Liberals. A 118% increase in 2015 was a Herculean challenge.

While the internal analysis of Lib Dem results was disappointing news for the movement, the national result for the other two major parties dominated the news, drowning out the dashed hopes inside the Liberal Democrats. A hung parliament had transpired, caused by the Conservative failure to achieve the 'magic 326' MPs necessary for a majority Tory administration. Despite their enormous investment of time, effort and media support, Cameron had not delivered the swing achieved by Thatcher in 1979 against a flagging Labour administration.

The Liberal Democrat leadership was protected from immediate internal attack by the hung Parliament and its delicious uncertainties. Cameron also focused on the task in hand, and did not expose himself to analysis of why the Tories had not won an overall majority. As long as he could secure the title of Prime Minister he would probably get away with it.

The deal

The inconclusive outcome swept any navel-gazing on the performance of the parties aside, in deference to urgent pressure to commence negotiations. As far as the media was concerned, the question was whether a deal between two or more parties could lead to a stable government.

For a very large proportion of the Lib Dem rank and file, under any normal circumstances a coalition with the Conservatives would have been anathema. However, the electoral mathematics made any other option problematic and unstable. No other combination provided a two-party coalition with a stable majority, which required 326 or more MPs on the government benches of the Commons.

A deal with Labour would need other parties to support a coalition, because Labour plus Liberal Democrat MPs did not add up to 326. A multi-party 'rainbow coalition' was considered unwieldy, given the different pressures between three or more parties. Besides, senior Labour spokespeople themselves scuppered the prospect of Labour in government. Former Labour home secretary David Blunkett forcefully argued that the best thing for Labour was to reconstruct in opposition. Others concurred.

By Monday, four days after the election, many people outside the inter-party talks were openly accepting the political necessity of a coalition between Conservatives and Liberal Democrats.

Others have written in more detail about the nature of the negotiations in the period. Rob Wilson, Conservative MP for Reading East, interviewed about 60 individuals from the main political parties, and published his findings in a work called *Five Days to Power*. He reveals a number of rather surprising facts. For example, a month before Nick Clegg had pledged to scrap the 'dead weight of debt' caused by student tuition fees, plans were already afoot to abolish the policy rather than the fees.

Wilson states that, on 16 March, Clegg's chief of staff Danny Alexander had written a confidential document which appeared to abandon aspects of the Lib Dem opposition to increases in student tuition fees before the election had even taken place:

> On tuition fees we should seek agreement on part-time students and leave the rest. We will have clear yellow water with the other [parties] on raising the tuition fee cap, so let us not cause ourselves more headaches.[35]

This was somewhat at odds with the leader's public statement in a promotional video directed at students; 'You've got people leaving university with this dead weight of debt, around £24,000, round their neck,' Clegg had complained, as he went on to reiterate the

Lib Dem pledge to oppose tuition fees.[36] There was no hint publicly that he might support an increase.

In the negotiations themselves, the Lib Dems also abandoned their position on resisting deficit reduction in the first year of the new government, and conceded on a VAT increase. Wilson explains that a Clegg team member informed him:

> The thing that changed minds was George Osborne saying that he had seen the figures and it was quite horrific in real life as opposed to spin life.[37]

Interestingly, success in the talks was not regarded as a foregone conclusion. In March 2010, Danny Alexander – Clegg's chief of staff – had believed that a coalition with the Conservatives could split the Liberal Democrats and that tensions between the parties 'would make it all but impossible for a coalition to be sustainable if it were formed.' However, Chris Huhne strongly favoured a formal coalition, partly because he believed that the financial crisis facing the country required it. He believed that not to create a coalition could damage Lib Dem fortunes in future if the economy were not turned around. All three of these individuals were Orange Bookers.

David Laws, the prime architect of *The Orange Book*, and a senior member of Clegg's inner team, himself wrote an authoritative book about these momentous negotiations from the Liberal Democrat perspective. Called *22 Days in May*, it provides a lucid account of the progress of the discussions.[38] Laws had believed that the Conservatives would offer a coalition deal, and was eager to pursue one. He had, in fact, been invited to join the Conservative Party by George Osborne four years earlier. While he preferred to remain in the Liberal Democrats, this warmth of interaction undoubtedly eased the path for the coalition negotiations in May 2010.

The final agreement hammered out by the Liberal Democrat and Tory negotiating teams consisted of a number of specific policy commitments. It was a programme for government – an agenda for addressing the economic crisis facing the country. The initial agreement was published on 12 May 2010. It would be honed into a slicker document later that month – but the deal was done. (See Appendix 4)

At this point in proceedings, Nick Clegg played a crafty sleight of hand. He and Cameron gave the impression that the coalition was agreed. Clegg arrived at Downing Street in front of the country's broadcast media, to be greeted by the putative Prime Minister Cameron on the steps of Number 10. After waving for the cameras, Clegg and Cameron went inside. It was not energetically reported that this impression of coalition occurred *before* the deal had been formally endorsed by the Liberal Democrats' hastily arranged special conference.

The approval process for coalition had been originally designed a decade and a half earlier by then Lib Dem Federal Executive member Lembit Öpik, at the request of the president of the party, Robert Maclennan. In its original form the process – called Fast Reaction Early Decision (FRED) – had been created in anticipation of the prospect of a Lib-Lab coalition in 1997, should that election result have proved inconclusive. A derivative of FRED was applied in 2010, and a historic coalition was rubberstamped by the activist base. Clegg's clever 'push' – by meeting Cameron in Downing Street – created a visual incentive to inspire thoughts of what life could be like for the Lib Dems in power. By doing this before the special conference – held in Birmingham's National Exhibition Centre – Clegg increased the chances of a 'yes' from the party, in support of the work by the negotiating team. Clegg's expedient stunt probably also increased the consensus throughout the party as a whole.

After the almost unanimous 'yes' vote, Clegg spoke to the excited conference:

> It is five days since I accepted the position of Deputy Prime Minister. Just five days, and we now know there will be no ID

cards, no third runway at Heathrow, no more fingerprinting in schools without parents' consent, no more child detention. Changes Liberal Democrats have spent months, years, campaigning for, are happening. Promises we were making to people on their doorsteps just a few weeks ago are becoming realities. Fair taxes. The income tax threshold is now going to rise to £10,000. That is this Government's priority, not tax cuts for millionaires.

The best start at school for every child. Extra money is now going to be targeted to pupils who need it most. That is a huge leap in creating a truly mobile society. A new, sustainable economy. The banks are going to be taxed, the bonus culture is going to be cracked. And instead of pinning all our hopes on financial wizardry in the City of London we'll build a new economy where we rediscover our talents for building and making things again, with green industry given new prominence as we head towards a zero-carbon future.

New politics. Fixed-term parliaments – happening. The power of recall to get rid of corrupt MPs – happening. A cleanup of party funding, a clampdown on lobbying in Parliament, an elected House of Lords – all happening. Our Freedom Bill is going to come off our leaflets and go onto the statute book, ending gross state intrusion into people's everyday lives. Patients, parents, communities are all going to have a much greater say over the decisions that affect them. And voting reform is going to be put to the British people, in a referendum in which Liberal Democrats will fight to deliver real change. I know the stakes are high – for me personally, as well as the party. But I came into politics to change things, and that means taking risks. Real, big change never comes easy. So it would simply be wrong for us to let this chance of real change pass us by. The chance to transform politics, the chance to hardwire fairness into our society, the chance to change Britain for good.[39]

His speech was met with rapturous applause and a standing ovation, which for once was sincerely offered. There were tears.

While activists ascribed different importance to various policies, the single most significant constitutional policy commitment was a referendum on electoral reform – the political 'crown jewels' for the Lib Dems. It sweetened the bitter pill of coalition with their age-old Tory archrivals. If the coalition could change the voting system of the United Kingdom forever, then this deal was worth it.

On 18 May 2010 Parliament met for the first time since the general election, with Liberal Democrats in power for the first time since World War II. The battle for votes was over. The battle to do well in government had begun. Nick Clegg sat next to the Prime Minister, where no Liberal had been since the likes of Winston Churchill and David Lloyd George had graced the Commons. He had achieved the backing of a potentially reluctant party for a historic accord. Clegg had secured five Liberal Democrat Cabinet ministry positions and over a dozen junior ministry positions. He himself occupied the most senior role held by any Liberal in living memory: that of Deputy Prime Minister.

Summary

Despite their general optimism, many Liberal Democrats had been cautious about allowing themselves to believe that such a time would come in their political lifetime. But it had. People were moved by a sense of awe, pride and delight, having struggled for years to achieve for the movement a place in government.

This moment was the zenith, both for Nick Clegg's standing and for the organisation he led. No 'third party' leader in the history of British politics had ever presided over a negotiated coalition arrangement of this nature, in a manner which had carried his party with him and without an ignominious split.

In the days after the agreement, Nick Clegg's standing in the Liberal Democrats was supreme. Subsequent months would begin to tell a different story. But that was all to come. After the rollercoaster ride of the 2010 general election, 18 May 2010 brought peace and stability. As the new Parliament began, for the deputy prime minister, the Right Honourable Nicholas William Peter Clegg MP, it was his finest hour.

Chapter 4

A Year to Deliver

Eat Nick Clegg.
Poster, Student anti-tuition fees demonstration, November 2010

The months after the 2010 general election were relatively calm. The coalition settled down with remarkable cohesion. For the first time in decades two parties worked together effectively to govern. Even Labour seemed relieved by the new order as they settled back gratefully in the armchair of opposition, resting their weary body politic after a 13-year marathon which had left it breathless and browbeaten.

Everyone was more or less where they wanted to be – and even Clegg's opponents had to grudgingly accept that his captaincy looked like it had delivered precious results. Liberal Democrat ministers were regularly appearing on television to discuss the performance of the government as representatives *of* that government. The Rt Hon Nick Clegg sat next to the Prime Minister in the Commons, with his party colleagues joining him on the green benches at the front of the government side of the chamber. The Orange Bookers who had worked so hard to acquire power together were in a politically secure position. Five Liberal Democrats – all of them Orange Bookers – were Cabinet Ministers, sitting around the 'top table' of authority. Over a dozen colleagues held junior ministry positions.

This state of calm was not to last long. In politics – as in most matters relating to human activity – time's arrow has a habit of pointing away from the comfortable state of equilibrium, towards more troubled circumstances. It was no surprise to observers of politics to see a time of relative harmony giving way to more wild oscillations which characterise the fickleness of political fortune. But let's start with the happy times, and examine the achievements which the Liberal Democrat element of government cited as evidence of its effectiveness in government. Did the returns justify the coalition?

Taking credit

As part of the initiative to build the party's credibility as a powerful force in government, from June 2010 Liberal Democrats highlighted policy commitments which had been delivered, as measured against the manifesto that the party had stood on in the 2010 general election. For example, they promised to assist the lowest-paid by increasing the threshold at which citizens pay income tax to £10,000 a year.[1] In the first Budget, the threshold was indeed raised substantially.

Liberal Democrat literature and websites claimed that over three dozen manifesto commitments had been delivered – or were on their way to being delivered – in the first eight months of government. Here is an edited list of the claims made in 2010 regarding the party's achievements.

- An increase in the tax threshold for low-paid workers.
- A crackdown on tax avoidance and evasion.
- An increase in the rate of Capital Gains Tax to 28% for higher rate taxpayers.
- Restoration of the link between pensions and earnings.

A Year to Deliver

- No like-for-like replacement of Trident before 2015.
- Abolition of the Identity Card project.
- An end to child detention for immigration purposes.
- Scrapping Home Information Packs.
- Encouraging farmers to convert buildings into affordable housing.
- Plans to get prisoners to work regular hours, and compensate victims.
- Scrapping government offices for the regions.
- Proposals to create Neighbourhood Justice Panels.
- Proposals for restorative justice.
- Introduction of experimental drug recovery wings in prisons.
- New approaches for mentally ill offenders with improved treatment.
- A Local Sustainable Transport Fund for local transport authorities.
- Funding to support people at home after a spell in hospital.
- A requirement of energy companies to help poorer customers.
- Plans for renewable energy by 2050.
- A requirement for carbon capture for new coal-fired power stations.
- Protection of the overseas aid budget.
- Devolution of landfill tax, stamp duty and Scottish Income Tax.
- A Fixed-Term Parliaments Bill.
- A referendum on the Alternative Vote.
- Maintenance of free entry to national museums and galleries.
- Display of the Government Art Collection to the public.
- Extension of 15 hours' free early education to disadvantaged two-year-olds.
- Keeping the offer of 15 hours' early education for three- and four-year-olds.
- A week's respite care to carers working over 50 hours a week.

- Short break provision for disabled children and their families.
- Publication of anonymous versions of Serious Case Reviews.
- Commitment to abolish the compulsory retirement age.
- Commitment to ban wheel-clamping on private land.
- Investment of £2.5bn in the pupil premium.
- Introduction of simple reading checks at age 6.
- Proposals to tackle bullying with simplified guidance.
- Plans to encourage more mature entrants into teaching.
- Commitment to review primary and secondary National Curriculums.
- Procedures to enable parents to hold schools to account.
- Publication of information that underpins government statistical tables.
- Publication of 'families of schools' documents, grouping similar schools.
- Promoting sharing of best practice between schools.
- Commitment to give schools greater flexibility and freedom to set pay.
- Review of the curriculum of the Early Years Foundation Stage.
- Proposals to remove bureaucracy from schools.
- Commitment to replace Train to Gain with an 'SME-focused' programme.
- A bank levy to raise money from bank turnover.
- An increase in the child element of tax credits.
- Scrapping of the third runway at Heathrow.[2]

The party claimed its performance in government had been highly impressive. These and other projects were regularly cited in press releases and speeches by ministers and party spokespeople as evidence of the effectiveness of the Lib Dems in power.

There was, however, a problem. While the list of achievements was long, its impact on the party's fortunes was entirely dependent on the extent to which the public accepted that Liberal Democrats were specifically responsible for their delivery – and how much they cared about the things being delivered.

In a coalition environment, one of the great difficulties is to apportion credit and to show that, in the case of the Liberal Democrats, they had truly contributed to the delivery of these policies. The alternative view is that the increase in the tax threshold for the lowest paid would not have happened under a Tory-only administration. This supposition is supported by the conflict between the coalition partners over the idea of reducing the top rate of income tax – a Conservative proposal which was energetically opposed by the Liberal Democrats.

Also, the protection of the overseas budget was probably assisted to an extent by a Lib Dem commitment on the matter. However, the Tory minister in charge also seemed genuinely enthusiastic to sustain this expenditure. Over the summer, Conservative International Development Minister Andrew Mitchell said:

> My ambition is that over the next four years people will come to think across our country – in all parts of it – of Britain's fantastic development work around the poorest parts of the world with the same pride and satisfaction that they see in some of our great institutions like the armed forces and the monarchy. This is brilliant work that Britain is doing.[3]

However, there were frictions. Tory MP Peter Bone said:

> The idea that we are going to be a world superpower in overseas aid – I have no idea what that means. It is the sort of complete tosh you would expect from a Labour minister.[4]

Mitchell's intentions may have been assisted by a commitment on Lib Dem benches for that proposition. However, it cannot be denied that Mitchell may have made these comments irrespective of Liberal Democrat support. Given the backlash from some Tory supporters and papers, he may have been grateful for Lib Dem 'cover' for his position. The investment in the pupil premium was another fairly clear example of Lib Dem policy in action, and much was made of this as a significant 'win' for the party.

While the development aid policy might have been assisted by Lib Dem intervention, some other things listed by the Lib Dems as achievements would have occurred whether or not Liberal Democrats had been in coalition. For example, the Conservatives were going to abolish the plans to construct a third runway at Heathrow Airport anyway. They had already committed to abolition of Identity Cards, not least due to the phenomenal cost such a project carried with it. Increasing the freedom for schools to set pay for staff is not clearly associated with a Liberal Democrat narrative as opposed to a Tory one. Replacing 'Train to Gain' with a programme which related directly to Small and Medium-sized Enterprises – 'SMEs' – would probably have happened under a purely Conservative administration.

Whatever the party claimed, these sorts of considerations would affect the plausibility of the public genuinely giving credit to the Liberal Democrats for particular policy initiatives. While it is not wrong to take credit for policies which both parties would have implemented independently, it is not possible to argue that these occurred thanks specifically to the presence of the Liberal Democrats in government.

Secondly, a large number of the achievements were in fact 'tactical' rather than 'strategic'. Plans to encourage more mature entrants to teaching could gain the appreciation of people who enter that profession as a result, but this was not a core policy commitment. Similarly, publication of Serious Case Reviews and scrapping Government Offices for the Regions may have political merit, but they were not greatly understood or appreciated by the wider electorate. And how many people would change their vote to the Lib Dems specifically because they had secured the display of the Government Art Collection to the public?

Thus, the length of the list was less important than the number of truly 'voter significant' initiatives which affected a large proportion of the population – and which could plausibly be attributed as Liberal Democrat victories. For example, if the Lib Dems could show that they were the key force behind raising the tax threshold for the lowest paid, this might generate electoral benefit. On the other hand, claiming to have delayed the upgrading of the nuclear deterrent was not especially believable – because at a time of austerity the Conservatives and Labour would probably have delayed it anyway.

Who's in charge

There is another subtle – but enormously important – point about how the two parties approached the taking of credit. Liberal Democrats were eager to show their members, and the electorate, that they were good at government and making a difference. By contrast, the Conservatives did not appear to spend so much time, internally or externally, attempting to 'prove' that they were doing a good job. In fact, some Tory activists took a deliberately disparaging line about the coalition, treating the interference of the Lib Dems as something of an irritation: a distraction from their core Conservative agenda preventing them from delivering their agenda. As noted elsewhere, colourful Conservative MP Nadine Dorries even called on the Prime Minister to show the Liberal Democrats 'who is boss.'[5]

While it may be thought that this went some way to showing that Lib Dems were indeed influencing Government policy – a correct assumption – the actual effect appears to have been rather different. In the eyes of traditional Tory voters it hinted that Tories in Government were 'putting up with' the Liberal Democrat demands for influence and that this was simply the price that

Cameron had to pay to be in charge. In this way they were able to imply that Lib Dem policy achievements were a tolerable 'cost,' and not one which should unduly worry Conservatives. That line of argument was in stark contrast to the Lib Dem line, which sought to enthusiastically point to how much difference they were making. This strategy inadvertently conceded that they were the junior partner to the Tories, whom Lib Dems had to continuously persuade to take on ideas. The alternative view is that, over time, the two divergent approaches of the coalition partners created a very strong impression in the public mind that the Tories were leading the Government while the Liberal Democrats were doing their best to try to influence decisions, and sometimes even succeeding – to the mild irritation of their 'senior' partner.

There was another helpful side-effect here. In some areas, Conservatives were able to modify policy commitments which they had made, but which it very much suited them to abandon for reasons of expedience. For example, the postponement of the breathtakingly expensive upgrade to the nuclear deterrent was very prudent financially, but the Tories had overtly supported the upgrade. They could hold the Lib Dems responsible for a delay which they privately welcomed. Using the Liberal Democrats as a shield in these circumstances was a convenient protection against policies and expenditure which did not suit either coalition partner.

While these marketing considerations were important, another more actively corrosive problem soon faced the Liberal Democrats: the failure to carry through commitments which had played a major part in the Liberal Democrat's credo in the years running up to the coalition. Later, we will examine why these divergences from previously held commitments were able to happen. Let us first look at the beginnings of this phenomenon and, later, its consequences.

The first significant divergence from the comfortable peace was a vote on VAT. In the general election Liberal Democrats had strongly campaigned against a 20% rate, while the Conservatives had campaigned on a policy which amounted to saying: 'if elected to serve as the Government of the country, when it comes to VAT we'll, er, do whatever we decide to do when the time comes.'

When the time did come, to nobody's surprise a 20% rate was indeed proposed by the Conservative Chancellor George Osborne.[6]

As we have already noted, the Liberal Democrat opposition to the VAT increase had been a casualty of the coalition negotiations. As such, the leadership and senior portfolio holders in the Liberal Democrats felt obliged to honour the increase rather than the original Lib Dem policy. Most backbench Lib Dem MPs also swallowed hard and voted with their new coalition partners. Only two 'rebels' felt strongly enough to defy their whips: Bob Russell MP and Mike Hancock MP.

Their resistance was only distant: a rumbling, rather than a major rebellion, in the party. As for the rest, 'This is not what we promised,' said some. 'We can't do that,' said others. But they did. A YouGov/Brand Democracy poll published in the *Observer* newspaper on 27 June 2010 indicated that 48% of Lib Dem voters said they were less likely to vote for the party as a result of the U-turn on VAT.[7]

An even greater debacle followed. In November 2010 the debate turned to the subject of student tuition fees. In the run up to the general election, Lib Dem MPs had been actively badgered by the leadership to sign a pledge solemnly promising to oppose any increase in student fees, should they be brought before Parliament. The policy had proved highly popular, and had garnered considerable support amongst students, almost certainly making a measurable difference to the party's electoral fortunes.

Thus, when it was announced that the Lib Dem official position was to vote *for* increases in fees, there was a collective sense of betrayal which immediately translated into attacks from the student movement, open rebellion amongst certain MPs, and a sustained campaign of anger against a party which, until now, had

The Alternative View

enjoyed a uniquely benign relationship with the student movement. Tim Farron MP, in the non-Orange Book party presidential election campaign in November 2010, summed up the mood of many on a *Guardian* newspaper comments site: 'Fees are the poll tax of our generation and I cannot in good conscience vote for an increase.'[8]

As anger grew, so did the protests, some of which spilled over into violence. Perhaps the most dramatic placard to be seen at a march in London which said simply 'Eat Nick Clegg'. Others took a more moderate line, merely wanting Clegg to eat his words and honour the pledge. He didn't, and nor did most Lib Dem MPs. Many MPs were being fiercely lobbied in their constituencies. Those with higher education establishments in their constituencies received the brunt of this pressure. There was much soul-searching in the party – and amongst MPs.

On the day of the vote – 9 December 2010 – tensions were high and nobody was entirely certain of the extent to which Liberal Democrats would be willing to stand up against their leader's exhortations to vote for the increase in tuition fees.

In the event, 21 Lib Dems overtly defied Clegg and voted in opposition to the plans. The list included two former leaders – Kennedy and Campbell – plus party president Tim Farron, senior backbench rebel Greg Mulholland and all three Liberal Democrat MPs from Wales. A further eight abstained, three of these (including Chris Huhne) being 'out of the country.'[9] In terms of Orange Bookers – namely, those who had written for either *The Orange Book* or *Britain After Blair* – *13 out of 15 had voted for the proposal*, while the other two abstained. In contrast, *two thirds* of those who had *not* been associated with the Orange Book project had opposed the proposal and an additional six non-Orange Book MPs abstained (see Appendix 5).

The vote was carried by 323 to 302 – a government majority of just 21.[10] Had the Orange Bookers agreed to vote together against the proposal, their votes would have been sufficient to defeat it – or to prevent it from even being tabled, had the government collectively decided that it was not willing to suffer a defeat on the floor of the Commons. Thus the official Liberal Democrat decision to support the proposal had made the difference between its passing into law and its rejection.

The recriminations were dramatic and immediate. The country was treated to the ironic spectacle of the Liberal Democrats taking the lion's share of the blame for a policy which had arisen from the Conservatives' agenda. It appears that people had expected it from the Tories, but had also fully expected their Lib Dem coalition partners to stand firm on the pledge to oppose the change, as promised in the general election.

The reality looked very different, depending on where you were in the Lib Dem hierarchy. While those on the inside of the leader's circle were aware of the private document written by Danny Alexander before the election, indicating a willingness to compromise on the issue,[11] this had not been broadcast to the membership or the public. To them, it had been seen as a pledge without compromise. Now it had come to be regarded as a betrayal without a justification.

Almost immediately Liberal Democrats, already enduring a series of reversals in by-elections around the country, began to suffer a far greater and energetic rejection from their former supporters – many of whom represented precisely the types of families and individuals most likely to seek higher education qualifications.

On 6 January 2011, a YouGov poll put the Conservatives on 39%, Labour on 43% – and the Lib Dems on 7%. Just 3% of voters believed that the Lib Dems were being led by 'people of real talent,' compared to 27% for the Tories and 17% for Labour.[12]

The polling figures – and the spate of bad by-election results – strongly indicated that for all the claims made by the Liberal Democrats regarding delivery of their programme in government the public had drawn different conclusions. By contrast, the relatively good poll ratings for the Conservatives suggested that their approach towards the partnership with the Liberal Democrats – a regrettable price worth paying for the opportunity to remain in government – was proving effective.

Danger signs

As if to underline the level of malaise facing the party, a series of high-profile parliamentary by-elections went very badly. On 13 January 2011, a parliamentary by-election was held in Oldham East and Saddleworth. The Lib Dems had forced the by-election on the grounds of electoral impropriety by the previous Labour incumbent, Phil Woolas, whose election had been declared void on the basis of actions his campaign had taken in the course of the general election campaign in the previous year.

Labour held the seat with an increased majority – their vote rising from 32% to 42%. Ironically, the Lib Dems had failed to prevent Labour from increasing their share of vote and majority substantially... even though it had been the Lib Dems who had forced the by-election. The Lib Dem vote grew marginally by 0.3%. However, this must be assessed in the context of a sharp decline in the Tory vote from about 26% in May 2010 to 13% in the by-election.[13] Even though the Tory vote had *halved*, the Lib Dems had *'flatlined'*. It has been suggested, with some justification, that the Conservatives had deliberately campaigned gently to improve the chances for the Lib Dems to beat Labour. If this was the case, the actions of the coalition partners certainly did not deliver the result that the Lib Dems had hoped for.

Clegg had visited the constituency three times to support Liberal Democrat candidate Elwyn Watkins. The leader claimed that the party had 'brought the fight to Labour's front door in a way that will have confounded our critics.'[14] However, the result was not good news in any sense.

In March 2011 another Parliamentary by-election took place, this time in Barnsley Central. The sitting Labour MP, Eric Illsley, was sent to prison as a consequence of irregularities in his parliamentary expenses claims. Again, it was a test of the relative strength of the parties. In the May 2010 general election Labour had won comfortably, with 45% of the vote, with the Liberal Democrats in second place, marginally ahead of the Conservatives. On polling day, 3 March, Labour again held the seat comfortably, with 60.8% of the vote. But this result was far worse for the Liberal Democrats. Their vote declined from 17% in the general election to 4%, meaning that the party lost its deposit, falling beneath the 5% threshold which must be achieved to get the deposit back.[15]

The party had sunk from second place to sixth place. It had been beaten by Labour, UKIP, Conservatives, the BNP and a disgruntled independent candidate called Tony Devoy who was angry about 'out-of-touch politicians' and the 'Greed Agenda'.[16]

Shortly after the result was announced, Liberal Democrat candidate Dominic Carman was very candid: 'the voters here in Barnsley have given me and the Liberal Democrats a kicking. We can take it.'[17] It was true. The Lib Dems could take it. But it also raised worries about what might happen in the forthcoming May elections.

Summary

Despite the efforts to deliver meaningful results in government, the going had got very tough for the party in electoral terms. Its poor performance in the autumn of 2010 and at the start of 2011 brought a chill to the Liberal Democrat candidates. The by-election results, coupled with the polling evidence, were worrisome signs of the gathering storm clouds in advance of the dramatic events of 5 May 2011. That day was to be the first national test of the public's view of the first 12 months of the Liberal Democrats in government.

Nobody knew how the parties would do, but to say that it was to be a night of surprises would be to hugely understate the case.

Part 2

Falling Down

Politics is about swings and roundabouts. Sometimes it swings in your favour – other times you go round and round without really getting anywhere. What happened to the Lib Dems was something else completely. They fell off the swing, landed on the spinning roundabout and got catapulted off into the hedge. The last person who did a stunt like that was Harold Lloyd – except that he didn't actually fall off.

Pete Wishart MP, Scottish Nationalist, October 2011, on
Lib Dem performance in Scotland in 2011[1]

Chapter 5

A Night to Remember

What matter are real votes in real ballot boxes.
Liberal Democrat mantra

A *Night to Remember* was the name of the original film, made in black and white, chronicling the last hours of the doomed ship *Titanic* after it hit an iceberg in the North Atlantic on 15 April 1912. This is also the name which could have been given to a film chronicling the performance of the Lib Dems on 5 May 2011 in a host of important elections. It too could have been made in black and white, for there was precious little Lib Dem yellow to be seen on that evening of reversals for the hapless party. To up the ante, there was also a by-election in Leicester South that evening.

The seat had been briefly held by the likeable and hardworking Liberal Democrat MP Parmjit Singh Gill after a gaining the seat in a by-election in 2004. The seat was lost to Labour again in the 2005 general election. But, once again, there was a by-election, this time caused by the resignation of the sitting Labour MP, Sir Peter Soulsby. He had decided to pursue election to a new role as Mayor of Leicester.

The Alternative View

Context

All the signs had warned the Lib Dems that this night would be memorable, and for all the worst reasons. Since November 2010, the polling had been consistently poor for the party. Everyone was aware of the disastrous result in the Barnsley Central by-election, as well as a spate of bad results in local government by-elections. There was a great deal of criticism from sections of the community such as students and their families – groups who had voted Lib Dem in the past.

All in all, it was a bad time to face bad polls. As such, the huge swathe of elections scheduled for that May couldn't have come at a worse time. Due to the electoral cycle there was a tremendous amount at stake. England was holding its local council elections. The Scots and Welsh were voting for their Scottish Parliament and Welsh Assembly too. And, of course, there was the Leicester South by-election, which had attracted a visit by Clegg himself on 4 May – the day before polling day.

Everyone knew that ballot boxes spoke far louder than spin doctors ever could. There was no substitute for hard facts – for 'real votes in real ballot boxes,' a popular mantra for those who seek to dismiss unfavourable opinion polls. Of course, whether the real votes would help to assuage the doom and gloom about the polls would depend entirely on what those 'real votes' revealed.

The stakes were also high for the Labour Party and the Tories. Labour needed to show strong growth in numbers, in order to begin rebuilding its activist base in advance of the next general election. It was vaguely estimated that any result returning fewer than 800 extra Labour councillors would be disappointing for Ed Miliband and his party.

For the Conservatives, the situation was different. Parties in government tend to lose seats at local elections. Their goal was to not lose too many. A notional estimate of 'acceptable' casualties was put at 300 losses, which might be considered tolerable collateral damage for the prize of government.

For the Liberal Democrats, it was a different story. There was little doubt amongst activists that they would suffer net losses. The question was: 'how bad is bad?' Nobody really dared discuss figures, but the alternative view is that, if Lib Dem losses did not amount to more than around 300 by the end of the night, then – given the 1,800 seats they were defending – the party would have felt mildly bruised rather than badly battered. Again, it would be explained as the cost of government and a price worth paying. The Lib Dems also ran 19 councils, and they were hopeful – if not optimistic – about protecting this power base.

Before the polls closed, independent commentators forecast that both parties in Government – the Lib Dems and Conservatives – would fare poorly, to the benefit of Labour. The Tories were, after all, defending a set of historically good election results in 2007 – the last time this particular round of elections had been held. If the public were angry with, for example, the spending cuts, it was reasonable to assume that Tories and Lib Dems would take the pain together. The scene was set for the first great test of the coalition partners of government.

Results

Once the ballot boxes closed there was the usual lull, as commentators made the usual vapid comments about voter turnout and collectively suggested that it would be nice if everyone voted. This unenlightening chitchat about turnout is a time-filling ritual which occurs at every election, because of the delay between the close of polling and the first actual results.

Once the results began to trickle in, a picture quickly arose which confounded what the political pundits had predicted. It became clear that Labour had done well, though it was not immediately obvious whether they had done well enough to feel justified in calling it a victory. However, much more surprisingly, the Conservatives did not perform as anticipated. Nor did the Lib Dems.

The Alternative View

In local authorities where the party was defending a Lib Dem administration, things began to go very badly, very fast. As the votes added up, it was clear that the party was going to lose control of a number of its 'held' authorities. As the hours went by it was ever more obvious that the damage would be considerable.

By the time all the votes were in, the Lib Dems were facing humiliation. They had lost control in nine councils. Three Lib Dem-controlled authorities, Newcastle-upon-Tyne, Chesterfield and Kingston-upon-Hull, all went to Labour. Labour also secured a council majority in, the constituency home of Lib Dem leader Nick Clegg himself, ousting the minority Lib Dem group from power.[2]

In three more councils power was lost by the Lib Dems as the figures indicated 'No Overall Control' – meaning no party had an absolute majority of councillors on those authorities.

As this unfolded, there was another dynamic at play. What few people noticed on that fateful evening was that Labour weren't the only party to benefit from the Lib Dem implosion. Control of three councils – Lewes, North Norfolk and the Vale of White Horse – passed directly across from the Liberal Democrats to the Conservatives.[3] This meant that, as far as gaining councils off the Liberal Democrats was concerned, the Tories had been exactly as successful as Labour – though, collectively, the three Labour gains were regarded as more newsworthy.

Thus in sharp contrast to the Lib Dem meltdown the opposite story was the case for the Conservatives. Although they lost some seats and gained others, they finished the election in net control of three *more* councils than they had started with. There were now a total of 201 Tory-controlled councils across the country, far ahead of the 77 authorities Labour now controlled.

By the end of counting the next day, Labour had made over 800 gains at local council level. However, the Conservatives had totally confounded predictions. Far from losing ground, the Tories had gained more than 80 new seats.[4]

By contrast, for the liberal movement the evening's bad news story was inescapable. Out of 1,847 Lib Dem seats up for election they made net losses of 748 seats, mainly to Labour candidates but also to Tories.[5] The headline story was the Lib Dem failure at the polls. They had lost four out of every ten seats they were defending.

Before polling day, Lib Dems had run 22 authorities. After it, they ran 13.[6] Their share of the vote – 16% – was their worst local election result since 1980.[7] The party had lost one-fifth of its total complement of councillors – *in just one night*. With a total of about 3,100 councillors remaining across the country, this was the smallest council contingent the liberal movement had experienced in a quarter of a century.[8]

The one big disappointment for Labour was their failure to make the 'fightback' in Scotland which party leader Miliband had boldly predicted. The Scottish Nationalist Party secured an *absolute majority* of seats in Scottish Parliament – something which had been considered practically impossible up to that time. Even their leader – the First Minister of Scotland, Alex Salmond – had not dared to speak publicly of such a potential triumph.

However, even in Scotland the worst results were suffered by the Lib Dems. Their performance was disastrous and there was no way on earth to pretend otherwise. Liberal Democrat numbers sank from 16 seats to a meagre five. The Scottish Lib Dem vote had roughly halved, with 7.9% for individual candidates in constituencies. Of the 11 constituencies they held, nine were lost.[9] Due to the proportional system of election in Scotland (and Wales) there was also a 'list' vote, in which electors express their preference between parties rather than candidates. The Lib Dems achieved just over 5% of the vote in this ballot. This translated to three 'regional' list seats – a drop of two.[10] Tavish Scott, the Lib Dem leader in Scotland, announced his resignation two days after the election. He declined invitations from interviewers to tell Nick Clegg to do so too.

The Alternative View

Alex Salmond made great play of the fact that the electoral system for the Scottish Parliament had, to an extent, been designed explicitly to prevent the possibility of an overall majority for any one party – especially the SNP. Their victory was in stark contrast to the decline in Labour support and the catastrophic reversal suffered by the Lib Dems. It is clear that his achievement would have been impossible without the fall in Labour's vote and the virtual collapse of the Liberal Democrats.

The tale of woe was unrelenting. In Wales it was Labour – not the Welsh Nationalists – who made the greatest progress. They secured sufficient gains to sweep up 30 out of 60 Assembly seats.[11] Lib Dem support slumped from 14.8% in the constituencies to 10.6%. Because of the proportional system of election in Wales, which was the same as the system in Scotland, there was again a 'list' vote, in which electors express their preference between parties rather than candidates. This also fell – from 11.7% to 8%. Welsh Lib Dems started the night with six Welsh Assembly Members. They ended it with five: their worst result since the Welsh Assembly had been formed 12 years previously. The internal story was even worse. They had lost two out of three 'constituency' seats. The only reason that it didn't look even worse was that the 'list' seats went up from three to four as a crude form of compensation to balance things in the Assembly proportionately.[12] By contrast, their Conservative coalition partners again performed well, increasing their vote and their number of seats by two, one being gained directly from the Lib Dems.[13]

And what of the Leicester South by-election? This time around, the able and popular candidate, Zuffar Haq, protected the party's second place, achieving over 22% of the vote – 4.4% points down on the previous general election the year before. In the context of a dismal night, it was far from being the worst result of the evening.[14]

It must also be noted that, in the face of this storm of failure, one candidate delivered a miraculous, and almost unheralded, triumph. Dave Hodgson, the Mayor of Bedford, held his tenure comfortably, keeping the Conservatives in second place.[15] This poll employed a system of proportional representation, enabling the transfer of second preference votes until one candidate has more than 50%. Let us examine this particular event a little more.

Hodgson achieved 38% in the first round. This meant that, in terms of 'first preference' votes, 38 out of every 100 electors cast their ballot for him. When the ballot papers of the candidates with the lowest number of votes were transferred from the Labour, Independent and Green candidates, seven out of every 10 of those votes also went to Hodgson. This was in large part thanks to Hodgson's outstanding performance as a mayor: his vote had actually increased considerably since his original election to the position in a by-election in 2009.[16] This isolated example did show that left-leaning voters were still willing to 'transfer' to a Liberal Democrat candidate whom they regarded as politically acceptable, even at a time when the party as a whole had become deeply unpopular (to underline the difference between party support and personal popularity, note that there was even a net loss of one seat in Bedford on the day Hodgson was re-elected). This will become significant when we turn our attention to the question of leadership and the next general election.

'What matter are real votes in real ballot boxes.'

It had been Labour's night, but the headline story was that the Lib Dems had been the biggest losers, to such an extent that any attempt at a positive news spin was drowned out by the figures themselves. The party's press operation made an effort to highlight that the Liberal Democrats had fared better in those areas where they already had Members of Parliament. This was hardly surprising – by definition, if a party has done well in an area before, it is more likely to do so again.

However, even here there was a very patchy story to be told. In the city which Nick Clegg himself represented – Sheffield – Liberal Democrats lost nine seats in the local elections. The party lost control in their northern flagship authorities. There was no way to massage the fact that of the three largest parties in Britain the Liberal Democrats had taken a great beating. Overall, the other two parties had done well – and in the case of the Conservatives, surprisingly so. The Liberal Democrats stood alone in their misery.

Analysis

Electorally, 5 May 2011 underlined what had already become obvious in the lead-up to the polls. Liberal Democrats had suffered reverses in parliamentary by-elections, council seats, the number of councils run, the Welsh Assembly and the Scottish Parliament. While there were good results in a number of individual Lib Dem-held seats, including Westmorland and Lonsdale, Eastleigh, Colchester, Barnsley Central, Portsmouth and Poole[17] – as well as that stunning mayoral result in Bedford – this simply suggested that individual Lib Dem-held seats had the capacity to buck the national trend. Overall – and apart from these islands of strength – there seemed no opportunity for the party to make any inroads in places where they were not already well represented.

This time, there was no way for the party to soften the message of those real votes in real ballot boxes, except to claim that this was the price that had to be paid for courageous and important decisions to get the country back on track economically.

The alternative view is that, logically, this could not be the whole story. If the Lib Dems had suffered a night of defeats simply because of being in government, why, then, had their coalition partners – who, by definition, were accountable for exactly the same governmental programme – gained council seats and councils, suffering minor reversals in, but winning two more seats on the Welsh Assembly? Some of these gains had even been at the direct expense of the Lib Dems.

Labour Leader Ed Miliband was quick to suggest that the damage to Lib Dem fortunes was self-inflicted by virtue of their association with the Conservatives. At the same time, Conservatives revelled in their victories privately, while doing their best to maintain a dignified respect for the losses of their coalition partners in public. It was reported that Downing Street had explicitly told Tory ministers not to gloat in public over the results.[18] It is inconceivable that they did not quietly celebrate the weakening of the Lib Dems amongst themselves.

Peter Maughan, a Lib Dem councillor on Gateshead Council, and former parliamentary candidate in Blaydon and Newcastle North, summarised a commonly held view. 'We did it to ourselves. Unless they get their act in gear down there in, we're finished up here.'[19]

Another conversation, in the picturesque northern village of Wylam, near Gateshead, with a former Chair of the Northern Region Liberal Democrats, Phil Appleby, offered a similar analysis. 'If we insist on supping with the devil, there's no Angel of the North that's going to want to come and save our souls.' He suggested that an exorcism might do the trick, leaving it open as to which 'evil spirits' needed to be exorcised.[20]

A similar opinion was expressed at a campaigning meeting of Lib Dem activists in the Three Stags – a Kennington public house used by various Liberal Democrat and Labour members for informal political gatherings. The meeting was downbeat about the party's national performance. One activist suggested this was a ' moment'. A councillor from South London noted that, in 2012, London itself would have local and Greater London Authority elections, adding sombrely: 'The battle of Britain is over. The battle for Liberal London has begun.'

Summary

The catastrophic performance of the party in by-elections and the local elections of May 2011 was no real surprise. Their actuality was still a body blow. Real activists had lost real power, and there was no escape from the statistics. A restless Spring Conference with demonstrations outside it in Sheffield had hinted at trouble around the leader's own university constituency, Sheffield Hallam. These results strongly implied that he would have to increase the time he would have to spend in his own constituency in order to protect his own seat, lest this, too, became vulnerable at the next election.

The one crumb of comfort for Clegg and his team was that, in 2012, there would be a much smaller number of local council seats to be defended – and no regional elections in Scotland or Wales. However, a further loss of, say, 300 seats would be just as bad proportionately – and there was also the London Mayoralty and Authority elections to consider.

As far as the elections were concerned, there would be future occasions to win back lost seats. However, what could not be re-run in the medium term was the 'make or break' referendum on electoral reform. That plebiscite had been a cornerstone of the coalition agreement. The Lib Dems knew that if the referendum was lost, their dream of fair votes would also be lost – potentially for a generation. After all, Conservative and Labour activists were potentially comfortable with a continuation of the convenient status quo which had, for so long, undermined Liberal and then Lib Dem fortunes. This was to be the last piece of counting to be associated with 5 May.

As the referendum ballot papers were poured out onto tables, the counting began. Everyone on both sides knew that the stakes couldn't be higher.

Chapter 6

Paradise Lost

A miserable little compromise.
Nick Clegg, 22 April 2010

Play it again, Sam.
Paramount Pictures, 1972

With the Liberal Democrats in shock over the disastrous election results on 5 May, there was one more vital result which could save the day – a permanent change to the way in which MPs were elected to Parliament.

Since the Liberal Democrats were formed, they had persistently advocated the case for a change in how the British Parliament was elected. For the whole of the 20th century, and the beginning of the 21st, Members of the British Parliament had been elected by the 'first past the post' system of election. This system is very simple: all it requires the elector to do is to put an 'X' next to one of the candidates. The options usually consist of candidates from the Conservative, Labour and Liberal Democrat parties. Candidates standing for other parties – or as 'independents' – are also entitled to put their names forward for inclusion on the ballot paper. For

British parliamentary elections, there is no requirement to be affiliated to any particular political movement in order to participate as a candidate in the electoral process.

The process for inclusion on a ballot paper is not in itself particularly onerous. All it requires is the completion of a nomination form, whereby a prescribed number of individuals entitled to vote 'nominate' the candidate. There is also the need to pay a deposit which is then returned after the election, subject to the achievement of a threshold level of support, which, in 2011, was set at 5% – as it had been for decades. There was, therefore, no insuperable obstacle to candidature.

Small parties have made their mark in politics by intelligent use of the electoral system, even when this has not led to direct representation in the House of Commons. For example, the 'Campaign for Real Ale' – CAMRA – successfully instigated a resurgence in support for real ale without winning a single seat in Parliament. Their influence remained strong by proxy through intelligent use of advocates, such as Liberal Democrat MP for Leeds North West, Greg Mulholland, a leading light in supporting their cause. CAMRA is a classic example of effective use of the electoral system to achieve a 'single issue campaign' result.[1]

This methodology can be applied successfully if the campaign is not overtly ideological in such a way that it stands to conflict with the philosophy of one party or another. Being a Conservative is no more a barrier to drinking real ale than being a Welsh Nationalist or an Ulster Unionist. However, the approach does not work for political movements such as liberalism. Ideologies cannot usually 'piggyback' on each other, because, unlike single issue pressure groups, they tend to conflict at a fundamental level with other political parties. Therefore it is not possible for liberals to operate effectively from outside Parliament, because finding advocates to represent the case – as CAMRA did – is not practicable in the same sense. Liberals must be represented in Parliament directly, not indirectly, because a conservative is not a liberal, even if he likes the same ales.

This brings us to the issue which has dogged political progress for the liberal movement for political generations. In order for liberalism to flourish in Parliament, it must win votes. Yet to do that, it must succeed against the main competing political movements, which, for most of the last century, were Conservative and Labour. Despite the fact that Liberals had formed the Government at the turn of the 20th century, they had a very long way to go to have any chance of regaining that exalted status at the turn of the 21st.

This is where the party's frustration with the first past the post electoral system comes into play. In this system, the winner simply requires more votes than any other candidate to win. However, the winner does *not* require more than half of *all* the votes cast. They do not need an absolute majority. If a candidate achieves even one single more vote than the other candidates, they are elected.

In 1997, Liberal Democrat Mark Oaten was elected as MP for Winchester with a majority of only 2 votes over his Conservative opponent, Gerry Malone. Oaten's share of the vote was 42%, which is known as a 'simple majority' and not an 'absolute majority' – defined as 'half the total vote plus one' or more votes. Even though he had less than half the total vote, he had more than anyone else and was declared elected. The Conservatives used a legal procedure to successfully force a by-election, which they then went on to lose by a much greater margin. In the by-election, the Lib Dems secured 68%.[2] With that majority, Oaten would have won under any system.

In May 2010, Sinn Fein candidate Michelle Gildernew was elected MP for Fermanagh and South Tyrone with a majority of just 4 votes. Once again, this is what is known as a 'simple majority,' because, at 45.5%, it was less than 'half plus one' of the total vote.[3] If there had been a transfer of votes to see who had the support of more than half the electorate, who knows whether Gildernew would have won or not. Nevertheless, her electoral status was exactly the same as that of Labour MP for East Ham Stephen Timms, who secured the country's largest majority of 27,826 – which, at 70.4% of the vote, was an absolute majority.[4]

In perhaps one of the quirkiest results of recent history, another former Liberal MP, the late Sir Russell Johnson, benefited enormously from the 'simple majority' nature of the British parliamentary electoral system. In the UK general election of 9 April 1992, he managed to narrowly hold his parliamentary seat of Inverness, Nairn and Lochabar, scraping back into office after securing a result where the four main contenders – Liberal Democrat, Labour, SNP and Conservative – were outrageously closely spaced, achieving 26%, 25%, 25% and 23% respectively, with the Greens on 1.5%. The inimitable Sir Russell held his seat with a majority of just 458 votes over his second-placed rival – and a percentage just 3.4 points greater than the fourth-placed candidate.[5] So, at the micro-political level of constituency results, even the Liberal Democrats have occasionally benefited from the first past the post voting arrangement. However, in general, the system has worked against the liberal movement.

The reason there is a disparity between what happens locally and what happens nationally is subtle, but relatively easy to explain. At a local level, liberals are able to pool their limited resources into a particular seat. Whether the individual resources are related to political activism, manipulating local campaigning circumstances, the prowess of the candidate or just good fortune, such factors can sway a local electorate to deliver a result in that locality which might be at variance from the general national trend.

Such considerations have also been relevant in the election of 'local heroes' who stand as independents, such as Martin Bell, who gained the formerly safe Tory seat of Tatton in 1997, following a high profile campaign to oust the sitting MP – Neil Hamilton – on grounds of probity. So, also, a medical practitioner, Richard Taylor, defeated a sitting Labour Minister, David Lock, in the 2001 general election on the basis of defending the local health services of Wyre Forest.

In the case of both Martin Bell and Richard Taylor, the Liberal Democrats did not field a candidate (with, nor did Labour), thereby boosting the Independent candidate's chances of victory in both cases, by reducing the competition and not splitting the vote against the incumbent defending his seat.

Bell did not stand again in Tatton in 2001, and the seat reverted to the Conservatives. However, he moved to the seat of Brentwood and Ongar, where Liberal Democrats refused to stand aside for Bell in his new chosen constituency. The seat was lost to the boisterous Conservative Eric Pickles, whose vote share of 38% gave him a 'simple majority,' over Bell's 32%. The total of Bell's vote plus the Lib Dem vote came to 47%.[6] The split vote against him gave perky Pickles the edge – and the seat.

When the Liberal Democrats again fielded a candidate in Wyre Forest in 2010, Taylor lost his seat by a majority of less than the Lib Dem vote.[7] All the same, Taylor would probably have won in 2001 with or without a Lib Dem opponent. Nevertheless, his parliamentary career showed how, under first past the post, consideration of local circumstances could deliver a result at variance with the national trend – in this case through the manipulation of the candidate list.

As this straightforward analysis shows, the characteristics of the existing electoral system presented a double-edged sword for the Liberal Democrats. On the one hand, the requirement to achieve merely a 'simple majority' means that, with focus on a local campaign and some tactical power play, such as not fielding a candidate against a sympathetic independent with a better chance of winning a seat, Lib Dems could determine the result in a seat, even if they could not win it themselves. The other edge of the sword was writ large in Brentwood and Ongar, where, theoretically at least, Bell or the Lib Dem could have defeated the Tory candidate Pickles, but their mutual refusal to give way to each other was instrumental in presenting the Conservatives with victory.

The arduous task of competing at a local level, considering local circumstances and delivering seats on a constituency-by-constituency basis, has defined liberal campaigning for decades. This has often been described within Liberal Democrat circles as 'winning the ground war'. Liberals and Liberal Democrats secured a large number of by-election victories in just this way, when they focused huge resources on a very small geographical area to overwhelm their competitors. Liberals learned to cope with the circumstances of the electoral system and won through.

The difficulty for Liberal Democrats always hinged on the reverse side of the same consideration. While it may have been possible to 'win the ground war' in specific localities, the party simply lacked the resources to win the ground war everywhere, due to the enormous resources that this required. Human and financial investment at that level was unsustainable at a national level. The concept of 'targeting' is known to every Lib Dem activist for this very reason.

It was also the cause of a recurring quest within the Liberal Democrat movement – how to 'win the air war'. This media campaign relied on macro-political commentary and support in the press and broadcast media, as opposed to depending almost entirely on leaflets delivered by party workers – as well as local campaigning activity.

Liberal Democrats have long held the belief that both Labour and the Conservatives have held a significant advantage in terms of the 'air war' for three reasons. Firstly, Conservatives and Labour have enjoyed more publicly-expressed support from large media proprietors who – whether out of ideology or expedience – tended to back the Conservatives and Labour in preference to the Lib Dems. There have been exceptions, such as *The Independent* and

The Guardian. Both papers were more sympathetic to the Lib Dems, especially in the early 21st century. However, the centre of media gravity never lay with the Liberal Democrats during a general election.

Secondly, Liberal Democrats persistently achieved significantly lower levels of political funding versus the other two main parties. This expenditure differential meant that, ever since the Liberal Democrats were formed, in general elections Labour and Conservatives spent many times more money on their campaigns than did the Lib Dems, and this necessarily impacted on their respective ability to purchase 'air time' in all its different forms.

Thirdly, because the electoral system favoured the Conservatives and Labour over the Liberal Democrats, a 'self-fulfilling prophecy' choked the party's prospects: 'I would vote Lib Dem, but I know they can't win, so I'll vote for one of the others.' Liberal Democrats were fond of publishing surveys which showed that if all the people who said they would vote Lib Dem if they thought the party could win *did* that then the Party *would* win. This argument did not achieve much leverage in any British general election up to and including 2011. However, it was an argument deeply rooted in the first past the post electoral system, where people did not want to risk 'wasting' their vote on the Lib Dems, lest another party candidate whom they liked even less was elected by default.

Therefore, it is obvious why the Liberal Democrats sought a change in the electoral system. They aspired to a system which swept away the argument that voting Liberal Democrat was a wasted vote. They desired a system in which electors could vote for Lib Dem candidates, safe in the knowledge that doing so would not risk letting in another candidate whom they liked the least by default.

If the Lib Dems could secure such a change, the party expected that it could also garner more attention from the media. In the new environment, they would feel obliged to take more heed of Liberal

Democrat activity – if only because these politicians would be far more likely to occupy a position of power. Lib Dems did receive an uplift in attention once they entered the coalition with the Conservatives, which supports this logic.

To summarise, the key drivers for Liberal Democrat support for a more proportional system of election were: firstly, the removal of the 'Lib Dems are a wasted vote' argument; secondly, greater media attention as a result; and thirdly, the potential for greater funding given the greater potential influence the party would have in a proportionately elected Parliament.

Footnote on funding

Whether the party would also achieve an increase in funding if the electoral system changed depended to an extent on the relative influence of the party. Thus, securing AV – which would unquestionably increase the importance of the Lib Dems as a party of power – had financial implications too.

If party funding could be significantly improved as a result of the Liberal Democrat presence in government, then it was reasonable to expect more funding for the party with a 'Yes' vote in the referendum. If a 'No' vote transpired, then Liberal Democrats would not be seen as so potentially influential. Even if the Liberal Democrats were influential in the coalition, there would be no guarantee that this would be sustained after 2015.

Should the AV referendum deliver no change, Liberal Democrats might be seen as a poor investment – precisely because investing in them could increase the 'risk' of a hung parliament in an unpredictable way. This might not be particularly attractive to funders who could prefer to invest in parties certain to win more seats than the Lib Dems. The outcome of the AV referendum would be of great importance for budgets as a result.

Separately, if the party improved its financial circumstances compared to the same point in the previous electoral cycle (2008), even without a 'Yes' vote in the AV referendum, then influence and profile in coalition would have proved themselves attractive to funders. If not, either a perceived lack of power, a lack of popularity or a negative prognosis in terms of the next election would contribute to this poor performance.

What kind of system?

Liberal Democrats spend a great deal of time discussing various electoral systems, and nuances within them. There is a mass of literature available to those who wish to study the options in detail. For the purposes of the alternative view, it is sufficient to outline the principles and preferred option of the majority – though not the totality – of the Liberal Democrat movement. For that, why not go to the font of information in this field, the Electoral Reform Society?[8]

Here's a brief look at the key elements Liberal Democrats sought in a proportionate system. They were ones which removed what the party perceived as discrimination against itself – and discrimination towards the Conservative and Labour parties. First past the post offered local advantages to campaigners on occasion, but usually worked against the Liberal Democrats and minor parties. A system reflecting share of votes – rather than which party secured the most votes in each seat – was more desirable to Lib Dems. For perspective, in the 2010 general election, Conservatives secured 36% of the vote and 47% of the seats in the House of Commons. Labour achieved 29% of the vote and 40% of the seats. Meanwhile, Liberal Democrats secured 23% of the vote and 9% of the seats.[9] It was hardly surprising that Liberal Democrats were a bit irate about the system.

Most Lib Dems preferred the 'Multi-Seat Single Transferable Vote' method of election. In this version, electors voted for a party list of candidates, and then the votes were used to give a proportionate number of elected politicians. In theory, if the party A receives 30%

of the votes, it also gets 30% of the seats. If the Lib Dems receive 20% of the votes, they receive 20% of the seats. This is the purpose of the 'multi-seat' element of the system. By having many Members of Parliament for much larger constituencies than at present, MPs can be divided up proportionately. The system is already used for European parliamentary elections. Its introduction resulted in a much larger representation of Liberal Democrats in the European Parliament, with a jump from two seats to 10 seats as a direct result of the change, even though the Lib Dem vote declined from 16% to 12% in this same period.[10] The Liberal Democrats were therefore highly motivated to promote a Multi-seat Single Transferable Vote system of election for the British Parliament. However, their potential coalition partners had other ideas.

The AV deal

Just as Liberal Democrats wished to see a dramatic change in the electoral system, so also the Conservatives wanted as little change as possible. They had made the same calculations and recognised that what benefited the Lib Dems did not benefit them. It is probable – though unproved in testimony – that internal party strategists on the Conservative side also recognised that a more natural coalition alliance in other electoral circumstances would be between the Liberal Democrats and Labour, not Liberal Democrats and Conservatives. They were as aware as everyone else that a key driver behind the coalition arrangement had been the mathematical outcome of the general election, which had made it all but impossible for any other stable partnership of parties to be forged. It is hardly surprising, then, that most Conservatives were not supportive of a change in the electoral system since it meant that they could end up excluded from power in future.

Nevertheless, the negotiations between the Liberal Democrats and the Conservatives required a consideration of commitment to some form of electoral reform. This imperative was the progenitor for what was ultimately agreed – a referendum on the Alternative Vote system.

The Alternative Vote system is not the same as Multi-Seat Single Transferable Vote. With the Alternative Vote, the constituencies remain unchanged. In other words, there is one elected representative per constituency, not a number of representatives jointly covering a larger area, as is the case in the European constituencies. The change is therefore not concerning constituencies, but, rather, how many votes you need to win an existing constituency. A 'simple majority' would no longer be enough because with AV having more votes than anyone else is not sufficient. Having more votes than everyone else *put together* becomes the new threshold: '50% plus one.' That's roughly twice as much as Sir Russell Johnson MP got in his photo-finish election result in 1992.

For electors, the change is about how one marks the ballot paper. Instead of putting an 'X' next to their preferred choice of candidate, they are encouraged to put a '1' next to the name, followed by a '2' next to their second favourite candidate, a '3' next to their third and so on until they have no further preferences.

With AV, when the votes are counted, if there is one candidate with more than 50% of the vote then they are the winner. Even under AV Steven Timms, who achieved 70.4% in his constituency in 2010, would have been declared the winner after one count of the votes; but under AV Sir Russell Johnson, in 1992, would not. As Sir Russell achieved just 26% of the vote, the candidate with the fewest votes would have been eliminated and their votes redistributed according to the second preferences – the '2s.' In this example, the candidates with the fewest votes would have been successively eliminated until one achieved more than 50% of the vote. It may or may not have been Sir Russell, but the point about an 'absolute majority' – 50% plus one – is that it provides a legitimacy which, it could be argued, a 'simple majority' of 26% does not.

For Liberal Democrats as a collective movement, the Alternative Vote (AV) system was not the party's preferred choice. But it was the best offer on the table, and, in the early days of the new coalition arrangement, they accepted it as a step forward. To be more precise, what was in fact on offer was a referendum on AV... not AV itself. Fatefully, the party negotiators agreed to hold this referendum on the same day as the 2011 local elections for England and the regional government elections for Wales, Scotland and Northern Ireland.

Now all the Lib Dems had to do was get the country to vote 'Yes' in the referendum. This may not have appeared to be that great a challenge in the fledgling campaign. After all, AV was a very modest change to the existing voting system. In terms of physical effort, the AV system would demand a few extra seconds from electors versus first past the post. In terms of intellectual challenge, it was no great leap forward either. As the coalition's Liberal Democrat junior minister Jeremy Browne commented while waiting to be interviewed on College Green outside Parliament in the run-up to the referendum, 'if you can count to four, then you can understand AV.'[11] It was a refreshingly simple explanation.

Nevertheless there was public opposition to the proposed change from Conservatives who knew that it wasn't biased in their favour, as the current system was. They openly criticised a system which could potentially prevent them from getting a majority again. They did not wish to share power with other parties, including the Lib Dems, if they could possibly avoid it. They preferred to operate alone. Having agreed to the referendum, they set about campaigning for a 'No' vote.

Officially, the Labour Party backed the 'Yes' campaign. Leader Ed Miliband participated in debates and did his part to 'look positive' about the reform. His party didn't share his enthusiasm, and a number of Labour MPs and councillors openly opposed the proposals.

For many months, the public at large were magnificently lethargic about the AV referendum. It failed to excite citizens, even if politically-minded activists were motivated about raising the issue on doorsteps. For much of 2010, the referendum occupied much less airtime than the tussles occurring on the *X Factor* reality TV talent show. Those interested in politics were more worried about the economy and other matters. Polling on the question was also equivocal, with both sides believing that they could win. Some polls indicated a lead for the 'Yes' campaign while others did the opposite.

As the referendum approached, the level of interest increased. At the same time, the opposing referendum campaign teams became fractious, bad-tempered and highly personal. The 'No' campaign resorted to threatening the nation with pictures of Nick Clegg – warning that, if they voted 'Yes,' Clegg and his Liberal Democrat buddies would be in power a great deal more of the time. This annoyed Lib Dems in no small measure, and a shouting match developed, spilling over into at least one Cabinet meeting, with Huhne reportedly lashing out at Cameron's involvement in the 'No' campaign.

As the campaign developed to a tetchy finale, it was clear that most of the country neither understood nor cared about voting reform. Even intelligent people were at a loss to understand it, while others saw it as an opportunity to punish the Lib Dems for 'selling out' to the Tories. They cited disappointment on policy issues, such as tuition fees, in aid of their decision to oppose the proposed change to the electoral system. The media made fun of the alleged complexity of the proposed system and it became fashionable to say that it was all too complicated and too much trouble to bother with.

The 'No' campaigners also repeatedly revelled in citing Clegg's own words about the AV system to erode support for a 'Yes,' claiming that even the prime advocate of AV had described it as 'a grubby little compromise'. It was true that Clegg had described the proposed system as a compromise, but further analysis shows the degree to which his words were both misrepresented and altered. Context is key.

In the run up to the 2010 general election, Clegg had discussed his conditions for electoral reform with the *Independent* newspaper:

> The Labour Party assumes that changes to the electoral system are like crumbs for the Liberal Democrats from the Labour table. I am not going to settle for a miserable little compromise thrashed out by the Labour Party.[12]

Clegg was arguing for something he called Alternative Vote Plus, which was different to the Alternative Vote system. However, he also said, in the same interview:

> AV is a baby step in the right direction – only because nothing can be worse than the status quo.[13]

The 'No' campaign didn't worry too much about context and quickly distilled the phrase 'miserable little compromise' into a mantra that they could use repeatedly to further damage the 'Yes' vote. Soon people were saying that Clegg regarded AV as a 'grubby little compromise'. The alternative view could find no direct evidence that Clegg had ever used that specific phrase, and he certainly did not use it in his interview with *The Independent* in April 2010. It is easy to find indirect references to Clegg's use of this term but not direct ones. The wording attributed to Clegg appears to be a mischievous distortion, taken out of context from Clegg's original interview with *The Independent*. Labour MP Emily Thornberry certainly did use this phrase a lot, as did others.[14] But, just as nobody in the epic film *Casablanca* ever said 'Play it again, Sam' (this, in fact, the name of a film starring Woody Allen), so also attributing the 'grubby little compromise' quote to Clegg owed more to Chinese whispers than it did to the Lib Dem leader.[15]

None of this made much difference. On 26 April 2010 Jonathan

Freedland of the *Guardian* paper was careful to use the correct terminology – and he also provided a fair context for Clegg's comment.[16] But from then on, the grubby little phrase appeared everywhere; it was attributed to Clegg; and nobody much cared if he had said it or not.

Despite an increasingly consistent set of indicators suggesting a rejection of AV by the electorate, right up to the last week of campaigning, confusion, scepticism, partisanship and turnout were variables beyond the capacity of pollsters to conclusively evaluate. All eyes were on the actual results as they emerged from the count.

'X' marks the spot

As the counting was carried out and the figures were reported, the outcome was beyond contention. The country had not been persuaded to move from what it knew to what the Lib Dems preferred. To the distress of the pioneers of electoral reform, the final result left no doubt: 32% voted 'Yes,' and 68% had voted 'No'.[17] Electoral reform was dead in the water, with less than a third of the voting electorate supporting the change. First past the post was here to stay, at least for the medium term. There would be no chance at all to replay this ballot before 2015.

Unlike council seats, which come up every four years, this ballot had kicked 'fair votes' into the long grass for as much as a political generation. A second referendum in the short term would look hectoring, and would almost certainly guarantee another 'No'.

Whatever the future held, there was evidently no prospect of any further debate about electoral reform as far as the coalition partnership was concerned. Cameron's gambit had risked his personal credibility with his AV-sceptic members. But his risk had paid off and left him in a strengthened position; he had effectively delivered his part of the deal – a referendum on a change to the electoral system – to Nick Clegg and the Liberal Democrats. Yet

Cameron had also presided over a wholesale rejection of change, causing him to stand tall in the eyes of his Tory party faithful.

Clegg had the opposite problem. He had been at the helm when a cherished policy had been thrown to the lions by the electorate. Worse still, this had been done according to a referendum on a date agreed by his own negotiating team.

It has yet to be established whether the opponents of AV were fully conscious, in 2010, of the benefits of holding the poll on the same day as the local government elections. Whether or not they were, it is probable that holding the referendum on the same day served to strengthen the Conservative vote by encouraging a greater turnout amongst right-leaning electors who strongly opposed the change. Not only had the referendum been lost by the Liberal Democrats; holding it on that particular day had probably caused the Lib Dems even greater local election losses than they would have suffered without the albatross of holding the AV referendum at the same time. As it was, Tories filed in to vote 'No' to electoral reform, and 'Yes' for Tory candidates while they happened to be at the polling booth anyway.

Whatever the level of sophistication in the timing of the ballot, the outcome was disastrous for the Lib Dems. The referendum had been a crucial element of the coalition agreement – a golden chance to make the elections fairer in a way that could remove some of the bias against Lib Dems in elections too. Now, the party was unquestionably doomed to fight according to the first past the post system at the next general election. Given its election performance in the first 12 months of the coalition, the prospect of living under a system which overtly favoured Labour and Tory candidates was nothing to relish.

Naturally, attention turned in part towards the Lib Dem involvement in the campaign. Accusations floated vaguely in the general direction of the leadership: there was a feeling that if Clegg had magically 'made himself more popular,' things might have been different. This fledgling dissatisfaction was not coherently formed. Official spokespeople condemned the personal nature of the attacks against Clegg by the 'No' campaign. Others blamed Labour for not trying hard enough to support the change. Nothing much came of these various attempts to pin the blame on an individual organisation or politician.

This prompts the important question: could the leadership have done things differently? Was there an alternative path which had been ignored? With the 'double whammy' of electoral disaster in the local government polls and the resounding failure in the AV referendum, the movement which had delivered Clegg to power – the Orange Book caucus – had not delivered on the heady expectations of only a year ago to the party. This was the second year in which the party had fallen short of what the activists had hoped for.

The anti-Clegg campaign

The highly personalised nature of the anti-Clegg marketing strategy was both ironic and poignant. It was ironic because a very large proportion of those propagating those negative and personalised views were, in fact, associated with the very coalition partners with whom Clegg had entered into a professional relationship in May 2010 – the Tories. And it was poignant simply because, once again, negative campaigning techniques had entered the political ring in the context of both Nick Clegg as an individual and the Liberal Democrats as a party force. It was a methodology which had reared its head in the 2007 Lib Dem leadership election. Now it was coming back to roost from the outside in.

In keeping with this aspect of the campaign, it is worth returning again to news reports which emanated from the Cabinet just before the poll, indicating that Liberal Democrat Orange Booker and Cabinet member Chris Huhne had launched a vitriolic outburst against Conservative fellow Cabinet members in the run-up to the crucial AV vote.[18] It was rumoured – especially in party circles – that Huhne's venom was a precursor to a leadership challenge in anticipation of a disastrous result in the AV referendum, and also in the local elections.[19]

Whatever the motivation, this was cautious evidence once again that at least one of the very most senior Liberal Democrats in the party was willing to quite publicly express negative views about Tory colleagues. It was in stark contrast to views expressed by the Lib Dem Deputy Prime Minister himself – who was, at around the same time, carelessly recorded bemoaning the degree to which he and the Conservative Prime Minister agreed, and how this could turn out to be a difficulty in future televised debates.[20]

From the point of view of consistency, the apparent willingness of some Liberal Democrats to take an aggressively negative view of coalition colleagues in the Cabinet, while others were taking an affectionately positive one in private, is further circumstantial evidence that there was, at that time, no collective position in the leading and ministerial circles of the Lib Dems on relations with the other party. Collective responsibility for stable government did not extend to a rigid rule of consistently supportive or indeed critical demeanour in inter-party discussions.

Whether Huhne's anger was planned or spontaneous is less important than the fact that it happened, and that it was not publicly condemned nor officially clarified by Liberal Democrat representatives is also significant. It hinted at a general acceptance by Orange Bookers, who, as we have seen, unanimously formed the five-strong Lib Dem contingent on the Cabinet, that a consistent approach was not obligatory. Whether this rang alarm bells amongst Conservative Cabinet ministers was not recorded. But it was surely an indication of what might recur in the event of a difficult and highly pressurised political crisis facing the Liberal Democrats at a future date. The capacity for vitriol was clearly there, and the conditions to provoke it were, at least vaguely, predictable.

Summary

Internal frictions within the coalition Cabinet reflected internal frictions in the party. Members were beginning to question the Liberal Democrat leadership's approach, and looking for ways to make sense of what had just happened. Until now, either such questioning had not seemed relevant to the rank and file or thoughts about it had not been methodically formed. To some, they had almost seemed taboo. But now there was a little more willingness to say things to the press about what had gone wrong and what the leadership needed to do to put it right.

Central to the alternative view is a consideration of the reasons for the defeat in the polls and in the AV referendum. Why was it that such a central tenet of Liberal Democrat ideology had been lost by such a large margin? Had it truly been impossible for the party to manage the campaign in a more effective manner? And what was the relationship between this defeat and what had happened in the local elections on the same day? This investigation leads to some conclusions which have implications for the party – and the leadership – up to 2015 and beyond.

Chapter 7

Orange Bookends

If freedom means anything, it must surely include the freedom to engage in activities which others may consider unwise.
David Laws, 2004

Company cultures are like country cultures. Never try to change one. Try, instead, to work with what you've got.
Professor Peter Drucker, Management Consultant

With the poor election results and defeat in the referendum, discussion turned to asking: why did years of effort and steady progress by the Liberal Democrats turn into losses so fast – and so dramatically? While the simplest answer offered was 'this is the price that the Lib Dems have to pay in the short term for a seat in Government,' the alternative view challenges this assumption.

If holding office in government were the only reason, then the Conservatives – the larger partner in the coalition agreement – would have fared far worse in the very same elections. In fact, they gained over 80 seats, while Liberal Democrats lost over 700. Nor did Prime Minister Cameron suffer a great slump in the polls as Clegg had done: there is an asymmetry in the relative damage incurred by the two parties, indicating that merely laying the blame at the door of 'being in government' is both simplistic and naïve. The Conservatives had also been successful in securing a 'No' vote in the AV referendum with a majority of two to one, using a good deal of overtly anti-Lib Dem propaganda to attempt to negatively skew voter perceptions.

Was part of the problem to do with the ruling Orange Book group? For much of the previous four decades, something of a left-leaning, softly libertarian narrative had been pervasive throughout most of the party, from the passive member through to the leadership. Could it be that the Orange Bookers' approach to the question of 'narrative' had somehow influenced the party's performance? When the Orange Bookers had succeeded in gaining authority within the party had they even done so with the explicit backing of the membership and supporter base for a particular worldview?

Let's recall what *The Orange Book* was. First of all, its cover spoke volumes about its intent. It showed a woman standing on a stepladder over-painting an off-white or yellowish wall with bright and bold orange, suggesting that a rebranding of liberalism was its creators' aim. With only a small patch to complete, it suggested that her work was nearly done. The bold black letters of the subtitle confirmed the goal – *Reclaiming Liberalism*.

In 2007, the leadership election had been between two members of that same Orange Book faction: Clegg and Huhne. Thus, there was no real ideological debate about the Orange Book itself, because 'there was no alternative'. This prevented the Orange Book viewpoint from being the subject of particular scrutiny, because it was not something which differentiated the candidates. The issue facing the membership had been centred on which Orange Book representative was the best one, not whether the Orange Book philosophy was the right one. The election bypassed the need for the two candidates to outline the ideology because it could be assumed that they both shared it, whatever 'it' was. This is why the campaign was fought on the basis of personality and human factors, not philosophical or strategic ones. It was an 'incomplete' campaign as either candidate could win without having to justify their different philosophies. Let's fill in that blank now by asking: what, in fact, is the Orange Book narrative?

Orange Book Unlimited

The Orange Book was the brainchild of one very impressive MP and thinker, David Laws, and one very successful industrialist and party supporter, Paul Marshall. These two individuals collaborated together on their Orange Book project, with the intention of defining this new agenda for the Liberal Democrats in the 21st century. *The Orange Book* was published in 2004.

Marshall had a very clear view of what he was trying to achieve. In the introduction to *The Orange Book*, Marshall explained:

> the views expressed are those of the individual authors and are not necessarily party policy. However, taken together, they do represent a hard-headed, coherent whole, which illuminates the practical relevance of Liberalism, classical and 'New,' to contemporary problems.

He concluded, 'Taken together, they offer a strong and radical agenda for reform.'[1]

David Laws shared 's clarity of purpose – as well as having a very precise philosophical viewpoint of his own. His economic ideas appeared to broadly agree with those which Marshall lucidly expounded. Laws also outlined his social-liberal outlook with laudable clarity. For example, of his libertarian viewpoint he wrote:

> If freedom means anything, it must surely include the freedom to engage in activities which others may consider unwise, provided the 'externalities' do not impose unreasonable costs on the rest of us. This includes smoking, overeating, not exercising, driving 'off road' cars in cities, even winning goldfish at fairs. A Liberal society is one in which people should be free to 'make their own mistakes.' The Liberal Democrats must surely be rigorous in applying the principles of personal liberalism in the future.[2]

This was visibly different to David Cameron's viewpoint, as we shall see when we take a look at 'muscular liberalism'. Laws' worldview would lead to different outcomes – confirming that both Laws and Cameron had meaningful but divergent positions – because the application of either narrative meant measurably different policy solutions for society's problems. As such, whether one agreed with them or not, they were both standpoints of substance.

Marshall and Laws coordinated a group of Liberal Democrats, primarily from the parliamentary party of MPs, to contribute to their Orange Book project. These included future leader Nick Clegg, plus other soon-to-be senior members of the leadership team – such as Vince Cable and Chris Huhne. Many were known to be ambitious personally, and made no secret of this fact.

Not much has been written or said about the motivations of those who agreed to write for *The Orange Book*. Whatever these aspirations were, the publication of the first volume had the effect of immediately creating the impression of a caucus within the party which stood apart from the rest. The Orange Book became a group to which one either pointedly belonged – or did not. Whatever Laws and Marshall wished for their initiative in philosophical terms, they had constructed a very visible political vehicle for its participants.

Lib Dem ministers and the Orange Book

The extent to which the two volumes of the Orange Book project defined who would be on the inside by 2011 is remarkable. Here are the chapter headings in *The Orange Book* – the first of the two volumes – and the authors of each:

1. David Laws MP, 'Reclaiming Liberalism: a liberal agenda for the Liberal Democrats'
2. Edward Davey MP, 'Liberalism and localism'
3. Nick Clegg MP, 'Europe: a Liberal future'
4. Chris Huhne MP, 'Global governance, legitimacy and renewal'
5. Vince Cable MP, 'Liberal economics and social justice'
6. Susan Kramer MP, 'Harnessing the market to achieve environmental goals'
7. David Laws MP, 'UK health services: a liberal agenda for reform'
8. Mark Oaten MP, 'Tough Liberalism: a liberal approach to cutting crime'
9. Steve Webb MP and Jo Holland, 'Children, the family and the state: a liberal agenda'
10. Paul Marshall, 'Pension reform: a settlement for a new century'[3]

Of the Members of Parliament involved in the writing of the original book, *all six* who were still MPs in 2010 held ministerial roles in the coalition. The two who did not were no longer MPs. One, Mark Oaten, stood down in the 2010 general election and the other, Susan Kramer, lost her seat to the Conservatives, also in 2010. In fact, Clegg appointed Kramer to the House of Lords, after which Kramer stood in the 2010 party presidential elections, losing narrowly to non-Orange Booker Tim Farron MP.

Given the success rate in terms of achieving high office, writing for *The Orange Book* was therefore a very good career move indeed. Building on the success of their first volume, they did it again in 2006. That was the year when the sequel to *The Orange Book* was published – *Britain After Blair*. The cover was clearly designed to confirm that this was a close cousin of the first *Orange Book* – a second volume in the project which Laws and Marshall had instigated. This time, a man with a brush was close to finishing the task of painting over Prime Minister Tony Blair's face, replacing it with the same even orange hue which had beamed out from the first volume. The subtitle on this occasion was *A Liberal Agenda*.

Here are the names of the contributors to *Britain After Blair*:

1. Julian Astle and Alasdair Murray, 'Blair's Britain: an audit'
2. Vince Cable MP, 'The economy: future assets, future liabilities'
3. Edward Davey MP and Julia Goldsworthy MP, 'Productivity: a more measured approach'
4. Sarah Teather MP, 'Education: expanding opportunities, increasing mobility'
5. Jo Swinson, 'Quality of life: the pursuit of happiness'
6. David Laws MP, 'Welfare reform: from dependency to opportunity'
7. Danny Alexander MP, 'Employment: freedom, responsibility and economic activity'
8. Andrew Stunell MP, 'Housing: the elephant in the room'
9. Nick Clegg MP, 'Crime and anti-social behaviour: a liberal priority'
10. Jeremy Browne MP, 'Police reform: increasing accountability and effectiveness'
11. Lynne Featherstone MP, 'Race relations: bridging communities'
12. David Howarth MP, 'Energy: a sustainable, non-nuclear future'
13. Alastair Carmichael MP, 'Transport: the missing link'
14. Michael Moore MP, 'International affairs: no such thing as abroad'
15. Simon Hughes MP, 'Democracy: towards a new constitutional settlement'[4]

Of the 13 contributors to the chapters of this book who were still MPs in May 2010, no less than 11 secured ministerial roles when the coalition was created in 2010. Only Simon Hughes and Jo Swinson did not. However, Simon Hughes was elected Liberal Democrat Deputy Leader, and Jo Swinson was appointed Parliamentary Private Secretary to Cabinet Minister Vince Cable. And there's more. *All seven Liberal Democrat MPs who had at some point served on the Cabinet by Spring 2012 had written for one or both of the Orange Book volumes* (see Appendix 6). Furthermore, all four Lib Dem MPs who had written for both *The Orange Book* and *Britain After Blair* were serving – or had served – on the Cabinet by that date.

The Orange Book and *Britain After Blair* were therefore very good tools for predicting the chances of an individual's likelihood of securing a senior position in the party after the 2010 general election. By the end of 2010, only six Liberal Democrat MPs who were ministers – and excluding the junior government whips – had *not* contributed to either *The Orange Book* or *Britain After Blair*.

Statistically by Spring 2012, and even after the mini reshuffle caused by Huhne's resignation, MPs who had written for the books had a *better than four out of five chance* of being a minister in 2010, while those MPs who did not contribute had a *less than one in five chance* of being a minister – and, at that point, a 0% probability of being in the Cabinet.

No new Orange Bookers were being proactively 'created' – and, short of producing another volume to follow *The Orange Book* and *Britain After Blair*, it would require a new mechanism to identify them, if the existing Orange Bookers did wish to generate a dynasty. Therefore these remarkable statistics were bound to gravitate more towards the non-Orange Bookers over time – through the usual mixing which occurs as roles are passed round, individuals resign, are fired or promoted or leave Parliament altogether. However, it is a testimony to the power of the Orange Book caucus that they had maintained such a steady grip on power in the party so comprehensively, and for such a considerable proportion of the five-year Parliamentary term, without being challenged by any other organised caucus.

Orange Book is not consistent

Did the collective success of Orange Bookers in securing ministerial positions arise from a collective worldview, as one might imagine for such a fabulously successful powerbase? After all, being an Orange Booker certainly boosted promotion prospects and the likelihood of high office. It would be reasonable to assume that this was because the caucus shared some kind of philosophical agenda which caused the Orange Bookers to support each other for ideological reasons.

Now we begin to see the weakness of *The Orange Book* and *Britain After Blair* versus Paul Marshall's ambition to create a 'hard-headed, coherent whole'.[5]

The truth is that many of the ideas were stimulating and creative but they did not add up to a 'big picture'. Some of them were blatantly contradictory. Perhaps because the Orange Book narrative was never tested in a leadership election in which both candidates were already signed up to it, the Orange Book agenda had not been 'shaken down' – or forced to become philosophically robust and consistent. Philosophies which have not been tested are always at risk of such flaws. These weaknesses can lie dormant in opposition, where philosophies are not placed under such great stress. However, inconsistencies take on great significance in government. Let's have a look to see how consistent the Orange Book agenda actually was. Whatever the intentions of its progenitors, there was no doubt that by 2010 the Orange Book was the single most powerful element in the party's leadership and ministerial team. How much philosophical cohesion was there in the party's most powerful group – and the one which had predominantly represented the movement in government since May 2010?

Orange Bookends

David Laws' contributions were consistently deeply thought out and assiduously argued. Even those who did not agree with his worldviews could hardly have faulted the thoroughness with which he presented his case, nor seriously have challenged its internal consistency. Laws understood the potential of the Orange Book narrative better than anyone else. Maybe, if he had led the project in a more intellectually 'hierarchical' way – and demanded consistency between contributors – the caucus could have crystallized around a shared core agenda. Having said that, it might also have made the project impossibly demanding and prevented its formation at all. Either way, he did not assume this kind of driving role, preferring a *laissez-faire* approach to contributions. Thus, inconsistency was not a limiting condition, whether or not he had intended this to be the case at the start.

In the run-up to the 2010 general election, there was no catalyst to drive the fermentation of the Orange Bookers into a cohesive, philosophically bound whole. It was never actively required to make the step from being a *vehicle* serving the ambitions and personal ideologies of its members to being a *movement* serving the collective shared vision of the group. Laws cannot be blamed for this. He had no duty to bond the Orange Bookers around shared values. After all, he was not the party leader or the elected head of the caucus. But this also meant that the group could never work to a single core narrative, because – even as its members graced the corridors of power – it had not been specifically encouraged to generate one.

The consequences are predictable. Throughout their contributions, there is a high degree of consistency in what Laws and Marshall wrote, indicating that they had worked closely together on their ideas and direction. However, the wider group of contributors did not display this same commonality of thought. A patient reading of both books quickly reveals the extent to which many of the contributions are something of a shopping list rather than a narrative, while other parts are blatantly contradictory. To say that there are contradictions is not to say that these are unintelligent works.

In fact, the contributors offer a lot to think about. Jeremy Browne makes the case against democratising elements of the police force:

> I do not think it is appropriate to elect police officers. They have an independent and impartial role that would sit very uneasily with the inevitable requirements of seeking elected office.[6]

Lynne Featherstone considered a very radical proposal for schools founded on different faiths: 'why can we not have collaboration between faith schools? Or even co-sited faith schools?'[7] Jo Swinson makes the case for more sympathetic approaches to mental illness. 'Mental health would become a bigger political priority if quality of life became a key indicator.'[8] Both books are populated with these kinds of engaging ideas, and they are worth reading – as a set of individual concepts.

However, it is the lack of consistency and the overt contradictions which are most problematic. It is not that individuals in these examples should have been prevented from making their proposals. It is simply that, since these contradictions were never ironed out, the Orange Book could not form a collective narrative for the party. Nor are all the conflicts stark matters of logic – some are nuances of priority, or tone. Yet, together, they add up to the absence of a clear direction. Let's have a look.

Mark Oaten advocated the empowerment of prison inmates in a positive way:

> A Dutch prison officer once explained the simple principle behind an extremely successful prison education project that was running: 'if you give a prisoner something simple and stupid to do, he will react stupidly. But if you give him something meaningful to do, you get a meaningful response.'[9]

Meanwhile, Clegg extolled the virtue of a different approach involving non-custodial penalties:

> Offenders should be seen out painting, sweeping, litter picking, planting trees and cleaning graffiti – so fixing the damage they've done, doing hard work and making life better for the communities in which they committed their crimes... A short custodial sentence for repeat offenders of these types of offences barely acts as a disincentive. The visible nature of a Public Punishment Sentence in the community, by contrast, can have a far greater deterrent effect.[10]

Although one spoke of prisoners and the other of non-prisoners, here the issue was one of tone. What did it mean to ensure that these offenders were 'seen out' doing these things? Why did the punishment need a 'visible nature'? How did that accord with Oaten's approval for respectful rehabilitation, not giving them 'something stupid to do'?

Steve Webb offered an interventionist agenda on matters relating to family and children. Justifying his argument on the basis of John Stuart Mill's harm principle (his chapter begins with a quote from John Stuart Mill) he believed that the state's authority could be used to promote family norms according to conventions that it considered appropriate for children. Webb wrote:

> as Liberals, we would be understandably nervous of using the power of the state to encourage particular family norms, but if the welfare of children is often enhanced where such family structures are adopted, we should not rule out such an approach.[11]

This implies the willingness to use the levers of power to encourage 'particular family norms'. In her contribution, Sarah Teather offered a different nuance:

> Policy intervention aimed at families and parenting presents uncomfortable challenges to liberals. We believe that families should be as independent and self-determining as possible and parents should be able to raise their children as they see fit.[12]

Teather goes on to ask 'what happens if the support parents are providing for their child means they are failing to reach their potential?'[13] Yet she appears to come to a different conclusion than the one drawn by Webb, preferring to focus on improving government programmes, such as the Sure Start initiative. She does not offer to use 'the power of the state' to 'encourage particular family norms' as Webb does. At no point does she seem to endorse intervening in family life as directly as in this way. Elsewhere Webb observes:

> Lone parents are also under considerable pressure from government to move off benefits and into paid employment, giving them still less time for their children.[14]

He adds:

> Based on the arguments we have advanced so far in this chapter, there would be a case for designing a tax/benefit system to make it more likely that children would be brought up in secure and stable homes, by both parents wherever possible.[15]

Meanwhile, David Laws muses:

> we need to do more to help lone parents back into employment and to create a culture in which work is seen as the appropriate avenue after the child has passed a threshold age. Employment of lone parents remains low – at around 56 per cent. Britain is highly unusual in allowing single parents to remain on income

support with no work requirements until the youngest child is 16 – this can mean parents staying out of the labour market for over twenty years. Beveridge's concept of responsibility is surely not consistent with people being able to draw benefits for so long without any obligation to seek work.[16]

Webb's position? 'Staying at home to bring up a child is... frequently looked down upon.'[17] Also:

> the pressures that any parent faces in spending enough time with a child are magnified when you are the only parent in the family home and you are also out at work for part or all of the week.[18]

The views of Webb and Laws are not criminally divergent – but they are never squared in the two volumes of the Orange Book project. What about nuclear power? Former MP David Howarth contributes an entire chapter, unambiguously titled: 'Energy: a sustainable, non-nuclear future'. In it he uses the first 10 pages to oppose the use of atomic energy:

> Nuclear is too expensive... Nuclear is not secure... Nuclear produces dangerous waste for which we don't have a solution... Far from encouraging diversity, nuclear power destroys it.[19]

Yet, in his ministerial role in government, Chris Huhne overtly supported the case for the next generation of nuclear power, despite being one of the most senior members of the Orange Book caucus. In direct contradiction to Howarth, Huhne told the Royal Society:

> Nuclear can be a vital and affordable means of providing low-carbon electricity. I believe nuclear electricity can and should

play a part in our energy future, provided that new nuclear is built without public subsidy.[20]

There are many more anomalies in the two volumes of the Orange Book project. Clegg bemoaned the dangers of revolutionary change in the European Union. Writing about the EU he states:

> Principle 1: Stop perpetual revolution.... it should be obvious that a process of relentless institutional revolution within the EU is guaranteed to inflame passions within.[21]

66 pages later in the very same book, Vince Cable observes:

> Mao Zedong may have been a tyrant, but his concept of 'permanent revolution' contained the crucial insight that state bureaucracies will always ossify and become self-serving without mechanisms to force self-criticism. In our gentler political climate radical, if less extreme, remedies are required both at a national and EU level.[22]

The contradiction needs no emphasis by us.

In her section, Susan Kramer writes: 'we have... proposed cuts in taxes such as VAT, shifting the burden to taxes on pollution.'[23] In the run-up to the 2010 election, Clegg was reported on an internal party website and elsewhere as taking a very firm line against VAT increases as well. Describing it as the 'Tories' £13bn VAT bombshell,' he said 'Let me repeat that: Our plans do not require a rise in VAT. The Tory plans do.'[24] Shortly after the advent of the coalition Liberal Democrats voted to increase VAT, on the pretext of helping to cut the government's deficit. Again, this condemns neither Kramer nor Clegg, but the inconsistency indicated that the VAT increases were never a 'red line' issue for the Orange Book leadership, despite the emphasis placed on it in the run-up to the general election.

To question whether these comparisons are taking quotes out of context would be to completely miss the point. Firstly, while we seek to share the content of the Orange Books in the spirit in which they were written, detractors could take a cynical approach and show the contradictions in starker terms. Clegg needs no reminding of the way that his words were twisted in grubby ways during the AV referendum. Secondly, an objective reading of the two Orange Book volumes does expose evident contradictions, in word and spirit. These are also to be found between what the books said in theory and what Orange Book ministers did in power – for instance on VAT. The Orange Book did not set out a 'clear liberal agenda for 21st-century politics,' as its creators had hoped on the back cover of the first volume.

That is why Davey and Goldsworthy argued in favour of 'limited drawdowns of pension savings'[25] while Marshall made the case for a 'compulsory funded pension scheme.'[26] It explains why Webb could raise concerns about government pressure on lone parents to go to work, while Laws inferred that a higher proportion ought to be in employment. It was a shopping list worthy of further debate, but not a blueprint for government.

Because the Orange Bookers were not bound to a shared agenda, this enabled its individual contributors to pursue their personal policy preferences when in power. There was no yardstick within the caucus by which to measure consistency. The Tories were pro-traditional family unit, pro-international intervention, pro-tough on crime and pro-nuclear. As such, individuals forming the Orange Book could find purchase for those elements of their own outlook which resonated with Conservative colleagues. Differences in the Lib Dem ministerial group could only be argued out on a case-by-case basis, and perhaps with reference to general Liberal Democrat policy and values. They could not be clarified with reference to the one thing three-quarters of Lib Dem ministers had in common – the Orange Book. Since all Lib Dem Cabinet ministers were Orange

Bookers, it would have been extremely helpful in underpinning a consistent narrative. That could have guaranteed the kind of consistency prevalent in the Tory party, which had a far more philosophically homogeneous ministerial core.

In the absence of a common philosophical guiding ethos, Lib Dem ministers were in danger of looking as if they were agreeing or opposing action points with their ministerial Tory counterparts on the basis of a proposal's individual merit, rather than strategically consistent factors relevant to liberalism.

The alternative view believes that this dynamic explains why Lib Dem ministers did not look like a cohesive vanguard of the Liberal Democrat movement, able to lucidly explain divergences from a core narrative in a transparent way acceptable to the membership. Given the right-leaning economic agenda of many Orange Bookers, and the authoritarian leanings of a number of those in power, this, in turn, facilitated the impression that Lib Dem ministers were drifting more towards the Conservative agenda and away from the traditional Lib Dem one – even if the individual ministers did not sense this drift themselves. As every sailor knows, with no steady reference point one can be unaware of the current that is quietly taking you off course.

The individual shopping lists began to be evolved individually in the various departmental silos. While one or two decisions did not redefine the party's image, the big picture formed by the mosaic of individual policies began to create a new impression of the party. It happened in a non-strategic, piecemeal way. There was no fanfare announcing the overall trend. Over time, the Liberal Democrat 'painting' started to change in character to citizens watching it from a distance. Yet it probably did not seem to be changing to those who were standing on the painting of government, and making their own individual brush marks on its enormous canvas.

Some of the conflicts held another tension. An alternative view suggests that overall reading of the two Orange Book volumes implied a potentially deeper conflict between its proponents and the party's more traditional economic outlook. For example, Cable promoted private management of care homes by 'mutuals'. He wrote:

> the most successful mutuals (from BUPA to the Nationwide Building Society to Linux computer systems) are disciplined commercial operations with a strong consumer service ethos backed by tight financial control and strong management.[27]

What he did not concede was that privatising care homes, in many cases, had meant that the 'mutual' enforced 'tight financial control' by reducing pay and conditions for the already low-paid staff. These poorly remunerated workers had enjoyed far better contractual terms from the local authority which previously ran the homes. This deterioration of working conditions for the lowest-paid in society directly contradicts the equitable distribution of wealth: a fundamental conflict with Liberal values. It also contradicted the party's continuing commitment to championing the fortunes of the lowest paid in society. Yet the willingness to shift towards 'mutuals' accorded well with the Tory ethos, namely to give more incentives for the rich to become richer, thus improving the quality of life for the poor as a byproduct through more and better job opportunities.

Ironically, as subsequent facts have proved, Vince Cable himself sat uneasily in the Conservative-led Cabinet, even claiming to some journalists that his resignation could destabilise it. He was also keen to intervene in a 'Labouresque' fashion against the proposed takeover by Sky of BSkyB in late 2010. This was a position which the membership approved of, but which was most certainly at odds with the Conservative ethos. It was with little grief that the Tories placed one of their own into position to consider various business matters relating to Murdoch's operations.

While the Orange Book did not have a clear philosophical narrative, its unspecific right-leaning economic 'centre of gravity' meant that it generally backed more free-market-based solutions than the traditional liberal movement had done for at least four decades. That covered everything from health provision to pensions, the environment, farming and even prisons. It was more compatible with Conservative thinking than the wider party.

In November 2010, Laws was reported on Liberal Democrat websites, political forums and elsewhere as having made a bold statement:

> Working with the Conservatives in government has led to the 'oranging' process going on at a rapid rate.[28]

Such was the import of his comment that, on 23 November, his words were even celebrated as the 'Quote of the Day' on the widely-read Guido Fawkes political blog.[29] Laws' comment would have been meaningless unless Laws believed that 'oranging' related to some kind of philosophy, or narrative, related to *The Orange Book* and, by inference, *Britain After Blair*. In the eyes of the group's creator, the Orange Bookers did indeed stand for something, and that something was happening in government. Thus the inconsistencies which had not been ironed out before the coalition represented a vagueness of mission which had been carried into government by the Orange Bookers. Their narrative would necessarily be defined by decisions, rather than the narrative determining what those decisions should be. Thus we can see the mechanism which enabled the party to look as if it were not guided by a clear philosophy: in some areas this was being worked out on a case-by-case basis as they went along. By comparison, the Conservatives had entered government with all of this clearly worked out.

Despite the ambitions of David Laws and Paul Marshall, the Orange Book foundered as a coherent new political philosophy –

because it wasn't one. Even to some contributors to *The Orange Book* it was really just a book with an orange cover – whose authors were a mutual support network, while achieving personal goals. In that scenario, as a sounding board for propositions and a way of marking the political territory, it didn't need to be consistent. But, by the same token, it couldn't lead the party's thinking because the authors had not agreed on what *they* thought.

It seems that there was a generally closer alignment in the Orange Books with Conservative economic thinking than there was with contemporary mainstream thinking in the Lib Dems regarding the free market. Market forces were more trusted by the Orange Book than by the wider membership. This may have caused Laws to feel that the 'oranging process' was going on at a rapid rate. Even if he was claiming that the Tories had been influenced by the Liberal Democrats, these things always work both ways. Had he been in office to guide the Liberal Democrat element of this interaction, things may have progressed with more clarity from the Lib Dem side. But accusations about his expenses denied David Laws the opportunity to continue as a Cabinet Minister. This was probably a factor which helped to leave these matters unresolved.

Orange teamwork

The party's performance was, by late 2010, clearly tied to the performance of the Orange Bookers. Once the coalition had been enacted, things started to go wrong for the Orange Bookers almost immediately – though the early attacks said more about the Orange Bookers' unwillingness to defend each other than it said about the Orange Book project itself.

Firstly, and of huge significance to the Orange Book caucus, David Laws himself had to leave the Cabinet following allegations about his expense claims. *At no point was there any suggestion that he had in any way broken the law.* He had occupied a role of central importance to the Cabinet with undoubted capabilities as an economist. Indeed, he was effectively the central player in the Orange Book's political development, having driven its creation with Marshall and promoted its intellectual dimension. During Laws' difficulties, his colleagues failed to show energetic commitment in coming to his defence, leaving a tiny number of senior voices to fight a losing battle in the media on his behalf. Laws stood down to return to the back bench, ready to face the process of addressing the allegations made against him.

To the apparent surprise of some Lib Dems and journalists, Laws' post was hurriedly filled by the relatively junior MP Danny Alexander. This promotion came as no shock to those who knew of his über-loyalism to Clegg as his chief of staff, and Alexander's impeccable Orange Book credentials.

When the long-running investigation into Laws' expenses finally led to his suspension from Parliament for a week, David Cameron spoke most warmly of his hopes that 'one day' Laws would return to office. 18 months after the general election, Laws had still not found the opportunity to return to the Cabinet as a Lib Dem minister.

A matter of days after Laws had left the Cabinet, Chris Huhne was exposed by a downmarket tabloid as having had an extramarital affair. Huhne rode the storm; but once again, there seemed to be little energy amongst his colleagues to defend him on what was evidently a matter entirely unrelated to his competence as a politician. This prompted some informal speculation outside the Orange Book clique about why the leadership acted in defence of 'one of their own' with such apparent indifference. Some expressed regret that the 'Establishment' of the party – which surely believed in the right of people to live 'free from conformity' – had failed to express this core value in support of a Cabinet minister when the chips were down.

The Orange Book caucus' behaviour towards Laws and Huhne was strikingly reflective of a dilemma faced in mountaineering.

In the words of a former climber, Brigg Taylor,

> mountaineering is in a sense a very selfish hobby. You sacrifice a lot of things for your interest, including friendships and even your family. Most people have never been in the extreme environment of a very high-altitude climbing expedition, where you have to balance collective goals with the wellbeing of all concerned.
>
> Sometimes that means the team has to make a brutal decision – and leave a member behind if it looks like more would be lost in a hopeless attempt to save them. These decisions have to be made fast and they are based on probabilities. However, leaving a trusted team member is a very big decision which no climber wants to make, and few will ever do it.[30]

The circumstances facing Laws and Huhne appeared to reflect these same challenging issues on the high peaks of politics. It was not clear whether the team had collectively decided that an offer of strong support was unhelpful or whether other considerations were at play. In any event, metaphorically nobody 'cut the rope' – so to speak – but it seemed to outsiders that both were left to in a sense pull *themselves* out of the political crevasse in order to stay in the team. Ultimately, Laws stood down shortly after the story about him had developed for some days.

Huhne remained in post until 3rd February, 2012, when he resigned his Cabinet seat after being formally charged with perverting the course of justice in relation to the speeding offence. His Cabinet position was backfilled by another Orange Booker, Ed Davey.

The question of mutual support arose again in December 2010 when Cable was caught in a sting operation by *Telegraph* newspaper journalists, apparently attempting to generate negative stories about Lib Dem ministers.[31] The *Telegraph* operatives misled Cable with regard to their reason for being in a surgery event held by Cable, in which he met the public and tried to assist them with various problems. The two girls secretly recorded conversations with him. They repeated the process with various other Lib Dem ministers. For clarity, it must be stressed that Cable expressly stated his presumption that the conversation was off the record. The *Telegraph* ignored this and recorded it anyway. The release of these secret 'off the record' recordings broke an ancient bond of trust between journalists and MPs, causing considerable reputational damage to *The Telegraph* itself, which was subsequently and very publicly censured by the Press Complaints Commission for its actions.[32]

However, Cable was also wounded: the issue in hand, a major proposed takeover by the Murdoch press, was removed from Cable's portfolio as a result of this incident. Later he admitted that he had considered resigning.[33] Once again, his leadership spent more time criticising Cable for his naivety than slamming *The Telegraph* for fracturing the relationship between journalists and politicians.[34] It had, after all, introduced a new element of suspicion to every MP's surgery in the country.

Compromising events are frequent in a world where the press fails to live up to the moral standards set for it. However, the interesting – and recurring – theme here is the Orange Book caucus' hesitance in defending another colleague in a difficult situation.

There was also the question of conflicting ambitions. Three of the eight MPs who contributed to the first Orange Book had already stood for the post of Leader by 2007 – Oaten, Huhne and Clegg. At least one – Davey – was said to have spoken of his ambition to do so. And one – Vince Cable – had already been 'acting leader' after Ming Campbell's sudden resignation. Thus five out of eight MPs who contributed to the first Orange Book had served as, stood for or been mooted as aspiring to the role of party leader. Personal ambition is not a contemptible motivation. But it does complicate relations in a ruling group.

Orange Bookers in power

As the months went by, the greatest shift in terms of public perceptions had occurred regarding the Deputy Prime Minister, Nick Clegg. One policy reversal particularly caused this. People were angry about the tuition fees debacle, a hammer blow striking at the heart of a critical element of former support for Lib Dems: students, their parents and academics.

During this phase, few in the party rallied round the Orange Bookers. Party activists were notably reticent in coming forward to support the establishment over this U-turn. An all-member ballot elected anti-tuition fees rebel MP Tim Farron, rather than Orange Booker Kramer, for party president. This is the only position apart from the leader elected by the whole membership. The alternative view believes that there was no mistaking the message being sent. After his election, Farron distanced himself from the Tories in his Spring Conference speech:

> As Conservative party leader David Cameron made speeches recently on what he said was the failure of multiculturalism; and then another expressing his view that the entire public sector should be opened up to private competition. Lots of people got worked up about those speeches. I didn't. As Conservative Party leader he has every right to say those things. And as Liberal Democrat President I have every right to say that he is wrong! If you listen to some, then apparently because I am in coalition with the Conservatives, or 'in bed with the Tories' then I must be a Tory. Are they mad? Look, for flip's sake, I share a bed with my wife, it doesn't make me a woman.[35]

Stories of Laws' personal difficulties had not shaken the membership – indeed, there appeared to be more sympathy for Laws amongst them than had been publicly expressed in Parliament by the leadership. But the activist base was more edgy about the Orange Bookers as a caucus. They were wedded to a different set of policies – the ones passed at conference. Few members followed policy debates in detail, but a lot of them placed themselves on the left of the spectrum. They were concerned that the Tories did not share the liberal movement's concern for fairness, an underlying value which had energised generations of activists with the liberal agenda since the 1800s. This included the equitable management of natural assets, such as land. They were therefore becoming wary regarding where the leadership might be taking the party.

The Orange Book leadership seemed aware of this issue and tried to get a 'Mansion Tax' into the coalition agreement. This would at least have begun to create a tax system based on land values – an age-old tenet of the liberal movement. There was also talk of using land tax proposals as a replacement for the 50% tax rate. It was clear that Conservatives weren't having this either. While there were other concessions in the coalition's actions, such as an increase in the tax thresholds, no fundamental redesign of the tax system was on the table.

By the summer of 2011 Conservative MPs were emboldened in their willingness to challenge the notion of a redistributive agenda. In September 2011 Charles Walker, Conservative Vice-Chair of the influential backbench 1922 Committee, claimed that most Tory MPs wanted the 50% tax rate for the richest people in the United Kingdom scrapped.[36] Chancellor Osborne also continued to maintain that the 50p rate had been a temporary measure.[37] Conservatives began publicly discussing the abolition of the 50% tax rate without any suggestion of replacing it with any other form of redistributive taxation. Liberal Democrats rejected the proposal, and the debate ended in stalemate, the status quo being retained. However, it was another example of the clarity with which the Conservatives had retained their core agenda as an interest group for the rich and empowered, even at a time when they were in coalition with another party which had traditionally stood against this self-serving philosophy. The Orange Bookers rejected the proposal, but only as a policy – they did not use the issue to begin to present themselves from the position of a philosophically robust counterpoint.

Conservatives returned to this demand for a cut in the 50% top rate during the Parliamentary session in September 2011. On the 7th of that month a group of economists called for its abolition, causing the left-leaning Lib Dem President to reject the proposal in forceful terms on television.

The tuition fees issue just kept coming back. It was used to show that Liberal Democrats had caved in to an elitist agenda which was diametrically opposed to pledges formally made by Lib Dem candidates in 2010. To many, it also appeared to contradict the ethos of fairness in the British education system, as the change doomed those wishing to improve themselves through higher education to years of debt, unless their families were able to pay for these bills upfront. This is a key reason why the tuition fees U-turn evoked such rage both inside and outside the party – something formally acknowledged by Clegg until as late as September 2011.

Backing Tory education policy was symbolic of the problem: this 'new liberalism' looked focused on the financial interests of the state, not the educational wellbeing of the individual and society as a whole. The shifting of assets from investing in education to cuts in expenditure offered little evidence of a desire to consider the equitable distribution of opportunity, and therefore had little traction with the left or traditional liberal elements of the party. The absence of a crystal-clear philosophical touchstone behind the Orange Bookers robbed them of the opportunity to provide a perspective which might have made this and other issues less irksome to members, who could only see the failure in terms of the policy. Clegg himself was exasperated with the issue, as he would make clear in his conference speech in September 2011. He lamented the difficulties of putting the policy forward in ways the public would accept. But the issue was not really about policy: it was about breaking a pledge.

Orange Book and local elections

While the Orange Bookers could reasonably claim to have been instrumental in raising the tax threshold – the income below which citizens don't have to pay any income tax – their opportunity to play on this interacted with talk of cuts in welfare payments by the coalition government. In line with Laws' hope of the 'oranging' of government policy, a 'Blue/Orange Book' economic-liberal approach appeared to operate in the coalition, while, unsurprisingly, a 'Red/Yellow' approach did not. This may have been another factor affecting voter opinions, especially in the north.

In the run-up to the May 2011 local elections, Liverpool Council pulled out of the 'Big Society' project that was launched in their very city, and Liberal Democrats across the north began to publicly oppose coalition decisions.

The new type of liberalism that emerged from the fusion of the Orange Book and the liberal Conservatives in Cameron's team found a new synthesis: 'muscular liberalism'. When Nick Clegg signed up to this in a speech in Luton on 3 March 2011 it was effectively the end of the Orange Book agenda as originally promoted, and its replacement by an absolutist, non-liberal construct which had been provided by the Conservatives. Curiously, the leadership failed to recognise that there was unlikely to be much grassroots support for this in the Liberal Democrats. It is so important to grasp what muscular liberalism represented that we devote the next chapter to it.

There was an additional slump of enthusiasm in the more purist elements of the activist base when Nick Clegg was attacked in the press a month after the Luton speech. It seemed to mark a tipping point – a moment when Clegg had knowingly sided ideologically with the Conservatives by endorsing an agenda which had been set *by* the Conservatives. Although little was said at that time, perhaps because of the feared negative impact in the upcoming May 2011 elections, Clegg's new agenda had little to do with liberalism as it had been traditionally perceived.

The results on 5 May confirmed the fears of Lib Dems who had supported the coalition but were unhappy at the lack of differentiation from Tory thinking. David Cameron had maintained the Conservative identity within the partnership. Lib Dems were perceived to have lost theirs. Considerable blame for the loss of the Alternative Vote referendum was also being laid at Clegg's door – on the premise that the 'No' campaign had succeeded in making the referendum, in part, an opportunity for a public expression of dissatisfaction with Clegg's personal performance.

Members see red

In the aftermath of the disastrous election results, three major considerations prevented an immediate open revolt: the impotence of the membership to challenge the leadership directly; a lack of appreciation that the Orange Book project did not have a shared core philosophy and that this was allowing the party to drift along on a policy-by-policy basis; and the absence of a non-Orange Book MP willing to stand against the leadership.

Candidates from the left and liberal wing of the party had their own reasons not to step up to the plate at that time. They decided to keep their powder dry and to see how things developed. It was a prudent calculation. The Orange Book clearly enjoyed sufficient strength to see off a challenge – and nobody wanted to risk messing up a leadership bid through bad timing. Even if a candidate could beat Clegg, why do it at a time of such difficulty for the party? It was better to let the current leader weather the worst of the storm... and wait.

Data from the doorstep

Further circumstantial evidence for the view that there had been a serious breakdown in support within the existing voter base was to be found on the doorstep. In polling carried out amongst party members in South London in July 2011, canvassing information suggested that at least one in 10 of those on the membership lists for London said that they no longer regarded themselves as members and intended to vote for others.[38] Localised canvassing is only a rough guide, but it does tend to support the other data available at the time.

On 28 July 2011 in Stanmore Park, a local authority by-election in North London returned 1,395 votes for the Conservative candidate, with the Liberal Democrats trailing in fourth place with 98 votes and 4% – behind Labour and an independent.[39] This was symbolic of the general weakness in the Lib Dem vote at the time, as witnessed in most of the other seats contested elsewhere on that Thursday evening, with only one showing an increase in support.[40]

In Islington's St Peter's ward on 11 August 2011, a hard-fought campaign with a strong candidate, David Sant, returned 19.8% for the Lib Dems, while Labour candidate Alice Perry achieved a winning 52.5%.[41] This reflected a loss of support of around one third for the Lib Dems, with Labour's vote up by half. As this seat had been billed as one of the most winnable in London against Labour – in an area which had even voted sympathetically for AV – the result was far from encouraging.

These results were typical. Evidence of the party's dismal electoral state was inescapably reflected on a weekly basis in by-election results around. There were occasional wins from as far afield as the South West of England and Keswick. But overall, there was little to celebrate. The Conservatives did not fare so badly, indicating once again that, despite standing on exactly the same record of government, Tories were not being punished but Liberal Democrats were.

Orange Mayor

The Mayor of London is the most powerful role in local government. It had typically been closely fought between Conservatives and Labour. Initially, the position was won by Ken Livingstone – but he lost to Boris Johnson in 2008. It was seen as another event in the slow death of New Labour between 2007 and 2010. The Liberal Democrats had always finished third.

The election is fought over an extended period with the selection of candidates taking place up to two years before the election. This is necessary because the election presents huge organisational challenges. It requires parties which are serious about winning to improve their vote in areas where they have no presence, because the election had always been so close. This put Labour under pressure to accumulate votes in the leafy suburbs of Bromley, while Conservatives had to make inroads in places like Newham where they were weak.

The Labour candidate selection took place in the summer of 2010, with Ken Livingstone beating former MP King for nomination. Boris Johnson was re-selected for the Tories in the same year.

The position for the Liberal Democrat selection was more complex. The Liberal Democrat nomination for 2012 was seen by some as a poisoned chalice due to the difficulties the party was experiencing. The nominee was, however, important because of the media exposure the role received. After her mayoral candidature, Liberal Democrat candidate Susan Kramer had gone on to be selected for a Parliamentary seat which she held for five years as MP.

In 2008, there was little competition for the nomination. It was widely seen as a success that a former senior member of the London Metropolitan Police Force, Brian Paddick, had stood as a credible candidate for the party. The 2012 selection was even more challenging because of the coalition. All the signs were that the

2012 campaign would be very difficult indeed. Various names came and went as the months passed by.

Lib Dem Baroness Floella Benjamin was mooted as a potential candidate in the press in August of 2010. Ultimately, Benjamin did not proceed with her nomination. Thus another high-profile individual was not on the shortlist.

After a series of delays, four individuals were approved as potential candidates: Mike Tuffrey, Brian Paddick, Brian Haley and Lembit Öpik.

Mike Tuffrey had a very longstanding career in the politics of the capital, most recently as a Greater London Authority (GLA) Assembly Member. Party activists such as former employee Mark Pack who wrote for the Internet appeared to back Tuffrey's campaign. A photo shoot was held at City Hall with Susan Kramer – an original contributor to the Orange Book – taking a leading role. She and Tuffrey also made a presentation in Kingston to local Liberal Democrats.

Brian Paddick, who had previously stated his intention not to stand again, announced that he would in fact put himself forward after all. The alternative view is that he was judged acceptable as a candidate by the leadership. On Monday 8 August radio station LBC asked Clegg who should be nominated. Clegg cited a focus on policy as key and played down the importance of 'celebrity'. Mike Tuffrey also appeared on a BBC London political news programme to discuss his candidature. By coincidence Simon Hughes, Deputy Leader of the Liberal Democrats, sat next to him on the programme. Hughes was not seen as a right-leaning member of the Orange Book caucus even though he had contributed an article to *Britain After Blair*. His presence nevertheless gave the accidental impression that Tuffrey was the 'Establishment' choice. As the campaign proceeded, rumours circulated that Paddick had even been asked to stand for the mayoralty by Clegg, though it will not come as a surprise that the alternative view has not been able to independently verify this.

On 2 September 2011, Paddick was announced the winner. Mike Tuffrey came second, with Haley in third place. Öpik had become so convinced he couldn't win that he had conceded defeat in the *Evening Standard* on the afternoon *before* the count. It was an accurate prediction: he came fourth and the Orange Book leadership had a candidate whom they appeared happy to work with. Interestingly, Paddick won despite Tuffrey's associations with the London Lib Dem 'Establishment,' including Susan Kramer, and even though Lib Dem Assembly Group leader Caroline Pidgeon had agreed to be his running-mate for Deputy Mayor. This suggested that incumbency was a powerful asset. Tuffrey was generous-spirited and conceded defeat with a smile, winning many friends through his gentle dignity. However, the facts spoke for themselves. Paddick had vanquished all others and headed into the Mayoralty race for a second time.

The implications were immediately obvious. Instead of maintaining an 'arm's-length' distance from the London mayoral election, the leadership now had a direct stake in the outcome of the May 2012 result. If Paddick performed well, and increased his vote from the 9.6% he achieved in 2008,[42] the Orange Book caucus could point to a turn-up in their fortunes, presenting this as a recovery from the dismal performance of May 2011. If the result showed further decline this would inevitably be seen as yet another failure for Orange Bookers. It increased the stakes for the 2012 election round, and linked Clegg closely to events on the London mayoral stage.

Upon his selection, Paddick announced his game plan, correctly recognising the challenge.

> My number one priority is to improve the image and standing of the party in the eyes of the public, with a view to securing the maximum number of votes for the Liberal Democrats in the 2012 elections and beyond. I am determined to work as a team

with the other candidates to present one distinctive Lib Dem agenda for London but we cannot do this without your help. That is why, over the next four months, I hope to visit every local party in London, to meet the activists whose support we rely on year after year and to raise as much money as possible for the campaign ahead.[43]

His comments were timely. He had to tackle the party's faltering image to improve his result from the last time. What he didn't say – but what everyone knew – was that the reputation of the leadership rode in part upon Paddick's performance.

Though polls go up as well as down, in early September 2011 the percentage of Londoners supporting the Liberal Democrats in the mayoral election was exceedingly low – far below the result in 2008. If that were not improved upon, there was a real risk that the Lib Dems would not make any progress in the numbers of GLA members they secured – which in 2011 stood at only three. If the number of Lib Dem GLA members reduced further – which was unlikely but possible – it could be very embarrassing for the leadership, due to the disproportionate focus on London politics in the national media.

Summary

The creators of the Orange Book project had clearly intended it to be a blueprint for the Liberal Democrat agenda in the 21st century. They had successfully marshalled a team of individuals into joining the group. The cost of membership was a written contribution to either *The Orange Book* or *Britain After Blair*. The prize of membership for most Orange Bookers was a ministerial position.

However, perhaps because the Orange Book narrative was not tested in the 2007 leadership election – since both candidates were Orange Bookers – the contributions which formed the two volumes contained many contradictions with no clear narrative, though the economic centre of gravity was clearly towards the right. This appears to have had the effect of causing ministers to judge policies on a case-by-case basis, allowing a degree of drift with the current of the Conservatives.

Even though the Orange Book agenda had overseen serious reversals in the party's fortunes, throughout 2011 they maintained a fortress mentality towards the key positions within the elected structures of the Liberal Democrats. They lost the presidency to a non-Orange Booker. The Mayoral and London elections were important to the reputation of the party, and the selection of Paddick increased the linkage between the result in 2012 and the leader.

Meanwhile, there continued to be a lack of coordination amongst potential opponents of the Orange Bookers. No organised section of the movement spoke openly of the need to rebuild a distinctive policy agenda for the Liberal Democrats without the Orange Bookers as an urgent priority.

Since February 2011, another theme had been drifting in and out of the consciousness of the organisation. The 'new' philosophy was being pushed forward by Cameron and Clegg. They had made mutually supportive speeches on the subject, just weeks apart. The name sounded good. It was the concept known as 'muscular liberalism'.

Chapter 8

Muscular Liberalism

But I ask you now to change your theme and sing to us of the making of the Wooden Horse... which my lord Odysseus contrived to introduce one day into the citadel of Troy as an ambuscade, manned by the warriors who then sacked the town.
Homer, The Odyssey, Book VIII.[1]

After May 2011, and the setbacks which activists endured at the polls, a general malaise inhabited the party. But there was no coherent debate about the extent to which the Liberal Democrat 'brand' risked losing its identity. Some felt that it would be inevitable that the arrangement with the Conservative Party would corrode the independence of the movement in the eyes of the public. Others did not share this concern, believing that as long as the Lib Dems followed party values and policy it would not erode the Liberal Democrat image. The more supportive of the Orange Bookers a member was, the less worried they were about the consequences of the coalition. It is telling that most members were worried.

In early 2011 a new concept arrived which, it was suggested by the leadership, would be attractive to the party: 'muscular liberalism.' This phrase quickly settled into the regular vocabulary of senior members of the party. The promotion of the idea finally seemed to mark an effort by the leadership to differentiate the Liberal Democrats from their Conservative bedfellows.

Some observers smelt a political rat. The alternative view is that, far from being a differentiator, the concept of muscular liberalism was a Trojan horse offered to the Liberal Democrats by the very movement from which the party was trying to stand apart. To pursue the concept of muscular liberalism, as outlined by both the Conservative Prime Minister and Liberal Democrat Deputy Prime Minister, was folly. It was, in fact, likely to generate a political *convergence* between the two parties. It offered an absolutist moral agenda which represented the antithesis of the relativist outlook which many regarded as emblematic of liberal thinking.

The alternative view asserts that action was needed to resist the moral framework offered to Liberal Democrats by Conservatives – because it would undermine the liberal movement in one of two ways. Either there would be a convergence towards the Tory agenda, with no time to recover the political position in the run-up to the next general election. Or there would be a schism between the leadership and membership, as the Orange Bookers pursued a morally 'absolutist' agenda in line with Conservative thinking while the traditional activist and support base remained wedded to a relativistic one and broke away, either officially or unofficially, from the Clegg agenda.

To see why this was so, let's take a revealing journey back to the origins of muscular liberalism, and see how it was relaunched many years later. The language used by its two loudest advocates is telling. Those 'loudest advocates' were David Cameron, who launched the concept in early 2011 in a speech he made in Munich, and Nick Clegg who responded in Luton some weeks later, warmly welcoming Cameron's new idea. So, where *did* the concept come from – and what did it mean?

Muscular Liberalism

Muscular liberalism's roots

While the current incarnation of 'muscular liberalism' was launched by David Cameron in early 2011, it appears to owe its roots to a related concept which was popularised as far back as the 1850s. This was 'muscular Christianity' – a phrase which, after limited use by various idealistic individuals, became much better known thanks to the work of an author called Charles Kingsley in 1857. Following a review of his writings by an approving clergyman, it became widely adopted.[2]

In the book *Tom Brown at Oxford*, originally published in 1861, there is this passage:

> The least of the muscular Christians has hold of the old chivalrous and Christian belief, that a man's body is given him to be trained and brought into subjection, and then used for the protection of the weak, the advancement of all righteous causes, and the subduing of the earth which God has given to the children of men.[3]

This in itself contained echoes of concepts in the Christian Bible linking physical exertion and muscularity with godliness.

Muscular Christianity had sufficient longevity to mature into an idea still in circulation in the early 20th century. In a volume called *Our Public Schools*, written by James George and Cotton Minchin in 1901, muscular Christianity is again described in stark but approving terms. They write:

> the spectacle of the Englishman going through the world with rifle in one hand and Bible in the other is laughable; but to Englishmen, who are neither idealists or logicians, it is not. We wish to see his skill with the one and his faith in the other strengthened and increased. If asked what our muscular Christianity has done, we point to the British Empire.[4]

As we shall see, the definition used by Cameron – who himself was a product of the same public school system under scrutiny by George and Minchin – bears a striking resemblance to this absolutist moral philosophy of the British spreading good around the world from a position of armed strength.

The alternative view holds that muscular liberalism is the descendent of muscular Christianity – and that neither serves the liberal cause well. This becomes obvious when we discover who was the most enthusiastic about the creed at around the time when Cameron delivered his Munich address – and Clegg gave his reply.

Muscular Christianity reinvented

Whether explicitly or implicitly, the present form of muscular Christianity appears to have been fermenting in, or near, the think tank Demos, which had originally been supportive of New Labour. It has more than a passing association with the ideology of the Tory Party. The founder-editor of 'muscularliberal.com' – Max Wind-Cowie – also happened to run the 'Progressive Conservatism' project at Demos.[5] We also find that the 25-strong advisory council of Demos – a policy thinktank – included George Osborne (Conservative), David Laws (Orange Book), David Willetts (Conservative), Danny Alexander (Orange Book), Vince Cable (Orange Book), Alan Milburn (Labour) and Jon Cruddas (Labour). Demos itself was headed by the former Labour MP James Parnell, and included George Osborne and three Orange Book Liberal Democrats on its advisory council.[6]

Wind-Cowie's own words underline the absolutist nature of the 'muscular liberalism' creed – a feature which places it much closer to the conservative mindset than the more relativistic liberal one. On 27 June 2011, writing on a Conservative website, he commented:

> When David Cameron announced that he wants his Government to pursue 'active, muscular liberalism' he was met

with a chorus of angst, anger and attitude. Opposition to Cameron's Munich speech, and to its policy implications, came in two guises. First up were those who claimed that it was somehow sinister, or at the very least oxymoronic, to be a 'muscular liberal' – that we have no business worrying about what British Muslims think, say or believe until they break the law. Second, but no less vociferous, were those critics who blasted the Prime Minister's supposed naivety about Islam. Muslims, this argument runs, cannot join the liberal mainstream of British society precisely because they are Muslims.

Fortunately for the Prime Minister, for all of us, both these lines of attack are profoundly flawed. British Muslims are more liberal, more tolerant and more open than they are often given credit for and this not only justifies Cameron's commitment to weeding out extremism in their leadership but it holds out hope of success in promoting better, deeper cultural and social integration more widely.[7]

This text offers a double revelation. Firstly, Wind-Cowie was enthusiastic about the definition of muscular liberalism as outlined by Cameron in his Munich speech. This is unsurprising given Wind-Cowie's links with the Conservative party. Secondly, he clearly opposes those who believe that 'we have no business worrying about what British Muslims think, say or believe until they break the law.' In other words, he believes that it *is* our business to worry about what British Muslims think, *even when it does not present a breach of the peace.* Here is strong support for an absolutist agenda, in which the Englishman can evaluate others' creeds, whether or not those creeds are causing actual harm. By contrast, traditional liberalism tends to tolerate ideas it may find offensive or intellectually worrisome, as long as there is no harm to a third party as a result. Liberals give the benefit of the doubt. A pedant may argue that *everything* we do affects everyone else in some way, but a liberal would apply their mind to setting limits to such a sweeping view and seek to respect diversity.

Wind-Cowie's aggressive perspective on muscular liberalism is further clarified by his criticism of the funding of the MCB – the Muslim Council of Britain. He says of them:

> With statements like 'gay partnerships undermine society' not only are 'Muslim leaders' such as the Muslim Council of Britain alienating the overwhelmingly kind and tolerant British mainstream but they are directly misrepresenting what their own community believe.

Wind-Cowie continues,

> Not only would David Cameron be doing gay people a favour by withdrawing funding, legitimacy and engagement from groups such as the MCB, but he'll be doing British Muslims a favour too.[8]

Wind-Cowie therefore asserts that muscular liberalism bestows upon government the moral authority to withdraw funding from an organisation like the MCB. So, let's see what the MCB actually stands for. It describes itself in these words:

> The Muslim Council of Britain is a national representative Muslim umbrella body with over 500 affiliated national, regional and local organisations, mosques, charities and schools. The MCB is pledged to work for the common good of society as a whole; encouraging individual Muslims and Muslim organisations to play a full and participatory role in public life.

Muscular Liberalism

Aims and Objectives:

1. To promote cooperation, consensus and unity on Muslim affairs in the UK.
2. To encourage and strengthen all existing efforts being made for the benefit of the Muslim community.
3. To work for a more enlightened appreciation of Islam and Muslims in the wider society.
4. To establish a position for the Muslim community within British society that is fair and based on due rights.
5. To work for the eradication of disadvantages and forms of discrimination faced by Muslims.
6. To foster better community relations and work for the good of society as a whole.[9]

Furthermore, under the 'Duty of Care' section of the MCB's 'Code of Conduct & Governance Protocols,' it states:

> All Concerned Members shall always conform to the laws governing the British Isles. However, this obligation shall not fetter the freedom of the MCB nor Concerned Members to evaluate the efficacy, necessity, or equity of any proposed or subsisting laws of the British Isles or any other jurisdiction.[10]

It could not be clearer. The MCB explicitly committed itself to respecting the laws of the land, while affirming its right to evaluate the implications of those laws upon the practice of beliefs that it upheld. Yet a proponent of the muscular liberalism ethos was calling for the withdrawal of funding from the MCB on the basis of its views on homosexuality. This is not trivial given the commentator's central role in the promotion of muscular liberalism.

It would be remarkable if muscular liberalism and muscular Christianity bore such a close resemblance simply out of coincidence. Digging deeper, there is still more to discover. In June 2011 Wind-Cowie made the case for taking a very specific approach towards those at one end of the social and economic scale.

> There is such a thing as the 'deserving poor' and we'd be serving them a whole lot better if we had the gumption to admit it.[11]

The alternative view is that Wind-Cowie was being perfectly consistent with Tory thinking – and Cameron's own controversial comments about this matter, which we have covered earlier. However, Wind-Cowie's – and Cameron's – picture of muscular liberalism appeared to diverge sharply from the Liberal Democrat movement's perspective. The new idea was rooted in an absolutist, 19th-century, Christian and British imperialist view. However much the Tories may have liked it, this was far from the bedrock of the traditional liberal movement.

When Clegg spoke in favour of muscular liberalism, he was praising an import from the philosophical narrative of the Conservatives. As Wind-Cowie's words on the subject confirm, it was evidently not a concept which would ever have been created by the liberal movement. It had been gift-wrapped and presented to Liberal Democrats by a man who felt a natural affinity with the Tories. It risked drawing liberal policy making away from the party's moral 'centre of gravity' towards a conservative one.

To confirm this picture, we need only examine Cameron's view of muscular liberalism, as explained in the Prime Minister's Munich speech on 5 February 2011. Speaking primarily with Muslim extremists in mind, Cameron said:

> we must stop these groups from reaching people in publicly-funded institutions like universities or even, in the British case,

prisons. Now, some say, this is not compatible with free speech and intellectual inquiry. Well, I say, would you take the same view if these were right-wing extremists recruiting on our campuses? Would you advocate inaction if Christian fundamentalists who believed that Muslims are the enemy were leading prayer groups in our prisons? And to those who say these non-violent extremists are actually helping to keep young, vulnerable men away from violence, I say nonsense.

Cameron continued:

> Frankly, we need a lot less of the passive tolerance of recent years and a much more active, muscular liberalism. A passively tolerant society says to its citizens, as long as you obey the law we will just leave you alone. It stands neutral between different values. But I believe a genuinely liberal country does much more; it believes in certain values and actively promotes them.[12]

Cameron's definition would have received posthumous praise from the long-departed advocates of muscular Christianity. But where was the Liberal Democracy in all this? For example, Cameron's muscular liberalism necessitated a no-platform policy on student campuses for non-violent extremists. This was in direct contradiction to Liberal Democrat principles on free speech – and entirely at odds with a vote opposing no platform which had been passed by Liberal Democrat conference delegates less than two years earlier, coincidentally as part of a motion which also reiterated the party's opposition to student tuition fees.[13]

The problem here was stark and simple. Even if Lib Dems attempted to redefine muscular liberalism for themselves, Cameron's definition would prevail amongst Conservatives – and large elements in the media. As Clegg never tired of pointing out, the media were not especially sympathetic to the Lib Dems. Faced with taking the

Tory line or the Liberal Democrat line, strategists didn't have to think very long to work out what line they'd take. Muscular liberalism was convenient because it was Conservative ideology dressed up in 'liberal-sounding' words. If the Lib Dems went along with it, that would certainly make things easier between the two parties – but for all the wrong reasons as far as the liberal movement was concerned. To maintain a separate image from the Conservatives, the best thing the party could do was reject muscular liberalism.

What did it mean for policy? A controversial example occurred in 2009, when a racist foreign speaker – Geert Wilders – was denied entry to the UK under a Labour government. Chris Huhne agreed with the ban. He told *The Independent*:

> there has to be a dividing line between the right to freedom of speech and when it topples over into incitement to hatred and violence. In my opinion, Geert Wilders' revolting film *Fitna* crosses this line, as its shocking images of violence and emotional appeals to anti-Islamic feeling risk causing serious harm to others.[14]

In fact, Liberal Democrats stood on both sides of this issue – not least thanks to Liberal Democrat policy which opposed no platform, passed by Party Conference in March 2009. The policy stated that Conference endorsed a policy to

> Defend and strengthen academic freedom and free expression on campus by guaranteeing research and publication freedom and removing unjustified and arbitrary restrictions – such as 'No Platform' policies – on lawful association and lawful free expression.[15]

By contrast, Cameron would have had no difficulty with the matter. His muscular liberalism would have made the Wilders case clear-cut: a ban for sure. The threshold for exclusion would have been reduced to 'non-violent extremism'. Questions of serious harm did not come into it.

Clegg embraces muscular liberalism

Despite the evident contradictions in doing so, the leadership nevertheless took the decision to actively *promote* the new agenda. On Thursday 3 March 2011, Clegg made his own muscular speech in, giving fulsome support to muscular liberalism. The Deputy Prime Minister's speech was entitled 'An Open, Confident Society: The Application of Muscular Liberalism in a Multicultural Society.' In that speech he clearly embraced Cameron's muscular liberalism agenda, in words which would accurately describe muscular Christianity too. Here are excerpts from that speech.

> The Prime Minister has recently argued that we need to assert confidently our liberal values. I agree. Politicians have a huge responsibility to lead by example, and engage in the often difficult arguments around immigration, multiculturalism and liberty. That is why I think the PM was absolutely right to make his argument for 'muscular liberalism'.
>
> At all three levels – individual, community and society-wide – it is vital to pursue 'smart engagement'. This means calibrating Government action in the following ways:
>
> - targeting resources in a way that clearly promotes liberal objectives
> - maintaining a clear distinction between social policy and security policy
> - distinguishing between violent and non-violent extremism
> - supporting free speech, but taking the argument to the bigots; and

- implacably confronting violent extremism.

...

The third battleground against violent extremism is at the level of ideas, values and ideology. The dangerous ideas that underpin violent extremism must never be allowed to go unchallenged.

...

That is why I thought the PM's argument in favour of 'muscular liberalism' was absolutely right. Liberalism is not a passive, inert approach to politics. It requires engagement, assertion. Muscular liberals flex their muscles in open argument. There is nothing relativist about liberalism.

...

If we are truly confident about the strength of our liberal values we should be confident about their ability to defeat the inferior arguments of our opponents.

...

Equally, smart engagement means being extremely careful about decisions to proscribe individual organisations. There are occasions when that is the right course of action. I have to say that, for me, agreeing to the proscription of the Pakistani Taliban was a straightforward decision.

...

So: smart engagement in defence of an open society. An unending determination to keep doing the hard work of maintaining our liberal society at home. Encouraging the birth and growth of liberal societies abroad. Smart engagement, appropriate and proportionate, to take on extremist ideas, alongside a ruthless determination to find and punish those who promote or take to violence.

...

Violent extremists of all kinds are the enemies of open societies. We will wage an unceasing battle against them. And we will win.[16]

Muscular Liberalism

There are three vital revelations here. Firstly, Clegg's words clearly abandoned the concept of relativism, just as muscular Christianity had done over a century before. This was at odds with the liberal credo, where relativism clearly has a huge role. To say 'there is nothing relativist about liberalism' was to directly contradict an essential characteristic of the movement.

Secondly, although he did so conditionally, Clegg promoted the 'proscribing' of organisations – in other words, prohibiting them. Adding this to his backing of Cameron's speech, it meant that he potentially agreed with the Prime Minister's intention to ban non-violent groups to help enforce liberal values. Again, this is at odds with a liberal relativist position, but in line with an absolutist agenda, in just the terms Cameron had outlined in his Munich address when he spoke of less passive tolerance and more active, muscular liberalism. Cameron was clearly advocating a no-platform policy for non-violent extremists, which directly contradicted Liberal Democrat policy. Clegg was agreeing with Cameron, in conflict with policy passed by his own party conference.

Thirdly, the *tone* of Clegg's speech seemed at odds with 'how liberals do things.' For example, consider his concluding comment:

> Violent extremists of all kinds are the enemies of open societies. We will wage an unceasing battle against them. And we will win.

This provides no margin for any positive engagement with violent extremists – only an 'unceasing battle' to be fought against them. How would this approach have played out in the Northern Ireland peace talks, where *engagement* with the 'violent extremists,' while they were still being violent and extreme, ultimately led to the peace accord? Clegg's words did not fit the reality of reconciliation as practiced in those peace negotiations. Nor did it resonate with the generally tolerant, inclusive – and relativistic – attitude of the traditional liberal movement.

Was Clegg willing to differentially grade one group of terrorists as 'better' or 'worse' than another? If so, this contradicts the absolutist agenda that Cameron had laid out so clearly and which Clegg had emphatically endorsed: 'I think the PM was absolutely right to make his argument for "muscular liberalism".' Their vision would never have delivered peace in Northern Ireland. These matters require a deeper and more empathic understanding of motivations and grievances than Clegg's and Cameron's stark statements implied. The great strength of former Northern Ireland Secretary of State, Mo Mowlam, was that she practiced the exact opposite of Clegg and Cameron's muscular liberalism policy. She engaged with people who were still – and had long been – associated with violence. In her own words:

> There was no metaphorical gun at my head... Putting my case face-to-face, arguing it through with them, I thought was the best way to do it.[17]

The engagement was positive and solution-based, with no talk of an 'unceasing battle' against them. An accord was found and the violence ended.

In dramatic contrast, Clegg underlined his conviction that the battleground against violent extremism is at the level of ideas, values and ideology. The dangerous ideas that underpin violent extremism must never be allowed to go unchallenged.

His absolutist position was belligerent – the primary focus being to challenge all ideas, values and ideology. None of these were challenged in Northern Ireland. The solutions resulted from a challenge to *methodology*, not ideology, which was, in fact, respected as part of the process. Clegg's words would lead one to forget that, even at the height of the Troubles, an ongoing dialogue occurred between terrorist groups such as the IRA and the British government.

Applying the principles of muscular liberalism to foreign policy, it is easy to see that there would be no prospect of dialogue with international terrorist groups such as al-Qaeda, or insurgents such as the Taliban. An absolutist position simply rules it out. The alternative view is that, far from securing victory over foes, this tub-thumping robustness risks *increasing* the resolve of the 'enemy' to stand and fight – potentially through self-sacrifice and attrition – because it gives them no negotiating alternative.

After Clegg had made his speech, his words increased the strain with sections of his party. These liberals did not accept his brand of muscular liberalism. If Clegg was serious about it, he had made a strategic break with traditional elements of the liberal movement. Yet Clegg seemed either unconcerned about the consequences of embracing such an absolutist agenda – or simply unaware of what the concept actually meant: a level of ignorance which we dismiss as extremely unlikely.

Within weeks, 'muscular liberalism' had become a recurring phrase in the leadership's repertoire. Even after the poor results of 5 May, Clegg referred again to muscular liberalism in a speech made on 11 May to party activists in the National Liberal Club:

> In the next phase of the coalition, both partners will be able to be clearer in their identities, but equally clear about the need to support government policy. We will stand together, but not so closely that we stand in each other's shadow. You will see a strong liberal identity in a strong coalition government. You might even call it muscular liberalism.[18]

Ironically, since muscular liberalism was a *convergent* agenda, not a divergent one, in a very practical sense Clegg was committing his party to drawing closer to the Tories, not pulling away.

The Lib Dems had a great deal more to lose than the Conservatives from this convergence. Individuals employing the phrase in the Lib Dems needed either to agree a satisfactory redefinition with their Tory opposite numbers – which in practice was impossible because the Tories would certainly not be willing to compromise their ideology – or to reject it. After all, Liberal – not Tory – values were at odds with the concepts of muscular Christianity and muscular liberalism. The Lib Dems – not Tories – would get the blame. Muscular liberalism sat in the forecourt of liberalism, as the fabled Trojan horse had done, concealing a dangerous army ready to sack the party. In this state of uncertainty, the future of the movement's identity hung in the balance.

Summary

The Orange book subtitle had been *Reclaiming Liberalism*. Now, with this new concept, the Orange Book leadership was fighting against 'liberalism' as understood in any conventional sense. By mixing liberal democracy with the Conservatives' muscular liberalism, the Orange Book leadership had, by 2011, spawned a new type of hybrid conservatism under a different name. Its tenets were not in keeping with a relativist credo. Enforcing liberal values by excluding from the UK those who spoke against them in extreme terms was ironic in the extreme.

The implications for the party were very practical. Think again about the ban of Dutch Freedom Party MP Geert Wilders, who wished to show his controversial film – which links the Islamic holy book to terrorism – in the House of Lords. As long as people like him did not promote violence, Liberal Democrat opposition to no platform in March 2009 would have required that they be let in – or, at the very least, indicated that there was a case either way. Under the new policy of muscular liberalism, they would undoubtedly be banned.

Incidentally, Wilders had been invited by UK Independence Party peer Lord Pearson. The British Embassy contacted Wilders prior to his journey to inform him that he would be denied entry should he attempt to make the trip. Lord Pearson said 'we're coming to this from the angle of freedom of speech,' claiming that the Dutch politician 'must be allowed to say what he wants, he must answer questions and then everyone can make up their minds.'[19] The danger to the Lib Dems was a further incident with a less controversial speaker, where the UK Independence Party could appear as the defender of free speech while the Liberal Democrats looked like the censors. Liberalism does not offer a specific set of entry criteria precisely because it is not absolutist. The lowered bar of muscular liberalism appeared to be changing that.

Elsewhere, muscular liberalism would allow the state authority to take a stronger, more absolutist, line in imposing 'family values' – perhaps one reason why some Orange Bookers may have warmed to it. By contrast, libertarians rejected this as not compatible with liberalism.

Clegg was not alone in appearing to warm to muscular liberalism. Recall Huhne's comments in the *Orange Book* of 2004 about intervention on an international basis. Sharing his belief in the need for the United Nations to take a more assertive role, even when misdeeds are confined to national borders, he wrote:

> it has to change its approach to domestic sovereignty, which is set out in Article 2, paragraph 7 of the Charter forbidding intervention in the internal affairs of its members. UN members must have the collective capacity to challenge the sovereignty of other members for gross and persistent abuse of human rights, the denial of the right to peaceful coexistence of nations and communities, or wilful and widespread environmental damage.[20]

However well intentioned, Huhne's words seem more closely aligned with muscular Liberalism – and muscular Christianity – than the more traditional liberal internationalist tendency to coexist and negotiate solutions. Ironically, given that the United

States of America was, at the time of his comments, producing roughly a quarter of the world's pollution, despite having about 4% of the planet's human population,[21] this philosophy would endorse the invasion of America by Third World countries threatened with the ravages of climate change.

The alternative view is that Orange Book support for muscular liberalism was harming the party by contributing to the convergence of the Liberal Democrats with Conservatives – with the Lib Dems doing the 'converging'. What could stop it? A challenge to the leadership might have an impact. Yet there was still no cohesive opposition to the Orange Book caucus anywhere in the movement – despite the anomalies of muscular liberalism.

If Lib Dems were shepherded towards a creed provided for them by the Tories, could liberal traditionalists and leftwingers be expected to remain motivated to work for the party? There was a moment of truth looming in September 2011. The party's September conference was expected to reveal to a curious media what the activist base truly felt, how strongly, and in what numbers. Could this be the big test of Clegg's leadership?

Chapter 9

The Hollow Men

*This is the way the world ends
Not with a bang but a whimper.*
T.S. Eliot, 'The Hollow Men,' 1925

The Liberal Democrat conference of September 2011 was the first such event since the May 2011 local, Scottish and Welsh elections and the 'No' result in the referendum on the Alternative Vote system. All of these had gone very badly for the party but, until now, there had been no major convention where members could discuss it. The question was: how much dissent would be displayed by disgruntled party activists?

On the Sunday morning of Conference a march took place, organised primarily by public sector workers, worried about the impacts of the government's planned cuts on their future employment prospects. A small demonstration also occurred outside the security barriers of the International Conference Centre, the venue for the Lib Dem convention.

The delegates' mood that Sunday was subdued but dignified. After the shock of seeing demonstrations at the Sheffield conference in March 2011, delegates had got more used to the idea that, in government, there was likely to be more negative interest in the party than it had received in opposition. A ComRes poll, commissioned by the *Independent on Sunday* and *Daily Mirror* on the eve of Conference, revealed that just 47% of people who claimed to have voted Lib Dem in the past said that they would do so now.[1] This corresponded remarkably closely with data gleaned from informal canvassing in South London earlier on in the summer by a local activist. It was also backed up by other polls, such as the YouGov poll of 18 September, which put the Tories at 36%, Labour at 42% – and the Lib Dems on just 9%.[2]

Conferences are intended to boost a party's popular appeal. An important measure of the success of the event would be the change in the poll rating immediately after it, and also after Labour and the Conservatives had held theirs.

Some indications were there to suggest that activists were seeking to court the votes of left-leaning electors, which had been lost since the formation of the Conservative-Lib Dem coalition. A fringe meeting attended by Labour MPs discussed these matters, and there was plenty of talk in the bars about the future of the party in relation to its leftwing leanings.

At a conference rally on the Saturday night a number of speakers tried to lift the mood. One pointed to a couple of by-election wins. A Lib Dem junior minister tried to entertain the party with a series of jokes. This was received with some generosity in the hall, though predictably the media derided it as a poor attempt at stand-up comedy. It must be said that the material was somewhat dependent on the listener possessing a reasonable knowledge of the nuances of Lib Dem thinking, and this partly explained the failure of political commentators to grasp what was primarily intended as a pick-me-up for Lib Dem activists. Part of that boost was the fact that they were watching a real-life government minister on stage, something delegates still appreciated as a new development since May 2010.

The wisecracks may not have been necessary. It quickly

transpired that the mood of activists was far less downbeat than many had expected. Attitudes depended on local fortunes: there was more gloom from areas suffering the heaviest electoral losses. However, another hidden dynamic was at play. Some of the most disillusioned activists were not vocal at the conference – because they weren't there. They'd not bothered coming – an absence which skewed the atmosphere in a less negative direction than would otherwise have been the case.

The press were keen to highlight the apparent woes of the party across the country, and an ongoing debate was whether Clegg had drifted too far towards the Conservatives. While some loyalists insisted that this was not the case, even within the slightly reduced number of delegates a significant proportion felt that it was, though no journalist had the presence of mind to use the event to conduct a detailed poll of activists' attitudes.

Two speeches always stand out as key: the president's and the leader's. The president's role is to represent the interests of the membership. Although this speech receives wide media coverage, his target audience is mainly internal – the activist and membership base of the party. The leader's speech must also be palatable internally, but it needs to resonate with the wider public – to win over votes rather than just keep the party in good cheer. President Tim Farron and leader Nick Clegg both felt the pressure in these different ways. Farron was to speak on Sunday, and Clegg on Wednesday.

An interesting complication was that Farron had beaten the establishment Orange Book candidate – Susan Kramer – in the presidential election. He was not beholden for his authority to the Orange Bookers. By contrast, Clegg still needed the backing of the whole membership and his Parliamentary colleagues. A number of activists openly blamed him for the ills they had suffered at the ballot box. Clegg had been made aware of this by occasional shouts from the audience and criticisms levelled at him from the floor of the conference hall. Although delegates were becoming more candid about their reservations in regard to the party's performance, they still didn't seem to identify the Orange Bookers as the caucus at the centre of power within the party.

A series of informal comments illustrates the mood of the conference. One activist from a seat which had been lost in the South West in the general election said

> When I heard them saying 'look, we've just won these two by-elections,' I just thought 'shut up'.

Another was struggling through the increasingly complex procedure to get an entry pass as a result of the tightened security arrangements: 'it's ridiculous to make it so hard to get in there. They should have been grateful I'm here at all.'

On Sunday afternoon, the time had come for Tim Farron to give his presidential address. His text pulled no punches. He knew that his role was to stand up for members, while seeking to show the necessary loyalty to the leadership. He began by highlighting the anger that many felt at the new security arrangements whereby delegates would only be permitted to register for conference subject to that police check – something that libertarians found highly offensive in respect of their civil liberties. He then dealt with anger caused over the May 2011 results, and outlined his desire for differentiation with the Conservatives. Here are some of the key sections of his speech.

> So, well done – you all got past security clearance! I'm very grateful to the police, they've now provided me with all the detailed personal information on party members that I need in order to conduct a Stalinist purge. Basically anyone who actually passed security clearance without sign of being a subversive will be erased.

...

May's elections really were the bottom – at least they flipping well better had be! Okay, we got 16% of the vote and had some real successes around the country, but let's not fool ourselves. In much of the country we got slaughtered. In Scotland, in many of our great cities, in shire districts Liberal Democrats who have served their communities and worked their backsides off for years got their backsides kicked.

...

I stand with you; I am angry on your behalf; I take the responsibility and I absolutely will not insult you by claiming that this was collateral damage, or an understandable mid-term blip. Frankly, as your President, I owe you an apology. Politics is full of clichés. Perhaps the worst is that bit where you're on telly having to pretend everything's gone swimmingly on a bad election night. I had that job, and I have to confess that I didn't stick to the script. I didn't pretend it was alright really. 'Cos it wasn't.

...

These people are my friends. People who didn't deserve to lose. But who lost. I'm not going to explain them away, shrug and accept their defeat as an inevitable consequence.

...

You want me as president to sell the undiluted Liberal Democrat standpoint. Not to be an apologist for everything the coalition does... There's wonderful freedom in this role and I'm determined to use it! Unlike ministerial platform speeches, I don't have to show mine to Oliver Letwin in advance! But there are 18 Liberal Democrats who don't have the luxuries that I do.

...

Those 20 economists... who called for scrapping the 50p tax rate. They have many supporters in the Conservative party. But they are utterly wrong. Are we all in this together? Well, not if we give tax cuts to the rich! ... Giving a 10p tax cut to those who need it the least... would be morally repugnant.

...

My politics were formed in the 1980s amidst mass unemployment in the North of England... that government deliberately used unemployment as an economic tool to control spending and the unions.

...

I spent June and July away from Parliament after my wife had an operation... I was granted compassionate leave by the whips – who, let's be honest, didn't owe me any favours!

...

We are the first government party in history that doesn't have a single newspaper telling our side of the story... That our excellent message wasn't landing in the minds of the public highlighted an obvious danger for all of us who hold elected office.

...

Isn't it so often the same old story... you get elected, you spend lots of time with your... officers... your diary gets a bit too full to go out knocking on doors, so not only are you now listening to officials but you have stopped listening to normal people and so you forget what they sound like, what angers them, what impresses them, what they elected you to do in the first place so you make daft decisions and you get slaughtered in the local press and then you lose.

...

That can happen in Whitehall as well as the town hall! It can be a slippery slope. So what's the answer? I'll tell you what: a full-blooded return to the principles and the practice of community politics. And it needs to start now.

...

This conference must mark a renewal of the theory and practice of community politics... if our poll rating is currently 13%... that's about 14 times better than it was in 1989. Survival is what we do. We are the vehicle for a radical, green, tolerant, internationalist, progressive form of politics.

...

Going into coalition was absolutely the right thing for the country, but costly for the party. I'm in no doubt that being in coalition with the Tories has tainted us, our identity is blurred, many who support us are confused. They say: 'We thought you were against the Tories, why are you shacked up with them now?' If it's a marriage, well, it's a good-natured one, but I'm afraid it's temporary... It's not going to happen for 3 or 4 years but I'm afraid divorce is inevitable.

...

Now... the AV referendum. Electoral reform was within our grasp for the first time in our lifetimes, but was it for the last time?... We will bring in proportional representation for the Upper House... It is in the coalition agreement, it is not an optional part of the programme. It's a red line. In 2015, we must be electing a part of the upper house by proper PR. Not a miserable little compromise! The AV referendum... reminds us what we are up against. A Tory party owned and directed by the impossibly rich, a Labour party... led by a progressive but... owned by the forces of conservatism.

...

We must... never become part of the establishment... let's look at each other, look to each other, focus on the goal, tackle our opponents and stuff them. Get on with it![3]

Farron's speech received rapturous applause. He had echoed what delegates felt – the anger and concern about the future and not wanting to get too close to the Tories. He voiced the view of many that local election losses were caused by the party's activities in

Westminster. He separated himself from the rightwing establishment and highlighted his distance from the Orange Book with an oblique reference to his decision to vote against the leadership line on tuition fees: 'I was granted compassionate leave by the whips – who, let's be honest, didn't owe me any favours!'

Farron was careful to praise his ministerial colleagues, but his core message was to the movement's disillusioned activists, who were worried about further contraction: 'Survival is what we do.' He appealed to those who felt a distance from the leadership: 'I think that you want me as president to sell the undiluted Liberal Democrat standpoint. Not to be an apologist for everything the coalition does.'

Farron's focus on community politics connected with long-standing activists who had spend years pounding the streets, knocking on doors and keeping the faith even at the party's lowest ebb. His reference to the title of the Lishman/Greaves pamphlet on community politics was no accident:

> So what's the answer? I'll tell you what: a full-blooded return to the principles and the practice of community politics. And it needs to start now.

Farron was using the language of traditional liberals. It wafted over delegates like a warming breeze in a stuffy room. They felt heard and understood by *someone* in authority.

The wider public were less effusive. Following Farron's article in the *Guardian* newspaper reflecting the themes of his speech,[4] there was heavy criticism. Many attacked him as just another Liberal Democrat who could not be trusted any more. Referring to a comment Farron had made in his article, one erudite observer using the name 'Hermionegingold' retorted:

> 'Following May's somewhat disappointing election results' – September 18 2011. Tim Farron.

> 'The war situation has developed not necessarily to Japan's advantage' – August 15 1945. Emperor Hirohito.[5]

The cynicism showed a reticence to apply a discriminating outlook to the Lib Dems. After all, Farron seemed to be taking a contrite view in regard to the performance of the party and the problems which its relationship with the Conservatives was causing electorally. Thus he was, in some senses, agreeing with 'Hermionegingold's' rueful observation, though in different words. But, in truth, many members of the public felt that way. There was nothing that a single speech or one person could do to change that external perception instantly.

Three days later, the same pressures were on Clegg to deliver something which offered succour to this frustrated body of delegates. Clegg also had the chance to respond to the implicit challenge set by Farron about the importance of community politics. However, as leader, it was also his job – more than the president's – to make a positive impact beyond the confines of the hall. Here are key elements of his speech.

> Liberal Democrats, we have now been in Government for 500 days. Not easy, is it? ... I suspect none of us predicted just how tough it would turn out to be. We've lost support, we've lost councillors, and we lost a referendum. I know how painful it has been to face anger and frustration on the doorstep. Will it all be worth it in the end? It will be. And today I want to explain why.
> ...
> I want to pay tribute to you. Your resilience. Your grace under fire. I have been genuinely moved by your spirit and your strength. Thank you... Alex Cole-Hamilton, one of our defeated candidates... said that if losing was part payment for ending child detention then, as he said: 'I accept it, with all my heart.' That is the liberal spirit and that is something we will never lose.

...

As for all those seats we lost in May, let me tell you this: I won't rest, we won't rest, until we've won every single one of those seats back.

...

So we are strong. United. True to our values. Back in government and on your side... with hard choices every day... For liberals, the litmus test is always the national interest. Not doing the easy thing. Doing the right thing.

...

The most heart-wrenching for me, for all of us, was on university funding... I saw the anger. I have learned from it. And I know how much damage this has done to us as a party. By far the most painful part of our transition. From the easy promises of opposition to the invidious choices of Government. No matter how hard you work on... a policy, it's no good if the perception is wrong. We can say until we're blue in the face that no one will have to pay any fees as a student... but still people don't believe it. We did the best thing we could... But we failed to properly explain those dilemmas.

...

So we can keep the government to a liberal path. Anchor the government in the centre ground. We were absolutely right to stop the NHS bill in its tracks... No backdoor privatisation. No threat to the basic principles at the heart of our NHS.

...

The European Convention on Human Rights and the Human Rights Act are not... foreign impositions. These are British rights... The Human Rights Act... is here to stay.

...

We must move now beyond the reflexes of opposition to the responsibilities of government, and the opportunities... too. New social housing. Criminal justice reform. Fixed-term parliaments. Keeping our Post Offices open. House of Lords reform. Better mental health care. Safer banks. Income tax down for ordinary workers. Capital gains tax up for the rich. Compulsory retirement scrapped. Pensions protected by a triple lock. ID cards: history. Child detention: ended.

...

Equal marriage, straight or gay. More power for consumers over the energy companies. Calling time on rewards for failure in boardrooms... New powers to turn empty homes back into family homes. A five hundred million pound investment in growth. Liberal achievements from a liberal party of government.

...

I know I have had all the advantages – good school, great parents... This will not be a liberal nation until every citizen can thrive and prosper, until birth is no longer destiny, until every child is free to rise.

...

We have to push ahead with the government's rehabilitation revolution: punishment that sticks, that changes behaviour... I want the criminal to look their victims in the eye, to see the consequences of their actions, and to put them right... there will be community payback projects in every city affected... we are investing in drug recovery wings in our prisons. Tackling gang culture. Tougher community penalties. Effective justice. Restorative justice... a two-week summer school helping them to catch up in Maths and English.

...

Protecting the schools budget. A two and a half billion pound Pupil Premium by the end of the parliament. More investment in early years education: 15 hours for all three and four-year-olds. New provision for the poorest two-year-olds. All steps towards a society where nobody is 'enslaved by poverty, ignorance or conformity'. Towards a liberal society... Not easy, but right.

> ...
> Our values are strong. Our instincts are good: reason not prejudice. Compassion not greed. Hope not fear. Britain is our home. We will make it safe and strong. These are our children. We will tear down every barrier they face. And this is our future. We start building it today.[6]

Clegg's speech received a standing ovation – a long established etiquette for all leaders' speeches. Compared to previous speeches, the ovation was polite and dutiful, rather than a spontaneous expression of enthusiasm. Although Clegg had recognised the troubles caused by the tuition fees U-turn, he appeared to believe that the problem lay in the projection of the changed policy, rather than the U-turn itself. It seemed that he *still* did not accept that the breach of trust on a pledge was key to why many had turned their backs on the party.

Conference was little lifted by the checklist nature of the achievements Clegg cited. Tax changes were indeed worthy. Other points were of less significance to the hall, and the wider population. A list has to be relevant to electors. Not everything prompted applause, indicating the limited extent to which the list inspired delegates.

There was another issue. Despite a great deal of discussion of the importance of community politics – and new policy calling for a return to this trusty liberal methodology – Clegg did not mention community politics once in the entirety of his speech. This was a very serious omission. The party had suffered heavy losses, and ongoing defeats in by-elections. Yet Clegg left out the most important tool at the party's disposal. This was particularly serious because most of those attending Conference would be returning to exactly this activity the next day. Even now, the leadership seemed unconcerned about encouraging the party faithful against the losses 'on the ground.' Nevertheless, on the upside he had added an additional target to his already heady goal of doubling the number of MPs held by the party:

> And as for all those seats we lost in May, let me tell you this: I won't rest, we won't rest, until we've won every single one of those seats back.

As the audience left to return to their local constituencies and wards there was no sense that the party had turned a corner. While Clegg had much to say about the difficulties of doing the 'right thing' for the country, he had not said the right things about community politics. And once again, his was a list of results, but one which had no core narrative.

Clegg had clearly acknowledged the pain felt by the party faithful in electoral terms. Yet his remedy was to pin the party's fortunes on jam tomorrow, meaning progress in the next general election – as well as his new goal of winning back all the lost council seats, a target without a timetable. But how could the party make jam tomorrow if it had let the fruit rot in the fields today? Only by planting a new crop of community politics immediately could there be a harvest of recovery in the near future.

Without a formal commitment to rebuilding the party through community politics from the leadership, a further decline in the 2012 local elections seemed a real possibility. Although there would be less than half as many Lib Dem seats at stake in May 2012 than there had been in 2011, a real danger existed that many of these would be lost specifically because the priority of the Clegg administration still did not primarily focus on victory in this local tier of politics.

There was a final problem. Clegg had once again sounded keen to prove that the Lib Dems were influencing the Conservatives in government. This inevitably made him sound as if he was conceding the role of 'senior partner' to his Tory colleagues. It was an error of presentation which the Conservatives would never contemplate, nor allow their leader to even hint at.

The feedback on the Internet was not good. On the *New Statesman* website one commented: 'Words Nick... just words.'[7] On *The Guardian*'s website, another commented:

> Clegg has really shown his true colour – blue, and it is quite clear now that he had no intention of going into coalition with Labour and had planned to join the Tories no matter what. This confirms that he has lied to us all this time and Nick Clegg has also confirmed that his party represents the right of centre. At least now the left-leaning vote won't be split.[8]

This observation summed up the problem. To the left wing, Clegg was now a pariah who would not be able to win back the lost left-leaning voters – so important to the Liberal Democrats in many seats.

Summary

Perhaps the feedback from the public is best summarised by a comment posted on 18th September, by someone calling themselves 'Stardancer69'. The post had actually been provoked by Farron's *Guardian* article some days before Clegg's speech. Yet it encapsulates the general view of those who responded to the conference coverage: 'Hollow words from the hollow President of a hollow political party.'[9] So, just a few lines from T.S. Eliot's 'The Hollow Men' seem quite apposite:

> We are the hollow men
> We are the stuffed men
> Leaning together
> Headpiece filled with straw. Alas!
> Our dried voices, when

The Hollow Men

> We whisper together
> Are quiet and meaningless
> As wind in dry grass
> Or rats' feet over broken glass
> In our dry cellar
> ...
> *This is the way the world ends*
> *This is the way the world ends*
> *This is the way the world ends*
> *Not with a bang but a whimper.*[10]

While Farron's speech had catalysed this reply, it summed up the general mood in the Internet world. A YouGov poll of 23 September 2011, shortly after the close of the Lib Dem conference, gave the following ratings. Conservatives: 36%. Labour: 42%. Liberal Democrats: 11%.[11] The support for the Lib Dems had therefore increased by 2% across its conference week. However, on 7 October, at the end of the conference season, the party had sunk back to 9% in the same YouGov poll – indicating no net lift in its fortunes as a result of conference, with the Tories 2% up and Labour steady.[12] Since the Lib Dems were in by far the worst position, this was of the greatest concern to them. It summed up the challenge of securing any improvement amongst disillusioned voters who had turned away.

Clegg's speech had been no disaster 'on the day,' but it left the door open for more grumbling and dissent. This was the last thing Clegg needed for the months ahead. To his advantage, the membership still had not coalesced into forming a specific opposition to his leadership or to the Orange Bookers as a whole.

Delegates left the hall edgily, concerned that they had not heard words to assure them that there would be clear water between the Liberal Democrats and the Tories. The alternative view holds that there *was* a way to achieve this. It would mean energetically re-embracing the campaigning methodology which the conference had approved: the theory and practice of community politics. Only then would the benefits of a clear narrative, image and policies bear the fruits on which Clegg had pinned his success: a doubling of MPs and the recovery of council seats to pre-May 2011 levels.

Part 3

Moving on

So what's the answer? I'll tell you what: a full-blooded return to the principles and the practice of community politics. And it needs to start now.

Party President, 18 September 2011

Chapter 10

Focus on Community Politics

All politics is local.
Tip O'Neill, former Speaker, US House of Representatives

Lib Dems don't end up in Parliament. They *clamber* up to it. A local party makes the ascent as a team, forming political pyramids from the ground up. The base is formed by the local members and activists – those foot-soldiers who lay the greatest foundations they can sustain. Then there are the local officers, the campaign managers and the councillors. At the summit stands just one person. If the pyramid is high enough, they can reach up to find purchase on the green benches of the Commons.

This is how it always used to be for liberals. Those at the top traditionally started at the bottom, and learned the ropes along the way. When they made it to the pinnacle of the pyramid, they carried with them a respect for all that had gone before – leafleting, canvassing, and everything it takes to make a local difference to local people.

More recently, there have been changes. A divergence has crept in from what has traditionally been perceived as the Liberal Democrat way up. What's happened and what, if anything, has it meant for the movement?

Community politics

The alternative view believes that, with a leadership in which few have passed through the process of serving at a council level, priorities have altered. Other routes to office have become available to members. These new paths risk a diminution of the link between power and pavement politics, as it is known. If the grassroots is not where you started to look up, it won't look the same for those looking down.

By 2011, the number of councillors had fallen to the lowest level held by the party since 1986. This risked throttling the movement of on-the-ground activists which it so desperately needed in order to continue the party's historical relationship with the communities it served – as well as acting as the foundation for political activity at a local level: the pyramids which act as means of ascent in constituencies. This latter methodology has been at the heart of how Liberal Democrats gained and held seats, with a strong correlation between local government strength and advancement in terms of parliamentary, and other elected, seats.

Community politics in its current guise was explicitly rolled out within the Liberal movement over a period beginning in about 1970. In that year, the Liberal Assembly in Eastbourne adopted 'Community Politics' as a strategic approach to build the party's influence and electoral success through focused, local campaigning. Various works were produced.[1] Former Liberal activist Peter Hain wrote *Community Politics* in 1975, prior to joining Labour and rising to the status of a Labour Cabinet Minister many years later.

However, it was a seminal document published in August 1980 which was perceived as bringing together many of the strands of community politics. Known humbly as 'ALC Campaign Booklet Number 12' (ALC stood for 'Association of Liberal Councillors'), it was authored by long standing Liberal Party activists Gordon Lishman and Bernard Greaves. Its working title was 'The theory and practice of community politics,' and it sought to provide activists with a clear, comprehensive and compelling thesis in support of releasing the individual and unique potential of each citizen through 'voluntary, mutual and co-operative enterprise within relevant communities.'[2] Since it is easy to access this booklet to this day, we have not reproduced large tracts from it. The alternative view's aim is to provide a route back to best practice, not to reinvent it or to republish everything that has ever been written about the subjects. But the ethos is very much worth revisiting.

Every successful business knows the importance of intimate contact with its clients. The true strength of the 'brand' is the relationship that it has with its customers. Personal association with a firm means that you keep going back – as long as you trust the service. It's no different in politics. If the elector feels that they know you, trust you and can rely on you, then they 'buy' your services with their vote. It is less likely that newspaper articles, personal attacks or distant difficulties will rob you of your local relationship or your seat. If thousands of individual activists and councillors are all building such relationships, then the party can grow in a way which is simply impossible to achieve through a television screen, a party political broadcast or a Commons debate.

The tenets of Lishman, Greaves and others' work have provided local political activists with reliable guidelines for community politics ever since. In an article written by the party president in September 2011, he reflected many of the elements of that work.[3] In the words of Tip O'Neill, the former Speaker of the United States House of Representatives, 'All politics is local' – a piece of advice he learned from his father after young Tip lost a local council election early in his career. It was wisdom that he never took for granted again.[4]

Context in 2010

Disciples of community politics had a rough time in the unlucky 13 months that began in April 2010. Their pain was very local and very real. In fact, the elections of 2010 were marked by two conflicting emotions for Liberal Democrats on the ground, operating far from the high-powered corridors of Westminster. These emotions were hope and despair. They gained hope from 'Cleggmania' and the one in 14 chance that the bookies gave the party of being the largest grouping in Parliament.

Many community campaigners had for years simply got on with their local work, not daring to dream or believe that national power would occur in their lifetime. They saw themselves as predominantly local or opposition politicians. Briefly, in April 2010 grassroots campaigners felt there could be a chance that events would turn in their favour. The nearest remotely similar situation had occurred in the early 1980s when Liberal Party leader David Steel had exhorted his members and supporters to think big.

> 'I am the first Liberal leader in a generation to say at a party conference: "return to your constituencies and prepare for government."'[5]

When Steel made his announcement the general election was far off. Everyone understood that this was a call for the activist base to increase their local campaigning in preparation for it. In their hearts, few took Steel's prediction literally – after all, he offered no timescale for the period of time over which the preparation was to take place. But he did speak to the party faithful in tones that appeared empathic to the plight of the leafleter, the canvasser and the local candidate. By contrast, the surge of support in 2010 had occurred a few short weeks before polling. There was a real sense that something could happen... that it might be too late for the Conservatives to respond and claw back their vote.

When the big guns of the anti-Liberal Democrat press began firing, that hope was shot down. Yet the hope of an unexpected turn of events was not quickly abandoned. Grassroots campaigners did their best to deliver a big leap forward.

However, even in this moment of opportunity, left-leaning activists could sense that Clegg's own vitriolic anti-Labour commentary – and personalised attacks on Labour Prime Minister Gordon Brown – implied that a coalition with the Conservatives was more likely than one with Labour. Though this was not known by much of the party at the time, those likely to negotiate an agreement, such as David Laws and Chris Huhne, had already decided that they favoured the Conservatives over Labour.

To those who had closely studied the Orange Bookers, it did not seem likely that any post-election arrangement envisaged by the leadership would lead to the implementation of a radical left-leaning platform. However, to the community-based activists all of these thoughts were far from their concerns. The duty was to ply their local trade to help win as many seats as the party possibly could.

In Parliamentary terms, instead of progress there was a decline in seats for the first time since 1992. However, less widely reported were the results of the local election which took place on the same day. These were quite poor. Of approximately 870 council seats that the party was defending, it ended up about 142 seats down by the end of the night, meaning that about one in six seats slipped away from the Liberal Democrats.[6] This was not prominently reported, because the drama of a hung parliament held centre stage. But it was a significant knockback for local activists, even as the parliamentary party stood poised to enter government.

The dangers of this under-performance are writ large within the detail of the 2010 results. Although Liberal Democrats were only one authority down in terms of 'overall control,' this was made up of three gains and four losses. We find an interesting correlation in the gains. The three 'gained' authorities were two seats with Lib Dem MPs up to 2010 – Winchester and Cheltenham – and the target seat of Burnley, which was not held by the Lib Dems.[7] It is no coincidence that the Liberal Democrats gained an MP in. The Lib Dem MP in Cheltenham also held his seat. Although

The Alternative View

Winchester was lost to the Conservatives the Lib Dems had a strong vote, though it was evidently insufficient to hold the seat.

The four authorities which were 'lost' by the party comprised Richmond-upon-Thames (to Conservative control), Liverpool (to Labour control), and Rochdale and Sheffield (to 'No Overall Control').[8] And what of the Parliamentary seats? The parliamentary seat relating to Richmond-upon-Thames was lost by the Liberal Democrat MP to a Conservative.[9] Rochdale was also lost by the Lib Dems and gained by Labour. And the Lib Dems made no Parliamentary gains in Liverpool or Sheffield – though Clegg's own vote in Sheffield Hallam was very strong.[10]

Basically, the gains and losses of MPs roughly correlate with the gains and losses of councillors. This is no shock to experienced local Liberal Democrat activists. The evidence of this relationship is writ large in the history of the party. It is a matter of record that the biggest jump that the Liberal Democrats had enjoyed in Parliamentary seats occurred in 1997.[11] At exactly the same time the Lib Dems held well over 5,000 local government seats, the most in the history of the Lib Dems. They were, in fact, the second party of local government from 1995-1998, ahead of the Conservatives during this period.[12]

The importance of the correlation between Liberal Democrat Parliamentary performance and council representation cannot be overstated. Two out of the three gained authorities shared a geographical area with a Parliamentary victory. Two out of the four lost authorities shared a geographical area with Parliamentary defeats. It was simple: where the party made progress at local authority level, the chances of Parliamentary success were increased. Where the party suffered reversals at local authority level the chances of Parliamentary success were reduced. Indeed, the same phenomenon was observable in other Lib Dem seats – such as Montgomeryshire, where the Lib Dems had suffered losses and the Conservatives had made progress in the local elections which had occurred in 2008, two years prior to the general election.[13]

This phenomenon is more pronounced for the Lib Dems than for Labour or Conservatives. The Tories actually lost seven councils and went down by roughly the same number of councillors on polling day as the Lib Dems; but gained 96 seats in Parliament.[14] Labour gained 17 councils and hundreds of council seats but lost 90 MPs.[15] It's obvious that, in comparison to the other parties, Liberal Democrats are more dependent on local authority strength for their parliamentary fortunes.

Are the local authority and Westminster parliamentary results simply measuring some other cause, which makes these election results go up and down together? Yes, that's slightly true. Overall popularity is also a factor which affects both at once. But it's far from being the whole story. In fact, the council performance is actually a *driver* of success, rather than just a *measure* of it. And the better the party does locally, the more it drives its own success nationally. Let's journey back to 1970, when the Liberal party faced oblivion with 7.5% of the vote and six MPs.[16] The story of its salvation proves beyond all doubt that, for Lib Dems, victory begins on the doorstep, in local campaigns by local politicians for local people.

Community politics as a foundation

Those with long experience of campaigning knew the reason for the party's longevity and survival: community politics. The trusty 'Focus' leaflet played a central role. Back in the 1970s, before the days of word processors and laser printers, activists would tap out their messages on a creaky typewriter, cut out the paragraphs with scissors, glue them down on a bit of paper and march off enthusiastically to the local printer who'd run off a couple of thousand copies for the plucky activists. If they had the money, the activist would pay a bit more to get the leaflets folded. Otherwise, that was a job they'd do by hand. The characterful Truro Liberal MP, David Penhaligon, summed up the strategy: 'If you have something to say, write it on a piece of paper and stick it through a letterbox.'[17] Liberals knew exactly what he meant, and did exactly what he recommended.

This method was all about raising local issues to generate support and win council seats, which were then converted to parliamentary seats. The approach suited the activist base well. Community politics had won the party many parliamentary seats, even when there was little support from the central party machine. Some of the triumphant constituencies had not even been treated as 'targets'. It could be said that community politicians raised money locally and largely bankrolled their own activities. That is largely true to this day. Without that self-funding capability, the organisation would have foundered long ago.

The drawback was that once one community had been won by the Lib Dems often little effort was made to help neighbouring councils. By the same token, the desire to seize the Parliamentary seat enthuses local activists. However, the possibility of winning control of a larger and different authority, such as the Greater London Authority – or GLA – is too esoteric to encourage many activists to campaign seriously in boroughs in which they do not live. This effect is also seen in the counties of England, where, for very pragmatic reasons of targeting, activists in towns rarely help in neighbouring rural areas unless boundary changes make them part of their local constituencies.

These resisting forces slowed down the spread of Liberal Democracy. They led to situations where a majority Lib Dem council bordered another with no Lib Dem seats at all. However, Lib Dems rarely took a parliamentary seat unless they first won the council. This is why it is evident that the party cannot take power nationally unless it also grows to become the first party of local government – or a close second – prior to the general election. If Clegg were to have any chance of achieving his target of doubling the number of parliamentary seats by 2015, he therefore would have to focus primarily on building up the *council* base first – and in enough seats to make this a possibility. In Clegg's case, that meant strong council representation in at least 124 constituencies. In 1997, Labour's great victory was built on a local council base which was twice that of the Tories. As we have noted, in that year the Liberal Democrats also had more local councillors than the Conservatives. By the same token, in 2010 the Tory local government base comfortably exceeded Labour by about two to one; while the Liberal Democrat decline in MPs between 2005 and 2010 roughly reflected its proportionate decline in councillors.

For Labour, Conservatives and the Liberal Democrats, the correlation is fairly consistent: the size of a party's local council base is indicative of its performance in general elections. But while the others can buck the trend occasionally, with sporadic deviations between council performance and parliamentary performance, the Lib Dems seem tied into a council-and-Parliament relationship where the linkage is far more rigid. Again, this is because, while Tories and Labour have the benefit of benign support in the media, most of the support the Lib Dems garner is 'home-grown' – it's created by the Liberal Democrats themselves. For them, more than for any other major party, 'all politics is local.'

How can the council base be rebuilt? If the party is to win councillors in areas where it has none, the quickest shortcut is for them to receive help from nearby Lib Dem local parties which have already got councillors. Then success can be carried across from one area to the next. However, to do any good in the next general election, it would also have to become an urgent and extremely high priority for the Lib Dem leadership for the entire period between then and the previous general election. Investment in the local government base needs to be continuous and intensive.

By 2011, the health of the council base had become a gaping chasm. The party had to engage on the ground to protect its existing local assets and make the interrelationship between more and less active areas into a much more functional and proactive one. When a Focus leaflet was needed in an 'out-of-borough' area the activists tended to view their neighbouring colleagues as customers who may be given a 'favourable deal,' rather than as members of the same organisation who deserved an investment of time and effort. It's easy to see why. Local groups are primarily focused on their own progress and survival, so it is natural that other groups are a secondary priority. Still, for Clegg to have any chance of averting a further decline and delivering growth, he needed to facilitate that transfer of knowledge across borough boundaries. This was particularly the case where there was no 'precept' – or automatic contribution – coming from councillors out of the money they received as a result of their election to office. Precept had become the backbone of funding for serious Lib Dem organisations. Without it, paying for election software and leaflets would be a serious problem.

Parliamentary by-elections

What was stopping the central party from doing more to help build the crucial local community politics base? One issue was the focus on parliamentary by-elections. The party had fought over seventy of these since 1987. Enormous effort and expense had been invested in the belief that good performances in these elections were important in building the party's fortunes overall. The result? By 2010, of the 35 net gains made since 1987 the party held just two seats, Brent Central and Eastleigh, which had been gained in by-elections and then held continuously ever since; a very small number of other seats can be added if the record is taken back to the early 1970s. All of the others were lost – at least for a period – at subsequent general elections.

There were tactical attractions for focusing on by-elections in the past, when the party had fewer than two dozen MPs and each individual victory was a substantial addition to Liberal, Liberal Democrat or SDP numbers. At that point the public relations benefits were also of considerable importance, especially between 1987 and 1992 when the party was experiencing very poor poll ratings, worse even than those in 2011. It is possible – but not proven – that its victory in Eastbourne in 1990 assisted with its recovery.

The alternative view is that, with the far greater Lib Dem parliamentary presence by 2012, a much greater return would now be achieved by investing the money in building up local campaigning infrastructure and resisting the temptation to expend vast amounts on those by-election seats which even if won would be unlikely to be won again at the subsequent general election. We also suggest that those which were lost and subsequently gained back in later elections were regained by patient investment of time and effort – exactly the type of investment in local infrastructure that we are recommending as an alternative to major by-election expenditure in seats which would not otherwise be targeted.

The sums under consideration are substantial. For example, the party is said to have spent £93,000 on the by-election in Oldham East and Saddleworth, for no particularly useful return in regard to votes or public image in the long term.[18]

It would be reasonable to assume that the party was spending nearly £100,000 where it campaigned hard. This investment would provide important returns if the seats were won and held. Between the 2005 and 2010 general elections, none of the by-elections had any feature that made them look as though they would lead to seats that would be held at the subsequent general election; yet vast resources were poured into them.

It follows that the Liberal Democrats simply cannot expect to recover on the basis of individual by-election victories, even if winning one were possible at any given time – an additional problem facing the party since the commencement of the coalition. This reality is contrary to the emphasis placed on support for by-election victories by a number of party organisers, who regularly exhorted the membership to invest time and money in by-election campaigns. It is the data, not prejudice or romantic attachment to the 'glamour' and 'gamble' of by-elections, which causes the alternative view to suggest that, regardless of the immediate headlines, it was not justifiable to make such enormous investments in parliamentary by-elections. By and large, these gains had been fleeting – and quickly lost.

However, not spending money on by-elections would provide considerable extra resources for community politics. The party's by-election investment could then have been refocused anywhere the movement had a real chance of winning a council seat – especially where the candidates agreed to pay a 'precept' if elected. This would be even more valuable if the party had no existing candidates in that local authority.

The figures suggest that the party paid more per vote to lose in Crewe and Nantwich than Obama did his presidency. The alternative view is that this level of investment was not a good way to spend resources. The by-elections of Crewe and Nantwich, Ealing Southall and Norwich North had very high budgets. On those three by-elections alone it is likely that the party spent in excess of £250,000.

Until the Liberal Democrats found a way of spending money on over half the total number of seats in Parliament – the number necessary for the Liberal Democrats to win an overall majority – the party was necessarily limiting itself to being a minority in the Commons. This spending had to go hand in hand with investment in the local government base – the best way to create a winnable parliamentary seat. By 2011, the party was not making enough progress in its local government base to have any serious prospect of making the sort of growth the leadership had committed to.

On 10 August 2011, speaking to an assembled group of members and interested individuals in London, leader Nick Clegg summed up the leadership's position regarding the difficulties facing the local activist base as follows: 'sure, we made mistakes – of course we do – but long-term it's absolutely right,' adding 'long term is no good if you're fighting a by-election next Thursday.'[19] In other words, the pain of losing locally now would be worth it in the end. The alternative view suggests that this very approach more or less guaranteed that Clegg would not deliver his targets at a parliamentary level, because the foundations to build them on had crumbled away. However, note also that Clegg's observation implied his belief that it would be unacceptable to take strategic policy initiatives in government which harmed the party's prospects in the *long* term; on this, the alternative view strongly agrees with Clegg's viewpoint.

Turning again to the short and medium term, why did current leadership feel willing to sacrifice the performance of the party in local elections – if the performance of the party in national elections was so dependent upon it? A look at the biographies of the Orange Bookers provides a very interesting answer.

The Orange Book and community politics

To what extent did Liberal Democrat MPs rise to Parliament through local activism, followed by a period of service on a local authority, and then ascent to the House of Commons? This route underpinned a personal commitment to community politics in those who served in Parliament. Even the few who did not take this route, such as Charles Kennedy – who in 1983 sprang a surprise victory in Ross, Skye & Lochaber over a Conservative minister – generally held their seats through strong local campaigning, operating within their constituencies as 'super-councillors'.

However, since the advent of the Proportional Representation system for the European elections, a new route opened up which obviated the 'need' for a spell in the rank and file of local authority elections and service.

Before the Liberal Democrats secured a change in the electoral system to the European Parliament, there was rarely a practical alternative to 'earning your stripes' at the local level then convincing local party members of the merits of selecting a proven local activist for the Parliamentary seat. Of the 42 MPs after May 2010 who had not written for either *The Orange Book* or *Britain After Blair*, 31 had served as councillors.[20] Thus the great majority were steeped in the local campaigning ethos. These MPs formed a 'critical mass' who intuitively grasped the importance of the local government base, and did their best to support it in their own constituencies and elsewhere. It was an accepted part of their duties.

However, of the 15 MPs in Parliament after 2010 who had contributed to *The Orange Book* or *Britain After Blair* only three MPs had served as councillors, the rest having percolated into Parliament through other routes. The key paths they took were: serving as a staff member to an existing MP; serving as a member of staff to the party; or moving from the European Parliament to a 'held' Lib Dem seat in the British Parliament.

None of the six Liberal Democrats who had served as Cabinet ministers – Clegg, Huhne, Cable, Laws, Alexander or Moore – are recorded as serving as a Liberal or Liberal Democrat councillor. Of these, only Vince Cable had ever been a councillor – and that was for Labour in the 1970s. These people did not owe their success to the local authority route. The party leader had never served in local government, and had not worked for a Liberal Democrat MP on the way to becoming one himself.

The difference in experience is stark and, we suggest, significant. Amongst non-Orange Bookers, 74% had served as councillors prior to becoming MPs. Amongst the 21 MPs and peers recorded in the list of 'ministers' (which includes whips) on the Liberal Democrat official website in October 2011 the figure was 43%.[21] Only 20% of contributors to *The Orange Book* or *Britain After Blair* had served as councillors. And of Lib Dem Cabinet ministers – all of whom were also Orange Bookers – the proportion who had served as Liberals or Lib Dems on a local authority was... 0%: the traditional route to Parliament for Liberals and Liberal Democrats – through service at local authority level – *had not been the one used by any of those in the most senior positions that the Lib Dems held in government.*[22]

It is the alternative view that their means of ascent within the Liberal Democrat party – to the highest levels of seniority in government – through a non-councillor route was profoundly important. It had altered the way the most powerful Orange Bookers in government regarded the integral nature of local government campaigning. Clegg had praised those who had lost their seats for the greater good:

> We've lost support, we've lost councillors, and we lost a referendum. I know how painful it has been to face anger and frustration on the doorstep. Will it all be worth it in the end? It will be.[23]

Clegg's words contrasted with the president, the spokesperson for the membership:

> I absolutely will not insult you by claiming that this was collateral damage, or an understandable mid-term blip.[24]

Clegg was clearly asking the party to accept a degree of attrition at the ballot box of local government if that was the cost of making tough decisions in power. His recurring phrase was that the party had to make the choices that were 'not easy, but right.' Yet, if this alternative analysis is correct, the loss of council seats was 'not easy, but *wrong.*'

There were financial implications too. Fewer seats reduced the flow of 'precept' funds into local parties for campaigning. With the national party spending funds on by-elections and head office functions, it meant that the required cash in hard-to-win seats was eroded. New – and previously held – seats had to be won for the party to gain power in its own right, or indeed make any progress. In effect, by allowing the council and local activist base to erode, the party would seriously diminish its ability to fight its corner, because many of the previous activists – motivated by local success and local community politics – would no longer be there to contribute financially or physically to the targets the leadership had committed itself to.

A degree of political efficacy would still be in evidence in held seats where a Liberal Democrat MP was in post. Yet even there a loss of councillors would harm the local organisation's ability to campaign. It is almost impossible to overstate the dangers that this presented to the party's continued representation in Parliament, let alone its ability to gain more seats in areas where the Liberal Democrats had no MP, fewer councillors and too little money to turn things around.

Following the poor results in the Scottish parliamentary and Welsh Assembly elections, it is clear that the attrition was not limited to local government alone. Furthermore, there was every reason for the Liberal Democrats to be deeply apprehensive in advance of the next European Elections in 2014. In a proportional system, Liberal Democrats were heavily dependent on the overall vote. With little or no capacity to campaign in areas where they had lost a large swathe of their on-the-ground activist base, the likely resurgence of Labour support as well as an assertive and driven UK Independence Party (UKIP) led by charismatic and popular leader Nigel Farage all presented dangers to Lib Dem fortunes. UKIP had even begun to construct a more liberal agenda towards freedom of speech: it was they who had invited controversial speaker Geert Wilders to the UK in 2009. Meanwhile, in 2011 Lib Dem and Tory leaders spoke of muscular liberalism and an absolutist agenda which seemed to embrace 'no platform' policies towards non-violent extremists.

Unless the leadership succeeded in rebuilding the campaigning strength of the party, where this had been lost or seriously diminished, it was becoming hard to see how the damage could be repaired in advance of these European and British parliamentary elections in 2014 and 2015 respectively. The apparent tolerance of a profound reduction in the local council base is explicable given the means of ascent of the current leadership. But there was a real – and ironic – danger that the very route that the leader had used – namely the European one – would be constricted through a loss of MEPs.

If this cycle of contraction continued far enough the leadership's ability to prevent further erosion and build a recovery would eventually fall below a critical mass of activists from which, in the short term, it would not recover. Then the party would find itself fighting to protect islands of support, while large parts of Britain lay fallow and untended by the liberal movement. It is hard to predict what that critical mass might be. It does exist, as the Canadian Progressive Conservative Party found out in 1993, when they declined from an overall majority in the Parliament to just *two* seats – in a *single* election. Their vote contracted from 43% to 16% in that ballot.[25] Liberal Democrats should heed that event – in autumn 2011, the proportionate decrease in their poll ratings bore a strong resemblance to the Canadian Progressive Conservatives in Canada in 1993, and the party would be prudent to look at the lessons to be learned from that remarkable collapse.

Reprioritising community politics

It is worth considering whether those who want to win seats in Parliament ought to have served for a period of time in a council seat. This stricture would stop the practice of what is known as 'descending angels' usurping the chances of local rising politicians to secure seats. If the only way into Parliament is by first showing experience of at least standing in a council election – as, indeed,

Huhne had done in the early 1980s – it will necessarily drive a lot more activity at that level and improve the integration between local and parliamentary campaigning. This is something that the party has repeatedly expressed its commitment to, but which has never seemed more distant than in 2011.

In 2011, the party president began actively promoting a return to the principles of community politics. Tim Farron had earned his stripes through years of effort in student politics, then as a party activist and finally as a central component in building the Lib Dem local government base in the seat that he eventually gained from the Conservatives in 2001. He summarised his vision in an article published in the *Guardian* newspaper in September 2011. Entitled 'Community is our priority,' it sought to recommit the party to the traditional methods of community politics so beloved of the activist base. Farron reflected many of the original views expressed in the work of Greaves and Lishman, and paid homage to a motion passed in 1970 at the Liberal convention. Here is an edited version of Farron's *Guardian* article.

> The Liberal party's worst setback in our 60-year march back to relevance was arguably in 1970, when we found ourselves with just 6% of the vote and a mere six MPs, three of whom had a majority of fewer than 500 votes. Movers of that year's community politics motion at the Liberal assembly in Eastbourne wanted to demonstrate and articulate the Liberal party's ideology. Concerted action among party activists putting the theory into practice saved the Liberal party. Its councillor base expanded quickly after and the party made five by-election gains: Rochdale, Berwick, Isle of Ely, Sutton and Cheam and Ripon. In the two 1974 general elections the Liberals' share of the national vote trebled.
>
> ...
>
> Community politicians immerse themselves in their

communities – empowering people to take action over the issues they face rather than the alternative, where politics is 'done to' communities. Community politics is not just what liberals do, it's part of who they are.

...

This commitment to the theory and practice of community politics has sustained the party throughout the turbulence of much of the postwar period, amid the revivals, the plateaux and the occasional flirtations with oblivion.

...

Following May's somewhat disappointing election results our resources must once again be tuned towards the advance of community politics. Activists on the ground, policy development, funding, campaign resources and the themes underpinning the work plans of the party's committees must all come under the overriding priority of a rebirth of community politics.

...

Lib Dems who are council leaders, council cabinet members, ministers or advisers need to be in the vanguard of a new community politics movement.

...

Being in power, at local or at national level, has an understandable tendency to suck you away from reality. There is a finite amount of time in everyone's day, so if you run your council, or if you are a minister, the time you spend fulfilling those roles can displace the time you previously spent campaigning.

...

The consequence of this is that you stop communicating as a campaigner, and corporate, desk-bound work makes you miss the issues that people are concerned about, the language they use and how they react to things.

> ...
> In council chambers and government offices we develop relationships with officers and civil servants. If they are our only real contact, we risk becoming completely out of touch. This is a dangerous habit, but it's easy to get hooked.
> ...
> So we must take control of our diaries. Community politics is our priority. That is why the practice of community politics is even more important for those who are in power. You can become part of the administration but you must never become the establishment; you must carry on campaigning against things and for things, but always alongside and within your community, and never falling for the arrogance that power can lure you into.[26]

Community politics is the movement's 'storm cellar,' the safe house from which it can again expand. However, that would need a concerted effort from the entire organisation, moving the focus away from parliamentary by-elections and the 'air war' – as the media campaigns were often called – back to the 'ground war,' a battle for hearts and minds with leaflets and canvassers and local campaigns. This was the one methodology which could help as long as it was urgently deployed. If the leadership ignored his exhortation they did so at the peril of movement. They would then be held responsible for continued contraction.

Summary

The logic of this section is clear. The Liberal Democrats would be wise to transfer financial and human resources away from the 'air war' and back to the 'ground war,' where hearts and minds are converted through the application of the trusted methods of community politics. Specifically, consideration should be given to the following five steps.

1. The Liberal Democrats should recommit to the long-term aim of being the leading party in local government, as the key stepping stone to winning a parliamentary majority.
2. The party should transfer resources from parliamentary by-elections to local authority ward activity.
3. The party should provide funding for literature and canvassing-related information technology in wards where there is an activist but no 'precept-paying councillor.'
4. There should be a presumption that all Prospective Parliamentary Candidates in target seats have at least stood in a local election and, ideally, served as a councillor.
5. The party should not engage in strategic policy initiatives at a national level that damage its *long-term* ability to win council seats.

The alternative view makes these specific suggestions as a result of our analysis. It must be right for the Liberal Democrats to make specific changes to the party's mode of operation to ensure the vision of a return to these tried and tested techniques, so that methods which protected the movement from oblivion in the past are once again promoted to a status that helps the organisation achieve growth and security.

These issues were not the only considerations which the Liberal Democrats needed to clarify as they sought a way through their ongoing difficulties in 2011. Questions of leadership inevitably arose, and it is to these that we now proceed.

Chapter 11

Focus on Narrative

Give us clear vision that we may know where to stand and what to stand for – because unless we stand for something we shall fall for anything.
Peter Marshall, Chaplain of the US Senate 1947-1949[1]

Politics has always been the art of the possible. Today it's too often the art of the probable – tinkering around the edges without any greater vision, without a sense of optimism and imagination.
US Senator John Kerry[2]

People are more inclined to be drawn in if their leader has a compelling vision. Great leaders help people get in touch with their own aspirations and then will help them forge those aspirations into a personal vision.
Emeritus Professor John Kotter[3]

This chapter and the following ones are all focused on constructing a robust narrative for the party, which is then developed into a clear image and a consistent policy agenda, prior to being sold through inspirational leadership.

An 'image' is different from a 'narrative,' a 'policy' and 'leadership.' The alternative view offers these definitions. 'Narrative' is the movement's worldview – a description of its ideal society in terms of what happens in it, how it happens and the values that its citizens display in their behaviour. 'Policies' are the specific individual things that the movement wants to implement, which collectively build the society that the narrative envisions. 'Leadership' is the act of focusing the movement on a common narrative, and inspiring it to win over hearts and minds to the worldview and policies which deliver it. 'Image' is the style which the movement displays in its projection of its narrative, policy and leadership, and can be described in marketing terms as the movement's 'branding.' Let's start with the narrative – which must underpin everything else.

Different coalition approaches to narrative

From the outset of the coalition, the Conservatives were good at projecting a narrative in a way that the Liberal Democrats were not. A look at some actual examples vividly illustrates the two divergent approaches.

During the second half of 2011, there was an active effort by senior Liberal Democrats to attempt to create distance between their image and that of their coalition partners. For example, on 3 September 2011, Liberal Democrat Baroness Shirley Williams challenged Conservative plans for the National Health Service, saying:

> The remarkable vision of the 1945 Attlee government, of a public service free at the point of need for all the people of England, should not be allowed to die.[4]

On 19 September 2011 at the Lib Dem party conference, Cabinet Minister Vince Cable launched an attack on Tory tax proposals:

> Some believe that if taxes on the wealthy are cut, new revenue will miraculously appear. I think their reasoning is this – all those British billionaires who demonstrate their patriotism by hiding from the taxman in Monaco or some Caribbean bolthole will rush back to pay more tax but at a lower rate. Pull the other one.[5]

While each individual attack was in line with Liberal Democrat thinking, they did not collectively add up to a common message – a united front which branded the party in a unique and indelible fashion.

By contrast, the Conservatives had succeeded in doing just this. They steadily adhered to their traditional Tory agenda, such as tax cuts favouring the most wealthy. One example was the Tory desire to abolish the top rate of tax – which had been raised by the previous Labour government to 50% for those earning over £150,000 per annum. On 7 September 2011, Conservative Communities Minister Eric Pickles said in a BBC Radio 4 interview that

> There is a strong case to say this isn't actually contributing very much and on balance is probably doing more damage than good. When the Chancellor judges the time is right to do so, then we should get rid of it.[6]

Again, Liberal Democrats responded appropriately. Chris Huhne said

> If the cut in the top rate of tax is just a way of helping the Conservatives' friends in the City to put their feet up, then forget it.[7]

The Alternative View

Lib Dem Chief Secretary to the Treasury Danny Alexander added:

> The wealthiest can afford to pay their fair share at a time of difficulty for the country and we need to make sure they continue to do so.[8]

The party president made an oblique reference to recent civil disorder:

> The super-rich don't need to go down Ealing High Street nicking tellies in order to demonstrate their contempt for society. They demonstrate their contempt by not paying taxes. And let's be honest, we are sharing power with a bunch of people who think that this is OK.[9]

However, the Conservatives were playing a crafty game – one which was advantageous to them in various respects. Their game consistently sustained their narrative, sometimes eroding that of the Lib Dems at the same time. An example of their clever play occurred on 10 September 2011. William Hague delivered a salvo against his coalition partners, claiming that the Conservative relationship with the Liberal Democrats was causing the United Kingdom to remain closer to the European Union than a purely Conservative government would have done if governing alone.[10] While this might appear to be no more than a lament, the Tory agenda was more sophisticated than that.

Firstly, by 2011 support for further integration with the EU was firmly opposed by many voters – and most Conservatives. Yet the United Kingdom had provided considerable amounts to bail out the faltering eurozone. Since the Liberal Democrats were the most pro-Europe of the three major parties, vaguely blaming them for the government's European financial commitments partly protected the Tories from attack, to the detriment of their coalition partners. It gave the impression that a Conservative-only administration would not have been so embroiled in the Euro mess.

Secondly, Clegg himself had been a Member of the European Parliament. He had a stated record of supporting further integration. Any negativity towards this issue could not easily be sidestepped by a party which he led.

Thirdly, the Conservatives had identified the growing plausibility of the UK Independence Party (UKIP) – headed by the highly effective Nigel Farage. To align the Conservatives on the Eurosceptic side of the European debate would partly counter potential UKIP advances in the European Elections scheduled for 2014. The Tories hoped to insulate themselves from UKIP inroads, leaving Liberal Democrats vulnerable to taking the flak.

This approach over the European Union was typical of the Tory methodology. It showed how they deftly contrasted themselves with their Liberal Democrat partners, by consistently returning to a core Tory narrative. In turn, their supporters felt less aggrieved about compromises compared to Liberal Democrat supporters. The variance in projection of narrative revealed a powerful asymmetry between the perceived sacrifices made by the Tories versus the Lib Dems.

The presentation of these sacrifices was qualitatively different in other respects too. Tories presented changes in policy either as minor or as some kind of regrettable necessity forced upon them by those meddling Lib Dems. The same could not be said of their coalition partners. More than once, Liberal Democrats were made to look as if they had 'sold out' to the Conservative agenda, for instance on cuts, health reform, student funding and foreign policy. There was genuine anger amongst former Lib Dem voters at the perceived shift towards the agenda of Cameron's Conservatives.

The Tories played another clever card. They presented some of the more attractive 'concessions' as Tory policy all along. This was the case with changes to the divisive Health Bill, parts of which were modified following dramatic criticisms of its original content by edgy Lib Dems after the May 2011 debacle. Conservative former Cabinet minister Stephen Dorrell, who chaired the Commons Health Committee, advised:

> It's important that the Conservative Party does not react to coalition initiatives by implying that every hardline initiative is a Tory initiative and every time there is a more imaginative initiative that's a Liberal Democrat initiative. That's in the Liberal Democrats' interests but quite a lot of the policies that are sometimes thought of as Liberal Democrat initiatives actually reflect a broad-based Tory tradition.[11]

It was an effective means of tempering the extent to which the Liberal Democrats succeeded in taking credit for influencing policy. Again, the Tory narrative was the starting point.

In a timely reminder of the Tory Party's irritation with the Liberal Democrats – whether synthetic or real – maverick Tory backbencher Nadine Dorries MP summed up the mood of many in her party. In Prime Minister's Questions on 7 September, she exhorted David Cameron to show Clegg 'who's the boss'. After contemplating an answer, Cameron said smiled and said wryly, 'I think I'm going to give up on this one.'[12] His mischievous confidence delighted colleagues and left Clegg, who was sitting beside him, with no opportunity to do anything other than acknowledge the response politely, leaving viewers to derive subliminal messages from the Tory bravado towards their partners.

Consistent Conservative messaging in many areas provides evidence of the benefit of maintaining a clear and consistent narrative in the eyes of the public – in stark contrast to the emphatic attempts of the Liberal Democrats to prove that they were both influential while bestowing a liberal flavour on the administration. These attempts were not translating themselves into a resonant message to those on the ground.

As long as the Lib Dems did not rely on a cogent core narrative as their starting point, however sound their individual comments, there was no guarantee of consistency in the 'mood music'. It left the impression that, by and large, the Tories were governing in line with their worldview, with a little help from their friends. They still looked Eurosceptic, sympathetic to privatisation and eager to cut taxes for the wealthy. They projected the hint that the only obstacle holding back further progress on this narrative was Liberal Democrat churlishness. Meanwhile, the Lib Dems looked as if they were running to keep up, while achieving limited concessions in minor areas. Tories made policy, and Lib Dems influenced those policies as best they could.

The alternative view is that this impression undervalues the true impact of Liberal Democrat ministers in government. Thanks to them, there was a greater emphasis on tax cuts for the poor. Steve Webb was highly credible in the Department of Work and Pensions. Vince Cable had recovered his stature in the business sector, following the difficulties that he had faced in December 2010. However, the collective effect of individual policy interventions did not paint an easily accessible 'Liberal Democrat Big Picture,' presenting a sufficiently consistent story in line with what voters wanted to see. The way back had to be a way forward which looked unmistakably Lib Dem – even from a distance, on the television screens and in tabloid papers.

Mike MacKenzie, a newly elected Scottish Nationalist Party (SNP) member of the Scottish Parliament, made the following observation over tea at the annual conference of the SNP, a party with no confusion whatever about its narrative: independence for Scotland. MacKenzie said:

> parties have lost their underpinning party ideology. Nobody knows what the parties stand for any more. Gordon Brown talked about a moral compass as a personal thing. But no moral

compass guides any of those parties. The SNP have core values that everybody understands, a core image that everybody understands and a core set of values close to the heart of Scottish people. It's as if the UK parties think politics is like selling ice cream in the summer. They're all trying to sell as much ice cream as they can, by crowding around the 'centre of the beach'. They need to express their core values to British people.[13]

He summarised the feeling of those who felt that parties were inclined to occupy a similar position in the political spectrum for the sake of votes, losing their identity in the process. While the alternative view would argue that the Conservatives did operate from a core narrative, we hold that the Lib Dems were not doing so, and therefore lay vulnerable to MacKenzie's criticism.

A collective narrative

The alternative view believes there was an urgent need for Liberal Democrats to re-establish a clear and consistent political narrative – one that the public could easily grasp as uniquely Liberal Democrat. Individual attacks on particular policies can only achieve that if it all adds up to a common and consistent message. The Conservatives were doing this very well – and the Lib Dems were not. Could the Liberal Democrats change this, and if so how?

Both coalition partners were defending precisely the same coalition record in government. One still operated from its worldview at the same time. It showed that there was no obstacle, at least in principle, to doing so even under the circumstances of coalition.

Was the relative difference in the size of the two parties an obstacle? In other words, could the 'smaller partner' in a coalition achieve a comparable clarity of message to the senior one? We find the answer within electoral events in the United Kingdom itself.

During the coalition arrangements between the Liberal

Democrats and Labour between 1999 and 2007, there was no evident obstacle to both parties campaigning and presenting themselves as individual movements. Certainly, the breathtaking contraction of the Liberal Democrats and Labour did not come at the end of a period of coalition. It happened after a period of minority government by the Scottish Nationalist Party, led by Alex Salmond.[14] Although there are various variables to be considered, the facts prove that there is no cast-iron relationship between being a 'junior party' in a coalition and suffering in terms of the party's image or electoral performance.

The Liberal Democrats flat-lined in terms of electoral performance in the Welsh Assembly, even though they were in coalition from 1999 to 2003. It made no difference to their performance for a full 12 years. Their decline occurred in 2011, after four years during which they had not been in a Welsh coalition of any sort.[15]

Another most interesting example is that of Northern Ireland. For reasons directly related to the peace process which ended decades of civil strife, the devolution arrangements were specifically designed to ensure power-sharing between parties. However, there has been no correlation between electoral success or failure and the relative strength of those parties in the power-sharing arrangements. For example, the Ulster Unionist Party lost ground to the Democratic Unionist Party for reasons entirely unrelated to size. So, also, the growth of Sinn Fein and the Alliance Party of Northern Ireland was not dependent on whether one or the other party had been a senior partner, a junior partner, or no partner at all.[16]

It follows that there is no binding reason to believe that the Liberal Democrats were doomed to be subsumed in the image of their larger coalition partner. Rather, the image of the party is based on the consistency of narrative shared by the individuals who speak and act for the party. If they speak with a common voice, to a common narrative using consistent language, this can create an identity separate to that of the 'government' as a collective unit.

Herein lies the difficulty for the Liberal Democrats. We have already analysed how the Orange Book caucus did not operate from a core narrative. It delivered personal success rather than a collective message. Whatever the good intentions of the key luminaries, most particularly David Laws, the movement was self-contradictory in principles and policies. It had no chance of creating a consistent image in government because it had no consistent vision of its own. As a movement within a movement, it could not project a clear and consistent story for the party because the Orange Bookers had no clear and consistent story for themselves.

A telling indication of the extent to which the Orange Bookers did not see themselves as a political creed was given by an MP who had contributed to the second volume – *Britain after Blair*. When he was described as an Orange Booker, he adamantly denied that this was so. He sincerely believed that his inclusion in the second volume did not associate him with the Orange Bookers. In 2011, a former MP and contributor to the first book and – briefly – party leadership candidate, Mark Oaten, remarked laconically:

> I was just asked to write something for it. We never met together, and if I'd realised where it was going to end up I'd have taken the whole thing more seriously.[17]

It was an important insight. Little wonder, then, that a distinctive political narrative has not been formulated by a leadership consisting almost exclusively of Orange Book members.

Summary

The alternative view is that the Liberal Democrats cannot hope to define a clear identity without building a clear, consistent story which the public can access. This requires a leadership bound together by a rock-solid narrative. The existence of a central grouping not formed around a shared worldview is a controlling weakness. Tories operate from their narrative viscerally. They do it because they all believe it. Only another deeply-shared sense of a common value system and worldview can compete with it sufficiently robustly to protect an alternative identity in government.

It is worth noting that should the Lib Dems achieve this it could generate tensions in the coalition. As long as only one narrative is at play – the Conservative one – there is no such tension. Once two conflicting narratives are present, the potential for ideological conflict increases. This is the cost of a more strongly defined Lib Dem identity, but the cost of not having one is moral anonymity.

It is an issue which cannot be rectified until the central ruling group is united ideologically, and around a narrative which the party identifies with. Can Orange Bookers deliver this? They must if their party is to recover under their leadership. However, this is not enough. They must also generate a consistent image to fit with the movement's worldview.

Chapter 12

Focus on Image

A brand is a living entity – and it is enriched or undermined cumulatively over time, the product of a thousand small gestures.
Michael Eisner, CEO, Disney[1]

This chapter is all about image. This is relevant to how individuals project the party's world vision, and how the party behaves as a whole. Let's be clear about what we mean by 'image'. An 'image' is different from a narrative in that it is the style in which the movement presents itself. For our purposes, in marketing terms the image can be regarded as the movement's 'branding'.

The party's image is also a bit like a personality. The actions and comments of all the individuals in the party add together like a tapestry, which provides an impressionistic picture of the personality of the whole. The leadership carry a particular responsibility in projecting the image, as these people have the highest profile and therefore add more to the tapestry than less prominent people in the movement. They are the nearest a party has to the personification of the 'body politic'. This is why praise and blame in regard to the actions of parties tend to be directed at leaders, and why members of the public often use the name of the leader almost interchangeably with the name of the party: 'I'm not voting for Blair again' was synonymous with 'I'm not voting for Labour again,' apart from in his Sedgefield constituency where they voted for or against the man himself.

Do not mix up character with personality. Character relates to someone's values and outlook, and has more to do with narrative. Personality relates to the impression someone projects onto others, regardless of their moral worth, and has more to do with image. One can have a 'bad' character and a nice personality – which could make a person a 'beguiling brigand'. Alternatively, one could have a 'good' character and an introverted personality – which could make a person an 'honourable wallflower'. So since character is about narrative and image is about personality, the ideal combination for a party – or a person – is a fine character and a great personality.

To effectively project an image the party must know its own personality, and grasp how wider society can best be shown it in an appealing way. Again, this puts a duty on the leadership. It is their role to help the whole movement project that personality, in a consistent way which makes sense to citizens who would potentially warm to it. If the party were a real person, it would ask: how do I make friends and influence people in keeping with my values and worldview?

Others may wish to separate these considerations in different ways. That's all well and good, but the alternative view will use these working definitions to offer an achievable actionable plan for progress.

In the words of American industrialist Tom Chappell:

> Success means never letting the competition define you. Instead, you have to define yourself based on a point of view you care deeply about.[2]

His words are right for business – and politics. It also means you need to know who you are in the context of others whom you interact with and who influence you. So let's get to know the two other 'big personalities' in British politics, Labour and Conservative, to provide a context for the Lib Dem image.

Image in terms of the Nolan Chart

Once in a while, a tremendously useful new tool surfaces from the volumes of academic political commentary. One such tool is the Nolan Chart.

The personality of the Liberal Democrats is very different to Labour and the Conservatives. But, until the end of the 1960s, it was very hard to explain *why* or *how* it seemed different. The left-right spectrum had been the dominant tool for the analysis of political views since the French Revolution – with no real alternative. It wasn't sophisticated enough to describe a three-cornered political world. A straight line missed out an entire dimension which had become extremely important in understanding the reality of British politics since the 1920s. The left-right model made political reporting easy for journalists and newspapers, which traditionally preferred a binary approach to the subject. It also meant that it was almost impossible for people to properly appreciate what was really going on in terms of the relative personalities – or images – of the three main British political parties.

David Nolan came to the rescue. In 1970 a new method, the Nolan Chart, produced by the political theorist David Nolan, came to prominence.[3] This had not only a Left-Right axis, but also a Statist-Libertarian axis.[4] Rather than giving only two options, with the liberals sitting between them, this more intelligent analytical tool helped liberals to begin to be understood as distinct from both the Labour and Conservative parties.

This comes as little surprise to anybody with a neutral view of the three main political movements. There are many similarities between Labour and Conservative – which had been described as 'Butskellism' in the 1950s,[5] and 'consensus politics' in the period following the election of David Cameron as leader of the Conservative Party. The work of the group Political Compass helped to propagate this evolving assessment and to inform the political debate. Their annual report, showing the views of political parties, illustrated an ever-closer alignment between the Labour and Conservative Parties.[6]

The analysis itself is intriguingly simple. It looks at attitudes towards personal freedom and economic freedom. To be deliberately provocative, the alternative view suggests that Conservatives like economic freedom but are not particularly motivated by personal freedom. The Labour Party likes the idea of personal freedom, to a limited extent, but is averse to economic freedom: it should be said that even Labour's claimed liking of personal freedom has to some extent been eroded by the introduction of authoritarian policies, such as increasing powers of police detention, surveillance and the use of bans to reduce harms such as smoking in public places. The liberal view has traditionally been to support both personal and economic freedom. The key to creating a liberal image is to find a 'branding' that reflects the array of personal and economic freedoms in a way that is consistent with the party's moral narrative and its consequent policy positions.

It could be said that one of the successes of the Tory party in the period between Thatcher's election as Prime Minister in 1979 and Blair's departure in 2007 had been to move Labour towards the Tories in terms of the Nolan Chart. This did not mean that the philosophical centre of gravity of Labour had shifted. The narrative was in a sense at odds with the image, causing Blair considerable problems with his own membership. But his decision to shift the personality of Labour towards where the Tories were on the Nolan Chart had paid off in three consecutive elections. The convergence between those two parties had left a space for an alternative voice – for a party with an image which was manifestly different to Labour and the Conservatives. Yet it did not seem that the Liberal Democrats in government were taking the opportunity to be that voice – despite their greatly elevated status on the political stage. Why not?

The alternative view suggests that, in terms of the Nolan Chart, there is no particular libertarian centre of gravity for the Orange Bookers running the party, while the commentary of *The Orange Book* and *Britain After Blair* qualitatively indicates a rightwing preference for economic policy. Up to 2011, the only contemporary attempt to measure the party's MPs in terms of social liberalism had been conducted by the think-tank Liberal Vision. Their report did not show up a striking pattern in regard to the Orange Bookers as far as libertarianism was concerned. Of those who had served as Lib Dem Cabinet ministers by October 2011, Vince Cable was identified as the second *least* liberal MP in the party, and David Laws as the second *most* liberal, with Huhne, Clegg, Alexander and Moore somewhere in the middle.[7] Although the research methodology was, by its own admission, only indicative rather than watertight, it offered limited circumstantial evidence of the lack of a common position in regard to social policy.

If Laws had remained in the Cabinet, this might have served to increase tensions in the Cabinet. His highly liberal views on social issues were confirmed in his contribution to the Orange Book and *also* by the Liberal Vision research. Without him, the Lib Dem Cabinet team was notably less liberal, with either a neutral or – if one applies the Liberal Vision findings literally – marginally authoritarian skew on social policy. Added to this was their apparently right-of-centre economic positioning. These factors made it easier for the Cabinet to operate than if the Tories had been faced with, for example, five clearly-focused libertarian leftwingers.

The alternative view suggests that the party at large has tended in recent years to back a fairly liberal approach to civil liberties, and left-leaning policies for the economy. This appears to define the wider party's personality – inasmuch as these things can be objectively judged. Policy motions at conference would tend to support this assessment. And now we begin to see the issue. Orange Bookers could sit relatively comfortably with Conservatives on the Cabinet – because those five individuals did not come to the table with a strongly libertarian position on social matters, and could tolerate a right skew economically. But these very same things were likely to cause stress to the party at large, as the image that the leadership projected in government reflected their own social and economic positioning, *even if they didn't have a clear view of it themselves.* The results of policy decisions would necessarily paint a picture which would be hard to see close up, but easy to see from a distance. This picture would directly impact on the party's image.

If this assessment is correct, it indicates the challenge facing the party in terms of personality. Courage in coalition requires a robustness to paint a consistent Lib Dem picture, even if this risks causing tensions with coalition partners. In reality, there was little likelihood of a breakdown in the coalition in the short term: Conservatives and Lib Dems had no political incentive to walk away in the early stages. So tensions caused by a more assertive Lib Dem image would not be 'dangerous' to the government.

Let's remember that the Conservatives themselves had continued to operate from the place in the Nolan Chart which fitted their leadership, their membership and their voter base. For them, there was no real contradiction between what they felt as a political movement and what they were able to do as a party in government. The absence of similar clarity amongst the Lib Dem Cabinet Ministers simply meant that conflicts of positioning were less likely to occur. That was not a good reason for the Lib Dems to remain bashful in regard to presenting a shared personality for the party. As the efforts of ministers to differentiate themselves in regard to individual policy issues showed, they concurred with our view. But they needed to do it collectively – to present the same image together. Otherwise there was a risk that the general comments of the individual ministers would not help to carve out that distinctly Liberal Democrat image which the party so badly needed.

This theory is certainly a view in line with the thoughts of former Lib Dem MP for Ludlow Matt Green. He suggested:

> all parties are 'trending' to the centre. The competition seems to be on who makes the best manager. The choice for the electorate is extremely limited – it's difficult to see where the next big idea is coming from.[8]

The alternative view believes that clarity on positioning in terms of the Nolan Chart goes a long way towards untangling the kind of blurred distinctions which Green had insightfully identified.

Self-knowledge can help a party to find its image by helping it to find itself. This rids it of the pressure to 'shuffle towards the others,' in the misplaced search for a political comfort zone in which one avoids getting attacked, mainly by not doing anything interesting enough to be attacked for. Ironically, the absence of interest itself leads to disengagement by the electorate, thereby realising the very outcome that unadventurous leaders seek to avoid.

Return to policies which other parties cannot offer

Getting the image right means being able to connect up the brand with the policies that go with the narrative. It is a far more proactive place to anchor the policymaking process than, for example, opposing things just to look different, trying to work out each policy on a case-by-case basis or – worst of all – going along with policies in order not to upset one's coalition partners.

In power, Liberal Democrat ministers have occasionally defended policies which are clearly at odds with Liberal Democrat policy. The U-turn on tuition fees, the concept of an absolutist agenda based on the Tory concept of muscular liberalism and the initial acquiescence to changes in the National Health Service are examples of this. If the first thought always related to narrative, the second to image and the third to policy, then these issues would not arise in the same way. It would still be the case that ministers have to compromise. But doing so would be far more tolerable to the movement if this were transparently highlighted in terms of its narrative, image and long-term interests.

Can it work? Yes. Whether consciously or intuitively, this was exactly what the Tories had done from the first day of the coalition. Their transparency protected the Conservative leadership from the fractious problems which had dogged the Liberal Democrats over the same period.

Community-based image

As we will consider in the next chapter, there are well-established reasons to believe that, uniquely of the three main political movements, the Liberal Democrats are superbly well-placed to develop an image anchored in the communities they represent. As far as image goes we suggest that, as long as the local mechanics can be made to work – which they demonstrably can, given the history of the Liberal movement from around 1970 – then an image heavily based on the profile of the party in local government is the single strongest starting point for a resilient and distinctive organisational 'personality'.

The Alternative Vote referendum indicated, circumstantially at least, that elements of the public used the vote to punish the party for what they regarded as a betrayal in policy terms. Consider the performance of the SNP, where they found a true resonance with the public by presenting themselves as a palatable alternative to their competitors. They achieved this to such a degree that they secured the almost unimaginable triumph of a majority of the seats in the Scottish Parliament. They were true to their narrative, displayed an attractive personality – personified by their larger-than-life leader, Alex Salmond – and carried that all the way through to their policies.

What can be done to use campaigning techniques to reposition the Lib Dems in a more distinctive and favourable light? Let's have a look.

Image versus the Conservatives

We've reviewed the mechanics of a party's image, and the reasons why there seemed to be a difficulty for the Lib Dems in coalition. Let's consider the remedies in a practical sense.

Shortly after the 2011 local elections, speaking to a press gallery lunch in Parliament, Conservative Culture Minister Jeremy Hunt said:

> this is an unbelievably radical government: if we achieve any one of our main projects, then we can be more proud than any government since Margaret Thatcher's.[9]

No Orange Bookers were in attendance to pass comment on Hunt's observation. However, to the majority of the membership, Hunt's words indicated precisely why many Lib Dems felt so uneasy about a close association with the Tories. The idea of Thatcher's regime as something to be proud of was anathema to most Lib Dem activists. Recall that Cameron himself had been full of praise for Thatcher, and never flinched from sharing his belief that she had been one of the greatest Prime Ministers of all time.[10] Such comments highlighted the emphatic need for Lib Dems to reassert a separate identity.

As we have seen, this could not be achieved simply by opposing individual policies. The Conservatives had adeptly maintained their distinctive and traditional image by sticking to their narrative and building their policy agenda upon it, even while in league with the Liberal Democrats. Cameron's interpretation of muscular liberalism was a classic gambit to tie the Liberal Democrats into the mindset of Conservative absolutism. Their tolerance of their Lib Dem partners was repeatedly highlighted as a necessary evil, as shown in comments from the back bench. Their ruthless progress at the cost of Lib Dem seats in local and regional elections belied their underlying – and perfectly legitimate – commitment to press on with a Tory agenda while doing their best to corrode the fighting power of their coalition partner.

The current leadership had not provided this differentiation with sufficient clarity – to stand firm on a point of principle, even at the cost of straining the coalition. Indeed, careless words by the Deputy Prime Minister to Cameron when he was still being 'wired for sound' by the media proved his view that he felt little difference of view from the Prime Minister.[11] As Clegg himself had said on occasion, it was not necessary to be rude to a coalition partner. However, it *was* necessary to be firm, and to know and show why the two parties were not one party.

It follows that the Lib Dems have to match the robustness of the Conservative narrative, image and policy agenda with a similarly strong construction of their own. That would infer the need to avoid muscular liberalism, for this would clearly corrode the party's independent image. Also, it would seem prudent to take on the Conservatives in a much more assertive way at the local level, where the image can be constructed directly with the public. The alternative view suggests that all of this can be assisted by a visible willingness to stand the party's ground on totemic issues projected consistently by all its spokespeople. This would, over time, reveal the divergence of ideologies – which is desperately important for the Lib Dem identity.

Positivity of messages

A further element in generating a more 'Liberal Democrat' image for the party is the tone of campaigning pursued by its senior members. The alternative view argues that a negative tone has entered the party's campaigning style. This has become systemic and its use – internally and externally – distracts from the values and, potentially, the cohesion of the party.

The alternative view defines 'negative campaigning' as follows: 'attempting to improve one's own electoral standing by actively highlighting negative factors pertaining to one or more opponents in such a way as to diminish their standing, thus, by default, improving one's own chances of success.'

In more crude terms, it is basically the practice of 'talking yourself up' by 'running others down'.

For years, party literature and spokespeople have attempted to present a tone of moral superiority in comparison to the more cynical approaches of their two main rivals. As recently as April 2011, Chris Huhne and others expressed their displeasure at the negative leaflets and 'trashing' tactics of the 'No' campaign in the Alternative Vote referendum, which, he claimed, the Prime Minister was not using his powers to prevent.[12]

This kind of complaint was nothing new. Liberal Democrats have traditionally attacked other parties for embracing the concept of negative campaigning. Some months before the 2001 general election, the BBC reported:

> Liberal Democrat leaders have promised not use a single negative poster or party political broadcast during the next election campaign. And they have challenged Tony Blair and William Hague to conduct television debates with opponents and to base the campaign on policies, not personalities. The bold promise came from Lib Dem election campaign leader Lord Razzall during a rallying call at the party's conference...

The Lib Dems, he said, would have a campaign that was honest, confident and positive.[13]

In March 2005, before that year's general election, BBC News reported that Charles Kennedy 'has insisted he will not engage in negative or personalised campaigning, claiming the British people are turned off by that style of politics.'[14]

In the next month, Kennedy made another speech pledging the party to positive campaigning. As reported in *The Daily Mail*, Kennedy told a rally:

> I am not going to spend these next few weeks talking Britain down. I am going to be addressing people's hopes, not playing on people's fears, and that is going to be the positive message from the Liberal Democrats during this campaign.[15]

Again, five years later, Senior Lib Dems admonished the Conservatives for allegedly attempting to instigate a negative campaign again Nick Clegg. *The Guardian* reported:

> Pressure was mounting on the Tories today to disclose whether anyone in the party had encouraged rightwing newspapers to publish negative stories about Nick Clegg. The Liberal Democrat leader's chief of staff, Danny Alexander, accused the Tories of orchestrating a smear campaign, and urged George Osborne, the campaign coordinator, to 'come clean' about the involvement of Conservative central office.
>
> *The Guardian* revealed today that senior Tories had summoned journalists to the party's Millbank offices on Monday to discuss Tory tactics. Alexander called on the shadow chancellor to detail what role he and his staff had played.
>
> 'I think that now what it looks like is that the first act that Team Cameron took after his pledge to redouble the positive

was to try and orchestrate a media smear campaign against us which had the effect of quadrupling the negative,' Alexander said. 'George Osborne needs to come clean as to whether he himself was personally responsible for this negative smear campaign... It reflects a panic in the old political establishment that they are in a battle for survival.'[16]

Despite these repeated implicit and explicit commitments to a positive campaigning tone, a look at the facts indicates that negative campaigning has been in evidence, at least sporadically, in Liberal Democrat activity. The sanctimony does not work if the party's own tone does not itself live up to its 'holier than thou' image.

Unfortunately, there have been skirmishes where those directly or indirectly associated with the Liberal Democrats did not necessarily live up to these standards themselves. *The Daily Mirror*'s journalist Kevin Maguire wrote the following series of comments on the social networking site Twitter:

> *On train a bloke's boasting on mobile he got Evening Standard to claim Lab has secret plans to shut Kingston Hospital (9.57, 27 Jan)*

> *He's 'a manifesto to write'. Tory? Wearing Hibs scarf. Clocking his details. May sneak photo to track down. Or could always ask! (10.01, 27 Jan)*

> *This is the Kingston hospital scare bloke. Anyone know him? He's a loud mouth in public places http://tweetphoto.com/9705183 (11.42, 27 Jan)*

> *Ta all Tweeters. Hospital phone man ID'd as Lib Dem activist... He should stop SHOUTING on trains (15.22, 27 Jan)*[17]

This related to a controversial campaign which suggested that Kingston Hospital was threatened with closure. Since Kingston Hospital was not closed, and this particular gambit did not seem to have anything to do with any real threat of closure, we suggest that the tactics were not in keeping with the kind of image that the party ought to be projecting. If one 'cries wolf' over fanciful threats, then when a genuine threat arises the party is less likely to be believed. Negative campaigning therefore appears highly undesirable for the Liberal Democrat image – and the alternative view proposes that it is not employed as a campaign tool.

Another episode, reported in the run-up to the 2010 general election, was even more intriguing. This time it was not so much about 'crying wolf' as 'lone wolf'. Under the title 'Liberal Democrat denies Richmond Park and North Kingston Tory infiltration plot,' the *Surrey Comet* paper published a story revealing that an individual associated with the Liberal Democrats had allegedly tried to volunteer to 'deliver leaflets and do "data entry" for the Tory campaign.' The individual denied this. When asked about the matter, the Liberal Democrat candidate who was defending the parliamentary seat responded 'I'm fighting a fair and honest campaign' and claimed that the activist in question had 'never been a member of my campaign team and has never been authorised to do anything on my behalf.' The individual in question went on to advertise his services as a 'Freelance communications and market research consultant'. He claimed that a speciality was 'negative campaigning' on his LinkedIn profile – an online curriculum vitae. Over a year later, the ex-parliamentarian was still listing that lone wolf as a Facebook 'friend.'[18]

As a postscript to the story it is interesting to note the thoughts of the Conservative MP Zac Goldsmith, who gained the seat from the Liberal Democrats in the 2010 election. He commented with a considerable degree of circumspection:

Whatever happened back then, I personally think it did not help the Lib Dems. In fact, the story as it appeared probably cost them votes and gained my campaign some support. I really don't have an opinion about who was involved and what, if anything, happened – and I've not personally set out to find out. As a general point, and not specifically about my local experience, I would say that it's risky to make a big play on positive campaigning if you don't actively and energetically distance yourself from cynicism and negativity at the same time.[19]

As well as concerns over using negative campaigning externally, the alternative view questions whether negative campaigning of the type outlined is indeed acceptable by Liberal Democrat Party members in internal elections. Consideration should be made of whether this harms the image of the party as a whole. Those using negative campaigning within the party give the impression of disregarding sentiments expressed by Charles Kennedy, Tim Razzall and Danny Alexander. The alternative view concurs with their view – that negative campaigning is corrosive, for the reasons they have outlined.

There is a risk that negative campaigning may arise again in the context of a leadership struggle, as it did between Huhne and Clegg in the previous campaign. If so, it would be a regrettable distraction from the creation of a positive image for the party. For Liberal Democrats to look better than their rivals they ought not to enter into caustic internecine disputes which leave a lasting bitterness afterwards. Positive 'branding' takes time to bed down. This cannot be achieved if members spend time negatively attacking each other on a highly personal basis. We suggest that the use of negative campaigning by all three major parties has been partly responsible for the low esteem in which politics as a whole is held. However, this is a larger subject for a future time.

As a postscript, in an ironic twist Clegg exacted a small and entertaining 'revenge' against Chris Huhne himself for the negative campaigning that Clegg endured during the 2007 leadership election. Allegations were made that Huhne had passed penalty points for a driving offence onto his wife. The claims emerged at a time when some believed that Huhne was preparing to launch a leadership bid against Clegg, following the party's poor performance in the May 2011 elections; *it should be emphasised that this suggestion has never held the status of more than a rumour.* We have not investigated it as it is only relevant to context, but not to the narrative of our thesis. At a Press Gallery lunch in the House of Commons, the devil got inside Clegg, who said before an audience of media professionals: 'Whatever people say about Chris Huhne, I don't know any politician better at getting his points across.' Clegg revealed to the delighted audience the insight that this quip was in retaliation for the 'Calamity Clegg' adage bestowed upon him by the Huhne campaign during the leadership election.[20]

Litigation?

Being positive is not the same as being soft. An alternative view proposes that the Lib Dems ought to be more litigious externally against libel and slander. There is no lack of honour in doing so. It would simply give sharper teeth to the defence of the party's image. Lib Dems have shown reticence over going to court. It has made the Lib Dems a potentially easy target for unscrupulous elements in the media. The leadership might consider taking a stronger line in challenging libel by opponents and the media. Of course, there is financial risk in doing so. But there is a reputational risk in *not* doing so. The alternative view holds that the party has been too reticent to defend its image. That image has a value and therefore, on occasion, ought to justify legal investment when it is seriously threatened.

Summary

Narrative is the movement's worldview, and is essential before any cohesive policy agenda can be constructed. Image is the movement's branding, as must be promoted by the leadership to win over hearts and minds.

These elements add up to a logical approach to generating and promoting the movement's core reason for existing. The Tories have stayed true to their narrative, as we see through how they project their image and policies. Their leadership navigates compromises in coalition in a transparent and open way, which has not challenged the organisation or its electorate to feel seriously betrayed. The Liberal Democrats need to do so too.

Using the Nolan Chart as a guide the party needs to identify its political positioning and have the courage to assert its identity independently of its coalition partner, even if the Conservatives dislike this resurgence of its coalition partner's authority.

Positive campaigning appears more in tune with the Lib Dem narrative and image than negative campaigning. Also, a greater emphasis is required on local community politics, which lies at the heart of much of what the movement stands for and its historic image. The arguments for building the image on this foundation are unequivocal. In the same way, the need for policies which reflect a challenging and inspirationally liberal agenda is a compelling, inspirational opportunity to help reinvigorate the party.

Chapter 13

Focus on Policy

It is right that we should be a party of lively debate, for debate of this type is the mark of a confident and growing party that expects to be at the heart of government.

Rt Hon Charles Kennedy MP, Liberal Democrat Leader,
foreword to The Orange Book, 2004

An alternative view believes that a policy agenda built on the unshakable foundation of a clear worldview and presented through a distinctly Liberal Democrat image is needed to begin shaping the Liberal Democrat proposition in local and national elections. Without this, as the party orbits around its Tory coalition partner its lack of a cohesive Orange Book narrative increases the gravitational pull of its partner. Over time, this risks drawing the party ever closer. A strong independent policy agenda acts as a very practical resisting force to keep things in equilibrium.

As members of a coalition government, the leadership naturally feel inclined to argue for coalition policies as part of their 'collective responsibility'. However, this is dangerous if the Orange Book do not, as a group, measure policy decisions against some reference point which reflects the liberal worldview. By contrast, the

Conservatives do have a Tory worldview and it is evident that this assists them with the consistency of their message.

The imperative to act on policy

A party can only preserve its independence of thought by operating from an 'ideological constant,' hence the recurring emphasis on narrative which informs the image and policies. This ought to have been clear to the leadership throughout the coalition project; however, while David Laws and Paul Marshall did understand this, the Orange Bookers as a group did not apply it to the operation of their caucus – either because they did not want to or, more probably, because they did not consider this to be the purpose of the grouping.

In the absence of that anchor, the risk of friction increased. The Party Conference – long touted as the sovereign policy-making forum of the Liberal Democrats – passed and supported policies that were then contradicted by subsequent decisions made by Lib Dems in government.

The leadership's obligations to the coalition have a very understandable human 'damping effect' on the extent to which ministers in the two parties want to challenge each other over differences of world view and policy. However, it ought to act as no barrier to the wider party, which needs to exercise its freedom to seek purely Liberal Democrat solutions. This does not conflict with coexistence in the coalition. After all, the leadership has offered repeated reassurances that there is no prospect of a coalition pact at the next election. So the Lib Dems *must* promote their own distinctive policies as a separate party.

It is wrong to think that the Lib Dem ministers are in the best position to generate party policy which stands apart from the coalition. The alternative view argues the exact opposite: ministers are not in an easy position to form policies because of the pressures of collective responsibility in power. This creates an observed desire to converge towards mutually acceptable and actionable plans. It is, however, the duty of the leadership to ensure and promote independence of policymaking. In the specific case as it pertained in 2011, where the leader is also the Deputy Prime Minister, this becomes difficult – or indeed almost impossible – because of those same pressures of coalition. In chapter 16 we look at an elegant solution to this issue which would ensure that the parties could work together but think apart from each other. So, what *should* it be thinking?

The 2010 manifesto

There are opportunities for imaginative developments. For instance, should we tax in new ways – such as taxing the negative consequences of actions, even accepting that this could cause pressure against the party from one interest group or another? This is no great diversion from the 'polluter pays' principle so often promoted by the party in the past. With a little thought and inspiration, many similar ideas could help define the party's positioning quite distinctly from the Tories and Labour.

Additionally, there is a need for consistency and a firm liberal base. Where there are clashes between different instincts within the party, there always needs to be a return to unchanging liberal values to resolve them. Again, the 'polluter pays' principle is a relevant example of a principle which guides policy. Another opportunity for true liberals is to jettison the illiberal habit of introducing 'blanket bans,' which tend to lack honing and owe more to authoritarian bigotry than to enlightened liberal policymaking.

Clashes are also obvious in areas related to religious issues, animal rights and narcotics regulation where the party's liberal line has sometimes been at odds with the inclination to produce policies which are 'popular' or 'fashionable'. It's obviously highly desirable to be electable! However, expedience can lead to the accusation of weakness if the pressure to be populist seriously compromises the intellectual and moral rigour of policymaking. Ironically, in power the opposite has tended to be the case, with the Lib Dems supporting altered states of policy which are *less* popular than the party's own manifesto commitments; the U-turn on tuition fees was a case in point, and one which also had the debilitating effect of inclining people to say that they 'don't know what the Lib Dems stand for,' because of the divergence between pledges and actions.

Creating a distinct policy agenda need not be a great struggle. This project is primarily a matter of *rediscovering* it, rather than creating a new one. There is an excellent starting point: the 2010 manifesto. That document was painstakingly created upon a clear and liberal base – and most candidates and activists at the time felt that the policymakers of 2010 had got it about right. The switch in policy by the leadership on tuition fees and the criticisms that this caused are symbolic of the importance of integrity in the Liberal Democrat movement.

Let's work through some examples of policymaking. We're not trying to rewrite the Lib Dem 2010 manifesto. Instead, we're illustrating how we believe the process should work. We attempt to anchor the ideas to a core narrative and express them in keeping with a consistent image. The exercise should be helpful in clarifying the methodology we're proposing. Perhaps you will enjoy – or be intrigued by – some of the policy ideas too.

Incidentally, despite the need for a degree of compromise in coalition, *compromise has no place in policymaking*. This ought to be focused entirely on what Liberal Democrats believe – without diluting their positions in deference to the narrative of another party. Policymaking and deal-making are two different things. Thus, it is perfectly acceptable – indeed it is mandatory! – for liberal policymakers to shun illiberal solutions. It frees the movement's thinking to look at the ideal solutions for a liberal society, rather than the limitations of government in partnership. It also assists

Lib Dems in terms of projecting their public identity, separate from both Conservatives and Labour. Full-blooded liberal-minded solutions serve the movement better than 'Liberal Lite' ideas which might sit comfortably with the other parties. This, again, is why those not in government are in the best position to focus on the vision for the future rather than the expedience of the present.

So, let's create a narrative and image. These reflect the actual views of those involved in the alternative view, but remember that this is illustrative. The aim is primarily to show how it works, and it is perfectly legitimate for others to take a different view, as long as the methodology is clear.

Alternative view narrative

'We strive to create a society in which people are free to live their lives as they see fit, on condition that they do not cause direct or intentional harm to others – and as long as they demonstrably understand the harm that they might cause themselves. Citizens are at liberty to live in unconventional ways which others may even find offensive or immoral; negative opinions of others should not prevent people from being able to pursue their own lifestyle choices. Nobody will be judged on behaviours or views on the basis that they fail to conform with the norm, as long as their outlook and behaviour does not prevent them from carrying out their professional and social responsibilities. Society will be based on the assumption that most people will do the right thing most of the time, and that it can withstand the actions of the few who don't. Risk will be managed, and a small increase in risk of harm will be accepted as a cost of liberty, because people have the right to make mistakes and do things which are bad for them. There will be a presumption against prohibition. There will also be a presumption in favour of peaceful co-existence and negotiated settlements, even with conflicting ideologies.'

Alternative view image

'We will project a positive attitude towards campaigning, and resist negative campaigning at all costs. We aim to expand the influence of the movement through spirited and creative argument – using the force of our case, as opposed to status, patronage or coercion. We try to see the best in others, accepting their flaws as an endearing part of our imperfect world. We celebrate the creative quirks of the human race with warmth and empathy. We tolerate mistakes which are made in good faith, and give people second chances. We believe in paying our dues and working very hard. On the Nolan Chart we place ourselves as strongly libertarian in social policy and left-of-centre in economic policy.'

Alternative view policymaking

So, those are the narrative and image elements we're going to work from. Let's have a look around policy itself. All of these are supposed to fit the narrative and image we have outlined. A good exercise is to ask: do the policies truly fit the narrative and image? This will improve one's familiarity with the technique, even if it risks showing up errors of thinking by the authors! In this limited selection we have represented policies which may resonate with the left – where the bulk of the party's lost votes reside. In saying that we feel this is more natural territory for liberals we are also saying that the authors of the alternative view feel most comfortable there.

This observation is more important than it may at first seem. Any policymaker creates ideas in line with their own worldview, whether they are consciously aware of it or not. That is why it is so useful to be clear about a person's – or a group's – narrative before embarking on policymaking. To know the paradigms in the room saves a lot of time clarifying why people are disagreeing later. This is also why the Orange Bookers, who had no collective discussion of narrative amongst themselves in the writing of *The Orange Book* and *Britain After Blair*, worked loosely to some common ideas which many – but not all – of them subliminally shared – for example, a right-leaning economic agenda. Because they did not discuss their narrative explicitly, they never formed a solid strategic foundation for Orange Book policymaking. Some rightwing views represent a majority in the Orange Book – but a minority view in the party. Because this was never explicitly stated, it had not been discussed in the wider party, and probably not beyond the inner sanctum of the leadership itself; and perhaps not even there.

Again, remember that these ideas are primarily to stimulate debate. In a future work, the alternative view will generate a cohesive and complete set of proposals. Given that this is not the prime goal of our current analysis, the policy discussion here is not offered as a complete programme for government.

Redistribution of wealth

The bedrock of the party's original reason for existing is fairness. In economic and social terms, distribution of wealth is a key element. The alternative view's narrative embodies the belief that having the legal right to make personal choices is meaningless if you don't have the cash to see them through. There's no point in theoretically deciding to feed your family on steak instead of turnips if you haven't got the money to buy either. In a similar vein, having the right to go swimming is irrelevant if one can't afford the entry fee to the public baths. In the real world, liberty goes hand in hand with the economic means to pay for at least a proportion of one's choices. This is why we strongly support redistribution of wealth.

The question is how to redistribute it, and how much to redistribute. Those who believe that there should be limits to the maximum differential between the richest and the poorest in society will conflict with those who believe in everyone's freedom to earn as much as they can. And both can argue their case from a libertarian perspective: the freedom to be rich versus the freedom to make financially independent choices.

So, how much *is* enough to be free from the shackles of poverty? What about millionaires who exercise more freedom than those who can't pay their rent? Liberalism can't proscribe on this – even regarding maximum differentials between rich and poor. 'Geolibertarians' offer a formula which provides an indicative answer. It is the amount of land rent, mineral and communally owned assets divided by the population.[1] It would be good for the party to either formally accept or reject this kind of formulation – having no opinion is the worst opinion.

Conservatives know where they stand because their narrative is related to this question. They argue against what they see as the suppressive impact of capping personal wealth, and want to reduce the 50% top rate of tax so the wealthy can get richer, creating jobs for poor people as a handy byproduct. Lib Dems oppose this, preferring to send the money directly to the poor. It's an ideological difference. The clearer the Lib Dems can be about their narrative, the more this sort of debate can provide a clear branding for the party in comparison to the Conservatives.

In 2010, the party proposed a substantial reduction of tax on those earning less than the median income, by raising the threshold for paying any income tax to £10,000. At 2010 incomes, that would remove large numbers of people from taxation altogether. The party proposed to fund this policy with a tax on properties with values in excess of £2 million.[2] This property tax is a close relative to the land tax proposed by Churchill and Lloyd George in the People's Budget of 1909.[3]

Both the old and new policies appear inspired by the same ideals, referred to as something called 'Georgism,' or 'Geonomics'.[4] This name had nothing to do with Lloyd George, but had everything to do with a 19th-century American economist with political aspirations called Henry George who suggested that nature's treasures – including minerals and land – belong to the people. Although others such as John Stuart Mill and David Ricardo shared similar thoughts, Henry George popularised the ideas in a book called *Progress and Poverty* in 1879.[5] It quickly led to the promotion of these ideas. Essentially, he argued that tax on land value was preferable to taxes on economic activity and income because it would share the wealth of the land amongst the people, and reduce the disincentives to work which income tax created.

The leadership of the party, Clegg, Huhne and Cable, were all members of ALTER, the party's land tax group.[6] The party chose the name 'Mansion Tax' for their proposal, partly as a marketing gimmick. The name was vague, since it made no distinction between whether the value of the 'mansion' was based on the building itself or the land on which it was built. The ethical argument for the tax – which is that it is based on wealth not created by the individual but by society – was slightly obscured as a result, even though in many ways that was the neo-Georgist 'Liberal Active Ingredient' which justified the whole policy.

The Georgist principle can be made to apply to business land. That's because this land gains its value from the population living in the area and from facilities provided by government. Perhaps it should be the starting point for reform of the tax system. Business land has huge value in the UK and businesses such as supermarkets hold 'land banks' which represent a store of wealth. A tax on business land would allow the Georgist principle to be applied, redistributing the value of land by converting the asset into income to alleviate the tax burden on low-income workers. To be clear, it is the unimproved value of land which is taxed: its value without buildings on it. This approach could be taken a radical step further.

Why not build new towns, taxing the land at its 'unimproved value'? That tax revenue could then used to provide a universal benefit to all individuals in the new town. Should an individual become, say, unemployed, the tax is kept by the local council to provide services, reducing the need for the welfare state to intervene in matters relating to council tax and other local provision. This would also remove the unfairness of unemployed people living in large properties having their council tax paid by the 'working poor,' as is currently the case.

There is a good working model related to Georgism. It's alive and well. In the 1970s significant oil revenues began accruing to the State of Alaska. In 1982, the governor, Jay Hammond, created the Alaska Permanent Fund, to control some of the oil and property revenues generated. It pays a 'dividend' each year to qualifying residents: those who were living in the state in the previous year *and have not committed a crime.* It is now accepted that it would be political suicide for an Alaskan politician to propose closing the scheme![7]

There may have been an unintended consequence related to crime. The year *before* the dividend was introduced marked the maximum extent of property crime, which had risen steadily from 1960 (1,544 offences per 100,000 citizens) to 1981 (5,979 per 100,000 citizens). Following the issuing of the dividend, the rate of property crime fell steadily, and had halved by 2009 (2,852 per 100,000). Property crime rates fell faster in Alaska since 1982 than across the rest of the United States.[8] It is interesting to consider whether a similar mechanism would have had an impact on the likelihood of the rioters to commit theft, and on crime in general in the United Kingdom. Figures for aggravated assault in Alaska actually rose, suggested that the dividend may be a disincentive for premeditated crime, but did little to address 'moments of madness'.[9]

It's worth comparing the dividend to the 's Jobseeker's Allowance. Up to a point, this is a financial incentive *not* to work, because of the interrelation between increasing earnings and losing benefits. By contrast, the citizen's dividend is retained by the jobseeker even when work arrives. It makes self-employment more attractive for people on low incomes. Because they don't lose their citizen's dividend, they aren't 'punished' for showing enterprise. This change might materially enhance the prospect of people 'owning' their financial decisions rather than handing them to the state. Some will make poor choices – a cost of liberty – but the safety net can be smaller because it will need to catch fewer people.

There are other creative debates the liberal movement could hold in terms of tax. What is the best way to stimulate initiative? How fair is it to tax earned income? Should unearned income be taxed at a greater rate? Is a minimum income appropriate, or should it be replaced with a more Georgist approach? After all, minimum wage is different because it's a payment for labour, not a sharing out of the wealth of the land. Could part of the UK's oil revenues form the basis for paying a citizen's dividend, as they do in Alaska? In 2009-10 the UK made £6,491 million from North Sea Oil. Were the Government minded to do so, it could use this as the basis for such a fund, though the figures per head would be relatively low compared to Alaska.[10]

Would the savings in reduced crime thanks to a citizen's dividend outweigh the cost of the scheme? What about regional variations in income – should these affect the payments or would that make people move to the places where the payments are greatest? The alternative view will return to these issues in a future volume. The liberal movement is well placed to have these debates because it is not shackled to the preferences of the very wealthy, nor to a conventional leftwing ideology.

Crime and punishment

Mark Oaten's contribution to the first Orange Book offered a farsighted and rehabilitative programme for dealing with crime. He observed the weakness of the current prison-based system, and the failure of the prison service to make a sufficient contribution to rehabilitation.[11]

Oaten's concept of JALE was very much in line with progressive thoughts which the alternative view strongly backs. JALE stands for: Justice – for victims of crime; Assessment – of the needs which, if met, would stop an offender from reoffending; Learning – educating the offender in relevant skills to deliver the assessed needs; Exit – a multi-agency approach to prisoner release.[12] Oaten's views are miles ahead of the current UK penal system. They should be revisited and promoted by the Liberal Democrats in and outside government. Working forward from a core narrative is key to making sense of a policy like this, because it impacts directly on questions of personal liberty, values and, within this, the relationship between prison, punishment and rehabilitation.

On another matter, riots and looting across the United Kingdom in early August 2011 led some to question how the level of criminal activity might be reduced. The political element of the riots was very limited. To a large extent the riots represented a chance for those who wished to obtain electrical goods and fashion items to obtain them without paying. Initially, the looters were implicitly presented by the press to be poor and uneducated. However, once the cases came to court it became clear that many had jobs. In one case, the driver of a vehicle containing stolen goods was found to be living in a million-pound house.[13] Another was a teaching assistant.[14] The impression given was that those engaging in property crime did so because they thought that the risk was worth taking for the reward that would be gained.

Looters made significant efforts to avoid the police, to target shops with high-value items, and to cover their faces. Some travelled significant distances, often by car, to reach the target area. There were a hard core of looters who took large amounts of goods. Most took a bag of goods – only as much as they could carry in their arms. If the looters were weighing up the odds and taking small amounts of goods, the question was: what could be done to restore order on a long term basis – to deter individuals from making the calculation that crime would pay? A 'citizen's dividend' would allow for a direct compensation to be paid to victims of crime from the offender's share, thereby increasing the options for restorative justice. It could also act as a disincentive to offend in the first place if the amount that you can steal is less than the amount of citizen's dividend that you lose – assuming, of course, that you are actually prosecuted.

A level playing field for education

Another key plank of policy could be the move towards free education for those at university. The question of funding is central. It can be funded by the introduction of new taxation – or a reduction in spending in other areas. A third and serious alternative is to abandon the target of sending half the population to college – which might be regarded as dogmatic rather than necessary. 50% was an arbitrary goal and there is nothing in principle to commend it above 40% or even 30%.

It is also obvious to many that the Lib Dems need to energetically address the leadership's U-turn on the pledge to oppose tuition fees. Note that the party policy did not change, despite the actions of its MPs. Thus the Liberal Democrats as a movement were still pledged to abolish tuition fees,[15] even though some of their elected representatives did the opposite in Parliament. The core issue here is the breaking of what had been presented as a totemic pledge. A degree of 'face' is at stake for certain individuals on this matter. Yet the cost to the party is very great if there is no assertive attempt to deal with the damage that the broken pledge has done to the party's reputation. This is covered in more detail in the following chapter.

Muscular liberalism? Big Society?

To maintain a separate identity from the Conservatives, it is self-evident that the party must generate its own narrative, not merely accept the definition of liberalism from the leader of another party. We looked at muscular liberalism in detail in Chapter 8. It is not a policy and must not be presented as one. Rather, it is an attempt by one party to interfere with the narrative of another.

The Alternative View

What about the Conservative idea of the Big Society? Well, for a start, it's also *not* a policy. It's a process which some elements of the party have mixed up with community politics. Clegg himself said

> The prime minister has coined the phrase 'Big Society' while the Liberal Democrats tend to talk about community politics or just liberalism. But whatever the words we use, we are clear and united in our ambition to decentralise and disperse power in our society and that shared ambition is one of the bonds that will keep our coalition strong.[16]

The alternative view is that these two processes are, in fact, opposites. Community politics is about people doing what the government is not doing, so – by definition – community politics starts in opposition. The whole point of it is that the people run community activities because, for example, the council hasn't. Once a Lib Dem group acquires control of the local authority, it is to be hoped that they run the council properly so the work gets done. In a sense, this might be regarded as a definition: Lib Dems win *by doing community politics*, and then keep on winning *by doing their politics in the community*. Either way, they do not seek to 'fob off' their work to other community groups to reduce the burden on themselves or the council. There may even be partnerships, but this is a world apart from what the Big Society is about. The objective of the Big Society is to actively transfer work that can be done by the government or local councils to voluntary groups – who, they hope, will do it free of charge.

Take the example of a stream that is full of rubbish. Community politicians will clear the rubbish and then publicise to the electorate that this was done by local Lib Dems. They then seek to take control of the council by winning over voters through their good deeds. Once in control, they will ensure that council workers do it, so community politicians no longer need to do so outside the elected system. If they do it badly, other community politicians come along and get elected in the same way.

The Conservatives' approach – utilising the concept of the Big Society – would be to find a community group that would clear the rubbish from the stream. Community groups may oblige – perhaps they have their own agenda. A church or mosque, for example, may be prepared to manage a group of school children in order to simultaneously introduce them to their faith. It is not, however, expected that this group would criticise the council or take an active role in taking control of it. The intention with the Big Society is to farm the work out, as opposed to creating electoral changes in the local authority. As a result the Big Society and community politics are *polar opposites*. The Big Society idea was implemented in past Tory administrations, where they cut funding for local services which were then provided by philanthropic individuals at a local level.

Some of those Liberal Democrats who actively promoted the Big Society did not appear to understand this. They did not seem to appreciate the essence of what community politics is versus what the Big Society is. Note again the small percentage of Orange Book ministers who had been Liberal Democrat councillors – in the case of those who had served as Cabinet Ministers by autumn 2011, none. In the same way that muscular liberalism is a Trojan horse of Tory design, so also the Big Society is consistent with Conservative ideology but not with liberal thinking.

Liberal Democrats ought to be careful to avoid political booby-traps such as the Big Society and muscular liberalism as they go about constructing their policymaking agenda. As long as the party is clear about its true narrative, it is protected against this kind of sleight-of-hand by others.

Make peace, not war
If we are to enhance the living standards of the population then the United Kingdom needs to take a reality check on its military

escapades abroad. However, there are deeper liberal reasons to oppose the further intervention in scenarios such as. It is ultimately counterproductive, as proved time and again, to pick and choose the fights that the country engages in with no clear exit strategy and no clear mission objective.

Liberal Democrats must begin to speak against poorly thought-through military intervention on the basis of the political and human cost of what we do. The humanitarian argument is used randomly – and various countries engaged in human rights abuses experience military intervention, while others do not. An ethical foreign policy is consistent. This might cause tensions versus the absolutist agenda that Cameron and muscular liberalism support, that idea apparently derived from muscular Christianity: 'the Englishman going through the world with rifle in one hand and Bible in the other'.

Rather than simply subjugating the worries of the party to the clarion calls for offensive action from Conservative ministers, Lib Dems have the chance to take an ongoing stand on these matters. The Afghanistan debacle is a classic example of the poor forward thinking of British foreign policy. To imagine that the killing of Osama bin Laden would make any positive difference to the chances of victory in the conflict there was self-evidently fanciful. These claims owed more to the need for public relations victories and retribution than they did to the military effort.

Accepting that proponents of the British involvement in the Libyan Civil War in 2011 offered a humanitarian defence for the intervention, these matters are often less clear-cut than they may appear on the television news. If those who are being helped turn out to violate civil liberties and human rights in a similar fashion to those whom they seek to overthrow, then the intervention becomes morally grey. America has previously assisted fighters around the world who have failed to win the hearts and minds of their local populations. The liberal outlook ought therefore to enforce consistency of policy considerations by reference to the party's core narrative, which will ensure that it is consistent in determining what is right and wrong.

Sometimes military action is not the answer. Occasionally, it is preferable to promote co-existence with foes. There is a real opportunity to define the Lib Dems in different terms to the other parties here. Finding forms of peaceful coexistence is rooted in the Lib Dem aspiration of seeking conflict resolution without going to war. However, our observation is at odds to an extent with Chris Huhne's desire to increase the authority to intervene in nation states, as laid out in his thesis in the first Orange Book.[17]

The party needs to decide what it believes on these matters, at the 'worldview' level. The alternative view holds that it is better to seek negotiated solutions, including with groups such as al-Qaeda and the Taliban, than to seek military ones. This is in direct contradiction with Clegg's ' speech' supporting an absolutist approach towards terrorist organizations. The party has to make up its mind, because to hold two contradictory views at once erodes its image and the clarity of its message.

'Hypothecate! Hypothecate!'

One of the most boring words in the English language is 'hypothecation'. Most electors have no idea what it means, and the Liberal Democrats have never really made a successful effort to explain it. Hypothecation means making a link between collecting particular taxes and deciding where they are spent. By introducing a say to the taxpayer, spending is linked to the *will* of the taxpayer. An example would be in the case of allowing taxpayers to veto the use of taxes on militaristic investment.

The party needs to decide whether it thinks there is merit in this idea. It carries the risk that people would say 'no' to all expenditure in the interests of saving themselves money. While the problems of hypothecation might exceed the benefits, it is good to have a settled position.

Applied libertarianism

In keeping with the Liberal tradition of protecting innocent people from the actions of others, but permitting individuals to make bad but informed decisions for themselves, the party must reflect this value in its view of personal liberties. For example, smoking outdoors ought to be permissible. Its negative health effects are primarily experienced by the smoker rather than others – even including those close to the smoker. To ban smoking in outdoor public places would be as illiberal as banning the consumption of high-fat foods, overeating, or taking insufficient exercise. David Laws – the progenitor of the Orange Book – argued this same point forcefully.[18]

The alternative view agrees with Laws. The narrative that we laid out at the beginning of this section requires a liberal society to be one where people are permitted to make unwise decisions, as long as they demonstrably understand the possible results of those decisions. Riding a motorbike is more dangerous as a means of transport than driving a car, and if outdoor smoking is banned then motorcycles could reasonably be included in the list. But, in this scenario, cars – which also present a more dangerous choice than trains – ought also to be candidates for prohibition. This is the core problem with illiberal interventions on questions of personal liberty. The attempt by the state to protect people from themselves rapidly becomes an authoritarian and hectoring crusade where the government legislates against individual freedoms on a dictatorial basis. This tendency insidiously and quickly becomes a justification for ever more interference in the citizen's freedoms 'for their own good'.

The party needs to evolve a steely clarity on this matter. Sometimes a ban is the fashionable thing to do, even if liberal values point to the opposite outcome. Cameron has made comments on obesity, quoted in an earlier chapter, indicating his view that some personal harms are a person's own fault and that the government might consider reducing the support these people get as a result. Although there is a slightly contrived way to reconcile the two – for example, by saying 'you're free to smoke but we'll charge you for your hospital treatment' – Cameron's words imply a potential conflict between libertarianism as defined by Laws and conservatism as defined by Cameron. The party needs to determine its position on the basis of its narrative, and stand its ground. This is another key marker which can differentiate it from the Conservatives at a symbolic level.

Individuals do silly things. A liberal believes that they're allowed to, as long as there are not overt and wider consequences to third parties. The Liberal Democrats will do themselves favours if they have the intellectual and political arguments to take a strong line on personal liberty when the opportunities arise.

Freedom of speech

Given the importance of freedom of speech to a liberal society, it is very important that the party upholds its historical commitment to support people's right to make offensive speeches without censorship by the state. There is a harm principle to consider, but on the whole most speakers do not now evoke violence against others.

Since the party reaffirmed its opposition to no platform as recently as March 2009, this should be preserved as a central tenet of a Lib Dem manifesto. This stands in direct opposition to the absolutist and authoritarian muscular liberalism principle, and is another reason why that concept should not be adopted by the party.

Speeding privileges

Governments have a habit of attempting to enforce behaviour on drivers which they regard as desirable through the application of punitive threats, rather than offering rewards. This is reflective of the generally authoritarian approach which liberals have traditionally shunned.

One classic case in point is the remorseless and unpopular increase in speed restrictions, and associated penalties imposed upon private car drivers. It was ironic indeed that even as new traffic restrictions were being imposed upon the public a Labour government minister, Jack Straw, was pulled over following a breach of the UK speed limit by his driver. This in itself was not the remarkable point of the incident: rather, what rankled with the public was that his driver was not prosecuted.[19] Notwithstanding the detailed elements of the legal matter, it suggests that there is legitimate precedent in the eyes of the law for speeding in some circumstances.

There is nothing to prevent a liberal government from dramatically altering the relationship between good driving and the law, while doing away with what appear to be double standards to those outside the political system. Here's how.

If a driver has not had an accident or traffic conviction for five years, why not give them the dispensation to drive 5 miles per hour faster – in designated places and at designated times – for every year thereafter? The condition would be the maintenance of a clean licence and accident-free record. In this example, after 11 years, a driver with no accidents or convictions could legally drive on designated stretches of, say, the M6 motorway at 100mph (70mph + 5mph × 6 years = 30mph) at certain quiet times of the day – say between 10pm and 6am – as a reward for their careful conduct on the roads. After 15 years, they would have accrued 50 miles per hour of 'privileges' – enabling them to drive at up to 120 miles per hour.

This idea may seem odd – but that's only because it reverses the conventional coercive contract with the driver. It rewards good behaviour, and creates a powerful incentive to remain responsible and careful. The principle behind the policy is entirely in line with the liberal philosophy of empowering individuals, rather than incarcerating them under the burden of legislative restrictions. It works on the basis that people will care more about their privileges than they do about speeding points. While a small proportion of individuals will abuse any system, the great majority will work to operate in cooperation with the 'social contract' to preserve their privileges for 'good behaviour'.

This type of radical thinking is not really so radical if one accepts that the attractions of 'buy-in' are preferable to the threat of 'punishment'. It is also a potentially rich seam of differentiation between the liberal movement and the other two main parties. Emotional reactions to talk of speed limits can obscure logical debate. If it could be shown that this policy genuinely reduces accident and injury versus the current system, the right thing to do would be to introduce it.

Sexual freedom

A specific example is the issue of the freedom of individuals, over the age of majority, to engage in consensual sexual acts with one another. People have fallen foul of the law simply because they failed to appreciate the strange consequences of the laws as currently constituted. Liberals should campaign to propose policy distinct from the Conservatives and Labour – though it must be said that it is not clear where the Orange Book caucus stand on these issues. It is probable that they have contradictory views, which could be a cause for conflict within this group, and between elements of the Orange Bookers and the wider party.

An example of the illiberal approach that can occur was the 'Operation Spanner' case. In 1987 police obtained a video of consensual sadomasochistic practice by a group of homosexuals. None of those who took part required medical attention for their 'injuries'. The men were, however, taken to court by the Crown Prosecution Service on the basis that they had taken part in an 'assault'. The men's defence – that the acts were consensual – was dismissed by the courts, the House of Lords and also by the European Court of Human Rights. The sentences given out to the 16 men were in some cases severe. One man was given a four-and-a-half-year jail sentence.[20]

There have been a number of changes in the law, but nothing suggesting that consent makes sadomasochistic sexual activity legal. In fact, evidence points to the reverse. Section 63 of the Criminal Justice Act, introduced by the Labour Party in 2007, specified that taking a photograph of 'an act which results, or is likely to result, in serious injury to a person's anus, breasts or genitals' was illegal.[21] Though it doesn't sound like it, this definition is vague. The CPS website explains

> 'The words "serious injury" are not defined in the Act and would take their ordinary dictionary meaning and be a question of fact for the District Judge or jury.'[22]

The maximum penalty is two years for a crime which depends on interpretations – even though we see that there is no indication that lawmakers are even clear on exactly what their interpretation of the law was expected to be. It leaves this open to precedent – a dangerously random way to define civil liberties.

Since these matters are also likely to go to appeal, when prosecuting these cases the Government risks incurring huge costs. This is because libertarians see these issues as matters of human rights. They resist with all the powers at their disposal. It has been stated that the cost of prosecuting the 'Spanner' case alone was £4m.[23]

In another notorious case, a cartoon character was at the centre of a debate over what constituted a breach in the law: the infamous 'Tiger Porn' case of 2010. Sexual freedom activists showed how their determination to protect freedom could lead to a costly defeat for the Government. In this instance, Andrew Holland received a video clip which, according to the defendant, showed footage of a a woman having sex with an animated image of a tiger. At the end of the scene the tiger turns to the camera and says 'That beats doing Frosties ads for a living.'[24]

Incredibly, this was also taken up by the CPS. As it turned out, it was revealed that they had not listened to the soundtrack. After considerable expenditure of time, effort, and state funds, the case was then dropped, on the basis that the words illustrated that the scene was not real... as a real tiger cannot talk. As such, it was to be regarded as humour rather than pornography.[25]

This was not the end of the prosecution, however, as the CPS continued to prosecute the same individual for possession of another six-second clip – believed to have shown consensual sadomasochism. This time Holland pleaded guilty and was told that a custodial sentence was 'likely'. The Consenting Adult Action Network, and sexual rights organization Backlash, became involved. The plea was reversed. A robust defence was prepared, but on 6 August it was announced that the CPS had dropped the case anyway.[26]

This kind of activity by the state may be acceptable to other parties. After all, Labour drafted the ill-conceived law used for the prosecution. But it is surely a totemic point of difference between authoritarians and liberals.

The Conservative Party also does not have a good record on sexual freedom. In 1988, Thatcher's administration introduced enormously restrictive regulations concerning what teachers could and could not say to pupils about homosexuality. Section 28 of the Local Government Act stated that local authorities had to enforce the rule that teachers 'shall not intentionally promote homosexuality or publish material with the intention of promoting homosexuality'. It also stated that local authorities were no longer permitted to 'promote the teaching in any maintained school of the acceptability of homosexuality as a pretended family relationship.'[27] This homophobic legislation was subsequently repealed after the Tories lost office in 1997, but it is an indication from the recent past of outlooks which are entirely at variance with the thinking of the liberal movement, and most certainly of the alternative view.

It follows that here lies a distinct opportunity to carve out a liberal niche which can differentiate the party from the two other main parties. Naturally it will be necessary to base this on a clear party narrative, as no doubt some will feel awkward about questions of sexual policy – but personal liberties ought not to be negotiable for any liberal. Even if not everyone feels comfortable with the social or political implications of taking a stand in this area, the alternative view believes that it is the liberal movement's duty to do so.

Euthanasia

The alternative view's narrative directs us to the view that citizens should have the right to die with dignity – according to carefully regulated conditions. It is hard to see how, in a liberal society, dignity in death could be *anything other* than a personal choice, as opposed to something prohibited by the state – which is currently the case. Religious objections are sometimes raised. Again, a liberal absolutist agenda does not seem to accommodate the enforcement of one person's morals upon another person when the choice that the other person makes does not involve harm to others.

In reality, euthanasia already exists in the, for example through the administration of morphine to make terminally ill patients 'comfortable' in the last hours of their life. It would be better for the law to reflect the reality. It seems that this would be a campaign very much in line with liberal thinking. The Liberal Democrats could take a clear view on this, though it is likely that, for religious reasons, this would be a 'free vote' issue. We suggest, however, that the liberal case for voluntary euthanasia is not ambiguous.

Regulate drugs

The Lib Dems also need a philosophically credible position on narcotics and other drugs regulation. Drug policy is divisive only because it is controversial with the electorate and a reactionary media. Expedience has sometimes been the guiding motivation in determining Lib Dem – and other parties' – policies. The issue that they face is this: to construct drug policy around pragmatic concern for public reaction will not produce a policy that works logically in regard to its commitment to do the right thing based on value and data.

Much of the argument around drugs in the party, and in the media, looks at reactionary perceptions, rather than the realities. It is likely that, by treating drug users as patients rather than criminals, good policy can make a real difference and reduce the issue to manageable proportions – as well as de-stigmatising treatment. It is worth noting that the end of the prohibition of alcohol in the United States was managed very constructively with no medium-term negatives in terms of societal harm and, arguably, many advantages because the system became regulated, with an apparent moderation in the potency of the alcohol available under the regulated system.[28]

It is equally notable that in the time since narcotics prohibition was introduced in the UK in the early 1970s drug use has increased enormously. In the past it was possible for doctors in the UK to prescribe heroin to recorded addicts. In 1971, the Misuse of Drugs Act was carried into law. It prohibited the prescription of heroin. This has been the law ever since. In 2007, Professor Peter Reuter from the USA and Alex Stevens from the UK published research which made the situation breathtakingly clear. In 1975, shortly after the change in law prohibiting the prescription of heroin, there were 5,000 dependent heroin users in the UK. By 2007, the number of dependent heroin users had increased to an estimated 281,000.[29] The alternative view concludes that prohibition has utterly failed the country.

Conservative statements about drugs are often built around the idea that drugs are an absolute harm and should therefore be stopped at all cost. An argument based on classical liberalism starts from the principle that the individual owns their own body. This is a better starting point than the 'benefit to society' approach, which is hard to prove. The harm principle is at the party's core and relates very closely to questions of drugs policy. Progressive drugs law reform groups such as Transform[30] have long argued for a change in law. They have done so in ways which, we suggest, resonate strongly with the underlying values of the Liberal Democrats. Ironically, it is probable that the harm principle applies to prohibition itself; that the illegal nature of the supply chain is the main cause of the harm directly caused to third parties, due to the theft which goes with finding the money to 'feed' an addiction.

It would clearly be wise to look at all options in seeking a workable policy on drugs law reform. The key issue at present is that, while the party activists discuss policy changes, only a small number of its MPs do the same. For Liberal Democrats in government to actively champion the issue would be a tremendous contribution to the welfare of the British people. The party could be a rallying point for progressive thinkers to look at the options to move in a direction that would lessen the harm to society as a whole – in which drug usage would be treated as a public health issue rather than one of civil disorder.

The implication of the alternative view's narrative would appear to be, at the very least, to provide addicts with their drugs through the state. As we have noted, this has been tried in the UK before. Issues such as patients using some of their 'prescription' as a saleable asset can certainly be resolved. The schemes that run best consider undesirable consequences such as these before they arise. It can be done, and has been done elsewhere – and even in the UK before the Misuse of Drugs Act introduced the unsuccessful policy of prohibition.

Lib Dems reaffirmed a progressive policy on this issue in 2011. This called for an investigation into the laws in other countries which have taken a progressive approach and assessment of the optimum legal position regarding possession of controlled drugs for personal use.[31] This farsighted approach could be criticised by a reactionary press and through opportunistic attacks by rival parties. They might wrongly suggest that the state has no business supplying drugs to 'weak' addicts. That kind of attitude would be in line with Cameron's comments about obesity. Thus, it requires strong leadership, and a willingness to litigate in the face of potentially libellous reporting in the media. Without this robust confidence in a liberal positioning, the policy differentiation on this issue will remain feeble, as senior members continue to retreat from a logically-argued liberally sound position, instead of fighting on the facts – and the party's own policy.

As an early step, ministers could promote a limited trial of state-managed supply, to provide a critical differentiator between the Lib Dems and their more authoritarian political partner. It would give Liberal Democrats all they need to be in the vanguard of progress in a manner which also gives positive 'branding' for the party.

Summary

Every element of policy has been argued on the basis of the liberal narrative as the alternative view would define it. Some of the Orange Bookers, such as Laws, would warm to a number of these ideas. What matters most, however, is clarity – of thought and action based on a narrative, an image and a policy agenda which is entirely consistent. The 'no harm to others' criterion; creative changes to taxation; rewarding good behaviour rather than merely punishing the bad; seeing the best in people, not the worst; being driven by narrative rather than the media; respecting personal choice even when these choices may appear distasteful to others: these can form a crystal-clear policy agenda which could *only* belong to the Liberal Democrats.

The alternative view believes that this is the way to restore the party's unique, and sometimes controversial, identity in the eyes of the country. Some of it may not be that easy to explain, and may cause discomfort with illiberal elements in the government, and indeed in the party. But, as Nick Clegg made clear at the September 2011 Party Conference, for the Liberal Democrats it is about following the best path philosophically and morally: 'Not doing the easy thing. Doing the right thing.'

Chapter 14

Focus on Leadership

So I want to make something very clear today. Will I ever join a Conservative government? No.
Nick Clegg, conference speech, 9 March 2008

At a human level, this and the subsequent two chapters are uncomfortable to publish. As well as providing strategic guidelines on timeless issues relating to the leadership of a party, they inevitably impact on the actual individuals currently in leadership positions. Our goal is to tackle these issues head-on, and to provide useful pointers of assistance to the organisation and to the current – as well as future – leaders for the short, medium and long term.

The performance of the leadership team – and any leader – endures a combination of sensible observation, gossip and spurious conjecture in any party. Some people want to discuss the situation in reasonable terms. Others place commentary on political leadership in the same category as having a whinge about their favourite football team's manager. Much of what is reported – especially in an environment which is fed by a politically partial press – is unreliable.

In an effort to provide a more objective assessment, we now offer the alternative view regarding the strengths and weaknesses of the current leadership, and the probable character of the next one. The aim is to facilitate a constructive debate amongst the membership – and the leadership itself – on matters that have hitherto been unaddressed, and to an extent even treated as taboo. We assess the progress of the party from 2007 to the autumn of 2011, and draw conclusions from this analysis that are of relevance explicitly to the leadership.

We will see that many of the problems have the same answers: a clear narrative, image and policy agenda which are unmistakably Liberal Democrat and pursued at the local community politics level by the leadership and the organisation.

Orange rise to power

Let us review how it all happened. In 2007, when the Orange Bookers took hold of the levers of power in the party, they were quite clear about their intentions. These were apparent to anybody paying any attention to their actions and statements. Their three success strategies were: firstly, an ability to coalesce as a faction within the party for a considerable period; secondly, an audacity in pushing their rise to power internally; and thirdly, a willingness by the core leadership team to overwhelm internal opposition using whatever tools were expedient. These included the energetic promotion of candidates sympathetic to their caucus for various roles within the party.

An example of this new thinking was the speedy acquisition of power on a timescale almost unknown in the liberal movement. Traditionally, a serious leadership candidate would not attempt to stand early in their first term as an MP. Orange Book aspirant Chris Huhne challenged for the leadership within months of being elected to Parliament. He did well in the polling, losing with 42% of the votes to Ming Campbell's 58%.[1]

As we have already observed, the rise of the Orange Book caucus was greatly assisted by Ming Campbell's short tenure as leader. His early and sudden departure from the role was a necessary condition for the next, exclusively Orange Book, leadership election in December 2007, this time between Huhne and Clegg. In that fractious and highly personalised campaign, Huhne lost again, this time by the narrowest of margins: 49.4% to Clegg's 50.6%.[2] Clegg's majority of only 511 votes continued to vex Huhne supporters, who claimed that some of Huhne's votes were discounted owing to their late arrival at Headquarters through the fault of the Post Office and the Christmas mail backlog. However, this is a moot point as far as we are concerned in this analysis. What matters is that from the start of the 2007 leadership election the Orange Book was the only game in town. Whoever won individually, the Orange Bookers had taken control of the party.

After the announcement of Clegg's victory, and as if to underline his anticipated role in the new order, Huhne commented:

> Nick is going to be a great leader for the party. He has an enormous amount of warmth and energy to bring to this job... We have ahead of us some great successes. I look forward to participating as part of Nick's team to make sure the party goes from strength to strength.[3]

As leader of the party, and de facto head of the Orange Bookers, Clegg held primary responsibility for the consequences this new direction would bring to the movement. In the short term, it seemed a highly attractive position to be in. He had inherited a party that had grown strong in Parliament and still retained a substantial body of local councillors. Poll ratings had been satisfactory and people were sympathetic to the party's image.

From the perspective of the individual ambitions of its members, the Orange Book collective had demonstrated a devastatingly effective strategy. It was to be hoped that this would translate well in terms of driving the ambitions of the party as well.

Initially, they were impregnable. The potentially loudest

dissenting voices were themselves in the Orange Book fold. From their insuperable position, in the event of any attempted dissent, the Orange Book simply flicked the collective switches of solidarity, profile and power – using an acquiescent and suggestible press to drive home their advantage. The energy simply drained away from any prospective counter-offensive by Orange Book sceptics before they even had time to form into a structured opposition. There were never more than a few rogue voices here and there; interviewees criticising Clegg from a distance, achieving little purchase with their complaints.

It was only when a serious error was made on the tuition fees issue that a more strategic threat to the Orange Bookers looked as though it might emerge, perhaps in the form of opposition from the left within the party. Yet again, however, the main weapon of choice of the dissenters was disengagement rather than direct attack. The absence of an organised alternative voice in the autumn conference of 2011 indicated that, even then, the Orange Bookers enjoyed a powerful and relatively stable position of control.

The break with traditional liberalism

Non-Orange Booker Tim Farron's election as President in November 2010 was the first electoral failure for the Orange Bookers. As ever, context is key. In the autumn of 2010, a number of relatively purist libertarians and those regarding themselves as classical liberals were prepared to stand behind Orange Booker Susan Kramer for the presidency. This tendency was conditionally sympathetic to some of the ideas in the Orange Book. Surprisingly, Kramer did not show much enthusiasm for the support of the libertarians, and described herself as 'quite comfortable being seen as an Orange Book liberal,' adding,

> I'm not keen on the notion of rigid tests of purity. Anyone who does take on membership of a political party that wants to be in government does have to have some sense of the pragmatic. If some point of principle has hideous outcomes you don't do it.[4]

Kramer's comments seem to support the alternative view of the pragmatic nature of the Orange Book caucus. Her willingness to give way on a point of principle if it had 'hideous outcomes' contrasted sharply with those who believed that a point of principle is defined as something that is non-negotiable. However, given her viewpoint, it is perhaps unsurprising that she was at best lukewarm in response to specific approaches offering support from those associated with the libertarian – and it might be said more 'purist' – wing of the party.

The campaign fought on the Internet during that presidential campaign was also telling. The Kramer virtual campaign was judged by many to be of low quality – indeed, less slick than some which Lib Dem activists used in local campaigning. By contrast, the libertarian factions were controlling highly sophisticated aggregated blogs – and had high levels of video production. Their offer of help meant that it had been open to her to access some of that know-how. Thus, failing to engage with a libertarian element of the party had been a rare tactical error by the Orange Book caucus. It is possible that had these offers of help been more eagerly accepted the Orange Bookers might have secured the presidency.

Kramer's defeat was the first sign that the Orange Book hegemony was not insuperable. Thereafter, Clegg could no longer rely on the impregnable security of his immediate 'inner circle'. They had been beaten by a representative of that element which had even defied the whip by opposing tuition fees in the voting lobbies of Parliament.

What Clegg did next seemed to underline the point. Until 2011, he had presented his ideas as traditional liberalism. Then in

February 2011 he made his seminal ' speech' in support of the Conservative idea of 'muscular liberalism'.[5] His decision to do so immediately catalysed a strong and more focused negative reaction from the libertarian section of his own party. They did not accept this brand of liberalism offered to them by an opposing conservative-based ideology, and were not pleased that the leader saw merit in doing so. Whether or not it was intended to, what had looked like a missed opportunity by Kramer's presidential campaign appeared a more strategic rejection of the relativist libertarian agenda by Clegg.

With storm clouds looming for the Orange Book faction, it was becoming a challenge to prevent a drift away by those more traditional and long-serving liberal-minded activists who, out of loyalty, had offered milky support to the leadership until that point. While most members and activists did not study the words from his Luton speech in great detail, the poor May 2011 election results catalysed them, for the first time, to pass an active verdict on Clegg – and by implication on the Orange Book. But as before, the criticism was disorganised and sporadic. The federal conference in September 2011 could have been a fractious occasion for the leadership. Clegg escaped again, in part because a proportion of his critics had voted with their feet and simply stayed away from the conference.

Static Orange

The Orange Bookers had been lucky. So far, there had been no strategic rebellion against them. Apart from the wobble in the presidential election, their status appeared solid and sound. But this situation would not last indefinitely. When a challenge came, possibly as a result of further poor election results, the Orange Bookers would need to create a motivating narrative, improve their marketing strategy or pump up their defensive mechanisms. Even by autumn 2011 there was no palpable and proactive response to the negativity now emanating from the former Liberal Democrat voter base towards them, and towards Clegg in particular.

With a drive from the party conference and others to return to community politics, there was even a route map for the Orange Bookers' re-engagement with the grass roots – should they choose to accept it. But Clegg's conference speech seemed wedded to the existing approach, with not a single word about community politics in the entire script, which promised to do what was 'not easy, but right'. It was a call to arms along the existing route map with familiar lines of engagement. An imperative to act does not always carry with it the realisation that this is the case.

To Clegg's advantage, the rank-and-file membership – who, it must be remembered, had never fully signed up to Orange Book thinking in the first place – continued to remain tolerant of the leadership and left him to pursue his course. If there were those who had contemplated a challenge, they were watching from a distance, waiting for their opportunity and deciding that it was not yet time to act. The un-marshalled appeals by deposed councillors for support against Clegg seemed almost forgotten. Their words seemed neutered by the circumstances of their defeat. It was easy for them to be dismissed as mavericks of one kind or another. The Orange Bookers had been given repeated reprieves thanks to the lack of cohesion of any opposing movement with the party.

The alternative view would suggest that the Orange Book leadership ought to have been making the most of its freedom from any spirited challenge in the closing months of 2011 by reinventing itself to fit into the party's more traditional culture. All the signs of trouble were there, with hints of insurgency from amongst the Orange Bookers themselves. In the run-up to 5 May 2011 Huhne in particular had spoken up against various tactics used by the Conservatives in the AV referendum. This was interpreted by the media as a positioning action by Huhne in anticipation of another leadership bid, which had been rumoured since March,[6] though as we have noted this had not been officially confirmed by him or his supporters. His words may have also been an effort to insulate himself from the bruising which he probably anticipated – correctly – would occur on 5 May 2011.

Parties cannot easily buck the ebb and flow of political tides. Nor can individuals. But there were things that he could do to refashion his agenda over subsequent months.

One of the things people said about Clegg was that he did not sound like a Liberal Democrat. While he attempted, in his leader's speeches to the party, to press the relevant Lib Dem buttons, there grew an increasing and sustained scepticism about his true Lib Dem credentials as the months went by.

Peripheral criticisms – and ones not always directly relevant to his performance – added to the tone. Peter Maughan, former Lib Dem councillor, said in May 2011:

> I remember the party in 1990. Almost bankrupt, almost no members, but we struggled on. I didn't work so hard to see it all go up in blue smoke in 12 months.[7]

This and similar sentiments were a dark portent for feelings in the party. Clegg made it worse when he committed his infamous faux pas to Cameron. Forgetting that he was still connected to a live microphone, Clegg told a polite but silent Prime Minister

> 'If we keep doing this we won't find anything to bloody disagree about in the bloody TV debates!'[8]

It was the very worst thing he could have possibly said to David Cameron. His thoughts are not recorded, but it is likely that privately many Conservatives were very amused by the slip. The Lib Dem membership weren't laughing. It seemed to confirm what some already suspected: that Clegg felt a closer association with a Tory

Prime Minister than he did with elements of the Lib Dem membership, to whom he could certainly *not* say 'if we keep doing this we won't find anything to bloody disagree about.'

His gaffe offered a field day to satirists, with cartoons suggesting that Clegg was generally in service to the Tories and to the Prime Minister in particular. However fanciful, these derisive quips did reflect a public impression which, once acquired, became hard to shake off.

The fact that Clegg had, in the eyes of many, never been a grassroots activist also contrasted with other MPs. In an informal conversation about party matters in October 2011, former MP for Ludlow Matt Green made observations about this very tradition. It must be clearly emphasised that his comments were as part of a general discussion about party activism, and were explicitly offered as general perspectives on how the party can make progress. Green was not offering any kind of attack or criticism in relation to Nick Clegg. Green said:

> In my experience, the tried and tested way to get to Parliament was that you'd rise up through the ranks, first as a Focus deliverer, then as a local candidate, a councillor, as party officer and so on. It may not sound very glamorous to people, I know, but personally I got a lot out of it. And by the time you get to be an MP you appreciate what community politics is all about. Really, it's what we're about. That's exactly how Ashdown got there.[9]

Finally, there were a number of comments to interviewers which were clearly intended to humanise Clegg at a time when his personal ratings were at a very low level. On 7 April 2011, *New Statesman* published an article by Jemima Khan in which Clegg had said to her 'No, well look, I'm a human being, I'm not a punchbag – I've of course got feelings.'[10] He also claimed that he cried 'regularly to music,' and that his own children had asked him why students were angry with him. These comments did little to assuage the worries of the movement. They wanted a change in direction and regarded the results that the party was getting as a red alert, where red meant Labour.

The alternative view suggests that for Clegg to restore his reputation as a campaigner, and to address the list of issues which we have outlined here, the best approach would be a concerted commitment to the local community political base on which the movement is founded. This would not be glamorous, in the sense that it would require an authentic presence at the most basic level of campaigning. If Clegg were seen to fill in the missing experience of local government activity, over time this would go some way towards healing the rift between him and his critics. Interviews in which he was heard to re-emphasise this element of the party's activity would also assist. However it would have to be a sincere and ongoing commitment, as anything which looked like a tokenistic stunt for the benefit of the media could even make matters worse.

But this on its own is not enough. Clegg would also have to generate a narrative with which he could drive the party forward – and which finally gave the Orange Bookers a visibly liberal shared agenda and image.

Looking Lib Dem

In the May 2011 elections, some activists had shied away from using their leader's image in leaflets and campaign materials. There was a feeling in certain quarters that the Deputy Prime Minister was not an electoral asset in local authority seats, with strong feelings being privately voiced in the Welsh and Scottish elections.

During those elections, Clegg did travel around the country. However, the main problem was one of differentiation. The satirical commentators remorselessly drove this point home, continuing to characterise the Deputy Prime Minister as little more than a foot-soldier. It was also a recurring theme in the virtual world of

Internet chatter, most of which was deeply vitriolic and cynical about Clegg's performance. The problem of differentiation had occurred before – when a similar role was attributed to Liberal leader David Steel at the time of the fractious alliance with David Owen's SDP. On that occasion, people laughed wryly at the analogy, largely driven by the puppet-based programme *Spitting Image*.

The difference in 2011 was that people took a more malign view, specifically on account of the deviation from what had been perceived as a Lib Dem agenda, ranging from the tuition fees U-turn through to matters of taxation and NHS reform. Even reform of certain detention regulations was said to have been watered down versus Lib Dem ideology, though this latter accusation is in reality equivocal, given the complicated legislative and political environment that obtained at the time.

The challenge for a Lib Dem leadership in coalition was to work together, but look different. It could be done. The Conservatives, just as much in partnership with the Lib Dems, had managed to continue to look like Conservatives. By contrast, there was a commonly held view that the Lib Dems in partnership *also* looked like Conservatives. This analysis certainly suited the Tory and Labour newspapers. But it did not suit the Liberal Democrats at all.

The alternative view believes that a Liberal Democrat leadership has an obligation to speak, behave and act as Liberal Democrats, even at the cost of generating strain within the coalition itself. The last thing that voters or members wished to see was the metamorphosis of its leaders into close cousins of the high command of another party. Simon Hughes never left his Lib Dem – more specifically, liberal and left-leaning – credentials behind, even though he had contributed a section to the *Britain After Blair* volume of the *Orange Book* project. Greg Mulholland MP, John Leech MP, Bob Russell MP and a host of other Lib Dem MPs and peers remained distinctly liberal in their words and deeds. Meanwhile, the Conservatives had made no effort to embrace the Lib Dem image. As one member summed up at an informal gathering in South London relating to the mayoral elections in the summer of 2011:

> Nick's suit would fit Cameron very well. But I don't think they'll ever get Dave to wear a woolly jumper or sandals.

The last thing Clegg could afford to do was be a Tory lookalike. He knew this. As Clegg had said to Jemima Khan in his *New Statesman* interview, politics is business, not friendship and there was no space for sentimental social cohabitation between party leaders. The aim was to make a difference in government – but to do it while being a Lib Dem.

While Clegg made a spirited effort to provide distance between his position and David Cameron's stance on European financial matters in December of 2011, it was again on a policy issue. The alternative view recommends that true differentiation can only be achieved by a clear return to a Lib Dem narrative. It is a very specific problem which we are addressing here, and it has a very clear solution. In fact, it underlines the importance of doing the basics: getting the worldview right and building from there. This also informs the image, which will automatically look different versus the Conservatives if it is built up from the narrative.

Vote like a Lib Dem

There is great risk in adopting a party agenda offered by another party leader. After all, it's unlikely that such a gift is given with any altruistic intent. We have covered this concern as it relates to muscular liberalism, David Cameron's 'present' to the Lib Dems as a way of redefining what the Lib Dems stood for. As we have shown, the alternative view is that this Trojan horse was aimed at making the Lib Dems more acquiescent to the beat of a Tory drum. To some extent a shift had already happened: certain illiberal edicts regarding immigration all came wrapped up as part of that gift.

We need not dwell on this again as the implications are clear. Instead of accepting muscular liberalism from others, the alternative view recommends that the Lib Dem leadership return to a more traditional definition of liberalism, as found in the party's mission statement.[11] In this way, the party could live in partnership while displaying greater independence of thought and action.

It seemed wiser to offer this different kind of 'muscle' – robust liberalism, based on libertarian and left-leaning ideas, which seeks to redistribute wealth from the landed gentry in a way which is neither penal nor soft. Coupled to this, the celebration of a relativist frame of reference, as opposed to Cameron's – and, it seems, Clegg's – absolutist one, fits much more naturally with the mindset of the liberal movement. While this would be anathema to the strategists for Conservatism, for whom the vision is partly built on tolerance of inequalities and the enforcement of absolutes, it is precisely why an alternative approach could differentiate the Liberal Democrats from their coalition partners.

The Tories cannot be blamed for attempting to move the Lib Dems into a position which was helpful to the Conservatives. It's good politics. The fault line of demarcation was buried not by them but by the Liberal Democrats; the Conservatives merely provided the shovel. Courage wasn't what was missing. The same individuals who did the 'digging' in the Lib Dems had shown robustness within their own party to get their way. It is more likely that the attractions of government had a moderating or distracting effect on those directly installed in powerful positions; after all there were evident personal ambitions embodied in those at the centre of the Orange Bookers. This attainment of personal authority may have tempered, or even obscured, potential objections to the senior coalition partner's agenda.

Compromise is inevitable and indeed desirable in a coalition; the same is true in a non-coalition environment. However, that does not exonerate Lib Dems from needing to look like Lib Dems on key, totemic issues. Collective responsibility in Government was not an excuse for collective irresponsibility in caring for the party's core beliefs, such as a level playing field in higher educational opportunity, a free and non-discriminatory health service, an ethical foreign policy and opposition to no-platform policy. All these are *not* particularly negotiable in the eyes of the members. Unlike Kramer, the alternative view holds that points of principle are not negotiable. Trading them increases tensions within the party. The leadership ought to be very sensitive to this sensitivity.

Recovery

It was too late to quickly reverse the damage done up to October 2011. Further damage could be prevented by a more energetic defence of liberalism by the leadership in the ways we have covered. It was something that the party at large was crying out for. Its historical allies, such as the national student movement, needed to see it in abundance before the rifts between the party and its old friends could be healed.

Only the leadership could offer this change of direction voluntarily. If lower echelons of the party had to force this to happen it would lead to a standoff, and that could not end without loss of face and, in extremis, loss of confidence in the leader. A tipping point would then come when the party felt that the internal strife was less damaging than the external loss of support and direction. Even in 2011, some feared that this was the gloomy alternative if nothing was done to prevent it.

Tuition fees: a totemic issue

While the leader defended his position on tuition fees as recently as September 2011, the alternative view is that his position had been compromised by the material failure to keep to the pledge, regardless of the merits of the new policy. Many stated that the collateral damage to the party as a result of the U-turn on the pledge would diminish with time; however there are reasons to believe that this would not be the case in the timescale necessary to prevent a disastrous decline in the party's electoral performance. The issue of tuition fees of itself *would* fade in electoral importance, eventually; but the principle of being seen to break a totemic pledge was an issue of trust which would haunt the leader during future attempts to present a manifesto credibly.

As a former Liberal Democrat councillor from Gateshead said:

> It was an important issue because the one way in which we were seen as different from the other two parties was that we were honest. When we broke the pledge the electorate drew the conclusion that we were no different to the others, and in some senses worse, because people really had trusted us and voted for us on that basis.[12]

In other words, the damage to the leader from this and other compromised policy positions went way beyond the specific issues themselves.

An indication of the problems that the leader would face at the next general election arose in the AV campaign. In a NO2AV video that was evidently a personalised and thinly veiled parody of Nick Clegg, the Right Honourable Alan B'stard promises 'No more tuition fees of course, and free electricity for anyone.' When pressed by an associate who says 'you do realise we can't afford to do any of these things you're promising?' he responds,

> Of course we can't, you silly thing. We just say that we are going to make these changes then, when we get voted in, we'll just blame the other lot, saying that they stopped us doing it because it's all in the 'national interest.'[13]

However distressing these campaigning methods were to the 'Yes' campaign during the AV referendum, the leader must face the fact that the referendum was lost to a campaign that successfully employed these tactics. A leader who broke a pledge in 2010 and did not generate a plausible defence would face similar attacks on a wider gamut of policies in 2015.

It may be that the only solution for the leadership is an admission that the U-turn on tuition fees was wrong; unsurprisingly, this seemed to be most strongly felt in areas with higher education establishments in which the Liberal Democrats had electoral interests. Any Liberal Democrat leader, today or in the future, would benefit from showing their considered acceptance of this fact. Future leadership candidates will benefit from evidence of having opposed this deeply unpopular policy shift.

It has proved impossible to determine the view of the electorate on those MPs who abstained in the tuition fees vote. These individuals have to some extent put themselves at the mercy of their opponents' ability to portray abstention on the matter as weakness, or as de facto support for the U-turn. Prospective leadership candidates who abstained or who supported the U-turn gave a considerable hostage to fortune to those who kept to the party's pledge to oppose any increase.

At any rate, it seems desirable for the leadership to swallow hard and formally admit error on its U-turn over tuition fees. Without a public statement to remedy the loss of trust, party representatives, especially the leader and those who voted with him on the issue, would find it hard to make similar statements with credibility in future. It is easy to see how this difficulty would play out in a televised election debate. The more the current leadership resists this reality, the higher the pressure on the future leadership candidates to prove that they were trustworthy on this and, by inference, on other matters of principle, making the tuition fees issue more important than even the policy itself.

Stylistic issues

It is reflective of the injustices of our world that the third party leader must work harder, usually for less media coverage, impact and reward, than his counterparts in the Tories and Labour. That's just the way it is – but it leaves little latitude for own goals which undermine the leader's apparent capacity to lead in the eyes of his peers. Only a dogged and traditional loyalty to the leader protects them at times of stress. We offer three suggestions which may be helpful for any leadership in the maintenance of stability and unity, especially under a period of stress for the movement.

Firstly, the willingness of the Orange Book caucus to offer negative briefings against colleagues has been difficult to square with the underlying ethos of the more traditional party mode of operations. Few beyond the inner circle would find it acceptable to distance themselves from fellow party members on the grounds that they stood outside the Orange Book grouping. The alternative view believes that this cynical methodology ought to be abandoned.

Secondly, there needs to be tolerance for diverse styles of politics and character in the party. It could be said that the concentration of power on a small, exclusive team of individuals clearly connected at some level to the same tight Orange Book caucus also brought with it an exclusive mindset which kept some of the party's diversity on the outside. This is in marked contrast to, say, Charles Kennedy, who happily shared centre stage with others not in his ideological circle. He recognised that the party would become stronger by making the most of all its human resources. By contrast, offers of help from left-leaning and libertarian elements have on occasion been either ignored or rebuffed by the Orange Book ruling group.

History shows that energetic activists who are obstructed by authority will find a way round – or through. The byproduct of excluding willing volunteers is the creation of a dissatisfied army of 'hostages to fortune' waiting for their chance to fight back. Making enemies of disparate individuals also causes alliances to form amongst people whose shared grievance is a sense of not being valued by the establishment. The Orange Book risked doing this through their determined efforts to maintain control in all the key posts, and by not actively engaging with those who felt distanced by the Orange Bookers. This risked building the ferocity and momentum of the attack if it finally came to a challenge to the leadership.

Thirdly, another stylistic imperative is to abandon the bunker and take the fight to the country. This would mean facing head-on the most unpopular elements of one's actions, and engaging with those who had the most to say about them. It may not achieve a change of heart from opponents. But it wins respect and maintains a relationship with those who otherwise have no emotional motivation to stick with the leader's programme. Attempting a rapport with 'the awkward squad' is always more constructive than ignoring them. Clegg attempted to do this over the summer of 2011, but he met only a small number of members. Any leadership needs to actively understand the grievances of those whom they do not meet and reach out energetically to bring them back into the fold. This could even have been achieved by identifying 'ambassadors' from those parts of the organisation which were not close to the Orange Book. In the first 18 months of the coalition that opportunity had not been taken, even though it had been suggested.

Short-term survival

While we cover strategic questions of the succession to the current leadership in the medium and long term in the next chapter, here we cover measures relevant to its short-term survival. Leadership means showing an awareness of the factors pertaining to how others judge your performance. It is a test of the leader's empathy with the organisation to be aware of these. They serve as an important guide to the leader's perceived performance in the view of the membership to which they are answerable. The alternative view suggests that the key indicators are:

Focus on Leadership

- Party ratings
- Personal ratings
- Performance against stated electoral targets
- Membership growth
- Objective commentary from moderate party sources
- Existence of and convergence between leader and membership narratives

The best guide is altogether more personal: it is the view of those who stand neither to gain nor to lose from a leader's tenure or resignation. The opinion of these individuals is far more valuable than the opinion of those intimately linked with the leader's own circle. Neutral observers are also more valuable than the view of people with an interest in seeing the leader go, who may wish for a resignation so that they can have their chance to stand for office.

As is always the case, the next Lib Dem leader will be on probation versus the performance of an outgoing one. As such, the current leadership must be mindful of its performance in the context of potentially laying out the elements of its own demise and prompting the next leadership election. This largely depends on what happens in the intervening time to the party's fortunes, which is in part, but not in whole, in their control.

Clegg's future is dependent on whether he can build his credibility following the May 2011 debacle and the failure of the AV referendum to deliver change. However painful it may be to say this, the alternative view is that Clegg's personal unpopularity materially damaged the party's success because of the negative image that the third party had acquired under his leadership. While Clegg and his inner circle undoubtedly committed themselves to presenting the best image they could, in the words of Steven Covey: 'you can't talk yourself out of what you've behaved yourself into.'[14]

It's also worth remembering that for a leader to leave before they're pushed is seen as a noble and statesmanlike quality. It can restore a degree of dignity to the historical record of their performance. To hang on for too long removes even this opportunity for retrospective redemption. This is a last resort. The best outcome is for the existing leadership to repair its image.

All of these are relevant in the short term. They will determine whether the leader is in post for another year, or potentially two. Other, more massive, forces are likely to determine the timing of the succession after that time, and we will cover these in chapter 15.

Impact of factionalism on the leadership

Although it may not have seemed like it to outsiders, the previous Liberal Democrat leadership election in 2007 was entirely influenced by factionalism. There were only two candidates, *both* of whom were from the *same* Orange Book caucus. In this sense, the Orange Book grouping can be regarded as one of the most successful political vehicles of all time in the liberal movement – no candidate from outside the faction even attempted to defeat it. In retrospect, it may be the case that some on the Left regret not offering a left-leaning candidate. The absence of an ideologically left-leaning candidate is a moot point as far as the past is concerned, but it is not a moot point for the future. The significant factional activity outside that space occupied by the Orange Book leadership means that there is almost no possibility that the next leadership election will be fought within that caucus alone.

When might this happen? About three months after the 2011 local elections, *The Sunday Times* published polling information suggesting that only 35% of voters expected that Nick Clegg would still be party leader by the time of the next general election.[15] As such, this issue is not theoretical. It is an active issue which, if unaddressed, will not go away on its own. By the end of 2011, a new phenomenon was adding weight to this view: the rise of factions. This flourishing of political interest groups within the Liberal movement was inevitable; it was only a matter of time before groupings outside the Orange Bookers formed into cohesive units.

These party factions started to crystallise around the four quarters of the Nolan Chart, which is a way of assessing where individuals and groups are in terms of social and economic policy.[16] In chapter 12 we briefly considered the Nolan Chart. Here we take that analysis further and deeper, starting with the terms 'leftwing' and 'rightwing.'

Here is how we depict the Nolan Chart. Think of it as a large square, made up of four equally sized smaller squares or 'quadrants' (figure 1).

Socially libertarian & economically interventionist	*Socially libertarian* & economically non-interventionist
Socially authoritarian & economically interventionist	*Socially authoritarian* & economically non-interventionist

Figure 1: The Nolan Chart

The *top* squares – or quadrants – indicate a more socially libertarian policy approach. The *bottom* two quadrants indicate a more socially authoritarian policy approach. The two *left*-hand quadrants indicate an economically interventionist policy approach, meaning relatively high levels of intervention by the state in the operations of the economy and the redistribution of wealth. The two *right*-hand quadrants indicate an economically non-interventionist policy approach, meaning relatively low levels of intervention by the state in the operations of the economy and the redistribution of wealth. We suggest that economic non-interventionism is a broadly rightwing or Conservative agenda, and economic interventionism is a broadly leftwing or Labourite agenda. These definitions offer an intuitive way to discuss 'economic freedom,' a phrase associated with the Nolan Chart.[17]

Using them, we can categorise the four quadrants of the Nolan Chart as follows:

- *Top left quadrant*: socially libertarian; economically interventionist.
- *Top right quadrant*: socially libertarian; economically non-interventionist.
- *Bottom right quadrant:* socially authoritarian; economically interventionist.
- *Bottom left quadrant* socially authoritarian; economically non-interventionist.

We leave it to the reader to decide how interchangeable the phrases 'leftwing' and 'economically interventionist' are, and the same goes for 'rightwing' and 'economically non-interventionist.' However, as a working model these reflect ideologies associated with evolving factions in the liberal movement, and help us to predict what may occur in the run-up to the next leadership election.

The Nolan Chart is relative: for example, all major British political parties are *relatively* socially libertarian and economically non-interventionist compared to the Communist party of the former. The Nolan Chart is also relative when comparing individuals and groups within a party. It is a comparative methodology, not a measure of absolutes. Nevertheless, it offers a persuasive explanation of the internal dynamics of factional evolution in the Lib Dems between 2008 and 2012, as we shall now see.

The establishment of the Liberal Vision blog in 2009[18] was a significant attempt to own part of the Nolan Chart territory. This group was built on a classical libertarian social perspective, while backing economically non-interventionist approaches.[19] This puts it in the *top right-hand* quadrant of the Nolan Chart. Liberal Vision's rise was followed by another new faction, the Social Liberal Forum, at the party's spring conference in Harrogate in 2009.[20] This group proposed a more authoritarian social agenda and a relatively interventionist economic policy, placing it in the *lower left quadrant* of Nolan's analysis.[21]

Historically, factions have tended to wax and wane. The durability and growth of these two groups implies that they have a valued role. By 2012, they enjoyed influence as rallying points within the party for like-minded people.

Autumn 2011 was a point of acceleration for factionalism. The Social Liberal Forum ran its first conference, which was well-attended and had high-profile speakers.[22] The group also established regional groups in the North East.[23] For reference, Liberal Vision had been holding meetings at conferences and releasing challenging documents for some time, as we have already noted.

Where was the Orange Book caucus in terms of the Nolan Chart? As we saw in chapter 7, the grouping held internally contradictory views. One of its key proponents, David Laws, was overtly socially libertarian and economically non-interventionist. This places him in the *top right quadrant*. Yet shortly after the Liberal Democrats entered coalition, Laws resigned from the Cabinet. While Laws and the Conservatives clearly saw common ground on the economically non-interventionist agenda it is possible that, had Laws been there to steer the social narrative for the Orange Bookers, there might have been a more consistent and clearly defined liberal counterpoint to the Conservatives' relatively authoritarian (at least compared to the Liberal Democrats) social agenda.

With Laws on the back benches, the alternative view suggests that there was a convergence between the Liberal Democrat leadership and the Conservative party's social policies. This is demonstrated in Clegg's support for the absolutist creed of muscular liberalism, as discussed in chapter 8 and initially proposed by Cameron in his Munich speech of early 2011.[24] More generally, while the Orange Book project, as defined by Laws, appeared relatively socially libertarian, his viewpoints were not pursued with the same clarity by other members of the Orange Book grouping. For example, the leadership spoke up for prohibition of non-violent extremists[25] and stepped up a tonally more aggressive and pro-interventionist approach on international matters, rather as Huhne had proposed in his contribution to *The Orange Book*.[26]

Not everything that the Orange Bookers did pointed consistently towards a socially authoritarian and economically rightward shift. For example, the leadership spoke up to defend various perceived socially liberal causes, such as defending the Human Rights Act[27] and opposing child detention[28] (though the actual level of achievement for that policy stand is open to debate[29]). Also, as we saw in chapter 4, the Liberal Democrats succeeded in raising the threshold at which individuals pay tax. Great store was also made of the introduction of a 'pupil premium' to support younger people.[30] While one can always question the efficacy of such changes, the point is that the Orange Book leadership intended these things to happen, and that they reflected liberal, rather than conservative, thinking.

Nevertheless, it is the alternative view's judgement that, all things considered, the leadership had moved towards a more socially authoritarian agenda, compared with the more libertarian agenda of the Liberal Democrats as a whole. A key reason for this conclusion is the absolute clarity with which Clegg associated himself with the authoritarian ethos of Cameron's muscular liberalism.

Evidence of drift on economic policy was observed in the mercurial fortunes of the proposed 'mansion tax,' an idea similar to policies supported by economic interventionists. This totemic proposal was originally proposed by Lib Dems in 2009,[31] then apparently scaled back a couple of months later,[32] only to be resuscitated again in 2011, causing predictable frictions between the coalition partners.[33] The shift to and fro did not give the impression that the policy was a key part of the leadership's narrative.

Worse still, even before the election Orange Bookers had been discussing the abandonment of the party's (socially liberal *and* economically interventionist) opposition to the increase in student tuition fees.[34] The anger caused by the breaking of the pledge made by Lib Dems to oppose the rises is not the point here. The policy considered those dissuaded by the prospect of a huge burden of debt from entering higher education and supported them (a socially liberal policy) through a subsidy paid for from taxation (an economically interventionist policy). Regardless of the reasons for the abandonment of the policy, this served to move the Orange Book leadership to the right in economic terms, and away from the socially libertarian quadrant at the same time.

As we have seen, the Orange Book caucus as a corporate group tend towards less socially liberal territory in comparison to the party's MPs as a whole. The alternative view is that, relative to the liberal movement, the Orange Book leadership's comments and actions in government place it in the *bottom right quadrant*: socially authoritarian and economically non-interventionist. Again, regardless of the merits of this stance, the point is that the Orange Bookers' location on the Nolan Chart was away from the socially libertarian (and economically non-interventionist) position – where Laws had appeared to place himself – towards a socially more authoritarian (and once again economically non-interventionist) one, a shift from the *top right quadrant* to the *bottom right quadrant* of the Nolan Chart.

It is important to emphasise, once again, that the Nolan Chart is a relative measure. This means that it is perfectly possible for the Lib Dem leadership to be left of the Tories economically and libertarian versus the Tories on social policy, while *simultaneously* being right of the Liberal Democrats' collective economic viewpoint and authoritarian versus the Liberal Democrat party's 'centre of gravity' on social policy. We suggest that this was the case by early 2012.

If this is the case, then only one quadrant of the Nolan Chart lay unrepresented by a significant faction in the Liberal Democrats: the economically interventionist and socially libertarian one – the *top left quadrant*. Politics, like nature, abhors a vacuum. It seems likely that this vacuum will be filled by a faction providing a collective voice for this combination of views. The creation of a left-libertarian faction, and the alternative view that it may provide, would mean that all four quadrants had a voice in the party.

In the face of the rise of factions in the other three quadrants, it is quite possible that some Orange Bookers will feel a need to sharpen up the ideological positioning of their own caucus. This might catalyse the creation of a more clearly defined faction to formally represent the economically non-interventionist and socially authoritarian quadrant – the *bottom right quadrant* in the chart. This would be entirely logical, as up until now there has been no formal, cohesive narrative to bind the Orange Bookers together. However, the problem of internal contradictions amongst Orange Bookers may be so ingrained that even the advent of a formal faction to define a collective position may be doomed, as it could serve to further expose the differences within the Orange Book caucus itself – primarily between the leadership and others – rather than unite it around a common narrative.

Any such development would most likely occur in 2012, in response to the perceived progress of the other ideological groupings which by 2012 were busy consolidating their respective positions. A highly visible indication of this burgeoning process occurred three months before this time. On 31 October 2011, a group linked to the Social Liberal Forum published a letter in the Guardian supporting a proposal by the leftwing think tank Compass for 'Plan B' – an established shorthand term meaning the adoption of a more Labourite agenda involving less swingeing cuts in public spending than those approved by the Conservative-Liberal Democrat coalition. The letter was immediately interpreted as a challenge to the leadership.[35]

Liberal Vision responded with a measured counteroffensive. Specifically, the support of a Lib Dem Greater London Authority candidate, Stephen Knight, for the Social Liberal Forum's 'Plan B' caused complaints from individuals associated with the Liberal Vision grouping.[36] On the face of it, these complaints revolved around the link between the Social Liberal Forum, Compass and the Labour party, with the inference that these links were potentially compromising. However, at a deeper level this argument was a proxy for a debate concerning the extent to which Lib Dem members ought to associate openly with Labour. The party's national conferences in 2012 would doubtless be used by all sides to develop this discussion further. Again, the leadership would have to be mindful of this growing debate, as a move towards stronger links with Labour could compromise the existing leadership's authority.

The leadership had other reasons to take the rise of factions seriously, for ideology was not the sole driver in their evolution. Another dynamic was consideration of the next leadership campaign. By early 2012 each faction was, to a greater or lesser extent, positioning itself in ways which could make it a stakeholder in the fortunes of potential leadership candidates. MPs with an interest in standing would benefit from maintaining links with those groupings closest to their own positions, and therefore potentially willing to support a leadership bid.

In the case of the presidential election, Liberal Vision had already supported Orange Book candidate Baroness Kramer,[37] while the Social Liberal Forum had published a set of answers from the left-leaning candidate Tim Farron;[38] although the opportunity had been given for Kramer to respond to these questions, she apparently had not done so – certainly no answers were published.

These processes can be expected to occur again as the next leadership election looms.

All members have the chance to vote in the election of the party leader. With tens of thousands of members to persuade, the election contest is a huge operation similar to a parliamentary by-election in scale. Any credible campaign requires considerable human resources to achieve the momentum to win. Factions and leadership hopefuls know this. Their courtship is an informal omen that the movement corporately senses that a leadership election is pending. Again, this can create energy which itself hastens a leadership election, such that the momentum can eventually overwhelm the existing leadership's capacity to prevent it.

A contest between leadership contenders from different Nolan Chart quadrants would guarantee that the next leadership election would be more openly ideological than the 2007 campaign. Even if the candidates themselves were for some reason averse to doing so, party factions that lined up behind the candidates would demand ideological positioning statements from their chosen champions.

Is it possible to predict what the existent factions will do when the leadership election comes and, importantly, whether their actions will prompt an election? We can make some informed guesses. Members of the Orange Book caucus spoke at the Social Liberal Forum's conference. Bearing in mind the history of the 2007 election, where no candidate associated with the Left stood, it seems unlikely that the Social Liberal Forum would support an Orange Book candidate if they were strong enough to support one of their own. The only possible exception to this would be someone who technically belonged to the Orange Book caucus by virtue of having made a contribution to *The Orange Book* or *Britain After Blair* volumes, but who also held left-leaning economic views. By early 2012, none of these individuals occupied a position near the top centre of the Orange Book caucus.

The position with Liberal Vision is more complex. In the past they have supported a candidate with an economically non-interventionist approach and without clear classical liberal leanings on social policy; this is more or less what happened in the case of supporting Baroness Kramer in her unsuccessful presidential bid in 2010.

Clearly, prospective leadership candidates will have their own support bases but, as the leadership election draws closer, candidates will work behind the scenes connecting with factions – and with people who might create one – to garner support on the basis of their own standing in the Nolan Chart quadrants. The growth of factions, and the way that potential party leaders associate with them, will provide a crucial indication of how a leadership election will be fought out and where the party's ideological centre of gravity truly lies – an answer which was not provided by the exclusively Orange Book leadership election of 2007.

Even though influential factions were growing, in early 2012 the Orange Book caucus still held tightly to the reigns of power. However, by this point, the development of competing factions in the party was too advanced to be stopped by anyone. Thus, the Orange Book hegemony could not be relied upon to deliver another leader. Moreover, it could not even be certain of resisting the pressure of being bounced into a leadership election.

Thus, in the event of an election, simply being an Orange Booker would no longer assure any candidate of victory and, depending on the perceived performance of Orange Bookers in government, might even serve to act as a negative which potential Orange Book candidates would have to address. This concern could act as a key motivator for ambitious Orange Bookers to set up a faction representing their agenda in an ideologically consistent way, providing distance from the perceived failings of an incumbent individual or team.

The alternative view holds that the majority of the party is on the left of the Orange Book leadership. Were they able to effectively reach out to the factions beyond their own, for example to the Social Liberal Forum, it could provide a wider power base in the event of a serious push against the existing leadership. Huhne and Cable had both spoken at the Social Liberal Forum conference in June 2011. However, the rise of alternative factions presents those in power with the growing potential of a forceful challenge to which there is no easy or obvious response.

Coalition: the leader's options

There is a view that the best interests of the leader and party might necessitate withdrawal from coalition – that to remain in the coalition up to the next general election would spell disaster for its electoral chances. This argument rests on the assumption that Labour voters might return to the Lib Dems if the Liberal Democrats break their partnership with the Conservatives, perhaps as a result of a policy split on a totemic issue – such as controversial reforms of the National Health Service, which were already causing friction between the coalition partners in early 2012.

It doesn't hold water. There is no reason to think that simply breaking the coalition would achieve this. For one thing, Labour won't deal with Clegg as leader because of his attacks on Gordon Brown in the past, which we'll cover in the next chapter. So there is no reason to think that he could preside over a return of those left-leaning votes. At the same time, he would be blamed by the Tories for bringing down a stable coalition and reneging on another major promise, the commitment to keep it going till 2015. Even in May 2011, the Tories made significant gains while the Liberal Democrats lost a catastrophic number of seats, many to Conservatives. Despite the coalition, there was no loyalty towards Lib Dems amongst the right-leaning electorate. While the ill-judged (from the Liberal Democrats' perspective) holding of the AV poll on the same day as the local elections may have lifted the Tory vote, the fact is that in those areas where Lib Dems were challenging Labour no solid lift in the Lib Dem vote took place from tactical voting by Conservative supporters.

However, the party has to do something to protect its interest. By 2011 the Liberal Democrats had lost much of its left-leaning vote to other parties, most notably Labour. In 2011 the loss of Lib Dem support was roughly inversely proportional to the gain in Labour support: they went up by 7% and Lib Dems went down by 8%.[39] The party would clearly need to reverse this to recover to the level of the 2010 general election. Remember that while the share of vote in 2010 was better than in the previous general election the share of seats was unimpressive, with a net decline in numbers. Thus, this would be a relatively modest ambition compared to the gains made in 1997, 2001 and 2005. However, Clegg had publicly committed to doubling the number of MPs by the next election. Even holding 57 seats would fall far short of his target of that. However, the harsh reality is that even to 'flatline' the party requires a considerable recovery. In no 'early withdrawal' scenario does it seem possible for the party led by the current leader to 'find' those votes. This is the bind that Clegg faces. Any suggestion of another coalition with the Tories would be the death knell for the tactical Labour vote. Conversely, an early breakdown of the coalition simply causes further bad press and attacks against the Lib Dems for pulling stumps on the coalition government. While staying in won't win Conservative votes either it buys time, and that is what the Liberal Democrats desperately need to build a recovery.

If the party's performance in future elections is catastrophic – at least as bad as 2011 – then the temptation to withdraw increases. However, even then it is not right for Clegg to pull out. He must play for time. From here on in, the analysis is tied up with succession scenarios, so we'll look at the rest of the possibilities in the next chapter. But, as far as the current leadership is concerned, the alternative view sees no situation where early withdrawal from the partnership is a sensible option for Clegg or the Liberal Democrats.

Electoral pacts?

What about doing a deal for votes, brokered by the two party leaders of the Conservatives and Liberal Democrats? Any such pact would effectively tie both parties into a promise of coalition after the election. This is a non-starter which would not assist Clegg or the party.

It is probable that any such pact would be rejected by a membership already uneasy with the existing coalition. A limited pact – where the Conservatives do not field candidates against, say, Lib Dem ministers – would cause further damage to those Liberal Democrat MPs not protected by the pact. Again, it would be improbable that the wider party would accept this arrangement; if so, this would cause stress to internal party cohesion whilst again giving Labour a very mighty stick with which to batter the Liberal Democrats and, in all probability, throttling any chance of a tactical vote from Labour supporters in Tory-Lib Dem marginals. As such, it would be extremely unwise for the leadership to propose any potential electoral pact with the Conservatives. Again, we will look at the extraordinary problems related to electoral pacts when we look at succession scenarios.

What if the Orange Book leadership persuaded the Conservative leadership to agree informal mutual support – or non-aggression – in the next general election? For the Liberal Democrats, this strategy would be equally foolish. It would also be as bad as committing the party to promising another Tory-Lib Dem coalition, guaranteeing that the left-leaning vote would not back Liberal Democrat candidates. After all, if you are anti-Tory, why vote tactically for the Lib Dems to keep the Tories out when the Tories themselves are saying that this helps to keep the Tories in? Any suggestion of a pact by the Conservatives will ensure that left-leaning voters support whichever candidate offers the best chance of defeating the Conservative *and* the Liberal Democrat. Since many Lib Dem MPs depend on the tactical Labour vote to hold or gain seats against Conservative challengers, the ironic but obvious consequence of an electoral pact *with* the Tories would be a loss of many Lib Dem seats *to* the Tories. Also, electors would be more likely to shift directly from Tory to Labour without stopping at the Liberal Democrats, since this would be regarded as 'the same as voting Tory.' This switch across from Conservative to Labour at the cost of Lib Dems has been observed before, for example in a number of seats in 1997.

Either way, unless Tories and Lib Dems agree not to field candidates against each other – which is a coalition agreement by any other name – there is no plausible scenario in which the Liberal Democrats would benefit from an electoral pact with the Conservatives (except in the vanishingly unlikely scenario where the Conservatives are polling at lower levels than Liberal Democrats, in which case the problem is reversed, to the benefit of the Lib Dems. However, given the relative strength of the two parties at local government level, this will not be the case).

As can be seen, there is no advantage in any attempt by the leadership to secure a formal or informal pact with its coalition partner. Indeed, there may be a tactical incentive for *Conservatives* to unilaterally promote the prospect of a Tory-Lib Dem alliance. This could frighten off left-leaning Lib Dem voters in Conservative-Liberal Democrat marginals, thus improving the chances of Conservative gains at a cost to their former coalition partners!

It is just about conceivable that a *very* targeted campaign could deliver a sufficient number of tactical Conservative votes to Liberal Democrat candidates in particular seats, such as Clegg's constituency of Sheffield Hallam. However, this self-protecting act would be regarded in a very dim light inside and outside the party, and the reputational cost would be colossal.

Incidentally, for the avoidance of doubt, party leaders Clegg and Cameron both rejected any suggestion of an electoral pact in the 2015 general election. This is hardly surprising. The Tories frequently show an antipathy towards the coalition, seeing it as nothing more than a useful marriage of convenience. They would very likely 'file for divorce' once a favourable situation arose to give them an overall majority. The Lib Dem president used similar 'divorce' language in his Conference speech in September 2011.

The implication for the leadership is obvious: to even maintain its numbers in the Commons, it must 'go it alone' and appeal to left-leaning voters in seats where those votes are essential for a Lib Dem victory. Therefore, the current leadership must provide a plausible narrative that left-leaning electors can genuinely accept. That means guaranteeing that Lib Dems will not back a Tory administration for a further five years after the next election. This is hard for the current party administration. This narrative would have to credibly offer the *prospect* of a Lib-Lab coalition as a possible outcome of the election, otherwise the only conclusion that the public would draw is that voting Lib Dem gives a Tory government. The logic is self-evident.

Can the current leadership deliver this message to left-leaning voters? Since Clegg already promised that the Liberal Democrats would support the current Tory coalition for the full five-year term, there appears to be no opportunity for distance between Lib Dems and Conservatives until electioneering has begun, by which time there will be little time to create meaningful distance between the leaders and parties.

Clegg has one more presentational problem. There will be mischief on words that he has used in the past. In his first leader's speech in 2008, Clegg said:

> The day before I was elected leader, Mr Cameron suggested we join them. He talked about a 'progressive alliance.' This talk of

alliances comes up a lot, doesn't it? Everyone wants to be in our gang. So I want to make something very clear today. Will I ever join a Conservative government? No.

This has already been used against Clegg, though the use of it is a little unfair. He made the same point about Labour immediately afterwards in his speech:

Will I ever join a Labour government? No. I will never allow the Liberal Democrats to be a mere annex to another party's agenda.[40]

The use of 'never' makes the phrase in relation to both Tories and Labour sound somewhat absolute – and it can be made to look as if Clegg did a U-turn. However, a more generous interpretation would be that Clegg meant that he would not join either party mid-term, if Labour or Conservatives held an absolute majority in Parliament. He went on to say: 'Am I interested in building a new type of government? Yes. Based on pluralism instead of one party rule? Yes.'[41] Taking that charitable interpretation, this is a useful commitment, as it means that Clegg ruled out any prospect of joining a majority Tory – or Labour – administration after the next election if such a deal were offered.

While we give his words this generous treatment here, it is likely that others will be less benign. Again, therefore, there is a potential electioneering issue here.

To overcome the considerable obstacle of over-association with the Tory movement is an imperative for the current leadership if they are to provide a plausible footing for the next general election. Otherwise, they will distance leftwing supporters, so essential to even maintaining what the party won in 2010.

There is a way forward: to split the role of government and party leadership. It is one of the scenarios which we will cover in the next chapter, which preserves the coalition as well as potentially restoring credibility with the Left. Of course, the current leadership might have a plan of its own to achieve this in a different way. By the end of 2011, nobody had heard it what it was.

Factors that count for the next leadership

We conclude this section with an alternative view of the factors likely to determine the identity of the next leader. After 5 May 2011 the Clegg administration began operating under greater pressure, generated by the public's rejection of candidates and, gravely, of electoral reform. Both were of great significance to the party, and to Clegg's tenure. May 2011 also raised the stakes over the continued viability of the Liberal movement as a strong national force in the short term. With so much at stake for so many people, the opportunity for further error had become more limited. It is worth looking ahead in case there is a sudden change in leadership, as there was twice between January 2006 and December 2007.

The analysis of factors influencing the next leadership election has no particular name in mind, for that is not the alternative view's remit. These factors follow logically from the narrative outlined in our analysis, and the research done in its compilation. It is a 'best guess' about what will matter when the leadership election occurs. Nor is it necessarily the case that one person will have all of these factors in abundance. It is our best assessment of what is likely to determine the suitability of future leadership candidates to the membership.

1. The next leader will be capable of generating an absolutely clear narrative – or worldview – which resonates with the membership at an instinctive and visceral level. This narrative will unite the party, and attract back lost voters, primarily from the Left.
2. The next leader will stand on a platform of generating a distinctively liberal image, based on the narrative and core values of the Liberal Democrats.

3. The next leader will have credibility on the student tuition fees issue, either by having opposed them in a vote in Parliament or by offering a plausible reason why they did not do so. To say that it was the cost of coalition is unlikely to be sufficient because many Lib Dem MPs did vote against it.
4. The next leader will be personally popular with electors who formerly voted for the Liberal Democrats, but who either abstained or voted against the party on subsequent occasions, particularly from May 2011 onwards.
5. The next leader will have a demonstrable history of community politics, ascending from the rank and file, and will probably have served as an elected Liberal Democrat councillor.
6. The next leader will not be accused of 'looking like a Tory.'
7. The next leader will be able to plausibly reject the prospect of another Conservative-Liberal Democrat coalition for the term beginning immediately after the next general election.

There is no real criterion pertaining to experience of the Commons. Clegg himself had only been in Parliament for two years when he became leader in 2007.

These speculations are exactly that, but they are the best estimate possible with the information available. All seven factors are based on an assessment of what we think will matter to members. Politics is unpredictable because there are too many variables for the future to be solved in a mathematical fashion. It is possible that a miraculous policy achievement will transform the current leadership's fortunes and alter the set of factors relevant to the next leadership election. These unknowns are what make the future... unknowable.

Summary

For the Liberal Democrats to recover some or all of their position, they need to restore credibility on their promises – which means direct attention to the damaged good faith caused by the U-turn on tuition fees and other policies. This requires robustness on totemic issues. It also demands a visible rejection of Cameron's concept of muscular liberalism. Lib Dems in Parliament need to vote as Liberal Democrats, even if this places a strain on the coalition. There is no imperative to terminate the coalition in 2011, but at the same time the party must find ways to re-attract its left-leaning vote rather than simply hoping for the whimsical scenario of 'Alarm Clock Britain' voters rising up to save the party from further decline. All of these considerations help to inform the likely factors which will count in the next leadership election.

In October 2011, the *Independent* newspaper published an article about likely successors to Clegg. The article stated that:

> Clegg has insisted he will lead it into the next election but there is speculation that he may quit in 2014 to become Britain's European Commissioner.[42]

Early signs of media interest in the Liberal Democrat succession were all there, and reflected findings that the alternative view has uncovered. The article also increased the importance of Liberal Democrats leading the debate over succession, rather than being led into it by the media.

Tied to questions of leadership are inevitable questions of succession. However uncomfortable this subject may be, it is less healthy to avoid it. Options need to be aired in the interests of predictability and transparency, two values which the party promotes externally and which it should display internally. Resisting the succession debate would be an act of denial in ugly contrast to the long, collectivist and fundamentally philanthropic history of the Liberal movement. Beginning it now is an honest and liberal way of doing these things.

Chapter 15

Succession Scenarios

It is not the critic who counts; not the man who points out how the strong man stumbles, or where the doer of deeds could have done better. The credit belongs to the man who is actually in the arena.
Theodore Roosevelt, 26th American President, 23 April 1910

There is no indispensable man.
Franklin D. Roosevelt, 32nd American President, 3 November 1932

The alternative view has no illusions of glory or grandeur in our thesis regarding scenarios relating to the succession of the leadership. American President Theodore Roosevelt's words ring true across the ages. Those who act in good faith in the public interest deserve the respect of their fellow citizen for making a noble contribution to the society they serve. But this does not preclude the need to take a dispassionate look at the realities of succession, for the reasons that his successor, Franklin D. Roosevelt, observed 22 years later.

Here we consider mechanisms that will precipitate a change in leadership. These are all derived from an objective investigation of political realities facing the party. Other possible scenarios have been analysed, and none of them pass muster in terms of plausibility. We believe that one of the following possibilities will necessarily occur.

Nick Clegg has argued that a coalition which lasts for the full five years of the current Parliament is in the best interests of the country – and, at the end of this five-year period, to the benefit of the party as well. The clear implication is that Nick Clegg will not seek to break away from the coalition before the 2015 general election. This will continue to be a contentious commitment, given the challenges that the coalition has caused in terms of the party's electoral performance – and given potential strains in the coalition itself. However, as we have already seen, Clegg's commitment is logical, not just in terms of honouring a promise but also because an early end to the coalition appears to be electorally damaging to the party. Labour and Conservatives have more to gain from a premature breakdown of the partnership than the Liberal Democrats. However, we must look at the implications for the leadership in the event of a breakdown because it is a possibility.

We assume that Clegg intends to remain the Deputy Prime Minister till the end of the coalition. He has given no notice of any other plan. We also assume that the next election will be fought without electoral pacts between any of the three main parties. This has been the explicit commitment by Clegg and Cameron. Once again, however, we will investigate the hypothetical scenario in which electoral pacts are introduced in the context of the leadership (we looked at this in the context of the party's best interests in the last chapter).

Timing for a change in leadership is a core issue for any party. So, we will also ask: what would happen if Clegg were to resign at different points of the electoral cycle? We also come to a clear conclusion: the right thing to do is to split the roles of Deputy Prime Minister and party leader well in advance of the General Election. Indeed, there is nothing to stop this split being made now.

While the scenarios we explore are founded on the actual situation facing the Liberal Democrats in the 2010-2014/5 electoral cycle these will play out again and again in the years ahead, with different names in the leading roles and perhaps different coalition partners. Thus much of our analysis will continue to be relevant in the political environment in the years ahead – especially should a proportional system of election be introduced for the British Parliament.

Internal party context

In his consultation sessions around the country with the membership in the summer of 2011, Clegg acknowledged the difficulties facing the party in the short term. He perceived that the period of political recovery could be four years, up to the scheduled date of the next general election – 2015. Clegg made clear that he hoped the organisation would be willing to endure a degree of contraction in the local government base in exchange for a recovery by 2015 and success in.

However, Clegg had also set himself the target of doubling the number of MPs the party. His deadline – 'the election after next' – was set prior to the 2010 election, meaning that 2015 was the target date for achieving a total of at least 124 MPs.[1] So we have a clear measure, defined by the leader himself. In September 2011, he added another target – to rebuild the council base up to its size in 2010.[2]

As we have shown, given the slight contraction of the number of MPs in 2010, the catastrophic performance of the Liberal Democrats in the 2011 elections and the generally poor subsequent results in local by-elections, there was little prospect of the party even holding its complement of seats at 57, let alone *increasing* it by 67 seats in one election. This required a jump in seats not achieved by the liberal movement since 1923 – and even then only at the cost of another collapsing party, the National Liberals.

For Clegg to miss his own target by 67 seats or more would mean that he had underperformed versus his own goal by a very great margin. This would be immensely disappointing compared to the high hopes that the Clegg leadership had stirred up in the party during the run-up to the May 2010 general election and, before that, in his own leadership election campaign. This on its own might cause an objective observer to judge Clegg's chances of remaining in office as slim. However, his ability to achieve the parliamentary target technically remains an open question until the day after the next election. It is *theoretically* possible that he would still achieve his target. We will not pursue this question further or try to second-guess his ability to deliver this target, because the point has been amply covered. Furthermore, for reasons that we will come to shortly, the alternative view regards it as unlikely that Clegg would lead the party into the next general election, so a long debate about these goals would seem pointless. If he did serve to the election as leader, it does seem probable that he would have to resign immediately after it, having led the party out of government. This is the normal etiquette. However we note that Clegg's new goal – to win back the lost council seats – may be more salient to his short-term survival as leader than the parliamentary one.

Relevant general factors

Three factors seem particularly important as the party heads towards the next General Election. They affect each scenario to varying degrees.

Firstly, in the previous chapter we analysed the reasons why it would be extremely foolish for the Liberal Democrats to even suggest the possibility of another coalition with the Conservatives for a second parliamentary term, because of the undoubted collateral damage that this would cause to the party's votes – whether or not the Orange Book were in control. Our research indicates that anything other than a clear rejection of the possibility of another Tory-Lib Dem coalition would guarantee a decline in the number of Lib Dem MPs. This positioning option is therefore effectively closed to the leader, regardless of who that leader is. Nor would arguments that another Lib Dem-Con coalition would be 'good for the country' restore the lost left-leaning vote.

Secondly, Labour would not countenance a coalition with the Liberal Democrats as long as Clegg were in charge. Clegg made this a certainty with his own adamant demand for Brown's resignation as a precondition of any arrangement with Labour in 2010. If Clegg were to lead the party into the next general election, any offer or suggestion of a coalition with Labour would be rejected as long as the party were still under his premiership. A left-leaning partnership would not be seen as plausible by political commentators or the media under Clegg. Thus, as well as being unable to offer a coalition with the Tories for electoral reasons, Clegg could not offer the prospect of coalition with Labour for political reasons.

Given the first and second points, the only feasible line that a Clegg-led campaign could take would be to promise one of two things: either a Lib Dem-*led* government – and even then Labour would call for his resignation if it were to be a partnership – or a promise to stay in opposition. He would have no other practicable positions – unless, perhaps, he stated publicly that in the event of a hung parliament favouring a left-leaning partnership he would stand down. Without that commitment, the suggestion would be rejected out of hand.

Thirdly, if Clegg were to resign prior to the general election the timing and nature of that resignation could have serious implications for the party's ability to campaign and win votes. It could even precipitate a general election *before* 2015, at a time which could be extremely disadvantageous to the Liberal Democrats, as we shall see.

An alternative view places the timing of a change in leadership between May 2012 at the earliest and December 2014 at the latest. From our analysis, it will become clear why delaying the transition beyond that date is likely to harm the party's fortunes at the next general election – and why a leadership election in 2014 is also a little dangerous. Here are the possible succession scenarios as we see them.

The next leadership election is likely to be prompted by:

1. Local election performance from May 2012 onwards.
2. Breakdown of the coalition from summer 2012 onwards.
3. General election strategy concerns from 2013 onwards.
4. Boundary changes from 2014 onwards.
5. A *coup d'état* at any time.

Electoral performance from May 2012 onwards

If the party's immediate electoral performance continues in line with the May 2011 results, internal pressure is likely to force the selection of a new leader in the shorter rather than the longer term. On the other hand, in the event of a profound recovery in the popularity of the party, and of the leader, there is the prospect that the current administration can continue for the medium term.

Although it is tempting to leave these matters vague for fear of being wrong, it is better to offer more specific guidelines – even if others subsequently prefer to insert different numbers in our model. We suggest the following parameters. In any of the local election rounds in the years up to 2014, if the party holds – or makes net gains in – its net number of councillors, the leadership is safe from a short-term challenge. If losses are less than 40% – the level of attrition in May 2011[3] – then the leadership is vulnerable. If losses exceed 40% of seats being defended, a challenge to the leadership becomes very likely.

Perhaps the membership may feel that the party's results cannot be improved upon at these elections – under *any* leader. The alternative view regards this as unlikely and asserts that poor results are not a given. It seems that the leadership believes this too – which is why in September 2011 Clegg committed himself to regaining the local government seats lost in May of that year. The number of seats being contested varies from year to year, so numerically, the absolute number of seats won or lost does not lend itself easily to relative comparisons. But the proportion of seats lost – or gained – is what matters. To be pedantic, the relative performance four years before might also be taken into account, but up to 2010 the party's poll ratings were more or less steady give or take a few percent so this probably isn't necessary.[4] The proportionate change is therefore a good indicator of whether things have improved versus previous elections. The same considerations apply to the local elections in 2012, 2013 and 2014.

Research reveals that, in 2011, Lib Dem council candidates fared best in a number of Lib Dem-held parliamentary seats. However, the Lib Dems suffered devastating losses in the Welsh Assembly (two out of three constituency seats lost)[5] and Scotland's Parliament (nine out of 11 constituency seats lost).[6] Thus it is perilous to assume that even consolidating 'the seats that Lib Dems have got' will be achievable in the current political environment. If 2011 were repeated at a general election, the Lib Dems would fall considerably, as the political betting pundits were predicting throughout 2011. Since they have a pecuniary interest in predicting the outcomes, it is sometimes instructive to see what they are saying.[7] The probability of significant gains against Conservative and Labour candidates would be tiny.

Without a turnaround in the local government performance, a poor result in the next general election would be ever more likely. Note that our analysis is not focused on Clegg's aim of doubling the number of seats. We are only considering the challenge of holding what they have got.

The mechanism in the scenario of continuing poor local election results is grassroots anger. These activists would be inclined to call for Clegg's departure, though the nearer the next election the more likely that MPs will also instigate some kind of intervention in the interests of improving their own chances of holding their seats.

In terms of the European elections, we speculate that matching or exceeding the result in 2009 (13.7%)[8] will bolster the leadership's position. A loss of support will make the leadership more vulnerable to challenge. A decline of more than one third of the vote – so the party receives less than, say, 9% – will put the present leadership under great pressure to stand down in advance of the general election if it has not already occurred by then. At that level of polling in the European elections we estimate that the party's general election performance would be heading towards the 16% ballpark. Also, that 33% loss of vote would put more than one third of sitting Liberal Democrat MPs at risk of losing their seats because of the way first past the post operates. Again, this could prompt a challenge from fearful MPs in advance of the general election.

The worst-case scenario would be one where the party is deeply dissatisfied with the performance of the leadership, but it does not believe that anyone else could do better. This would paralyse the movement into inaction and mean that whatever problems could have been resolved with a change at the top, for example by splitting the roles of Deputy Prime Minister and leader, would not be fixed.

Breakdown of the coalition from summer 2012 onwards

In the previous chapter, we considered why it was unwise for the Lib Dems to break the coalition early. But what if it *did* happen? What then for Clegg? Let's look at how it might happen, and the implications of a breakdown from the perspective of the leadership. It could be caused by pressure from activists following intolerable losses to the party in electoral terms. It could also be caused by insurmountable political difference between the coalition partners – perhaps deliberately by the Conservatives to cause an election.

Would the end of the coalition necessarily prompt the leader's resignation? Yes. While Clegg could resign from the leadership and continue productively as the Lib Dem Deputy Prime Minister, it is not a reciprocal situation. Resignation from the Deputy Prime Minister position to continue as leader would have no plausible campaigning value after his departure from government, together with his ministerial colleagues. Consider his ongoing electoral campaigning options after leaving the government before 2015. There are four things that Clegg could attempt:

- Express a willingness to broker another coalition with the Tories: this would be politically unpalatable to the membership and implausible to the public after the collapse of the previous coalition;
- Offer a deal with Labour: this would be rejected by Labour itself as long as Clegg was in power – a direct reciprocation to Clegg's demand for Gordon Brown's resignation prior to any possible deal with Labour in 2010;
- Promote the prospect of a Lib Dem majority government: this would be patently unrealistic under the first past the post system of election and given the party's local government strength – which cannot recover in time to make majority government a realistic possibility;
- Campaign on a platform of 'leading the party back into opposition': despite this being a possible outcome of the next general election, Clegg could not realistically campaign on this agenda. Opposition would be a period of renewal after government: no British government leader in decades continued to lead their party after transiting from government to opposition – and also Clegg's leadership would become untenable the moment the coalition collapsed.

Even if Labour were willing to accept a Clegg Lib Dem Party into a coalition – and they wouldn't – a new coalition with Labour simply would not be practicable without a general election. The electoral mathematics arising from the outcome of the 2010 general election make it impossible for any realistic combination of two parties other than Conservatives and Lib Dems to govern with stability. So, even if Clegg – or any new Lib Dem leader – wanted to, there is no way to form a stable majority administration with Labour prior to an election. Besides, from a political standpoint, it would not be in Labour's interests to do so, as they would gamble that an election might increase their presence in the Commons, partly at the Lib Dems' expense.

An end to the coalition thus infers a leadership election, and a search for someone able to regroup the party. The new leader could plausibly speak independently of the Tory-Lib Dem coalition and reach out to left-leaning voters, as long as they themselves had not been very closely associated with the partnership – or had somehow managed to distance themselves from it prior to the leadership election. They could even campaign on a positive, if perhaps deliberately vague, platform of rebuilding the party's electoral fortunes, even if that meant doing so from opposition.

Is there *any* scenario in which a break could be good for the party, or in which the existing leadership could continue? Since a breakdown – however problematic for the Lib Dems – is a possibility, let's make absolutely sure that we've analysed it from all angles – though that means looking at some scenarios which are a bit fanciful.

What if Clegg were to withdraw from the coalition, while attempting to retain some authority over the government? This might take the form of offering some kind of deal whereby the Liberal Democrats formally leave the coalition but negotiate with the Tories on a policy-by-policy basis – known as 'confidence and supply.' Clegg could then try to show that, in doing so, he had separated the Lib Dems from the Conservatives while still maintaining influence.

This is not likely to protect Clegg from the need to resign. Again, it is inconceivable that Labour would make this situation easy for the Liberal Democrats. We must always be mindful that Clegg's precedent – demanding Gordon Brown's resignation in 2010 – is still a score yet to be settled. Clegg could not realistically depend on any help from Labour in a 'confidence and supply' environment. After all, if Clegg broke the coalition, the Conservatives would fill all the positions with Tory ministers while Liberal Democrats physically joined Labour on the opposition benches; for Lib Dems to stay on the government benches with no government ministers would be the worst of both worlds, and a public relations disaster. As such, supporting the Tories, now facing his team who had relocated to the opposition benches of the Commons chamber, would make Clegg look like a puppet of Cameron, without even the benefit of having any ministers. Also, the etiquette point arises again: since Clegg would have led the Lib Dems out of government, the natural expectation would be for him to resign – though this is not a rule set in stone.

Another thought. In this scenario, if the Tories were strong in the polls, they could force an early election, at the cost of the 'deal-breaking' Lib Dems. Clegg would be branded the 'deal-breaker' to Tory voters, as he had previously committed the Liberal Democrats to sustaining the coalition right up to 2015. That would mean a further reduced chance of any fleeting Conservative votes coming over tactically for Liberal Democrats, since he and his party had shown themselves to be an unreliable partner in government. Again, Clegg's action would create a political harm with the right wing, while there would be no quarter given by Labour to him for the reasons that we've already considered. Again, his resignation would be the only responsible action, even if no immediate successor is apparent. After all, in this scenario, Clegg has no voter base to offer the party, and this would lock the Lib Dems down with their remaining core vote.

Does the fixed-term Parliament legislation make any difference? No. The fixed-term arrangements can easily be circumvented and the terms of the legislation can easily be used to corner the Lib Dems. To quote from the Parliamentary Services summary of the bill:

> The Bill fixes the date of the next General Election at 7 May 2015, and provides for five-year fixed terms. It includes provisions to allow the Prime Minister to alter the date by up to two months by Order. There are also two ways in which an election could be triggered before the end of the five-year term:
>
> - if a motion of no confidence is passed and no alternative government is found
> - or if a motion for an early general election is agreed either by at least two-thirds of the House or without division.[9]

There is no comfort in this for Lib Dems. On the one hand, in the event of a break in the coalition, Labour can call a motion of no confidence. If Lib Dems vote with the Tories against the motion of no confidence, they will be accused of propping up a minority Conservative government, meaning that left-leaning voters will have no reason to support them. Conversely, if they vote with Labour to bring down the Tories with the no-confidence motion, they will, at the very least, distance themselves from Tory voters in Lib Dem-Labour marginals even more than they already had. At this stage there would already be antagonism because the Lib Dems would have broken their promise to stay in the coalition till 2015. Thus, the lesser of evils would be to back the Labour no-confidence motion – in the hope of re-attracting left-leaning voters to the party. That is a tall hope given that the Lib Dem leader was, until recently before that point, also the 'number two' to a Tory Prime Minister. Abstention would be seen as weak and tantamount to backing the Conservative administration.

According to the legislation, if a no-confidence motion is passed parties have a fortnight to try to find a new arrangement which can garner the confidence of the House of Commons. If this did not occur, it would precipitate a general election, which could be highly damaging to the Lib Dems. All it takes is an ordinary, simple majority of MPs to pass the no-confidence motion. This actually makes the fixed-term legislation pointless as far any strategy to get out of the coalition is concerned. The mathematics of Parliament since the 2010 election mean that no other combination of two parties could govern with stability – apart from a Labour-Conservative partnership, which would not happen. Thus, either a new Lib Dem-Tory coalition would be formed or the country would go to the polls a fortnight later.

If the Conservatives were weak and Labour were strong Clegg would face the invidious question of a no-confidence vote against the Conservatives, knowing that the former coalition partner would retrench against the 'deal-breaking' Lib Dems as Labour retained the left-leaning votes on account of their polling strength. If the Tories were strong then Lib Dems would be squeezed by their strength at the polls, while again there would be little elasticity in the left-leaning vote, which would treat Clegg with suspicion.

What would Clegg instruct his colleagues to do? Back the Labour no-confidence motion, provoking Conservatives to shun the 'anti-Tory' Lib Dems? Vote with the Tories, against Labour's motion, making the break with the Tories appear merely tokenistic? Or abstain, which mathematically has the same effect of backing the Conservatives?

To summarise, for Clegg to break the coalition at a time when the Conservatives were strong could hasten a general election – with Cameron even having the latitude to send some of his own

MPs through the lobby to ensure that this was so. This would help the Tories, while doing nothing for Lib Dem support. For Clegg to break the coalition when Labour was strong would provoke a general election with little hope of lost left-leaning votes drifting back to the Lib Dems on the basis of this one gesture. In any of these scenarios the Tories would damn the Lib Dems as having betrayed them by leaving the coalition.

It follows that a 'Clegg-driven' break from the coalition is at the very least appallingly risky, except in the vanishingly unlikely scenario where the Liberal Democrats had somehow massively improved their polling performance at the cost of the other parties. In 2011, that seemed an unlikely scenario. The coalition could be a problem for the Lib Dems, but it was a problem that could not be solved by walking away from the arrangement.

Even if a resignation by Clegg might assist the left-leaning vote in the event of a coalition breakdown, this would be extremely dangerous during the collapse of the coalition. In fact, it may *prompt* a general election if others saw advantage in calling one while the Liberal Democrats were leaderless. During this period Lib Dems would leak support away to Labour *and* Conservatives. This is because both would generate 'scare stories' about who the next Lib Dem leader might be: the Tories would point to the most left-leaning candidate, and Labour to the most right-leaning candidate. Labour would also highlight the historical fact of the rightwing coalition. Meanwhile, Conservatives would cite the Lib Dems as unreliable: 'and who knows what the next leader's position will be on a coalition anyway?' All of this would occur as Lib Dem leadership candidates worked to differentiate themselves from each other in the party's electoral process. The party would be at risk of dreadfully mixed messages and competing personalities. Since, in the hierarchy of human behaviour, fear is a greater motivator than hope, the situation would be very off-putting to the electorate.

Also, who would speak for the party during the election and in televised debates? By precedent, it would be the Deputy Leader; in 2011 this was Simon Hughes. Hughes stood apart from the mainstream Orange Book. His style and opinions were more left-leaning. This fact might be the only redeeming feature for the party if an internal leadership election occurred during a general election, as Hughes might at least be heard by left-leaning voters.

To leave the timing of the succession to chance so that it might occur if the coalition collapsed would be very risky. More fundamentally, leaving the coalition does not save the leadership nor help the party if the leader and Deputy Prime Minister roles are not split. Without a managed departure by Clegg from the leadership – *but not necessarily from government* – a break could be catastrophic for the party because it could fall at the very worst time for the party.

Election strategy considerations 2012-2014

A 'joint slate' of Lib Dem and Conservative candidates has already been ruled out by both leaderships – and for very good reasons, as we saw in chapter 14. The coalition parties will compete at the next general election, under a first past the post system which does not favour the Lib Dems.

Liberal Democrats lost ground to Tories in the South of England and in Wales in May 2011. A repetition in a general election is quite possible. Where Lib Dems were second to Labour one may have hoped for Tory tactical votes, but there was no significant evidence of this in May 2011. There is no reason to think that Tories would be helpful to Lib Dems at the ballot box at the general election either.

Even without coalition breakdown, Labour will use the current Lib Dem leader's association with the Conservatives to attract former Lib Dem voters, as they did successfully in Northern England in 2011. They could raise the prospect of another Lib Dem coalition with the Conservatives, exhorting those who don't like the Tories to 'punish' Lib Dems for keeping Cameron in power.

Again, without a new leader it is hard to see how to create a sufficient discontinuity to create an authentic distance between the coalition government and the Lib Dem Party. In this scenario, the departure of Clegg from the leadership would leave the way open for the election of an individual who could re-attract the lost voters. Clegg's departure need not be a dramatic affair, nor one which heaps blame on him for issues facing the party at the ballot box. It simply becomes a sensible, politically smart change based on hard facts. In fact, if this is carried out during a period of stability for the coalition, splitting leadership from the Deputy Prime Ministership makes very good campaigning sense.

Furthermore, Clegg could then focus on delivering results in government, while the new party leader addressed challenges to the party, especially in an electoral sense in advance of the local and European elections, the latter unquestionably being a much greater challenge with the UK Independence Party working to become the primary alternative to Labour and Conservatives in the 2014 polls. A very poor result in the 2014 Euro-elections could be particularly harmful to Clegg if he were in charge at that point, given his association with the European Parliament, which had been his vehicle into. A new leader might provide something of a shield for Clegg, at the same time as focusing on resolving the issues facing the party in all the various elections.

Boundary changes from 2014

New constituency boundaries were proposed in October 2011, as part of the bill sponsored by Liberal Democrats Nick Clegg and Tom McNally. This was connected to legislation passed in association with the May 2011 AV referendum. This reduced the number of parliamentary seats from 650 to 600.[10] Conservatives believed that the new constituencies strongly favoured them, partly because of large reductions in the traditionally non-Tory Scotland and Wales.

In September 2011, Anthony Wells of UK Polling Report made an assessment of the impact on constituencies for. If the 2010 general election vote had occurred under the new boundaries, Wells estimated that Tories would have had five fewer seats, compared to 18 fewer for Labour and seven fewer for the Liberal Democrats. In percentage terms, that meant Tories would have lost only 2% of their seats; Labour would have lost 9%; and Liberal Democrats would have lost... 16%![11] Tories would have accrued further advantages from the reductions in Scotland and Wales, with Liberal Democrats losing perhaps three further seats, with an uncertain situation in Wales too. This meant that the total notional loss to the Lib Dem compliment of 57 seats could quite possibly be over one in six of all existing Liberal Democrat MPs! That was assuming that the party equalled the 23% share of the poll which it had secured in 2010. Overall, Labour were the second biggest losers in percentage terms, and with Conservatives losing by the fewest seats by a very great margin.

The Tory motivation for this change was plain to see. But it begged the question: with Liberal Democrats suffering such a massive loss of seats in the boundary changes, why on earth had the leadership allowed this change? Lib Dems affected by these reductions were naturally likely to become more rebellious and free-spirited in their actions in Parliament. Was this an example of Clegg's commitment to do what was 'not easy, but right'? Or had they simply not thought through the consequences to the party of the change? The bemusement was summed up by the succinct words of colourful Liberal Democrat MP for Leeds North West Greg Mulholland:

> When I saw the boundary changes I thought to myself, for ****'s sake, what were the party thinking? Couldn't they see what this was going do to the number of Lib Dem MPs?[12]

However unfathomable Lib Dem support for boundary changes

seemed, the new arrangements evidently made a general election much more attractive to the Tories. At their 2011 poll ratings, the Tories could form a majority government once the new constituencies were in place. If they could keep Lib Dems close in a 'non-aggression pact' until the new boundaries were active in 2014 they could then collapse the coalition and hold an early election. This might deliver for Cameron an overall majority, enabling him to govern without the nuisance of needing a coalition partner. Furthermore, if the Liberal Democrats could be provoked into making the break, events could play out as we outlined earlier. The Conservatives could do this by challenging the Lib Dems to vote for one or more Conservative policies which were utterly unacceptable to Lib Dems. One way or another, this provocation could quickly lead to a motion of no confidence, with all the pitfalls this brings to the door of Clegg and his party. If they achieved a gambit such as this, Conservatives could slam the Lib Dems as deal-breakers and try to cannibalise their support – while Labour kept hold of the left-leaning vote at the same time.

In this scenario – and unless the party can identify a way to win votes at the expense of the Conservatives – a close alliance with the tribal Conservatives becomes a potential death warrant to the coalition as soon as the new boundaries are in place in 2014. As Vince Cable said to Channel 4 News immediately after the AV debacle, 'we've been reminded that when they feel under pressure they are ruthless, calculating and really rather tribal.'[13] The same would be true if they sensed an opportunity to govern alone.

This danger makes January 2014 very important, as it is the first date at which the Tories might seriously consider provoking a breakdown in the coalition and a general election. If Clegg cannot deliver votes back to the party, as long as there are others who are considered more able to do so the alternative view believes that the current leader ought to stand down from the leadership in the run-up to the boundary changes, to enable his successor to become established enough to appeal to the leftwing vote in case of a snap election. Unless Clegg can prove his ability to re-engage that left-leaning electorate, it would be folly to continue to run the party once the boundaries make an election much more appealing to the Conservatives.

There is one further approach which could eliminate this danger altogether. If the Lib Dems were able to vote down the boundary changes then the Tories would have far less incentive to bring the date of the election forward. Time will tell whether this turned out to be feasible or whether, by late 2011, the commitment to boundaries had gone too far.

A *coup d'état*

A leadership election can be prompted by another potential candidate who evokes sufficient support from their colleagues to force the issue. An alternative view feels that this option is unlikely before 2013, and only then if the local election results prove to be a source of great concern. It is more likely that candidates will wait for other external factors to prompt discontent from the wider party, and then step forward once they can see that there is momentum. Being seen to pull down a leader is risky. If it fails, a long walk in the political wilderness is likely to be the penance.

There's an additional dilemma for would-be candidates, such as Chris Huhne. Firstly, any member of the Orange Bookers aspiring to power must be mindful that the removal of Clegg would draw attention to the Orange Book caucus led by him. Non-Orange Book candidates could legitimately challenge Orange Book candidates on the basis that they served the same agenda, and that this agenda had failed to deliver satisfactory results for the Lib Dems in the ballot box. Those associated with the Orange Book – for example, ministers – may decide that their best interests lie in sustaining Clegg's leadership as long as possible, in the hope that political circumstances will rehabilitate the caucus as a whole.

Nick Clegg was the man officially at the head of the coalition

The Alternative View

deal. He held the key relationship with the Prime Minister. Forcing Clegg to stand down speedily could therefore potentially harm the national interest by destabilising the government.

Ironically, Orange Book supporters, including Clegg and Huhne, actively participated in deposing former leader Charles Kennedy in January 2006. The alternative view is that their action was inappropriate then. It would be equally inappropriate to force the resignation of Clegg without a clear picture of the 'game plan' thereafter – such as the introduction of a clear narrative by someone clearly able to win back the lost voters. The construction of this kind of narrative did not happen after Kennedy's departure, nor upon Clegg's arrival. If Clegg could swiftly generate such a narrative, he might buy himself time as leader. But to truly avert a coup at some point, Clegg would need to demonstrate that he could rebuild the voter base. Otherwise, there would be increasing risks of a direct challenge right up to 2014, at which point it would become very probable indeed.

One potential 'wild card' coup could come from a disgruntled MP whose seat was being abolished thanks to the boundary changes. They'd have nothing to lose and could help themselves in their future endeavours by acting as a focal point for dissent. They could also look statesmanlike: 'It's nothing to do with the man, but the party needs a new vision and image which is separate to the coalition.' But, again, this is playing with fire. If momentum built behind this rebel yell, the rogue candidate could depose Clegg only to prompt his replacement with another Orange Booker. Unless they themselves won, they could perhaps change the leader's name while the political song remained the same. Of course, such is the nature of the beast that in this scenario the stalking horse could flush out others ready to run a full-power campaign to beat Clegg. Thus the rebel could indeed cause a revolution, even if they themselves could not win.

If significant momentum grew behind any one of these scenarios then the leadership could be forced into resigning – just as Kennedy was forced to do. By late 2011 there was still no cohesive opposition to the Orange Book leadership. Nevertheless, all of these possibilities were latent. It would only take an internal crisis to catalyse a challenge – maybe even from within the Orange Bookers themselves, as one or other offered themselves up as a safe pair of hands to guide the party out of the quagmire. In addition, if Clegg refused to resign from the leadership by 2014 then he could risk undermining the Orange Bookers as a unit, as they squabbled amongst themselves. And all the while, with the boundary changes looming, other ever more footloose MPs would be reviewing the situation.

If Clegg were forced to stand down in a coup it would be conceivable that the ministers he left behind could still continue in their roles. After all, Clegg had promised that the coalition would continue till the next general election. He might even be able to continue as Deputy Prime Minister – a position bestowed upon him by the Prime Minister, not the Liberal Democrats. However, a forced resignation would be ignominious and a very messy way to split the roles, while a coup would be especially dangerous if it happened at any time after the boundary changes because of the risk of an election. A handover before a potential general election would be far preferable to chaos at the top of the organisation during one.

Independent Scotland– a factor?

In a sense, the prospect of an independent Scotland is a factor which operates in a similar vein to the boundary changes, but with different implications. It does not directly prompt the resignation of the Liberal Democrat leader, but it could influence the date of the next general election, which would impact on Clegg if he were still in the role of leader at that point.

Everyone knew that the charismatic Scottish Nationalist Party leader – and First Minister of Scotland – Alex Salmond intended to hold a referendum on independence for his nation. He was just waiting for the right time. Polling carried out by ComRes and published in the *Independent* newspaper in October 2011 indicated that his chances were looking good with 49% saying 'Yes' to independence and 37% disagreeing.[14]

Despite their 'Unionist' credo, as far as Westminster were concerned it was in the Tory interest to see a 'Yes' vote. They never did well in Scotland and the disappearance of Scottish MPs from Westminster would markedly skew elections in what was left of Great Britain towards Tory majorities. Despite claiming to want to keep the kingdom united, they were also extremely pragmatic. How useful if Salmond won his referendum – especially if it did not appear to be anything to do with the Conservatives who, having emphatically opposed devolution in the past, had become supporters once the devolutionary settlements were in place. The prospect of a referendum in Scotland could therefore offer an ironic benefit to Conservatives.

A motivating factor influencing a 'Yes' vote in that nation could, at the same time, be the very fact that the Tories *were* in power in Westminster, and independence would liberate the mainly anti-Conservative Scots from ever being governed by them again.

How conceivable was it that the Conservatives might even attempt to facilitate all the details of the independence regulations prior to the referendum to encourage a 'Yes' vote? After all, if independence were introduced, the SNP and the Tories could both achieve benefits of power. In this scenario, Tories would have no further need for the Liberal Democrats, and once again the party would find itself in opposition. Clegg's resignation in this scenario would be little short of automatic, again in line with parliamentary etiquette for a leader who has led his party out of power. Furthermore, once the Tories could see a pathway to governing alone, it is hard to believe that they would not take it.

In reality, the Conservatives' visceral unionist tendencies are a powerful resisting force to any breakup. While there was clearly a divergence between its electoral interests and its unionist leanings, it was also clear that any such debate within the Conservative party would be held in private... though it would be highly surprising if party strategists had not quietly considered the matter.

Divide and rule

A leadership election serves no purpose in the event of a profound recovery in the popularity of the party, and of the leader. In this scenario, the current administration could safely continue in office up to a few months before the boundary changes. However, after that the Conservative interest is best served by cannibalising its junior partner's support base to secure an overall majority. The alternative view is that a Liberal Democrat Deputy Prime Minister who served under a Tory Prime Minister could not respond fast enough to differentiate the party. And proactively breaking the coalition is a non-starter for the reasons that we've looked at.

So we once again return to the compelling case for the division of the roles of party leader and Deputy Prime Minister. Nick Clegg could continue to rule in the government while leaving another person the role of party leader. Constitutionally, there is no stipulation which requires the Lib Dem Deputy Prime Minister to be the same person as the Lib Dem party leader. The two roles are politically independent. It is perfectly feasible for Clegg to play a leading role in government, while another individual plays a leading role in the party.

This splitting of roles has three other advantages.

Firstly, the separation of the Lib Dem leader and the Lib Dem Deputy Prime Minister provides a qualitative distinction between the roles. This resolves the confusion whereby, for example, comments primarily related to Clegg's governmental portfolio are interpreted as comments on behalf of the party. That is resolved if two people occupy one role each, instead of one person occupying both roles.

Secondly, a Lib Dem leader could campaign independently of the coalition's edicts. They could credibly generate messages which differentiate the parties even as the two govern together. The Tories achieve this through frequent statements by prominent Conservative spokespeople – ensuring that the Conservative narrative is regularly espoused. Empirically, it seems that the Liberal Democrats would do better to give their leader a freedom of expression to compete with the strength of messages that their coalition partner had become so adept at projecting.

Thirdly, the daily operational pressures of the role of Deputy Prime Minister make it virtually impossible for any one person to carry out those onerous functions at the same time as being the Liberal Democrat party leader. Running the country is not very compatible with running a party so heavily structured around democratic processes which demand an enormous commitment of time from the leader. By contrast, this is not the case for Conservative and Labour leaders. They are not tied into the intimate operational details of their parties in the way that the Liberal Democrat leader is. Without rewriting the Liberal Democrat constitution, the leader's role cannot be easily changed. As such, it is virtually impossible for anyone to be Deputy Prime Minister and Lib Dem party leader at once and do the jobs to their maximum potential.

Given the duties associated with being Deputy Prime Minister, the leader's role will unquestionably be the one at greater risk of compromise. This in turn can create serious difficulties, as members react to issues associated with a leader who is limited in the time that he can spend dealing with them. All of that can be avoided by splitting the roles. It also has the added benefit of enabling the leader to act as the guardian of the party's interests through the interface with the Deputy Prime Minister.

Splitting the roles is the only mechanism through which the coalition can realistically continue up to 2015, while also generating a visible separate identity for the Lib Dems from government and its coalition partners. For Clegg to continue as leader up to the dissolution of Parliament gives insufficient opportunity – or time – to do so. It is not realistic to believe, after having presided over the Lib Dem side of that partnership for a full five years, that 35 days would be enough to win back the lost left-leaning voters.

The leadership may find an as-yet-undiscovered and radical solution to alter the fortunes of the party. But good government is not it: a strong economic recovery may improve the government's popularity, but it does not help Lib Dems much because it's not a differentiator from the Tories. If the Liberal Democrat election performance does not improve by May 2013 at the very latest, an alternative view can see no other way to achieve what's best for the country – and the Liberal Democrats – than to split the roles, something which would make sense if it occurred now, and certainly not later than 2013.

Leadership election after 2015

If Clegg were able to remain leader till 2015 the only possible scenario would be his resignation immediately after the election. By 2011, it was obvious that he could not achieve his goal of doubling the number of MPs – a key promise that he made, and reiterated, for his leadership. Even if he presided over some growth, there were too many other factors which stood in the way – not least Labour's venom towards him and the lack of viability of a second coalition with the Tories. As such, the very longest he could delay his announcement of the intention to step down was already written in stone: the day before the next general election. There was no prospect whatsoever of a longer tenure.

By 2011 the party had declined to its lowest number of council seats since 1986, and had suffered its biggest numerical decline in

MPs since 1970. The next general election was not looking too promising. To continue to lead the party if Clegg and his Orange Book caucus had presided over poor results would be pointless and damaging to the party's development. At a subsidiary level, we have already noted the etiquette that when a party leaves government it usually means that the leader resigns. Clegg's views on this have never been publicly expressed, but the expectation that he would step down would itself be a big pressure to do so.

As a thought experiment, let's ask what would happen if Clegg still ran the party after the next general election and tried to make a coalition with the Tories. If they had an overall majority, he would be breaking his 2008 promise not to do so. If they were in minority, it is unrealistic to think that the party would buy it, especially if they had declined thanks to the previous one. The possibility of a split – as feared by Clegg's chief of staff, Danny Alexander, prior to the 2010 election – would become a very high probability, with the Left separating off or seeking new alliances outside the Lib Dem fold. Clegg couldn't carry through a second coalition deal with the Conservatives without incurring enormous collateral damage.

Conservatives might invite individuals from the Liberal Democrats, as they had done with David Laws. If this offer were extended to anyone, it would certainly be extended to Clegg himself. Again, none of these options protect Clegg's position as party leader. In any practical sense, therefore, even a gambit to continue in a Conservative partnership heralds the end of Clegg's leadership. Instead of splitting his roles, it could split the party.

Positioning of the new leader

As we have noted, a necessary – but not sufficient – condition for the electoral success of a new leader would be to reject coalition with Conservatives when the current coalition ends. This is crucial for left-leaning voters. It widens other options for the party, by plausibly opening up the theoretical possibility of an arrangement with Labour. A leader chosen before 2014 could have the time to ensure that a credible alternative view of the party restores its chances to perform well at all tiers by opening its appeal out to a wider electorate. Unless this action is taken, Liberal Democrats face a decline to their core vote. This appeared to be around 16% in May 2011, with many polls putting Lib Dem support at around 10% for much of the year.

Summary

Lib Dems need to refocus on their narrative, image, policy and leadership approach. Unless they do, they risk being corralled into a compromising electoral position by the Conservatives and Labour. The idea of collaboration between Liberal Democrats and Labour with Clegg as leader is a non-starter. The alternative view also believes that a Conservative-Liberal Democrat coalition after the next election, once the boundaries change to favour the Tories – and after five years of partnership – is politically implausible as far as the membership is concerned.

All the same, a leadership election is undesirable before the leadership has had the opportunity to try to reverse the party's fortunes to achieve positive growth in 2012. They should be given the time to revisit their political narrative and test it then and, if these results are promising, potentially also in 2013.

However, since the role of Deputy Prime Minister can be split from the role of leader, this should be done before 2014 – the time after which a general election might be called. Dividing up the two jobs offers a sensible, robust, practical solution to sustaining the coalition while liberating Lib Dems to rebuild the party's credibility with the essential left-leaning vote. Given the predatory nature of the Conservatives towards the Lib Dems in elections, even during the coalition, any attempt by Clegg to lead the party into the next general election – when he will inevitably miss his own growth targets anyway – would not be right for the movement. The leadership – and the party – need to consider which scenario best offers a managed succession in the interests of the country and the party. Splitting the two roles seems the most elegant.

We believe that Clegg's leadership will end in 2013-14, possibly with a coup to oust him catalysed by the grassroots up to 2014, or possibly by the parliamentary party from that time onwards. In the improbable scenario whereby he were to lead the party into the next general election he would resign immediately afterwards. There is no plausible circumstance in which he could extend his tenure beyond this time for all the reasons we have seen.

With the measurable decline in local government strength – a robust indicator of the likely outcome of the next general election – another leader needs time to re-attract lost votes while Clegg continues as Deputy Prime Minister till the end of the coalition.

However harsh this analysis may seem, it is impossible to construct any other realistic scenarios. A mature appraisal mitigates towards succession planning to ensure that the party's future is not harmed by the doubling up of two tremendously important roles in one person. Nick Clegg ought to relinquish the leadership of the party before the next election, and continue as Deputy Prime Minister. Our view can only be advisory, but we suspect that it will grow into a political imperative of its own accord if proactive steps are not taken. To deny this will simply damage the party's fortunes for no advantage to anyone except the two other main parties. Clegg can yet make a huge contribution to government on behalf of the Liberal Democrat agenda – but he cannot do it to his best ability as long as he is also attempting to lead the party.

Chapter 16

Clegg's Defence

My conscience is clear on one fundamental belief I have... it is that we're doing the right thing for the long term for the country – but I'm acutely aware we're facing difficulties in the short term as a party.
Nick Clegg, 10 August 2011

If we don't tell our story, then no-one else will.
Nick Clegg, 10 August 2011

The alternative view is determined to present a balanced thesis. In order to provide a flavour of the leader's own perspective on some of the matters we have discussed, we present an abridged summary of his comments from a question-and-answer session conducted in summer 2011.[1] The alternative view has limited itself to a few short observations at the end, which the reader is evidently at liberty to read or skip. Our comments in this chapter are deliberately not pivotal to the observations that we make in the final chapter.

Context

Nick Clegg commenced a series of meetings with party members and others on 10 August, 2011. This was the launch of his consultation exercise, with the intention of rebuilding his relationship with rank and file members. His goal was to discuss, with the activist base, the state of the party and its recent electoral difficulties, as well as the opportunities ahead. The aim was also to attempt to settle some of the discontent which had been brewing.

The approach taken by Clegg is highly instructive in helping us to understand his own grasp of the condition of the party, what had gone wrong and what was required to fix it. The alternative view felt it necessary to report Clegg in his own words as far as practicable, and to provide an appropriate platform for what he said in the session – even if not everything that he suggested or observed necessarily contributes, or is directly salient, to the thesis that we have put forward in our own analysis.

While others have sought to report Clegg's members' sessions from a particular angle, our report is intended to be neutral and indicative of the overall approach that he took to the issues under discussion. Clegg has also made most or all of these observations in other public forums. Nevertheless, we report it as it was, to give what we hope is an objective flavour of Clegg's engagement with the membership and members of the public in the summer of 2011.

Around 200 people attended the first meeting, which had been organised to take place at 1pm in the National Liberal Club's Lloyd George Room, in the heart of Whitehall.

Clegg's comments

Clegg began by outlining the purpose of the exercise.

> The reason this meeting was established in the first place was to spend some time with Liberal Democrats talking about the Liberal Democrats.

Clegg's Defence

He sought, early on, to acknowledge the growing concerns in the party.

> I'm acutely aware it's been a rollercoaster for the last year and a bit, and it's not been a wholly comfortable one for us.

Clegg cited the local election results. 'A large number of friends and colleagues lost seats in May.'

Clegg moved on to outline his core message – the journey the Liberal Democrats had taken into government, and the changes this had forced upon the movement.

'We used to be universally inoffensive.' However, in government this inoffensive image could no longer be maintained. 'We've had to make some divisive, and depressing, decisions,' Clegg said, 'at a time of unprecedented difficulty,' to assist in the task of 'restoring sense to public finances.' Clegg focused heavily on the economic challenges affecting policymaking, and the party's role in the decisions which had to be made to restore order to Britain's financial future.

> We face a very acute dilemma as a party, because we are having to extricate ourselves from a way of doing things at a time when things have gone spectacularly wrong.

He outlined the background to the economic problems.

> It was an illusion of prosperity, it was an illusion of growth... credit card debts that we couldn't repay... totally unsustainable property prices... the government borrowing money which they couldn't repay, spending money which they couldn't afford.

Pointing out that the housing market had collapsed, Clegg then extended the analysis beyond the actions of the previous administration.

> I think it's not just the Labour government... It goes back to the big bang in the 1980s... we have to deal with the IOUs.

He emphasised the need for a socially sustainable approach to the immediate future.

Then Clegg turned to the plight of the Liberal Democrats, aiming to separate the short-term difficulties from the longer-term agenda for the country and the party. 'Our problem, I think, as a party is, I believe, sure we made mistakes – of course we *do* – but long-term it's absolutely right.' He acknowledged that 'long-term is no good if you're fighting a by-election next Thursday.' And here Clegg began to offer a viewpoint which implied the need for the party not to lose its mettle.

> My conscience is clear on one fundamental belief I have... it is that we're doing the right thing for the long term for the country – but I'm acutely aware we're facing difficulties in the short term as a party.

Clegg highlighted his view of the fact that the Liberal Democrats had suffered the problem of being misrepresented.

> Labour lie about us... Just remember about Labour that if they were in government they would do almost exactly the same thing. For every £8 we're cutting they would have cut £7. It's treating people with contempt for Labour to pretend otherwise. Even after all these difficult decisions, we – this government, your government – will be spending about 41% of national wealth on public spending... roughly the same as 2009.

Clegg then turned to the national media, and particularly towards criticisms which had been levelled at the Lib Dems. 'The *Daily Mail* and *Guardian* have become almost interchangeable.' He claimed that the other parties had sympathetic supporters in the national media but the Liberal Democrats were persistently attacked, for partisan reasons, by those media outlets sympathetic to Labour and Conservative philosophies.

'If we're not self-confident as Lib Dems about what we're trying to do, nobody else is.' He was indignant about some of the claims he felt were being ranged against the party, particularly the 'absurd allegation that we're turning the clock back to the 1930s.' He also appealed to the common sense of the wider public about the challenges facing the country. 'I think there's a sort of big picture thing which I think people intuitively know – we're in a real mess and we're trying to get out of it.'

Clegg emphasised his desire not to leave a legacy of debt for the future. 'The generational thing is very important.' Clegg wanted to 'wipe the slate clean for the next generation.'

Then he turned to the achievements of the Liberal Democrats in government –

> specific things people don't hear about at all that we're doing in government that are really good: child care; 250,000 more apprenticeships because of Liberal Democrats in government; over one million people taken out of tax; the pensions-earnings link restored because of Liberal Democrats in government.

Clegg felt that the story was not being told in a manner favourable to the party.

> It's really important that we also tell the other side of the story which will make the difference.

In a wide ranging series of questions, Clegg was asked about very specific, tactical and general strategic matters. In response to concerns about the impact of the Welfare Reform Bill on disabled people who, the questioner claimed, would suffer a real cut in income, Clegg responded:

> On welfare changes I just need to know a little bit more about the specifics you've got in mind. You first simplify the benefits system and remove the disincentive to work... On the question of tests being applied to Invalidity Benefit, if you look at the figures – a very large number of people decided voluntarily they were no longer going to access IB.

Clegg claimed that this 'shows it's not wrong' to test people for Invalidity Benefit eligibility. He praised a fellow Liberal Democrat minister in the department concerned: 'Steve Webb at the Department for Work and Pensions is doing an exceptionally good job of it.' Clegg finished his answer by backing the reforms. 'I kind of rile against this idea that we should have left IB untouched.'

In response to criticism that Clegg had been insufficiently visible in the immediate aftermath of the so-called 'riots' in London in August 2011, which had just been brought under control the day before the session, Clegg replied,

> Well, I was around on Monday when I went to Tottenham and was very visible. Cameron returned on Monday night and we reconvened COBRA [the emergency planning committee of the British Government] on Tuesday night. I was not going to ring Cameron to say 'please could you stay away because I want to look in charge.' I totally get that it would be nice to think that I should be able to stand on the steps of Number 10 and say Nick Clegg's in charge. I'm not the PM – we didn't win the general election – we have 8% of MPs in.

Clegg said that, given the mathematics, it was not realistic to think of the Liberal Democrats being in a position to deliver all their manifesto commitments.

> Sorry, we're in a coalition government. When people said 'you didn't deliver your manifesto,' damn right we can't! We didn't win.

Clegg returned to the successes on childcare.

> I'm an absolute passionate believer in what we're doing for childcare, for early years education. I'm proud of the fact we've taken some very radical decisions.

Another questioner challenged the Liberal Democrat failure to lobby against UK military involvement UK military involvement in Libya against Colonel Gaddafi.

> Just imagine if Gaddafi had gone into Benghazi and said 'I'm going to go in and kill these people.' I'm an unashamed liberal internationalist – I'm a liberal interventionist when it's justified. You either believe that human rights are a universal concern or you don't. One of the things that define the Liberal [Democrat] party is our care for rights around the world. I think the moral and legal difference between what we're trying to do in Libya, with full legal evidence published by this government, utterly separates off what we're doing in Libya from Iraq.

Defending the intervention, Clegg said 'it would be a grave mistake for us to turn our backs on our long tradition… and turn our backs.'

Clegg then commented that he did not think that policy U-turns were a particular issue on the doorstep for activists canvassing for votes. 'I spend less time on the doorstep than I used to, but I would be surprised if that comes up a lot on the doorstep.' He also defended the position the party had taken in opposition to the

National Health Service reforms as originally laid out, and which had been originally implicitly supported by the party. 'On the NHS it would have been bone-headed to carry on given the objections.'

Clegg was then challenged about the close association of the Liberal Democrats with the Conservatives. The questioner said:

> I can understand the benefits of being in government and being a Lib Dem minister. You've had a go at bashing Labour. But my worry is really with the Tory party. I'm extremely concerned that we're supporting a government with the likes of Andrew Lansley... I think you've got to be a lot tougher... we've got a big problem all over London about reconnecting with young people... the joke early on in coalition was that we were the human shield for the Tories – there doesn't seem very much externally explaining what we're doing.

Clegg responded with a semi-joking quip about how the party made decisions. 'I'm just the leader of the party. I get my wrists slapped if I make this suggestion or that.' Then he developed his answer in a different direction.

> Let me be honest with you. Are we the human shield for the Tories? Am I carrying the can for bad news? How do we differentiate ourselves? Yes, some serious mistakes have been made over the last year. I think for a time we were completely in the wrong place politically, it was very personal against me. I certainly made clear I learned my lesson. I hope you've started to see a change. But it's not all me!

Clegg explained that there was

> a big difference in the culture of the leadership of Conservative Party and us. The Conservatives protect their leader – until they

slit their throat! We have a slightly different attitude towards leaders. We put up with leaders for years – constantly complaining about them!

The audience found this amusing and appeared to relate to the analogy.

Clegg continued, 'handling issues learned over last year, I find myself relaxed that we will be differentiated from the Conservatives.' He ridiculed the 'laughable suggestion that we could sort of mutate into each other.' Clegg cited the disagreement over 'who gets tax cuts first,' rich or poor. 'You can't open a newspaper these days without seeing traces of differences.' Clegg expressly dismissed the idea of negative campaigning against the Prime Minister.

> I won't indulge in it. There's no point in me as Deputy Prime Minister calling David Cameron names. We are in coalition with them. That is part of the deal. You can be different – you don't have to be rude.

Clegg also expected the public to be well able to understand the distinctions between the two parties, in a way which may not be apparent to political activists.

> We are abnormal – we're talking about politics. The vast majority of people aren't politicians. That balance between differentiation will become clear as daylight. It's a balance we can strike in the long run. If we prove the benefits of difficult decisions we take now, there will be many non-partisan people in the country who appreciate what we're doing.

Clegg added that there would be 'something seriously wrong' if the Liberal Democrats failed to get their message across in the forthcoming period.

He then returned to the bias he saw against the party in the media and elsewhere.

> Stop for a moment and think: what happens when Liberal Democrats go into government? The right and left hate that we're in government at all, unless you can rustle up some great newspaper proprietor who can bombard Liberal Democrat propaganda across the country. We are really, really upsetting the normal order of politics in this country. We're messing up the normal pendulum system, so of course it is a bit lonely.

But it was still up to the Liberal Democrats to sell their message. 'If we don't tell our story, then no-one else will.'

Another questioner asked if the party would be fighting the next general election in coalition, on the basis that ministers remain in post during an election, even after Parliament has been dissolved.

> We will fight the next general election as a fully independent party which has governed in this coalition for five years. Elections are fought about the future, not the past. If I were Labour, I'd fight the next election a bit like 1945.

Clegg suggested the Labour position would be to say that

> '"these people have done the difficult stuff," but that Labour should now be able to take over.'

Clegg explained the pressures of ministerial power, stating that 'we're quite overstretched in government.' He said he wanted the Lib Dems to

> start defining our own vision in future. I sometimes feel people forget the circumstances that led us to coalition in the first

place. There was mass unrest in Greece, a summit of European Union finance ministers. I was being telephoned over the weekend to say that if we didn't form a stable government within days, there would be a real risk of meltdown. Imagine what the alternative would have been like. We were on the precipice. I think we wouldn't have been forgiven for a generation. It would have been an unforgivable betrayal.

Clegg predicted the country would be out of the economic difficulties by 2015.

A questioner asked why the party could not be 'anti-Tory' and stay in government at the same time. Clegg did not offer a specific answer, but he may have felt that an earlier answer had already covered this point.

When tempted to criticise the BBC as being a 'part of Labour,' Clegg said it was 'very dangerous territory to try to start to tell the media how to do its job.'

Another questioner asked if the state of the world economy risked bringing down everything the government was doing economically. Clegg was sympathetic to the concern. Speaking of the international markets, he said

> we don't have any direct control on them. We are hugely interested in them making the reforms necessary to make the European Union stable, which means another step towards greater integration.

Clegg also cited '£18 billion investment in green energy' and said that 'Vince [Cable] has been very active [in that field]'.

Another inquiry related to constituency boundary changes which would have a big impact on Liberal Democrat fortunes. Clegg replied that

> the Boundary Commission will publish first drafts of what the maps will look like, and there will be a vote in the Commons and Lords. I think it is better to have constituencies which have roughly the same number of constituents in them – it is fair. I have heard apocalyptic scenarios about what will happen to my constituency in Sheffield.

His tone of voice on this issue appeared reassuring.

Asked if the target to double the number of MPs in the next general election still stood, Clegg replied:

> Doubling. Well yes. You know, let's just stick with it. We are in government but we lost MPs at the last election and we need to understand why we lost MPs. I know things went wrong in a few seats, but why didn't we win new seats? A week before the election we did a whole lot of telephone canvassing, and we were told we would win a dozen seats off Labour in the North. Something went seriously wrong. The answer that came back was absolutely universal, overwhelming and consistent: 'but these are difficult times and we don't think you're up to it. It's a time for grown-ups. We didn't think we could risk voting Liberal Democrat this time.' They didn't think we should govern.

A questioner again asked about differentiating from the other parties, commenting that it would be wrong to move to the left, and that the Liberal Democrats ought to be battling for the centre ground. The individual said that the Big Society was a social liberal idea and that 'Cameron got it straight out of the Orange Book – many modernising Tories have become liberals.'

Clegg replied,

> I have written pamphlets on this and I will do it again. I can't bear left-right language. We are not a 'leftwing' party or

'rightwing' party. We are quite... separate to the paternalising collectivism of Labour – and the pessimism of Conservatism. The three basic views of life in politics are the Conservative view: 'things should be conserved as they are'; the Labour view *was* a noble view – creation of the welfare state, emancipation of millions of working men and women with the state being a battering ram for a social programme; and the *liberal* view starts and finishes, above everything else, with a belief that we should cherish individuals. We are there to make sure that the full potential of each individual is achieved in society. We should not use... terms and distinctions which are not ours. At times of anxiety, we have a sane, sensible reasoned liberal voice in government.

After about an hour, the meeting concluded.

Commentary

Nick Clegg's style of presentation was authoritative and energetic. The alternative view believes that it is safe to assume that he achieved the same level of communicative ability elsewhere around the country.

He focused on themes which he had frequently returned to – long-term rewards from difficult decisions in government, with the harvest being reaped by the next general election in 2015. He had been careful to acknowledge the reversals in elections, including by-elections, and inferred that these were an interim cost – a point repeated in his speech to conference in September 2011.

Clegg was again very clear about his intention to remain in coalition up to the next general election, which he clearly believed would be in 2015. One questioner had insightfully observed that ministers continue executive roles during the election, to ensure that the country is still being governed. Clegg said that the party will have 'governed in this coalition for five years.' It seems fair to assume that Lib Dem ministers would therefore serve according to the normal etiquette; he did not suggest otherwise. If the coalition lasted for the full term, it is hard to see any other arrangement, without forcing a spurious Tory reshuffle on the eve of the election – which could easily backfire on Lib Dems who could then be labelled as 'deal-breakers'. Pulling out even a few months before the election would enable Conservatives to fill Lib Dem vacancies, 'proving' that they could govern alone – while attacking Lib Dems for putting party before country. It seems therefore that Clegg's plan was for Liberal Democrats to fight the Conservatives while running the country with them as ministers – at the same time as fighting Labour. This would be the obvious consequence of Clegg's five-year coalition commitment.

Clegg was clearly conscious of activists' concerns in regard to the May 2011 local election results. He appreciated worries about the coalition's impact on electoral fortunes, and the need for distinctiveness:

> 'We should not use… terms and distinctions which are not ours. At times of anxiety, we have a sane, sensible, reasoned liberal voice in government.'

The alternative view believes that 'muscular liberalism' fits Clegg's category of 'terms and distinctions which are not ours.' The alternative view holds that it is a Conservative construct defined by Cameron in early 2011 – and therefore should not be used by the Liberal Democrats.

Chapter 17

The Way Back

There is a tide in the affairs of men,
Which, taken at the flood, leads on to fortune;
Omitted, all the voyage of their life
Is bound in shallows and in miseries.
On such a full sea we are now afloat,
And we must take the current when it serves,
Or lose our ventures.

William Shakespeare, *Julius Caesar*, 1599

... with hard choices every day... For liberals, the litmus test is always the national interest. Not doing the easy thing. Doing the right thing.

Nick Clegg, 21 September 2011

The coalition brought with it a period of reversals and worry for the movement. After the advent of the pact, few spoke of visionary hopes for a radical majority Liberal Democrat government. There was a palpable downgrading of ambitions – to win back what had been lost in the recent past, rather than to forge ahead towards a

Liberal Democrat future. This chapter offers thoughts of a return to that inspired vision.

We hold that the only limits to the capacity of the organisation to finish what it started so long ago are self-confidence, resolve and a large dose of common sense. Our action steps are the logical conclusion of our analysis and embrace a deeply optimistic perspective for the liberal vision.

Our assumption is that the liberal movement is at its best when it finds inspiration in its long-term motivations, instead of wallowing in frustration at its short-term tribulations. Our analysis also indicates that the party's poor performance in the polls is not a 'given'. If the organisation takes the right structural and strategic decisions now, it can benefit enormously from its authority as a party in government. It can also build its narrative and image as a clear-minded counterpoint to the Tories, while expanding its campaigning capacity outside, especially at the local community level. The steps are not complicated. They just need application, methodical commitment and a team spirit, especially from the current leadership.

The starting point is creating a firm foundation – and doing so now, before the opportunity is lost: as Shakespeare's Julius Caesar observes, 'There is a tide in the affairs of men, which, taken at the flood, leads on to fortune.' Julius Caesar may be far from the minds of most activists, but the sentiments apply to them all. Everything has to be in place by 2014, the year in which the general election could occur if the Tories regard it as expedient to trigger one when the boundary changes which are so advantageous to them could come into force.

One more point. Despite the leadership's repeated reassurances to the membership that the rewards for good government will come in a few years, this is a shaky strategy. The prowess of Liberal Democrat ministers in the corridors of power will not deliver a stronger campaigning base – nor a clear narrative and image. Their role is implementation in government more than planning the strategic future of the party.

Members can point to Labour and Conservative councillors who sit where Lib Dems used to be, and watch the ministers – expectantly awaiting the plan to win these seats back. That plan must come from the party, not the government, and the role of the ministers has become blurred between the two.

Clegg promised that he would not rest until he delivered this in his September 2011 speech to conference.[1] The grassroots want that breakthrough – they want results which retrieve decades of local government advances which were lost in one night in May 2011. So, we now summarise what we believe constitutes the way back for the Liberal Democrats.

Focus on community politics

Clegg's prudent local government commitment to win back all the Liberal Democrat council seats lost in May 2011 becomes much more achievable with a clear narrative, image, policies and the demarcation of the leader's role from government.

Remember that 1997 was the Liberal Democrats' most successful general election since 1923 – and it coincided with a period during which Lib Dems were also the second party of local government.[2] The vision of a Liberal Democrat government lives in the leaflets, street activity and campaigns of local community politics. Steady advances at ward level build the triumphs of the movement as a force across the country.

The sure start for long-term growth is thus at the council level. Investing in local authority wards across the country sows the seeds for the harvest in the medium and long term much more than sporadic – largely unwinnable – parliamentary by-elections. It also nurtures an understanding in those advancing towards Westminster of what Tip O'Neill recalled in the words of his father, who told him 'all politics is local.' To a Liberal Democrat, the appreciation of the value of community politics is a priceless education. Winning parliamentary seats is almost a byproduct of this process. This is why the alternative view holds that it would be highly desirable for all who stand for Parliament to have necessarily at least stood as a local authority candidate prior to fighting a parliamentary constituency.

Focus on narrative

The party must begin refocusing on its narrative – the movement's worldview, a description of its ideal society in terms of what happens in it, how it happens and the values which its citizens display in their behaviour. This means re-establishing a clear and consistent vision – one which the public could easily grasp as uniquely Liberal Democrat. This is not about individual policies – the narrative underpins them all.

This will prevent the party from being overshadowed by its coalition partner. A common voice using consistent ideas creates a sense of identity and purpose, separate to the identity of the 'government' as a collective unit.

The Orange Book is not bound by any such narrative, even if some shared elements crop up – especially in terms of a right-leaning economic agenda. Nor is muscular liberalism a narrative for the party; it is a Trojan horse construct, offered to the Lib Dems for the convenience of the Tory agenda.

The party's true narrative binds and focuses the whole movement in a common, genuinely liberal, direction – so that its energy is directed towards the same vision. It is about truly valuing people, protecting their freedoms and liberating them from poverty, ignorance and conformity. It comes to life when the movement's representatives grasp it, believe in it and want to sell it to society. This common value system needs to be a foundation beneath everything else the movement does. It is the Liberal Democrats' reason for existing.

To rekindle the Liberal Democrats' narrative, the alternative view suggests a process of engagement with representatives of local government, Welsh and Scottish Parliaments, both chambers in the British Parliament and in the European Parliament, plus those involved in the interface between the party and the people – the grassroots activists. We envisage that by involving, say, 300 contributors across six months, and ensuring that the process is properly facilitated, a narrative can be constructed which will stand the test of time – built on core values which will evolve into pin-sharp clarity in the development process.

Focus on image

With its narrative established, the organisation can clarify its image – or branding – the style through which the movement projects itself, its people and policies. This is the party's personality.

The party needs to understand where it wants to sit on the Nolan Chart, a tool to identify the economic and social positioning of the organisation. Identifying this clearly can give the party great confidence in standing its ground, because it will know what that ground is. This prevents the party from being driven towards convergence with other parties through a lack of political clarity or the pressures of fashion. The party can then offer policies which others cannot – or dare not – offer. It will also protect the party from hostages to fortune, such as the tuition fees debacle, by guiding its chief practitioners to work according to that image and the narrative behind it.

The party can also hone its image to fit the operational methods which work best, such as community politics. This could form a central element in the personality of the party and how it is seen by others. If projected effectively, the image ensures that there is no question of Liberal Democrats ever being confused with Conservatives. It can also guarantee a positive campaigning ethos, as opposed to the flawed practice of negative campaigning.

The image will be resonant and compelling for those who are potentially sympathetic to the liberal cause.

Focus on policies

The alternative view has proposed some policies for consideration. However, what matters more than anything is that, once the narrative and image have been comprehensively established, the policy agenda needs to flow naturally from these. Perhaps some of those ideas put forward by the alternative view will find purchase, but that is a matter for the movement once it has clarified its narrative (its worldview) and image (its personality).

Focus on leadership

The alternative view is adamant that, to make the most of the breathtaking opportunity which being in government offers the organisation, it is vital to split the roles of Deputy Prime Minister and leader before 2014. No other solution will be sustainable up to the next election without considerable internal strife – and external damage to the party's fortunes.

A new leader can reach out more to voters on the left who largely returned to the Labour fold after 2010. A new leader can focus their team around creating and promoting the common narrative – the touchstone for the organisation's image and policies. The leadership team can devote themselves to sharing its crystal-clear agenda and policies with the country – with activists, members and the wider public. This provides the independence of word and deed which the party craves, and which differentiates it from the Conservatives with unambiguous precision.

Clegg as Deputy Prime Minister will be liberated to focus on maximising results by the ministerial team in government, ensuring that Liberal Democrat activity is fully in line with the party's narrative and image too. Where there is divergence in policy this can be done transparently, with an honest, logical explanation of the nature of the divergence, and its place in the overall context of its relevance to government from a Lib Dem perspective.

The leader and Deputy Prime Minister will work together to get the most out of the political opportunities that government provides – and the best out of the campaigning opportunities that the activist base supplies. This synergy has the capacity to turbocharge the effectiveness of the organisation, radiating from the centre out.

Tensions between the ministerial team and the leadership team should be regarded as a stimulant, not a curse. Such pressures test thinking and often lead to 'third alternatives' which can be far better than the 'first and second alternatives'. It is a highly productive model to create solutions – and it's wholly appropriate for a positive-minded movement such at the Liberal Democrats.

Some practicalities

By late 2011 the Liberal Democrat fall in the polls was at least 8 percentage points – primarily to the benefit of Labour. These votes must be either replaced or won back.

In an interesting gambit, Clegg evoked the peculiar vision of some mysterious legion of liberal-minded citizens, who might be persuaded to rise up and come to the party's assistance at the ballot box in its hour of need. Clegg has christened this enigmatic division of fellow travellers 'Alarm Clock Britain'.[3] The hope of redemption from this – up to now invisible and dormant – throng of citizens seems, to put it politely, a little fanciful. No methodology had been put in place to 'wake these people up' and get them to go and vote Lib Dem. Certainly, by late 2011, the evidence suggested that these supposed Lib Dem supporters had slept right through the alarm. It seems probable that more conventional sources of potential Lib Dem supporters need to be found.

Lib Dem strategists would also do well to remember that Conservatives who had not voted Liberal Democrat in the past are not likely to vote Liberal Democrat in future, regardless of the coalition. This was the experience in elections since May 2010 when the coalition began. The Right do not offer electoral salvation for their Lib Dem coalition partners. Thus Lib Dems are left with the need to win back left-leaning voters, lost at great cost to the Lib Dem local government base. This is a powerful pointer towards the kind of narrative which would work best for Liberal Democrats – one which resonates with the left of the Liberal Democrat support base.

Again, splitting the roles of Deputy Prime Minister and leader seems instrumental in making this possible. One heads the government team, where the Lib Dems – mostly Orange Bookers – have a reasonable working relationship with their coalition partners. In parallel, the leader heads the organisation's non-governmental activity externally, working with the president to build the party's campaigning base internally and win back votes which Clegg would not be able to access for the party. The triumvirate of Deputy Prime Minister, leader and president forms a tremendously powerful triangle of influence at the centre of the party, where the three roles are already clearly defined and offer no conflict of authority – since the Deputy Prime Minister's role is not written into the party's constitution.[4]

Under this arrangement, Clegg can also sustain the coalition arrangement for the full five-year term, as he promised, as the ministers can serve their time in power. Simultaneously, the leader can publicly lead preparations to run effective election campaigns at local and European levels, applying the concepts of community politics and creating a vibrant agenda for the general election. The messages will be clear-cut, distinctively liberal and free from the blurring of messages which being Deputy Prime Minister and leader at the same time had inadvertently caused.

What should Liberal Democrats aim for?

The Liberal Democrats should aim for power... as a government in their own right. Only a council of despair would abandon this long-term ambition, and much has been said by leaders of the past about the importance of cherishing this heartfelt aspiration for the future. By contrast, the dream of opposition is one loaded with a poverty of ambition, and, as a preferred destination, ought to be rejected.

American management guru Peter Drucker observed:

> Effective leadership is not about making speeches or being liked; leadership is defined by results, not attributes.[5]

Well, we know the leadership's medium-term targets, because Clegg has set them: 124 MPs and the winning back of the 748 council seats lost in May 2011. These are both extremely tall orders in the short term, and it may be that a degree of reassessment may be required with a change of leadership.

Reference to history gives us a clearer view of what is necessary for various parliamentary targets to be achieved. When the Lib Dems doubled their parliamentary representation in 1997, they entered the general election with over 5,000 local council seats – in second place behind Labour and ahead of the Conservatives.[6] In the run-up to 2001 it held 4,400 council seats. In the run-up to the 2005 general election, the figure was 4,700 seats.[7] In 2010 – when the number of MPs declined – the party had entered the election with under 4,100 seats.[8] By the end of 2011, it held just over 3,000.[9] The last time it had roughly that number of councillors, it held about two dozen MPs.[10]

The alternative view estimates that to have any chance of even holding the number of MPs it had after 2010 the Liberal Democrats need to hold over 4,000 local authority seats by the time of the next general election. To continue making growth, it needs over 4,400.

To make the kind of breakthroughs Clegg had committed to requires in excess of 6,000 seats, and probably nearer 6,500. To become the largest party in Parliament would require over 8,500 local authority seats. Others may wish to refine these estimates. Also, the 'spread' of councillors – in other words, how concentrated they are in particular constituencies – is important. Additionally, our analysis of the records seems to indicate a threshold of councillors above which the number of MPs increases at a *disproportionately* greater rate versus the increase in councillors. Notwithstanding these refinements, the crucial point the leadership needs to actively acknowledge is that MP gains are founded on local government success.

As such, Clegg's local government target is really only deliverable through the community politics route. The length of time it will take to do it is dependent on the speed with which the party refocuses on this target, and the effectiveness of the current and next leader at seeing through an effective strategy to re-attract the lost votes at a very local level.

Conditions for coalition

Liberal Democrats can strengthen their hand – and the accountability of their representatives in government – by taking a very strong line regarding the conditions for coalition. In March 2008 in his Conference speech, Nick Clegg promised that he would never allow the Lib Dems to become an 'annex to another party's agenda'.[11] A solid, principled set of conditions can help with this. The alternative view offers five conditions which would have the greatest efficacy if enshrined in the Liberal Democrat constitution.

1. No coalition with another party will be agreed if one party has secured an overall majority, except in time of war.
2. Up to three 'red line' policies will be included in a coalition agreement if they have been proposed by at least 20 local

constituency parties or 100 delegates, and have won a priority ballot from a list of policies individually approved for inclusion in a Conference referendum using the Single Transferable Vote system.
3. No individual may occupy the roles of leader and Deputy Prime Minister simultaneously.
4. There will be no electoral pacts with the Conservative or Labour parties.
5. For the first general election after 2010, there will be no coalition with the Conservatives.

The first condition reflects what we believe Clegg meant in 2008 when he ruled out joining the Conservatives and Labour. Given his subsequent actions, the only consistent way to interpret what he said is that he would never join an administration which already has an *overall majority*.

The second condition is a trust exercise. Having up to three 'red lines' guarantees electors a specific set of policies which will be delivered in any circumstance where the Liberal Democrats are in power. This addresses the question of broken commitments – which was so damaging in the tuition fees debacle. By involving Party Conference, the process becomes truly democratic and makes delegates into stakeholders – and thus ambassadors at a local level – should the party find itself in government. By making the three policies binding, negotiators have a strengthened hand.

The third one makes the splitting of the roles of Deputy Prime Minister and leader a constitutional requirement.

The fourth condition reflects the insanity of attempting an electoral pact with any party.

The fifth and final condition reflects a political imperative. The commitment to refuse a coalition with the Conservatives for one general election guarantees that voting Liberal Democrat does not mean getting Conservative. It would be better to cause a second election than to compromise the independence of the Lib Dems from the Tories at the next election. Nothing less will satisfactorily re-attract lost left-leaning voters, who will have lived under five years of a Conservative-Liberal Democrat coalition immediately prior to the election. Note also that, by and large, the tactical argument used by the Lib Dems around the country tends to be towards attracting Labour tactical votes rather than Tory tactical voters. As such, the party has little to lose in this strategy, not least given the apparent fact that Conservatives have not shown any real interest in assisting Lib Dems against Labour in Parliamentary by-elections or local elections.

Without the status of constitutional mandates this list of concessions lacks an anchor. They risk being traded for other concessions; their enshrinement is an insurance policy to assure the public that they will not be betrayed on these five conditions. Also, the liberal movement will make progress towards the systemic changes that it has fought for almost two centuries to see, by entering with a public, clear and transparent portfolio of up to three 'red lines' which cannot be abandoned.

Not doing the easy thing. Doing the right thing.

For those primarily dedicated to the collective achievement of a liberal recovery and progress beyond that, there is an urgent need to act swiftly before time's arrow swings away from the party, to point at the arbiter of fate instead. In the words of Nick Clegg himself, it is time to live up to the challenge to ensure that the movement is engaged in: 'Not doing the easy thing. Doing the right thing.'[12]

The mechanisms already exist, and have been used before to improve the party's future prospects 'from the ground up'. They revolve around the theory and practice of community politics. When this is coupled to a clear narrative, image and portfolio of policies, the formula delivers success.

A managed succession which splits the role of Deputy Prime Minister from a leadership election before 2014 will also mean that the Deputy Prime Minister Nick Clegg continues as a full member of the Liberal Democrat parliamentary party, fulfilling his promise to the country of a stable five-year coalition, while the leadership can operate in parallel to rebuild the party. This would also enable Nick Clegg to switch to the position of Britain's member of the European Commission replacing Catherine Ashton when the Baroso Commission concludes at the end of 2014. The alternative view is that Clegg should clarify whether this is his ambition at the earliest opportunity. This would enable the movement to voice its support for this sensible approach and it would allow the organisation to manage its succession in an orderly fashion. It is also crucial that it is clarified whether this is something that the Prime Minister would agree with. This is particularly important for the party as this patronage could allow for influence and control over him and it is therefore necessary that his intentions are made clear. Personally-orientated strategies by the current leadership may perhaps sustain it – at the very longest – to 2015. In practice, it cannot survive even a week beyond the next general election without announcing the intention to move on. The worst-case scenario is a messy power struggle fought out during an early general election in 2014, if the new 'Tory-friendly' boundaries are approved by Parliament.

So there is a way back, and it's not complicated. Indeed, it is elegant in the sense that a number of issues can be managed at once by thought-out, common-sense changes. The alternative view is optimistic about the future, but persuaded that what happens now will determine the quality of the recovery in the party at least up to 2015. The choices that the Liberal Democrats make up to 2013 will also determine the party's fortunes in the next general election. Failing to split the two roles held by Nick Clegg in 2011 will harm those chances. The leadership must generate an authentic and motivating narrative distinct from that of its coalition partner. The Orange Book does not have a shared narrative and Clegg has no time to create one. Only a leader working in parallel with him can complete this urgent task. This is not an easy thing to admit, but it is the right thing to do.

If those on the summit of government subjugate personal standing to the collective interest they may yet be heroes of liberalism. If they do not, they risk causing turbulence in the short term, potentially finding themselves swept aside as early as 2012. It is to be hoped that those who occupy the very highest office in the movement will put its interests first and work with the party to create a new and optimal division of labour.

The lessons of history confirm that in defence of its ultimate survival liberalism works hard to win the day. We propose that the current leadership considers these changes presented in that spirit – to create a new model at the summit of the movement, delivering powerful leadership, good government and an effective party. The alternative view well understands the very human feelings which such decisions evoke. Yet it is surely a sign of honour to make a selfless choice in the collective interest... and the mark of the greatest statesmen to do what is 'not easy, but right'. This is the way back for the Liberal Democrats.

References

Introduction
[1] 'Reinhold Messner: On top of the world,' *The Independent* (13 June 2006), http://www.independent.co.uk/news/people/profiles/reinhold-messner-on-top-of-the-world-482133.html, retrieved 24 November 2011.
[2] *The Orange Book: Reclaiming Liberalism*, eds. Paul Marshall and David Laws (Profile, 2004).
[3] *Britain After Blair: A Liberal Agenda*, eds. Marshall and Laws (Profile, 2006).

Chapter 1
[1] Peter Maughan, interview with the author (24 October 2011).
[2] George Monbiot, 'A Land Reform Manifesto' (22 February 1995), http://www.monbiot.com/1995/02/22/a-land-reform-manifesto/, retrieved 25 November 2011.
[3] George Orwell, 'As I Please,' *Tribune* (18 August 1944), http://orwell.ru/library/articles/As_I_Please/english/eaip_03, retrieved 25 November 2011.
[4] Tim Delaney, The March of Unreason: Science, Democracy and the New Fundamentalism (New York: Oxford University Press, 2005), p. 18.
[5] Thomas Hobbes, *Leviathan* [1651], ed. C.B. Macpherson (Harmondsworth: Penguin, 1968), p. 186.
[6] Ibid., p. 227.
[7] John Locke, *Two Treatises of Government* [1690] (Industrial Systems Research, 2009), p. 70.
[8] 'English Bill of Rights 1689,' http://avalon.law.yale.edu/17th_century/england.asp, retrieved 25 November 2011.
[9] Ibid.
[10] 'Liberal Party Election Manifesto 1959' (Liberal Publication Department, 1959), http://www.politicsresources.net/area/uk/man/lib59.htm, retrieved 21 November 2011.

[11] 'Liberal Party Election Manifesto 1964' (Liberal Publication Department, 1964), http://www.politicsresources.net/area/uk/man/lib64.htm, retrieved 21 November 2011.
[12] Andrew Whitehead, 'God Gave the Land to the People: the liberal 'Land Song',' http://www.historyworkshop.org.uk/the-land-song/, retrieved 21 November 2011 (see also Appendix 1).
[13] G. Lee, *The People's Budget: An Edwardian Tragedy* ((London: Shepheard-Walwyn, 2008), p. iv.
[14] Hansard HC (29 April 1909), cols. 481-482, http://hansard.millbanksystems.com/commons/1909/apr/29/urgent-social-problems, retrieved 22 December 2011.
[15] Ibid., cols. 509-510.
[16] Ibid., cols. 532-536.
[17] Author's personal testimony, canvassing during Peckham Ward, held on 7 July 2011, comment received on doorstep, 2nd July 2011.
[18] 'PM vows action to get addicts on benefits into work,' BBC News (21 April 2011), http://news.bbc.co.uk/news/vote2001/hi/english/newsid_1361000/1361458.stm, retrieved 25 November 2011.
[19] *The Times* (8 July 2008).
[20] 'David Cameron blasts druggies,' *The Sun* (8 July 2008).
[21] 'May: Scrap the Human Rights Act,' *The Sun* (2 October 2011).
[22] Declan Gaffney, 'David Cameron is stuck in a time warp on disability benefits,' *The Guardian* (28 July 2011).
[23] Leader's Speech, Conservative Party Conference (12 October 1990), http://www.youtube.com/watch?v=DQ6TgaPJcRo, retrieved 21 November 2011.
[24] Cf. 'Lib Dems plan warmer homes,' BBC News (31 May 2001), http://news.bbc.co.uk/news/vote2001/hi/english/newsid_1361000/1361458.stm, retrieved 25 November 2011.
[25] House of Commons Health Committee, 'Social Care: Written Evidence' (15 October 2009), Ev 152-3.
[26] 'Election Statistics: UK 1918-2007,' House of Commons Library Research Paper 08/12 (1 February 2008), p. 8.
[27] Ibid., p. 11.
[28] Ibid.
[29] Ibid.
[30] 'Local Elections 2011,' House of Commons Library Research Paper 11/43 (24 May 2011), p. 11.
[31] 'Conservative community mission statement' (6 April 2010), http://www.upmystreet.com/article/local-area/election-2010-conservative-mission-statement.html, retrieved 21 November 2011.

References

Chapter 2

[1] '1992 Liberal Democrat Election Manifesto,' http://www.libdemmanifesto.com/1992/1992-liberal-manifesto.shtml, retrieved 25 November 2011.

[2] 'Election Statistics: UK 1918-2007,' p. 11.

[3] Keith Laybourn, *Fifty Key Figures in Twentieth-Century British Politics* (Psychology Press, 2002), p. 180.

[4] 'Election Statistics: UK 1918-2007,' p. 11.

[5] Ibid., p. 57.

[6] Ibid., p. 12.

[7] Ibid.

[8] Ibid.

[9] Ibid.

[10] 'General Election Results, 7 June 2001,' House of Commons Library Research Paper 01/54 (18 June 2001), p. 7.

[11] 'Election Statistics: UK 1918-2007,' p. 57.

[12] Paddy Ashdown, 'The Chard Speech' (9 May 1992), http://www.liberalhistory.org.uk/item_single.php?item_id=82&item=history, retrieved 21 November 2011.

[13] Hansard HC (18 March 2003), col. 782.

[14] Ibid., col. 761.

[15] http://www.totalpolitics.com/speeches/war/war-on-iraq/33768/speech-to-antiwar-rally-hyde-park.thtml, retrieved 21 November 2011.

[16] Author's personal testimony (October 2011).

[17] 'Election Statistics: UK 1918-2007,' p. 11.

[18] 'General Election 2005,' House of Commons Library Research Paper 05/33 (10 March 2006), p. 49.

[19] 'Election Statistics: UK 1918-2007,' p. 11.

[20] 'The letter – and those who gave backing to it,' *The Scotsman* (7 January 2006), http://www.scotsman.com/news/politics/the_letter_and_those_who_gave_backing_to_it_1_687284, retrieved 21 November 2011 (see also Appendix 2).

[21] BBC online poll: 'Should Charles Kennedy continue as Lib Dem leader?' (6 January 2006), http://news.bbc.co.uk/1/hi/uk_politics/4587076.stm, retrieved 21 November 2011.

[22] 'YouGov survey results: Iraq War Tracker' (18 March 2003), http://www.yougov.co.uk/extranets/ygarchives/content/pdf/CLO020101003.pdf, retrieved 28 November 2011.

[23] 'Embattled Kennedy quits as leader,' BBC News (7 January 2006), http://news.bbc.co.uk/1/hi/uk_politics/4590688.stm, retrieved 21 November 2011.

[24] Ibid.
[25] Liberal Democrat Federal Constitution, http://www.libdems.org.uk/constitution.aspx, retrieved 21 November 2011.
[26] 'Election Statistics: UK 1918-2007,' p. 38.
[27] Kevin Maguire, 'Village life: Kevin Maguire eavesdrops on an unhappy Minger,' *New Statesman* (29 May 2006).
[28] 'In Full: Sir Menzies resignation,' BBC News (15 October 2007), http://news.bbc.co.uk/1/hi/uk_politics/7046010.stm, retrieved 25 November 2011.
[29] 'Chris Huhne targets "Calamity Clegg" for Lib Dem leadership,' *The Daily Mail* (19 November 2007), http://www.dailymail.co.uk/news/article-494873/Chris-Huhne-targets-Calamity-Clegg-Lib-Dem-leadership.html, retrieved 28 November 2011.
[30] Liberal Democrat Federal Constitution, ibid.

Chapter 3

[1] 'Local Elections 2011,' p. 9.
[2] Ibid., p. 6.
[3] Tim Castle, 'UK's Labour Party suffers big losses in local polls,' Reuters (Friday 5 June 2009), http://uk.reuters.com/article/2009/06/05/us-britain-politics-results-sb-idUKTRE55451V20090605, retrieved 26 November 2011.
[4] Ibid.
[5] Author's personal testimony (8 June 2009).
[6] 'Local Elections 2011,' p. 6.
[7] Ibid., p. 5.
[8] 'European Parliament Elections 2009,' House of Commons Library Research Paper 09/53 (17 June 2009), p. 2.
[9] Ibid., p. 6.
[10] 'Liberal Democrats back plans to scrap university tuition fees,' (Saturday 7 March 2009), http://www.libdems.org.uk/policy_motions_detail.aspx?title=Liberal_Democrats_back_plans_to_scrap_university_tuition_fees___&pPK=b5043fc9-2719-489a-9e0b-532ef2b05906, retrieved 21 November 2011 (see also Appendix 3).
[11] 'Clegg hires Thatcher campaign man,' BBC News (8 January 2008), http://news.bbc.co.uk/1/hi/uk_politics/7176792.stm, retrieved 21 November 2011.
[12] 'Election Statistics: UK 1918-2007,' p. 11.
[13] http://conservativehome.blogs.com/torydiary/images/misterambition.gif, retrieved 26 November 2011.
[14] 'Cameron praises "great" Thatcher,' BBC News (31 January 2008), http://news.bbc.co.uk/1/hi/uk_politics/7220424.stm, retrieved 21 November 2011.

References

[15] Jon Swaine, 'MPs' expenses system created in pact between Thatcher's ministers and Opposition,' *The Daily Telegraph* (23 November 2009).

[16] Patrick Hennessy, 'Tories plan £14bn cuts to red tape,' *The Sunday Telegraph* (12 August 2007).

[17] Hansard HC (18 March 2009), col. 952.

[18] Ibid.

[19] Vince Cable, Prime Minister's Questions, http://www.youtube.com/watch?v=P9ZErdQy96U, retrieved 21 November 2011.

[20] Piers Morgan, 'When Piers met Nick Clegg,' *GQ* (May 2008), http://www.gq-magazine.co.uk/comment/articles/2010-07/23/when-piers-met-nick-clegg/sex, retrieved 26 November 2011.

[21] 'The First Election Debate,' ITV1 (15 April 2010).

[22] YouGov survey (15 April 2010), http://today.yougov.co.uk/politics/instant-reactions-great-debate, retrieved 21 November 2011.

[23] 'Sky News Leaders' Debate,' (23 April 2010), http://news.sky.com/home/video/15614025, retrieved 21 November 2011.

[24] YouGov survey (22 April 2010), http://today.yougov.co.uk/politics/instant-reactions-great-debate2, retrieved 21 November 2011.

[25] 'The Prime Ministerial Debate,' http://www.telegraph.co.uk/news/newsvideo/uk-politics-video/7654197/BBC-leaders-debate-highlights.html, retrieved 21 November 2011.

[26] YouGov survey (29 April 2010), http://today.yougov.co.uk/politics/instant-reactions-final-debate, retrieved 21 November 2011.

[27] 'Polls Suggest Cameron Wins Final Debate,' Sky News (29 April 2010), http://news.sky.com/home/politics/article/15622529, retrieved 21 November 2011.

[28] 'General Election 2010,' Commons Library Research Paper 10/36 (2 February 2011), p. 1.

[29] 'Election Statistics: UK 1918-2007,' p. 11.

[30] 'Liberal Democrat target seats,' BBC News, http://news.bbc.co.uk/1/shared/election2010/results/targets/p_ld.stm, retrieved 28 November 2011.

[31] 'General Election 2010,' p. 32.

[32] 'Boundary changes affect Solihull,' BBC News (6 April 2010), http://news.bbc.co.uk/1/hi/england/west_midlands/8565268.stm, retrieved 28 November 2011.

[33] 'Election Statistics: UK 1918-2007,' p. 11.

[34] 'General Election 2010,' pp. 100-109.

[35] Rob Wilson MP, *Five Days to Power* (Biteback, 2010), quoted in Nicholas Watt, 'Revealed: Lib Dems planned before election to abandon tuition fees pledge,' *The Guardian* (12 November 2010),

http://www.guardian.co.uk/politics/2010/nov/12/lib-dems-tuition-fees-clegg, retrieved 22 December 2011.
[36] 'Nick Clegg on student funding' (27 April 2010), http://www.youtube.com/watch?v=Q_AMABsBNgw, retrieved 21 November 2011.
[37] Ibid.
[38] David Laws, 22 *Days in May* (Biteback, 2010).
[39] 'Liberal Democrat Conference approves Coalition Agreement' (16 May 2010), http://www.libdems.org.uk/latest_news_detail.aspx?pPK=a4cc7d74-959a-4c9f-a4b9-751a49315a0d&title=Liberal_Democrat_Conference_approves_Coalition_Agreement, retrieved 21 November 2011.

Chapter 4

[1] 'Liberal Democrat Manifesto 2010,' p. 13, http://network.libdems.org.uk/manifesto2010/libdem_manifesto_2010.pdf, retrieved 28 November 2011.
[2] 'Liberal Democrat achievements in Government,' pts. 1-7 (29 December 2010), http://www.freedomcentral.org.uk/2010/12/liberal-democrat-achievements-in-government-part-one.html, retrieved 21 November 2011.
[3] Jason Groves, 'Backlash as minister boasts "Be as proud of our £12bn foreign aid bill as you are of the Army",' *The Daily Mail* (6 June 2011).
[4] Ibid.
[5] Hansard HC (7 September 2011), col. 354.
[6] 'Budget: Osborne's 'tough' package puts VAT up to 20%,' BBC News (22 June 2010), http://www.bbc.co.uk/news/10371590, retrieved 28 November 2010.
[7] YouGov/Brand Democracy poll, *The Observer* (27 June 2010).
[8] Tim Farron, 'Tuition fees are the poll tax of our generation,' *The Guardian* (11 November 2011).
[9] See Appendix 5.
[10] Ibid.
[11] Nicholas Watt, 'Revealed: Lib Dems planned before election to abandon tuition fees pledge,' *The Guardian* (Friday 12 November 2010).
[12] YouGov poll (sample size: 1,862 adults), *The Sun* (6 January 2011).
[13] 'By-elections since 2010,' House of Commons Library Standard Note SN/SG/5833 (1 July 2011), p. 3.
[14] 'Labour celebrate victory in Oldham East by-election,' BBC News (14 January 2011).
[15] 'By-elections since 2010,' p. 4.
[16] 'Independent candidate hits out at public sector greed,' *The Barnsley Chronicle* (4 March 2011), http://www.barnsley-

References

chronicle.co.uk/news/article/3732/independent-candidate-hits-out-at-public-sector-greed, retrieved 28 November 2011.

[17] 'Lib Dems slump to sixth as Labour win Barnsley poll,' BBC News (3 March 2011).

Chapter 5

[1] Interview with the author (21 October 2011)

[2] 'Local Elections 2011,' p. 8.

[3] Ibid.

[4] Ibid., p. 9.

[5] Ibid.

[6] Ibid., p. 7.

[7] Ibid., p. 10.

[8] Ibid., p. 11.

[9] 'Scottish Parliament Elections,' House of Commons Library Research Paper 11/41 (24 May 2011), pp. 7, 10.

[10] Ibid.

[11] 'National Assembly for Wales Elections 2011,' House of Commons Research Paper 11/40 (19 May 2011), p. 2.

[12] Ibid.

[13] Ibid.

[14] 'By-elections since 2010,' p. 5.

[15] 'Local elections 2011,' p. 11.

[16] Jon Land, 'Lib Dems claim victory in Bedford mayor race,' 16 October 2009, http://www.24dash.com/news/Local_Government/2009-10-16-Lib-Dems-claim-victory-in-Bedford-mayor-race, retrieved 29 November 2011.

[17] 'Local elections 2011,' pp. 13-18.

[18] Nicholas Wyatt, 'AV and local elections: don't gloat in public, triumphal Tories told,' *The Guardian* (7 May 2011).

[19] Peter Maughan, interview with author (24 October 2011).

[20] Phil Appleby, interview with author (24 October 2011).

Chapter 6

[1] Cf. 'Greg Mulholland MP launches Cross Party Initiative to support pubs' (21 February 2008), http://www.camra.org.uk/page.aspx?o=271231, retrieved 21 November 2011.

[2] 'By-election results: 1997-2001,' House of Commons Information Office Factsheet M16 (September 2003), p. 9.

[3] 'General Election 2010,' p. 93.

[4] Ibid., p. 84.
[5] http://www.election.demon.co.uk/1983SC.html, retrieved 29 November 2011.
[6] 'General Election results, 7 June 2001,' p. 51.
[7] 'General Election 2010,' pp. 32, 109.
[8] Detailed information on all electoral systems is available at http://www.electoral-reform.org.uk (retrieved 21 November 2011).
[9] 'General Election 2010,' p. 7.
[10] ' Election Statistics 1918-2004,' House of Commons Library Research Paper 04/61 (28 July 2004), pp. 44-45.
[11] In conversation with the author (May 2011).
[12] Andrew Grice, 'I want to push this all the way, declares Clegg,' *The Independent* (22 April 2010).
[13] Ibid.
[14] 'AV voting referendum: Emily Thornberry's viewpoint,' BBC News (5 April 2011), http://www.bbc.co.uk/news/uk-politics-12913697, retrieved 21 November 2011.
[15] Marcus Wood, 'New AV system "worst of all compromises,"' This is South Devon, http://www.thisissouthdevon.co.uk/New-AV-worst-compromises/story-11691357-detail/story.html, retrieved 21 November 2011.
[16] Jonathan Freedland, 'AV: a crucial "baby step" if we are to break Britain's's electoral reform taboo,' *The Guardian* (26 April 2010).
[17] 'AV and electoral reform,' House of Commons Library Standard Note SN/PC/05317 (14 June 2011), p. 18.
[18] Tim Montgomerie, 'The latest stage of Huhne's leadership bid involves clash with Osborne in Cabinet,' Conservative Home (3 May 2011), http://conservativehome.blogs.com/thetorydiary/2011/05/the-latest-stage-of-huhnes-leadership-bid-involves-clash-with-osborne-in-cabinet.html, retrieved 21 November 2011.
[19] Cristina Odone, 'This is the moment Chris Huhne has been waiting for,' *The Telegraph* (6 May 2011).
[20] Duncan Robinson, 'Nick Clegg's on-mike gaffe,' *New Statesman* (24 March 2011).

Chapter 7

[1] *The Orange Book: Reclaiming Liberalism*, eds. Paul Marshall and David Laws (Profile, 2004), p. 17.
[2] Ibid., p. 25.
[3] Ibid., pp. vii-x.
[4] *Britain After Blair: A Liberal Agenda*, eds. and Laws (Profile, 2006), pp. vii-ix.
[5] *The Orange Book*, p. 3.
[6] *Britain After Blair*, p. 212.

References

[7] Ibid., p. 228.
[8] Ibid., p. 141.
[9] *The Orange Book*, p. 223.
[10] *Britain After Blair*, p. 198.
[11] Steve Webb and Jo Holland, *The Orange Book*, p. 249.
[12] *Britain After Blair*, p. 118.
[13] Ibid.
[14] Steve Webb and Jo Holland, *The Orange Book*, p. 240.
[15] Ibid., p. 260.
[16] Ibid., p. 159.
[17] Ibid., p. 243.
[18] Ibid, pp. 240-241.
[19] *Britain After Blair*, pp. 233-243.
[20] Jason Groves, 'Nuclear power is vital to our future, says Huhne in energy U-turn,' *The Daily Mail* (14 October 2011).
[21] *The Orange Book*, p. 83.
[22] Ibid., p. 149.
[23] Ibid., p. 180.
[24] Stephen Tall, 'Nick Clegg reveals Tories' £13bn VAT bombshell,' Liberal Democrat Voice (8 April 2010), http://www.libdemvoice.org/nick-clegg-reveals-tories-13bn-vat-bombshell-18755.html, retrieved 21 November 2011.
[25] Ed Davey and Alison Goldsworthy, *Britain After Blair*, p. 110.
[26] Paul Marshall, *The Orange Book*, p. 292.
[27] Ibid., pp. 161-162.
[28] Helen Duffett, 'In Government for all the right reasons: the David Laws interview,' Liberal Democrat Voice (23 November 2010), http://www.libdemvoice.org/in-government-for-all-the-right-reasons-the-david-laws-interview-22174.html, retrieved 21 November 2011.
[29] Guido Fawkes' Blog (23 November 2010), http://order-order.com/2010/11/page/5/, retrieved 21 November 2011.
[30] Interview with the author (22 December 2011).
[31] Holly Watt, ert Winnett and Heidi Blake, 'Vince Cable: I could bring down the government if I'm pushed,' *The Telegraph* (20 December 2010).
[32] 'Telegraph undercover Lib Dem story "broke press rules,"' BBC News (10 May 2011), http://www.bbc.co.uk/news/uk-13342013, retrieved 28 November 2011.
[33] 'Cable "Considered Quitting" Over BSkyB Row,' Sky News (18 April 2011), http://news.sky.com/home/politics/article/15974767, retrieved 21 November 2011.
[34] Holly Watt, ert Winnett and Heidi Blake, 'Nick Clegg says Vince Cable is "right to be embarrassed" about threat to bring down coalition,' *The Telegraph* (21 December 2011).

[35] 'Tim Farron's speech at the Liberal Democrat conference rally,' Liberal Democrat Voice (11 March 2011), http://www.libdemvoice.org/tim-farrons-speech-at-the-liberal-democrat-conference-rally-23394.html, retrieved 21 November 2011.

[36] Patrick Wintour and Polly Curtis, 'Row over ending of 50p tax rate threatens to spark Tory rebellion,' *The Guardian* (7 September 2011).

[37] Andrew Woodcock, '50p tax rate a "temporary measure,"' *The Independent* (7 September 2011).

[38] Canvassing evidence collected by authors in South London (July 2011).

[39] 'Stanmore Park Ward – by-election 2011,' http://www.harrow.gov.uk/info/687/elections_information/2349/stanmore_park_ward-by-election_2011/6, retrieved 22 December 2011.

[40] Liberal Democrat Voice (29 July 2011), http://www.libdemvoice.org/council-byelection-results-28-july-2011-24868.html, retrieved 18th December 2011.

[41] Andrew Johnson, 'St Peter's ward by-election result – Labour's Alice Perry cruises to win, as Lib Dem and Tory vote collapses,' *Islington Tribune* (12 August 2011), http://www.islingtontribune.com/news/2011/aug/st-peters-ward-election-result-labour%E2%80%99s-alice-perry-cruises-win-lib-dem-and-tory-vote-, retrieved 29 November 2011.

[42] BBC News, http://news.bbc.co.uk/1/shared/bsp/hi/elections/london/08/html/mayor.stm, retrieved 29 November 2011.

[43] Helen Duffett, 'Brian Paddick selected as Liberal Democrats' London Mayoral Candidate for 2012,' Liberal Democrat Voice (2 September 2011), http://www.libdemvoice.org/brian-paddick-selected-as-liberal-democrats-london-mayoral-candidate-for-2012-25129.html, retrieved 28 November 2011.

Chapter 8

[1] Trans. E.V. Rieu (Penguin, 1946).

[2] Jim Parry, *Sport and Spirituality: An Introduction* (Taylor and Francis, 2007), pp. 18-81.

[3] Thomas, Hughes, *Tom Brown at Oxford* (Ticknor and Fields, 1861), chapter 11.

[4] James George Cotton Minchin, *Our Public Schools,* page 113 (Sonnenschein, 1901).

[5] http://www.muscularliberal.com/contributors, retrieved 28 November 2011.

[6] Demos Staff overview: Advisory council, http://www.demos.co.uk/people?council_page=1&tab=council; http://www.demos.co.uk/people?council_page=2&tab=council; http://www.demos.co.uk/people?council_page=3&tab=council, retrieved 28 November 2011.

References

[7] Max Wind-Cowie, 'British Muslims are being misrepresented by a leadership that is more extreme and less tolerant than the vast majority of their number,' Conservative Home (27 June 2011), http://conservativehome.blogs.com/thinktankcentral/2011/06/max-wind-cowie-of-demos-british-muslims-are-being-misrepresented-by-a-leadership-that-is-more-extrem.html, retrieved 21 November 2011.

[8] Ibid.

[9] 'About MCB,' http://www.mcb.org.uk/aboutmcb.php, retrieved 21 November 2011.

[10] http://www.mcb.org.uk/downloads/MCB_CODE_&_PROTOCOLS_28.9.pdf, retrieved 21 November 2011.

[11] Max Wind-Cowie, 'There is such a thing as the deserving and undeserving poor,' Conservative Home (13 June 2011), http://conservativehome.blogs.com/platform/2011/06/max-wind-cowie-there-is-such-a-thing-as-the-deserving-and-undeserving-poor.html, retrieved 21 November 2011.

[12] David Cameron, Speech to the Munich Security Conference (5 February 2011), http://www.number10.gov.uk/news/pms-speech-at-munich-security-conference, retrieved 21 November 2011.

[13] 'Liberal Democrats back plans to scrap university tuition fees'.

[14] 'Chris Huhne: Geert Wilders should have been banned,' *The Independent* (13 February 2009).

[15] See Appendix 3.

[16] Nick Clegg, 'Nick Clegg speech: An Open, Confident Society' (3 March 2011), http://www.libdems.org.uk/speeches_detail.aspx?title=Nick_Clegg_speech%3a_An_Open%2c_Confident_Society&pPK=25e28e0b-a8e7-4104-ba5e-e860d752c31a, retrieved 21 November 2011.

[17] http://thinkexist.com/quotation/there-was-no-metaphorical-gun-at-my-head-putting/675844.html, retrieved 28 November 2011.

[18] Author's notes (10 August 2010) (see chapter 16).

[19] 'Dutch MP banned from entering UK,' BBC News (12 February 2009), http://news.bbc.co.uk/1/hi/uk_politics/7882953.stm, retrieved 21 November 2011.

[20] *The Orange Book*, p. 118.

[21] 'Report 5: How Do We Contribute Individually to Global Warming?', Hinkle Charitable Foundation, http://www.thehcf.org/emaila5.html, retrieved 28 November 2011.

Chapter 9

[1] John Rentoul, 'ComRes poll: Tories draw level with Labour,' *The Independent* (17 September 2011).

[2] YouGov survey (18 September 2011), http://today.yougov.co.uk/politics/update-16th-18th-sept-labour-lead-6, retrieved 21 November 2011.

[3] 'Tim Farron's speech to Liberal Democrat Autumn Conference' (18 September 2011),
http://www.libdems.org.uk/news_detail.aspx?title=Tim_Farron%E2%80%99s_speech_to_Liberal_Democrat_Autumn_Conference&pPK=b0e06ec1-1e1d-478a-b925-ddf6369b11a2, retrieved 21 November 2011.

[4] Tim Farron, 'Community is our priority,' *The Guardian* (19 September 2011), http://www.guardian.co.uk/commentisfree/2011/sep/18/liberal-democrats-local-politics-community?INTCMP=SRCH, retrieved 21 November 2011.

[5] Ibid.

[6] Nick Clegg, 'Nick Clegg's speech to Liberal Democrat Conference' (21 September 2011),
http://www.libdems.org.uk/speeches_detail.aspx?title=Nick_Clegg's_speech_to_Liberal_Democrat_Conference&pPK=00e086ba-d994-4146-bb14-60ce615d05eb, retrieved 21 November 2011.

[7] Comments on "Speech to Lib Dem conference, Birmingham, 21 September 2011,' *New Statesman* (21 September 2011), http://www.newstatesman.com/uk-politics/2011/09/government-liberal-economy, retrieved 21 November 2011.

[8] 'Liberal Democrats: not easy for Nick Clegg,' *The Guardian*,
http://www.guardian.co.uk/commentisfree/2011/sep/21/liberal-democrats-nick-clegg-editorial, retrieved 21 November 2011.

[9] http://www.guardian.co.uk/commentisfree/2011/sep/18/liberal-democrats-local-politics-community, retrieved 21 November 2011. Note again that this post was technically a response to the president's Guardian article some days before Clegg's speech, but the alternative view judges it to be representative of the opinion held by a significant sector of the population towards the party.

[10] http://aduni.org/~heather/occs/honors/Poem.htm, retrieved 3 December 2011.

[11] YouGov survey (23 September 2011),
http://cdn.yougov.com/today_uk_import/yg-archives-pol-sun-results-220911.pdf, retrieved 21 November 2011.

[12] YouGov survey (7 October 2011),
http://cdn.yougov.com/cumulus_uploads/document/2011-10-07/YG-Archives-Pol-ST-results-0710-091011.pdf, retrieved 21 November 2011.

Chapter 10

[1] See John Meadowcroft, 'Community Politics' (October 2003),
http://www.liberalhistory.org.uk/item_single.php?item_id=69&item=history, retrieved 21 November 2011.

References

[2] Bernard Greaves and Gordon Lishman, 'Theory and practice of community politics,' (ALC Campaign Booklet No. 12, 1980), http://www.cix.co.uk/~rosenstiel/aldc/commpol.htm, retrieved 21 November 2011.

[3] 'Community is our priority'.

[4] Charles P. Pierce, 'All Politics Is Still Local,' *Esquire* (29 September 2010), http://www.esquire.com/blogs/politics/all-politics-is-still-local, retrieved 29 November 2011.

[5] Ollie Stone-Lee, 'Conference season's greatest hits,' BBC News (10 September 2003), http://news.bbc.co.uk/1/hi/uk_politics/3185313.stm, retrieved 21 November 2011.

[6] 'Local Elections 2010,' House of Commons Library Research Paper 10/44 (22 June 2010), p. 5.

[7] Ibid., pp. 3-4.

[8] Ibid., p. 4.

[9] 'General Election 2010,' p. 34.

[10] Ibid., pp. 86-88.

[11] 'Election Statistics: UK 1918-2007,' p. 11.

[12] Ibid., p. 57.

[13] 'General Election 2010,' p. 92; 'Local Elections 2008,' p. 20. Note that in local elections the constituency of Montgomeryshire falls under Powys County Council.

[14] 'General Election 2010,' pp. 7, 64.

[15] Ibid.

[16] 'Election Statistics: 1918-2007,' p. 11.

[17] Variations are widely quoted; this version from http://www.trevox.co.uk/blog/1 (7 January 2011), retrieved 21 November 2011.

[18] Michael Crick, 'Lib Dems by-election parsimony exposed,' BBC News (8 April 2011), http://www.bbc.co.uk/blogs/newsnight/michaelcrick/2011/04/lib_dems_parsimony_exposed.html, retrieved 28 November 2011.

[19] Author's notes, London (10 August 2011).

[20] 'Liberal Democrat Members of Parliament,' http://www.libdems.org.uk/mps.aspx, retrieved 28 November 2011.

[21] 'Liberal Democrats in the Cabinet' (October 2011), http://www.libdems.org.uk/cabinet.aspx (see also Appendix 6), retrieved 21 November 2011.

[22] These conclusions have been drawn by extensive research into each individual MP using their own websites, written records and media biographies.

[23] 'Nick Clegg's speech to Liberal Democrat Conference'.
[24] 'Tim Farron's speech to Liberal Democrat Autumn Conference'.
[25] Richard Johnston et al, 'The Collapse of a Party System? The 1993 Canadian General Election' (September 1994), p. 2, http://www.electionstudies.org/conferences/1994Impact/1994Impact_JohnstonBlais.pdf, retrieved 21 November 2011.
[26] 'Community is our priority'.

Chapter 11

[1] http://www.brainyquote.com/quotes/authors/p/peter_marshall.html, retrieved 1 December 2011.

[2] Speech at the California Democratic State Convention, 14 March 2003 quoted in *Richmond Times-Dispatch* (27 June 2003), http://presrace.mgnetwork.com/index.cfm?SiteID=RTD&PackageID=43&fuseaction=article.main&ArticleID=2556&GroupID=173, retrieved 29 November 2011.

[3] http://www.alumni.hbs.edu/bulletin/2001/february/kotter.html, retrieved 29 November 2011.

[4] Toby elm, HHHelm, 'Shirley Williams plunges NHS reforms into fresh turmoil,' *The Guardian* (3 September 2011).

[5] 'Vince Cable's speech to Liberal Democrat Autumn Conference' (19 September 2011), http://www.libdems.org.uk/news_detail.aspx?title=Vince_Cable's_speech_to_Liberal_Democrat_Autumn_Conference&pPK=8f00035e-7adc-4bdd-bfd5-5d6105ae711d, retrieved 21 November 2011.

[6] Andrew Woodcock, '50p tax rate a "temporary measure,"' *The Independent* (7 September 2011).

[7] 'Chris Huhne warns Tories over axing 50p tax rate,' BBC News (11 September 2011), http://www.bbc.co.uk/news/uk-politics-14874049, retrieved 21 November 2011.

[8] Ibid.

[9] 'Tim Farron's speech to Liberal Democrat Autumn Conference'.

[10] James Forsyth, 'Hague says he's been held back on Europe by the Lib Dems' (10 September 2011).

[11] Nicholas Cecil, 'Don't let riots and euro push us to right, warn Tory moderates,' *London Evening Standard* (9 September 2011).

[12] Hansard HC (7 September 2011), col. 354.

[13] Interview with author (20 October 2011).

[14] 'Scottish Parliament Elections 2011,' House of Commons Library Research Paper 11/41 (24 May 2011), p. 3.

[15] 'National Assembly for Wales Elections 2011,' House of Commons Library Research Paper 11/40 (19 May 2011), pp. 1-2.

References

[16] 'Northern Ireland Assembly Elections 2011,' House of Commons Library Research paper 11/42 (24 May 2011), pp. 3, 6.
[17] Interview with the author (26 October 2011).

Chapter 12

[1] Quoted in Peter Fisk, *Marketing Genius* (Wiley, 2006), p. 152.
[2] Quoted in Adam Morgan, *Eating the Big Fish: How Challenger Brands Can Compete Against Brand Leaders* (Wiley, 2009), p. 80.
[3] David Nolan, 'Classifying and Analyzing Politico-Economic Systems,' *The Individualist* (January 1971), cited at Advocates for Self-Government (22 November 2010), http://theadvocates.org/blog/175, retrieved 29 November 2011.
[4] http://www.nolanchart.com/index.php, retrieved 3 December 2011.
[5] 'Butskellism,' Encyclopaedia Britannica definition, http://www.britannica.com/EBchecked/topic/1417052/Butskellism, retrieved 26 November 2011.
[6] Cf. 'UK Parties 2010 General Election,' Political Compass, http://www.politicalcompass.org/, retrieved 18 November 2011.
[7] 'How liberal are the Liberal Democrats?', Liberal Vision (September 2008), http://www.liberal-vision.org/wp-content/uploads/2009/03/liberal-vision-how-liberal-are-the-liberal-democrats.pdf, retrieved 18 November 2011.
[8] Interview with the author (13 October 2011).
[9] Author's notes (10 May 2011).
[10] 'Cameron praises "great" Thatcher,' BBC News.
[11] Duncan Robinson, 'Nick Clegg's on-mike gaffe,' *New Statesman* (24 March 2011).
[12] Patrick Wintour, 'David Cameron using AV to trash us, say Lib Dems,' *The Guardian* (1 May 2011).
[13] 'Lib Dems promise positive campaign,' BBC News (19 September 2001).
[14] 'Lib Dems promise positive campaign,' BBC News (22 March 2005).
[15] 'Kennedy promises positive campaign,' *The Daily Mail* (5 April 2005), http://www.dailymail.co.uk/news/article-343796/Kennedy-promises-positive-campaign.html, retrieved 18 November 2011.
[16] Allegra Stratton and Polly Curtis, 'Liberal Democrats turn heat on George Osborne over Nick Clegg smears,' *The Guardian* (23 April 2010).
[17] 'Loose Lips Sink Ships,' Guido Fawkes' blog (30 January, 2010), http://order-order.com/2010/01/30/loose-lips-sink-ships/, retrieved 18 November 2011.
[18] David Lindsell, 'Liberal Democrat denies Richmond Park and north Kingston Tory infiltration plot,' *The Surrey Comet* (12 April 2010).
[19] Interview with the author (18 December 2011).
[20] Author's notes (16 June 2011).

The Alternative View

Chapter 13

[1] Cf. Dan Sullivan, 'Who are the Geolibertarians?', http://geolib.com, retrieved 18 November 2011.

[2] Liberal Democrat Manifesto 2010, p. 14.

[3] Cf. 'People's Budget 1909,' Liberal Democrat History Group, http://www.liberalhistory.org.uk/item_single.php?item_id=46&item=history, retrieved 18 November 2011.

[4] Cf. 'Henry George Foundation Information,' Henry George Foundation, http://www.henrygeorgefoundation.org/henry-george-foundation-information/, retrieved 18 November 2011.

[5] Henry George, *Progress and Poverty* (Garden City, NY: Doubleday, 1879).

[6] ALTER, http://libdemsalter.org.uk/en/, retrieved 18 November 2011.

[7] Alanna Hartzok, 'The Alaska Permanent Fund: A Model of Resource Rents for Public Investment and Citizen Dividends' (14 November 2001), http://commonground-usa.net/alaska03.htm, retrieved 18 November 2011.

[8] 'Alaska Crime Rates 1960-2010,' http://www.disastercenter.com/crime/akcrime.htm, retrieved 18 November 2011.

[9] Ibid.

[10] Based on figures in 'North Sea Revenue,' http://www.scotland.gov.uk/Publications/2011/06/21144516/7, retrieved 18 November 2011.

[11] *The Orange Book*, pp. 212-213.

[12] Ibid., p. 213.

[13] Paul Bracchi, 'A star pupil from £1m home. How did she end up in the dock?', *The Daily Mail* (2 September 2011), http://www.dailymail.co.uk/news/article-2025068/UK-riots-Middle-class-rioters-revealed-including-Laura-Johnson-Natasha-Reid-Stefan-Hoyle.html, retrieved 30 November 2011.

[14] 'UK riots: Swift justice for London rioters in court,' BBC News (10 August 2011), http://www.bbc.co.uk/news/uk-14484239, retrieved 30 November 2011.

[15] 'Liberal Democrats back plans to scrap university tuition fees' (see also Appendix 3).

[16] Patrick Wintour and Polly Curtis, 'Nick Clegg says 'big society' same as liberalism,' *The Guardian* (13 December 2010).

[17] *The Orange Book*, p. 118.

[18] Ibid., p. 251.

[19] Paul Waugh, 'Straw's 103mph driver "must face prosecution,"' *The Independent* (22 July 2000).

[20] 'The History of the Spanner Case,' The Spanner Trust, http://www.spannertrust.org/documents/spannerhistory.asp, retrieved 18 November 2011.

References

[21] 'Extreme Pornography,' The Crown Prosecution Service, http://www.cps.gov.uk/legal/d_to_g/extreme_pornography/, retrieved 18 November 2011.
[22] Ibid.
[23] 'The History of the Spanner Case,' ibid.
[24] John Ozimek, ' UK prosecutors drop "tiger" sex video case,' *The Register* (6 January 2010), http://www.theregister.co.uk/2010/01/06/tiger_police/, retrieved 29 November 2011.
[25] Ibid.
[26] 'Tiger Porn defendant miscarriage of justice averted' (28 May 2010), http://www.backlash-uk.org.uk/wp/?page_id=856, rretrieved 18 November 2011; Jane Fae Ozimek, 'Extreme porn law on the ropes,' *The Register* (6 August 2010), http://www.theregister.co.uk/2010/08/06/tiger_freed, retrieved 18 November 2011.
[27] Section 28, Local Government Act 1988, http://www.legislation.gov.uk/ukpga/1988/9/section/28, retrieved 18 November 2011.
[28] Harry G. Levine and Craig Reinarman, *Alcohol prohibition and drug prohibition: Lessons from alcohol policy for drug policy* (Amsterdam: CEDRO, 2004), http://www.cedro-uva.org/lib/levine.alcohol.html, retrieved 29 November 2011.
[29] Peter Reuter and Alex Stevens, 'An Analysis of UK Drug Policy' (UK Drug Policy Commission, April 2007), p. 7.
[30] http://www.tdpf.org.uk/, retrieved 18 November 2011.
[31] 'LibDem Conference passes drugs motion,' Liberal Democrat Voice (19 September 2011), http://www.libdemvoice.org/libdem-conference-passes-drugs-motion-25314.html, retrieved 18 November 2011.

Chapter 14

[1] 'Leadership Elections: Liberal Democrats,' Commons Library Standard Note SN/PC/3872 (22 October 2007), p. 7.
[2] Ryan Cullen, 'Nick Clegg is the new Leader,' Liberal Democrat Voice (18 December 2007), http://www.libdemvoice.org/nick-clegg-is-the-new-leader-1841.html, retrieved 29 November 2011.
[3] BBC News (18 December 2007).
[4] 'Liberal Vision interviews Susan Kramer,' Liberal Vision (21 October 2010), http://www.liberal-vision.org/2010/10/21/liberal-vision-interviews-susan-kramer/, retrieved 18 November 2011.
[5] 'Nick Clegg speech: An Open, Confident Society,'
[6] 'Nick Clegg orders re-brand amid rumours of leadership challenge,' *The Telegraph* (26 March 2011).

[7] Interview with the author (October 2011).
[8] 'Nick Clegg's on-mike gaffe'.
[9] Interview with the author (October 2011).
[10] Jemima Khan, 'I'm not a punchbag – I have feelings,' *New Statesman* (7 April 2011).
[11] Liberal Democrat Federal Constitution: 'The Liberal Democrats exist to build and safeguard a fair, free and open society, in which we seek to balance the fundamental values of liberty, equality and community, and in which no-one shall be enslaved by poverty, ignorance or conformity,' http://www.libdems.org.uk/constitution.aspx, retrieved 18 November 2011.
[12] Councillor Peter Maughan, interview with the author, ibid.
[13] 'Alan B'stard: backroom deals and not delivering on promises,' YouTube, http://www.youtube.com/watch?v=8aUxilWb2Og, retrieved 18 November 2011.
[14] Quoted in Peter Fuda, 'Leadership Transformation: Creating Alignment from the Inside-out' (TAP, 2011), p. 22, http://www.tap.net.au/resources/TAP_WhitePaper_LeadershipTransformation.pdf, retrieved 1 December 2011.
[15] *The Sunday Times* (31 July 2011).
[16] David Nolan, 'Classifying and Analyzing Politico-Economic Systems,' *The Individualist* (January 1971), cited at Advocates for Self Government (22 November 2010), http://theadvocates.org/blog/175, retrieved 29 November 2011.
[17] 'Centerpiece of the Quiz: The Nolan Chart,' Advocates for Self Government, http://www.theadvocates.org/content/the-nolan-chart, retrieved 29 November 2011.
[18] Ed Joyce, 'Liberal Vision writes... New site, new vision,' Liberal Democrat Voice (12 May 2009), http://www.libdemvoice.org/liberal-vision-writes-new-site-new-vision-14399.html, retrieved 29 November 2011.
[19] 'Vision,' http://www.liberal-vision.org/vision/, retrieved 29 November 2011.
[20] 'Report from Social Liberal Forum launch,' Social Liberal Forum (9 March 2009), http://socialliberal.net/tag/harrogate/, retrieved 29 November 2011.
[21] 'What We Stand For,' Social Liberal Forum, http://socialliberal.net/about/what-we-stand-for/, retrieved 29 November 2011.
[22] 'SLF Conference: 18 June 2011,' Social Liberal Forum, http://socialliberal.net/about/slf-conference-18th-june-2011, retrieved 29 November 2011.
[23] 'SLF North East to hold first meeting,' Social Liberal Forum (10 November 2011), http://socialliberal.net/2011/11/10/slf-north-east-to-hold-first-meeting, retrieved 30 November 2011.
[24] David Cameron, 'Speech to the Munich Security Conference' (5 February 2011), http://www.number10.gov.uk/news/pms-speech-at-munich-security-conference, retrieved 29 November 2011.

References

[25] 'Nick Clegg speech: An Open, Confident Society.'

[26] *The Orange Book*, p. 116.

[27] 'Deputy PM Nick Clegg defends human rights laws', BBC News (26 August 2011), http://www.bbc.co.uk/news/uk-politics-14675318, retrieved 3 December 2011.

[28] Allegra Stratton, 'Nick Clegg to announce timetable for ending child detentions,' *The Guardian* (1 December 2010).

[29] Lisa Nandy, 'Nick Clegg dodges, again, the question of what he's doing to end child detention' (15 November 2011), http://www.leftfootforward.org/2011/11/nick-clegg-ending-child-detention-pledge/, retrieved 30 November 2011.

[30] 'Schools' pupil premium for England set at £430,' BBC News (12 December 2010), http://www.bbc.co.uk/news/education-11977844, retrieved 30 November 2011.

[31] Andrew Sparrow, 'Cable accused of planning unworkable mansion tax,' *The Guardian* (21 September 2009).

[32] Rosa Prince, 'Liberal Democrats backtrack over "mansion tax,"' *The Daily Telegraph* (30 November 2009).

[33] Andrew Sparrow, 'Eric Pickles reveals split in coalition over Lib Dems' "mansion tax,"' *The Guardian* (19 August 2011).

[34] Nicholas Watt, 'Revealed: Lib Dems planned before election to abandon tuition fees pledge,' *The Guardian* (12 November 2010).

[35] Patrick Wintour and Larry Elliott, 'Economic plan failing, grassroots Lib Dems say in first sign of revolt,' *The Guardian* (31 October 2011).

[36] Angela Harbutt, 'Errant Knight – a red in yellow clothing?', Liberal Vision (2 November 2011), http://www.liberal-vision.org/2011/11/02/are-labour-supporters-running-on-the-lib-dem-ticket, retrieved 30 November 2011.

[37] 'Party President election – vote Susan Kramer,' Liberal Vision (25 October 2010), http://www.liberal-vision.org/2010/10/25/party-president-election-%e2%80%93-vote-susan-kramer, retrieved 30 November 2011.

[38] 'Tim Farron responds to SLF questions on the party presidency,' Social Liberal Forum (3 November 2010), http://socialliberal.net/2010/11/03/tim-farron-responds-to-slf-questions-on-the-party-presidency, retrieved 30 November 2011.

[39] 'Local Elections 2011,' p. 6.

[40] 'Liverpool 2008: Nick Clegg's Leader's Speech' (9 March 2008), http://www.nickclegg.org.uk/speeches.aspx?pgNo=28, retrieved 18 November 2011.

[41] Ibid.

[42] Andrew Grice, 'Vince Cable emerges as Lib Dems' favourite – and candidate to succeed Nick Clegg,' *The Independent* (7 October 2011).

Chapter 15

[1] 'Clegg hires Thatcher campaign man,' BBC News.
[2] 'Liverpool 2008: Nick Clegg's Leader's Speech'.
[3] Rob Hayward, 'The Liberal Democrats lost 40% of the council seats they were defending but did much better in places where they had an incumbent MP,' Conservative Home (1 June 2011),
http://conservativehome.blogs.com/localgovernment/2011/06/rob-hayward-the-liberal-democrats-lost-40-of-the-council-seats-they-were-defending-but-did-much-bett.html, retrieved 30 November 2011.
[4] 'Local Elections 2011,' p. 6.
[5] 'National Assembly for Wales Elections 2011,' p. 2.
[6] 'Scottish Parliament Elections 2011', p. 10.
[7] For illustrative purposes we have taken an example from the political betting environment which does not take an overall view of the total UK compliment of MPs. This is because we do not seek to be tied into a specific prediction for the outcome of the next election at this stage – which will also be influenced by the outcome of Boundary Commission changes. Therefore, as an illustrative example of the genre, we cite 'General Election 2015: The (Very) Early Assessment' (Tuesday 20 September 2011),
http://politicalbetting.blogspot.com/2011/09/general-election-2015-very-early.html, retrieved 18 November 2011.
[8] 'European Parliament Elections 2009,' p. 7.
[9] 'Fixed-term Parliaments Bill 2010-11,' http://services.parliament.uk/bills/2010-11/fixedtermparliaments.html, retrieved 30 November 2011.
[10] Patrick Wintour, 'Plans to cut UK constituencies from 650 to 600 "could topple coalition,"' *The Guardian* (27 July 2011),
http://www.guardian.co.uk/politics/2011/jul/27/cutting-constituencies-could-topple-coalition, retrieved 30 November 2011.
[11] Anthony Wells, 'Projected effects of the boundary change' (13 September 2011), http://ukpollingreport.co.uk/blog/archives/4009, retrieved 18 November 2011.
[12] Interview with the author (1 November 2011).
[13] Channel 4 News (7 May 2011).
[14] ComRes poll, *The Independent* (15 October 2011).

Chapter 16

[1] Notes by author at a meeting between Nick Clegg and members of the party and the public, National Liberal Club, London (10 August 2011).

References

Chapter 17

[1] 'Nick Clegg's speech to Liberal Democrat Conference,' ibid.

[2] 'Election Statistics: 1918-2007,' pp. 11, 57.

[3] Patrick Wintour, 'Nick Clegg to speak up for "alarm clock Britain,"' *The Guardian* (11 January 2011), http://www.guardian.co.uk/politics/2011/jan/11/nick-clegg-alarm-clock-britain, retrieved 30 November 2011.

[4] Liberal Democrat Federal Constitution, ibid.

[5] Quoted in Armando Costa Pinto, 'Leadership, capacity building and governability in cooperatives' (UN, April 2011), p. 10, http://www.un.org/esa/socdev/social/meetings/egm11/documents/Costa%20Pinto-Leadership,%20capacity%20building.pdf, retrieved 30 November 2011. http://www.brainyquote.com/quotes/authors/p/peter_drucker.html, retrieved 18 November 2011.

[6] 'Election Statistics: 1918-2007,' p. 57.

[7] Ibid.

[8] 'Local elections 2009,' p. 12.

[9] 'Local elections 2011,' p. 7.

[10] 'Election Statistics: 1918-2007,' pp. 11, 57.

[11] 'Liverpool 2008: Nick Clegg's Leader's Speech'.

[12] 'Nick Clegg's speech to Liberal Democrat Conference'.

Appendices

Appendix 1

The Anthem of the Liberal Movement

The original 'Land Song' appears to have its roots in the Georgist land tax movement of the 1800s. The words – without attribution of a lyricist – were published in a document promoting tax reform in the 1880s. A recording made in 1910 achieved sales in the United Kingdom as a 78rpm gramophone record.

The tune is that of 'Marching through Georgia,' which was a favoured piece by the Union army of the American Civil War. The song is regarded as the Liberal anthem, and encapsulates the organisation's commitment to reform of land law. Its central message is that the land belongs to the people.

For more details, a good authority on the subject is Andrew Whitehead who has studied the song, its history and its lyrics extensively. He also provides further points of reference for this enduring song:

http://www.andrewwhitehead.net/the-land-song.html

The Land Song

Sound the call for freedom boys, and sound it far and wide,
March along to victory for God is on our side,
While the voice of nature thunders o'er the rising tide,
'God gave the land to the people!'

Chorus:

The land, the land, 'twas God who made the land,
The land, the land, the ground on which we stand,
Why should we be beggars with the ballot in our hand?
God made the land for the people.

Hark, the sound is spreading from the East and from the West,
Why should we work hard and let the landlords take the best?
Make them pay their taxes on the land just like the rest,
The land was meant for the people.

Clear the way for liberty, the land must all be free,
Liberals will not falter from the fight, tho' stern it be,
'Til the flag we love so well will fly from sea to sea
O'er the land that is free for the people.

The army now is marching on, the battle to begin,
The standard now is raised on high to face the battle din,
We'll never cease from fighting 'til victory we win,
And the land is free for the people.

Appendix 2

Ultimatum to Charles Kennedy

The following article was published on Saturday 7 January 2006 at 12.45am on *The Scotsman*'s website. It referred to a letter sent by 25 MPs calling for Charles to stand down as leader of the Liberal Democrats.

The letter – and those who gave backing to it

This is the statement issued by Liberal Democrat MPs Ed Davey and Sarah Teather, titled: '25 Lib Dem MPs who asked Charles Kennedy to reconsider his position.'

Mr Davey, the Education spokesman, read:

> I and my colleagues believe we need to make our personal positions clear.
>
> Everyone wishes to give Charles the weekend to reflect, and have expressed their sympathy and support for him in his battle with his serious medical condition.
>
> However, we felt we had to indicate what our personal intentions would be next week, given his statement yesterday.

> We have indicated to Charles Kennedy that we would no longer be prepared to serve under his leadership after this weekend.
>
> Following conversations over the last few days it is absolutely clear that a growing number of MPs agree with us.

Ms Teather added: 'I have reached the same conclusion as Ed Davey and I can say with absolute confidence that a further 23 of my colleagues also concur.'

The other 23 MPs are: Norman Baker, Tom Brake, Andrew George, Sandra Gidley, Norman Lamb, David Laws, Jeremy Browne, Alistair Carmichael (Orkney and Shetland), Nick Clegg, Tim Farron, Lynne Featherstone, Julia Goldsworthy, Chris Huhne, Evan Harris, John Pugh, Jo Swinson (Dunbartonshire East), Stephen Williams, Nick Harvey, Martin Horwood, Dan Rogerson, Adrian Sanders, Matthew Taylor and Jenny Willott.

Appendix 3

Full text of the motion passed on 7 March 2009, reaffirming the party's opposition to student tuition fees and also to no-platform policy.

F8 *Investing in Talent, Building the Economy* (Adult Further and Higher Education Policy Paper)

Conference believes that high quality education and training, accessible to all, is crucial to the achievement of a fair, free and open society, in that:
A. It helps people gain the skills, knowledge and aspiration to move out of poverty.
B. It develops their intellectual capabilities so that they can overcome ignorance.
C. It boosts their individual self-esteem so that they have the confidence to challenge conformity.
D. It improves the productivity of the nation and employers.
E. Above all, it widens people's horizons and opens up new choices and experiences to them.

Conference affirms that the key principles on which we base our adult further education and higher education policy should be:
i) The creation of a climbing frame for learning which provides for each student a choice of 'pathways' from basic skills to higher level qualifications and the opportunity at every stage to move sideways and upwards rather than just up a straight

ladder, mixing academic and practical learning to achieve success by following a variety of routes.
ii) The creation of a level playing field in which both tuition and maintenance support is offered equitably to those studying part-time and full-time, in adult further and higher education, and in universities, colleges and work-based settings.

Conference recalls that Liberal Democrats opposed the introduction of tuition fees and top-up fees, and reaffirms the policy of free tuition for first Higher Education degree qualifications, while also extending it to part-time students; this effectively extends the two-year entitlement given to young people in Policy Paper 89, Equality and Excellence, to an entitlement of up to five years free tuition for a qualification up to and including first degree level, to be taken full-time or part-time, as suits the individual.

Conference therefore endorses Policy Paper 90, Investing in Talent, Building the Economy, as a statement of the party's policies for Adult Further and Higher Education, and in particular welcomes proposals to:
1. Promote a coherent approach across the Adult FE and HE sectors by:
   a) Replacing the Higher Education Funding Council for England (HEFCA) and the Learning and Skills Council (LSC) with a single Council for Adult Skills and Higher Education, while transferring 16-19 LSC funding for education and training, including apprenticeships, to local authorities.
   b) Developing a credit-based framework for learning across the FE and HE sectors, using a modular system with funding following the student.
2. Improve opportunities for Adult Further Education by:
   a) Covering the full fee costs for first level 3 qualifications (e.g.

Appendix 3

A-levels, Advanced Apprenticeships and NVQ Level 3) for all adults (including those aged over 25).

b) Making maintenance grants available to adult first level 3 FE students at the same level and on the same means-tested basis as for full-time HE students.

c) Enhancing provision for Adult Community Education.

d) Redirecting resources from the employer-led Train to Gain programme into Adult Education, Adult FE, and Adult Apprenticeships.

3. Strengthen Adult Apprenticeships by:

    a) Fully funding the off-the-job training costs of apprenticeships.

    b) Developing a national application system for apprenticeships similar to the Universities and Colleges Admissions Service (UCAS).

4. Enhance university education and research by:

    a) Developing a common recognised teaching qualification for university lecturers which should first be introduced as an element of doctoral programmes to train all new entrants to university teaching, before ultimately being extended to all those teaching in HE.

    b) Developing doctoral programmes which better prepare graduates for the research world.

    c) Resisting moves to concentrate research in a handful of universities and creating mechanisms to ensure that strategically important new research areas are supported.

    d) Developing with the banks a Career Development Loan scheme to assist students to undertake postgraduate study.

5. Maximise opportunities for study at HE level, and reduce the long-term debt burden on students by:

    a) Abolishing fees for first Higher Education degree qualifications, whether studied full- or part-time.

    b) Improving access to Higher Education for under-

represented groups through transparent and fair admissions criteria which take into account educational background when considering attainment.
c) Reversing cuts to provision for study of Equivalent and Lower Qualifications.
d) Reforming the existing bursary scheme to make it available more fairly across universities on the basis of encouraging study of shortage subjects, and rewarding good performance at university.
6. Defend and strengthen academic freedom and free expression on campus by guaranteeing research and publication freedom and removing unjustified and arbitrary restrictions – such as 'No Platform' policies – on lawful association and lawful free expression.

Conference also notes that British participation rates in international education exchanges are amongst the lowest in Europe and declining; and affirms that time spend studying and working abroad facilitates intercultural dialogue, boosts independence and stimulates competitiveness.

Conference therefore calls for measures to encourage students and educators to take full advantage of opportunities to study and work abroad, such as the ERASMUS programme.

Applicability: England only

Appendix 4

Original coalition agreement 12 May 2010

This is the full text of the coalition agreement published by the Liberal Democrats and the Conservatives on 12 May 2010. This version has been derived from the BBC website at:

http://news.bbc.co.uk/1/hi/8677933.stm

The document was further refined and extended to form a comprehensive statement of the government's intentions in all areas of policy. A full PDF version of that document, issued in late May 2010, is available on the Cabinet Office website at:

http://www.cabinetoffice.gov.uk/sites/default/files/resources/coalition-agreement-may-2010_0.pdf

Full text of original agreement

This document sets out agreements reached between the Conservatives and Liberal Democrats on a range of issues. These are the issues that needed to be resolved between us in order for us to work together as a strong and stable government. It will be followed in due course by a final Coalition Agreement, covering the full range of policy and including foreign, defence and domestic policy issues not covered in this document.

The Alternative View

1. Deficit Reduction

The parties agree that deficit reduction and continuing to ensure economic recovery is the most urgent issue facing. We have therefore agreed that there will need to be:

- a significantly accelerated reduction in the structural deficit over the course of a Parliament, with the main burden of deficit reduction borne by reduced spending rather than increased taxes;
- arrangements that will protect those on low incomes from the effect of public-sector pay constraint and other spending constraints;
- and protection of jobs by stopping Labour's proposed jobs tax.

The parties agree that a plan for deficit reduction should be set out in an emergency budget within 50 days of the signing of any agreement; the parties note that the credibility of a plan on deficit reduction depends on its long-term deliverability, not just the depth of immediate cuts. New forecasts of growth and borrowing should be made by an independent Office for Budget Responsibility for this emergency budget.

The parties agree that modest cuts of £6 billion to non-frontline services can be made within the financial year 2010-11, subject to advice from the Treasury and the Bank of England on their feasibility and advisability. Some proportion of these savings can be used to support jobs, for example through the cancelling of some backdated demands for business rates. Other policies upon which we are agreed will further support job creation and green investment, such as work programmes for the unemployed and a green deal for energy efficiency investment.

The parties agree that reductions can be made to the Child Trust Fund and tax credits for higher earners.

2. Spending Review – NHS, Schools and a Fairer Society

The parties agree that a full Spending Review should be held, reporting this Autumn, following a fully consultative process involving all tiers of government and the private sector.

The parties agree that funding for the NHS should increase in real terms in each year of the Parliament, while recognising the impact this decision would have on other departments. The target of spending 0.7% of GNI on overseas aid will also remain in place.

We will fund a significant premium for disadvantaged pupils from outside the schools budget by reductions in spending elsewhere.

The parties commit to holding a full Strategic Security and Defence Review alongside the Spending Review with strong involvement of the Treasury.

The Government will be committed to the maintenance of Britain's nuclear deterrent, and have agreed that the renewal of Trident should be scrutinised to ensure value for money. Liberal Democrats will continue to make the case for alternatives. We will immediately play a strong role in the Nuclear Non-Proliferation Treaty Review Conference, and press for continued progress on multilateral disarmament.

The parties commit to establishing an independent commission to review the long-term affordability of public sector pensions, while protecting accrued rights.

We will restore the earnings link for the basic state pension from April 2011 with a 'triple guarantee' that pensions are raised by the higher of earnings, prices or 2.5%, as proposed by the Liberal Democrats.

3. Tax Measures

The parties agree that the personal allowance for income tax should be increased in order to help lower- and middle-income earners. We agree to announce in the first Budget a substantial increase in the personal allowance from April 2011, with the benefits focused on those with lower and middle incomes. This will be funded with the money that would have been used to pay for the increase in Employee National Insurance thresholds proposed by the Conservatives, as well as revenues from increases in Capital Gains Tax rates for non-business assets as described below. The increase in Employer National Insurance thresholds proposed by the Conservatives will go ahead in order to stop Labour's jobs tax. We also agree to a longer-term policy objective of further increasing the personal allowance to £10,000, making further real-terms steps each year towards this objective.

We agree that this should take priority over other tax cuts, including cuts to Inheritance Tax. We also agree that provision will be made for Liberal Democrat MPs to abstain on budget resolutions to introduce transferable tax allowances for married couples without prejudice to this coalition agreement.

The parties agree that a switch should be made to a per-plane, rather than per-passenger duty; a proportion of any increased revenues over time will be used to help fund increases in the personal allowance.

We further agree to seek a detailed agreement on taxing non-business capital gains at rates similar or close to those applied to income, with generous exemptions for entrepreneurial business activities.

The parties agree that tackling tax avoidance is essential for the new government, and that all efforts will be made to do so, including detailed development of Liberal Democrat proposals.

4. Banking Reform

The parties agree that reform to the banking system is essential to avoid a repeat of Labour's financial crisis, to promote a competitive economy, to sustain the recovery and to protect and sustain jobs.

We agree that a banking levy will be introduced. We will seek a detailed agreement on implementation.

Appendix 4

We agree to bring forward detailed proposals for robust action to tackle unacceptable bonuses in the financial services sector; in developing these proposals, we will ensure they are effective in reducing risk.

We agree to bring forward detailed proposals to foster diversity, promote mutuals and create a more competitive banking industry.

We agree that ensuring the flow of credit to viable SMEs is essential for supporting growth and should be a core priority for a new government, and we will work together to develop effective proposals to do so. This will include consideration of both a major loan guarantee scheme and the use of net lending targets for the nationalised banks.

The parties wish to reduce systemic risk in the banking system and will establish an independent commission to investigate the complex issue of separating retail and investment banking in a sustainable way; while recognising that this would take time to get right, the commission will be given an initial timeframe of one year to report.

The parties agree that the regulatory system needs reform to avoid a repeat of Labour's financial crisis. We agree to bring forward proposals to give the Bank of England control of macro-prudential regulation and oversight of micro-prudential regulation.

The parties also agree to rule out joining the European Single Currency during the duration of this agreement.

5. Immigration

We have agreed that there should be an annual limit on the number of non-EU economic migrants admitted into the UK to live and work. We will consider jointly the mechanism for implementing the limit. We will end the detention of children for immigration purposes.

6. Political Reform

The parties agree to the establishment of five year fixed-term parliaments. A Conservative-Liberal Democrat coalition government will put a binding motion before the House of Commons in the first days following this agreement stating that the next general election will be held on the first Thursday of May 2015. Following this motion, legislation will be brought forward to make provision for fixed-term parliaments of five years. This legislation will also provide for dissolution if 55% or more of the House votes in favour.

The parties will bring forward a Referendum Bill on electoral reform, which includes provision for the introduction of the Alternative Vote in the event of a positive result in the referendum, as well as for the creation of fewer and more equal-sized constituencies. Both parties will whip their Parliamentary Parties in both Houses to support a simple majority referendum on the Alternative Vote, without prejudice to the positions parties will take during such a referendum.

The parties will bring forward early legislation to introduce a power of recall, allowing voters to force a by-election where an MP was found to have engaged in serious wrongdoing and having had a petition calling for a by-election signed by 10% of his or her constituents.

We agree to establish a committee to bring forward proposals for a wholly or mainly elected upper chamber on the basis of proportional representation. The committee will come forward with a draft motion by December 2010. It is likely that this bill will advocate single long terms of office. It is also likely there will be a grandfathering system for current Peers. In the interim, Lords appointments will be made with the objective of creating a second chamber reflective of the share of the vote secured by the political parties in the last general election.

The parties will bring forward the proposals of the Wright

Committee for reform to the House of Commons in full – starting with the proposed committee for management of programmed business and including government business within its scope by the third year of the Parliament.

The parties agree to reduce electoral fraud by speeding up the implementation of individual voter registration.

We have agreed to establish a commission to consider the 'West Lothian question'.

The parties agree to the implementation of the Calman Commission proposals and the offer of a referendum on further Welsh devolution.

The parties will tackle lobbying through introducing a statutory register of lobbyists. We also agree to pursue a detailed agreement on limiting donations and reforming party funding in order to remove big money from politics.

The parties will promote the radical devolution of power and greater financial autonomy to local government and community groups. This will include a full review of local government finance.

7. Pensions and Welfare

The parties agree to phase out the default retirement age and hold a review to set the date at which the state pension age starts to rise to 66, although it will not be sooner than 2016 for men and 2020 for women. We agree to end the rules requiring compulsory annuitisation at 75.

We agree to implement the Parliamentary and Health Ombudsman's recommendation to make fair and transparent payments to Equitable Life policy holders, through an independent payment scheme, for their relative loss as a consequence of regulatory failure.

The parties agree to end all existing welfare-to-work programmes and to create a single welfare-to-work programme to help all unemployed people get back into work.

We agree that Jobseeker's Allowance claimants facing the most significant barriers to work should be referred to the aforementioned newly created welfare-to-work programme immediately, not after 12 months as is currently the case. We agree that Jobseeker's Allowance claimants aged under 25 should be referred to the programme after a maximum of six months.

The parties agree to realign contracts with welfare-to-work service providers to reflect more closely the results they achieve in getting people back into work.

We agree that the funding mechanism used by government to finance welfare-to-work programmes should be reformed to reflect the fact that initial investment delivers later savings in lower benefit expenditure.

We agree that receipt of benefits for those able to work should be conditional on the willingness to work.

8. Education
Schools
We agree to promote the reform of schools in order to ensure:
- that new providers can enter the state school system in response to parental demand;
- that all schools have greater freedom over curriculum;
- and that all schools are held properly accountable.

Higher education
We await Lord Browne's final report into higher education funding, and will judge its proposals against the need to:
- increase social mobility;
- take into account the impact on student debt;
- ensure a properly funded university sector;
- improve the quality of teaching;
- advance scholarship;
- and attract a higher proportion of students from disadvantaged backgrounds.

If the response of the Government to Lord Browne's report is one that Liberal Democrats cannot accept, then arrangements will be made to enable Liberal Democrat MPs to abstain in any vote.

9. Relations with the EU

We agree that the British Government will be a positive participant in the European Union, playing a strong and positive role with our partners, with the goal of ensuring that all the nations of Europe are equipped to face the challenges of the 21st century: global competitiveness, global warming and global poverty.

We agree that there should be no further transfer of sovereignty or powers over the course of the next Parliament. We will examine the balance of the EU's existing competences and will, in particular, work to limit the application of the Working Time Directive in the United Kingdom. We agree that we will amend the 1972 European Communities Act so that any proposed future Treaty that transferred areas of power, or competences, would be subject to a referendum on that Treaty – a 'referendum lock'. We will amend the 1972 European Communities Act so that the use of any passerelle would require primary legislation.

We will examine the case for a United Kingdom Sovereignty Bill to make it clear that ultimate authority remains with Parliament.

We agree that Britain will not join or prepare to join the Euro in this Parliament.

We agree that we will strongly defend the UK's national interests in the forthcoming EU budget negotiations and that the EU budget should only focus on those areas where the EU can add value.

We agree that we will press for the European Parliament only to have one seat, in Brussels.

We agree that we will approach forthcoming legislation in the area of criminal justice on a case-by-case basis, with a view to maximising our country's security, protecting Britain's civil liberties and preserving the integrity of our criminal justice system. Britain will not participate in the establishment of any European Public Prosecutor.

10. Civil Liberties
The parties agree to implement a full programme of measures to reverse the substantial erosion of civil liberties under the Labour Government and roll back state intrusion.
This will include:
- A Freedom or Great Repeal Bill.
- The scrapping of the ID card scheme, the National Identity register, the next generation of biometric passports and the Contact Point Database.
- Outlawing the fingerprinting of children at school without parental permission.
- The extension of the scope of the Freedom of Information Act to provide greater transparency.
- Adopting the protections of the Scottish model for the DNA database.
- The protection of historic freedoms through the defence of trial by jury.
- The restoration of rights to non-violent protest.
- The review of libel laws to protect freedom of speech.
- Safeguards against the misuse of anti-terrorism legislation.
- Further regulation of CCTV.
- Ending of storage of internet and email records without good reason.
- A new mechanism to prevent the proliferation of unnecessary new criminal offences.

11. Environment
The parties agree to implement a full programme of measures to fulfil our joint ambitions for a low-carbon and eco-friendly economy, including:

Appendix 4

- The establishment of a smart grid and the roll-out of smart meters.
- The full establishment of feed-in tariff systems in electricity – as well as the maintenance of banded ROCs.
- Measures to promote a huge increase in energy from waste through anaerobic digestion.
- The creation of a green investment bank.
- The provision of home energy improvement paid for by the savings from lower energy bills.
- Retention of energy performance certificates while scrapping HIPs.
- Measures to encourage marine energy.
- The establishment of an emissions performance standard that will prevent coal-fired power stations being built unless they are equipped with sufficient CCS to meet the emissions performance standard.
- The establishment of a high-speed rail network.
- The cancellation of the third runway at Heathrow.
- The refusal of additional runways at Gatwick and Stansted.
- The replacement of the Air Passenger Duty with a per flight duty.
- The provision of a floor price for carbon, as well as efforts to persuade the EU to move towards full auctioning of ETS permits.
- Measures to make the import or possession of illegal timber a criminal offence.
- Measures to promote green spaces and wildlife corridors in order to halt the loss of habitats and restore biodiversity.
- Mandating a national recharging network for electric and plug-in hybrid vehicles.
- Continuation of the present Government's proposals for public sector investment in CCS technology for four coal-fired power stations; and a specific commitment to reduce central

government carbon emissions by 10 per cent within 12 months.

We are agreed that we would seek to increase the target for energy from renewable sources, subject to the advice of the Climate Change Committee.

Liberal Democrats have long opposed any new nuclear construction. Conservatives, by contrast, are committed to allowing the replacement of existing nuclear power stations provided they are subject to the normal planning process for major projects (under a new national planning statement) and provided also that they receive no public subsidy.

We have agreed a process that will allow Liberal Democrats to maintain their opposition to nuclear power while permitting the government to bring forward the national planning statement for ratification by Parliament so that new nuclear construction becomes possible.

This process will involve:

- the government completing the drafting of a national planning statement and putting it before Parliament;
- specific agreement that a Liberal Democrat spokesman will speak against the planning statement, but that Liberal Democrat MPs will abstain;
- and clarity that this will not be regarded as an issue of confidence.

Appendix 5

Tuition fees vote

The vote on whether to permit universities in England to increase student tuition fees was held in the House of Commons on 9 December 2010. The vote was carried by 323 votes in favour to 302 against. The Liberal Democrats were officially instructed to vote for the proposal.

27 Liberal Democrat MPs voted for the motion. A further 21 voted against. Nine abstained. Six Conservatives also rebelled against their government line.

Of the 15 Liberal Democrat MPs who had contributed to *The Orange Book* or *Britain After Blair*, 13 – or 87% – voted for the proposals. Only Simon Hughes (who abstained) and Chris Huhne (who was not present for the vote) did not. None of those who had written for *The Orange Book* or *Britain After Blair* voted against the proposal.

For comparison, only 14 out of 42 non-*Orange Book/Britain After Blair* MPs – 33% – voted for the increase. 22 voted against and six abstained.

The votes of the Orange Bookers were sufficient to ensure the victory for the government. Had the Orange Book caucus voted against the proposals, it would have been defeated.

Source: Hansard HC, 9 December 2010, cols. 624-630.

Lib Dem MPs who voted for an increase in tuition fees (*Orange Book/Britain After Blair* contributors in bold)
Danny Alexander (Inverness, Nairn, Badenoch and Strathspey)
Norman Baker (Lewes)
Sir Alan Beith (Berwick-upon-Tweed)
Gordon Birtwistle (Burnley)
Tom Brake (Carshalton & Wallington)
Jeremy Browne (Taunton Deane)
Malcolm Bruce (Gordon)
Paul Burstow (Sutton & Cheam)
Vincent Cable (Twickenham)
Alistair Carmichael (Orkney & Shetland)
Nick Clegg (Sheffield Hallam)
Edward Davey (Kingston & Surbiton)
Lynne Featherstone (Hornsey & Wood Green)
Don Foster (Bath)
Stephen Gilbert (St Austell and Newquay)
Duncan Hames (Chippenham)
Nick Harvey (Devon North)
David Heath (Somerton & Frome)
John Hemming (Birmingham Yardley)
Norman Lamb (Norfolk North)
David Laws (Yeovil)
Michael Moore (Berwickshire, Roxburgh & Selkirk)
Andrew Stunell (Hazel Grove)
Jo Swinson (Dunbartonshire East)
Sarah Teather (Brent Central)
David Ward (Bradford East)
Steve Webb (Thornbury and Yate).

Appendix 5

Lib Dem Government whip – taken to have supported an increase in tuition fees
Government whip Mark Hunter (Cheadle) acted as a teller.

Lib Dem MPs who voted against an increase in tuition fees – the 'rebels'
(*Orange Book/Britain After Blair* contributors in bold)
Annette Brooke (Dorset Mid & Poole North)
Sir Menzies Campbell (Fife North East)
Michael Crockart (Edinburgh West)
Tim Farron (Westmorland & Lonsdale)
Andrew George (St Ives)
Mike Hancock (Portsmouth South)
Julian Huppert (Cambridge)
Charles Kennedy (Ross, Skye & Lochaber)
John Leech (Manchester Withington)
Stephen Lloyd (Eastbourne)
Greg Mulholland (Leeds North West)
John Pugh (Southport)
Alan Reid (Argyll & Bute)
Dan Rogerson (Cornwall North)
Bob Russell (Colchester)
Adrian Sanders (Torbay)
Ian Swales (Redcar)
Mark Williams (Ceredigion)
Roger Williams (Brecon and Radnorshire)
Jenny Willott (Cardiff Central)
Simon Wright (Norwich South).

The Alternative View

Lib Dems who abstained on an increase in tuition fees (*Orange Book/Britain After Blair* contributors in bold)
Lorely Burt (Solihull)
Martin Horwood (Cheltenham) (Abroad)
Simon Hughes (Bermondsey & Old Southwark)
Chris Huhne (Eastleigh) (Abroad)
Tessa Munt (Wells)
Sir Robert Smith (Aberdeenshire West and Kincardine) (Abroad)
John Thurso (Caithness, Sutherland & Easter Ross)
Stephen Williams (Bristol West)

Appendix 6

Liberal Democrat ministers

Figures have varied in different publications regarding how many ministers the Liberal Democrats actually have. This is because of debate about the status of government whips, who are categorised differently by different people. We include them in the list for completeness, but have only categorised the Deputy Chief Whip as a minister for our analysis.

We have also focused on the Commons, as no peers contributed to the Orange Book project. If we were to include the Lords as well, then two additional ministers would be included in our statistical analysis – Lords McNally and Shutt. However, we would also then have to include the total compliment of Lib Dem peers in the analysis, which would make the proportion of non-Orange Bookers who had achieved a ministry position even smaller – 8% including all Lib Dem government whips, and 6% excluding the junior whips. This compares to 86% of *Orange Book/Britain After Blair* contributors who held a ministry role at some point up to February 2012.

Here is the list of those categorised as ministers on the Liberal Democrat website as of February 2012. Note that David Laws was a Cabinet minister prior to his resignation in May 2010, after which he returned to the back bench. Chris Huhne resigned from the

Cabinet in February 2012, and his role was back-filled by another Oranger Booker – Ed Davey. Thus 100% of Lib Dem Cabinet ministers were still Orange Bookers at this point.

Current information is available online at:

http://www.libdems.org.uk/cabinet.aspx

Liberal Democrat Cabinet Ministers
(*Orange Book/Britain After Blair* contributors in bold)

Danny Alexander MP: Chief Secretary to the Treasury (from May 2010)
Vince Cable MP: Secretary of State for Business, Innovation and Skills
Nick Clegg MP: Deputy Prime Minister
Ed Davey MP: Secretary of State for Energy and Climate Change
(Chris Huhne: Secretary of State for Energy and Climate Change until 3rd February 2012)
(**David Laws MP: Chief Secretary to the Treasury until 29th May 2010**)
Michael Moore MP: Secretary of State for Scotland

Liberal Democrat ministers (including assistant government whips)
(*Orange Book/Britain After Blair* contributors in bold)

Norman Baker MP: Under Secretary of State for Department of Transport
Jeremy Browne MP: Minister of State for the Foreign and Commonwealth Office
Paul Burstow MP: Minister of State for the Department of Health
Alistair Carmichael MP: Deputy Chief Whip in the House of Commons

Appendix 6

Norman Lamb MP: Under Secretary of State for the Department of Business, Innovation and Skills
Lynne Featherstone MP: Under Secretary of State (Minister for Equalities) for the Home Office
Nick Harvey MP: Minister of State (Minister for the Armed Forces) for the Ministry of Defence
David Heath CBE MP: Secretary (Deputy Leader) to the Office of the Leader of the Commons
Mark Hunter MP: Assistant Government Whip
Jenny Willott MP: Assistant Government Whip
Lord McNally: Minister of State for the Ministry of Justice
Lord Shutt OBE: Deputy Chief Whip in the House of Lords
Andrew Stunell OBE MP: Under Secretary of State to the Department for Communities and Local Government
Sarah Teather MP: Minister of State to the Department for Education
Lord Wallace: Government Whip
Steve Webb MP: Minister of State for the Department of Work and Pensions

Biography

Lembit Öpik was born in Northern Ireland in 1965, to Estonian parents who fled to the UK to escape Stalin's oppressive regime. Following many years in student politics, as President at the University of Bristol Union and later as a member of the National Union of Students Executive, he went on to serve on Newcastle-upon-Tyne's City Council in the 1990s. In 1997 he was elected as the Liberal Democrat Member of Parliament for Montgomeryshire. In Parliament he served on the Lib Dem Shadow Cabinet in various roles, including as Shadow Housing Minister, Shadow Energy Minister, Shadow Secretary of State for Wales and Shadow Secretary of State for Northern Ireland, and also as leader of the Welsh Liberal Democrats. He was also a member of the Business select committee and the Agriculture select committee.

Lembit is a regular contributor in the public domain on political issues and has a profile which reaches far beyond the conventional bounds of the political media. His other work includes public speaking, political consultancy, training & development, journalism and entertainment programmes.

Ed Joyce

Born in Cheltenham in 1965, Ed Joyce joined the Young Liberals in 1979. Inspired by the left libertarianism of Roy Jenkins, Ed joined the Social Democratic Party – the SDP – at its formation, rising to a national position in the Young Social Democrats. He moved to the Liberal Democrats upon the SDP's merger with the Liberals.

Ed has held many roles, including conference delegate, ward organiser and activist – all at grassroots level. In 2007 he formed the libertarian Open Liberty Alliance with Lib Dem Councillor Gavin Webb. Following Webb's suspension from the party in 2008 he ran the successful 'Save the Stoke One' campaign which saw Webb's ultimate reinstatement.

Ed helped launch the Liberal Vision blog in 2009 and has been linked with the faction ever since. Like his brother, Andrew, he has served as a councillor – in the London Borough of Sutton, applying the theory and practice of community politics in his work.

Index

A

Abolition 81, 84, 148-9
Absolute majority 98-9, 107-8, 115, 309
Activists 5, 7, 36-7, 39, 63, 77, 97, 103, 121, 148, 178-80, 195-6, 201-2, 210-11, 320
Alcohol 45, 47, 271
Alternative Vote see AV
Alternative Vote system 115, 118, 177
Ambitions 45, 49, 51, 83, 133, 143, 146, 260, 277, 305, 355, 363
Anger 87-8, 163, 180, 182-3, 185-6, 209, 221, 299
Authoritarian 44, 58, 264, 269, 273, 295-9
AV (Alternative Vote) 5, 81, 114-20, 151-2, 236, 239
AV referendum 112-13, 116, 120-3, 126, 139, 183, 281, 289, 293, 328

B

Ballot 16, 49, 99, 101, 119-20, 211
Banks 61, 63-4, 76, 82
Battle 77, 103, 214, 241
Unceasing 170-2
BBC 47, 51, 56, 70, 239, 351
Bedford 25-6, 101-2
Benefits 13-14, 20, 98, 114, 120, 136-7, 163, 165, 192, 203, 222, 263, 290, 307, 348-9
Big Society 259-61, 352
Blair, Tony 4, 28, 36, 40, 46, 49, 58, 88, 130-2, 142, 154, 156, 208, 226, 232-3
Boundaries, new 329-30
Boundary changes 42, 71, 202, 318, 328-33, 335, 356
Breakthrough 29, 31, 33, 35, 37, 39, 41, 43, 45, 47, 49, 51, 53
Britain 17, 23, 29, 33, 46, 49, 62, 71, 83, 88, 102-3, 130-1, 136, 142, 208
British Government 172, 346
British Muslims 163-4
British Parliament 105, 114, 208, 315, 359
British politics 17, 22, 61, 77, 231
Brown, Gordon 61, 66, 68, 199, 223, 304
By-election victories 46, 110, 205
  Individual 205

By-elections 89-91, 95, 101-3, 107, 178, 180, 188, 204-7, 209, 214-5, 302, 344, 353, 357, 366.

C

Cabinet 6, 121-2, 131, 143-4, 233-4, 297

Cable, Vince 66-8, 141, 145-6, 208, 255, 304, 351

Cameron, David 19-20, 55, 60, 62-4, 67-9, 72, 75, 86, 120, 128, 144, 147, 151, 160-4, 166-8, 171, 232, 237-8, 264-5, 282, 286, 307-8, 346

Cameron's muscular liberalism 167, 172, 298

Campaigning 34, 61, 76, 116, 119, 201, 209, 213-14, 239, 252, 284
  Positive 240, 243, 245

Campbell, Ming 50-1, 66, 88, 146, 276

Campaign for Real Ale (CAMRA) 106

Candidates 2, 6, 47, 50, 99-101, 105-9, 111, 113, 115, 126-7, 151, 155-6, 206, 294, 302-3

Chart, Nolan 231-5, 245, 252, 295-7, 299, 302-3, 359

Child 76, 136-7, 187

Children 65, 129, 135-6, 161, 188, 283

Clarity 127, 143, 146, 148, 224, 234-5, 238, 263-4, 273, 297

Clegg, Nick 6-7, 49-52, 55, 66-71, 73-5, 77, 98-9, 102, 105, 117-21, 128-30, 150, 171-3, 188-92, 240, 277-84, 308-9, 314-17, 319-23, 325-8, 330-3, 337-40, 342-54, 360-5, 366-7.

Clegg administration 189, 310

Cleggmania 53, 69, 198

Clegg's Defence 341, 343, 345, 347, 349, 351, 353

Clegg's departure 320, 328

Clegg's leadership 176, 321, 338, 340
  Sustaining 331

Clegg's performance 68, 284

Clegg's speech 171, 188, 190-1

Coalition 72-5, 84-6, 112-13, 149-51, 183-4, 224-5, 248-50, 304-6, 314, 316-18, 320-8, 330-3, 337-40, 348-50, 364-5

Coalition agreement 104, 114, 120, 125, 148, 183, 224, 307, 362, 364

Coalition breakdown 326-7

Coalition government 150, 247, 305, 328, 347

Coalition negotiations 74, 87

Coalition partners 83, 86, 90, 97, 102-3, 218, 220-1, 224-5, 234-5, 238, 245, 287, 298, 307, 336-7
  Former 307, 325

Commons 37, 39, 50, 59, 64, 66, 72, 77, 79, 89, 195, 197, 206, 308, 311

Community politicians 202, 260-1

Community politics 39, 44, 183-5, 188-9, 195-7, 199, 201-3, 205-7, 209, 211-15, 260-1, 281, 283, 311, 357-9

Index

Practice of 8, 182, 184, 192-3, 196, 213-14, 366
Concept 19, 25, 110, 138, 157, 160-1, 166, 171, 173-4, 236, 239, 261, 265, 362
Conditions 5, 35, 43, 118, 122, 141, 251, 266, 277, 338, 342, 364-5
Conference 57, 148, 168, 177-80, 182, 188, 191-2, 234, 280, 297, 353, 357
Conservative administration 84, 325
Conservative agenda 85, 140, 221, 295
Conservative coalition partners 100
Conservative ethos 27, 141
Conservative Government 16, 28, 34, 220, 275, 308, 324
Conservative ideology 168, 261
Conservative image 27
Conservative leadership 236, 306
Conservative-led Government 6
Conservative-Liberal Democrat coalition 5, 300, 311, 339, 366
Conservative ministers 207, 262
Conservative movement 39
Conservative MPs 22, 148
Conservative outlook 17, 20, 23
Conservative Party 15, 18, 38, 74, 147, 159, 163, 181, 222, 232, 269, 297, 335, 348
Conservative policies 330
Conservative votes 36, 120, 305, 323
  Tactical 307
Conservatives 23-6, 36-8, 62-7, 69-72, 84-6, 89-91, 96-8, 109-14, 147-53, 198-200, 218-21, 231-4, 285-7, 306-7, 325-31
  Liberal 150
Conservatives and Labour 26, 85, 110-11, 153, 251, 267, 339, 365
Conservatives and Lib Dems 5, 73, 199, 234, 306, 322
Consistency 26, 122, 133-4, 140, 223, 225, 248-9, 262
Constituencies 88, 90, 99-100, 104, 109, 114-15, 196, 198, 202, 207-8, 329, 352, 364
Context 37, 90, 96, 100, 117-18, 121, 139, 197, 231, 243-4, 278, 293, 314, 342, 361
Contradictions 66, 133-4, 138-9, 156, 169
Control 13, 37, 61, 63, 98, 214, 256, 260, 277-8, 291, 293, 316, 346
Council base 202-3, 315
Council seats 39, 55, 57, 102, 119, 192, 199, 201-2, 206, 209, 211, 215, 363
  Local 104, 363
  Lost 189, 316
Councillors 37, 39, 57, 98-9, 103, 116, 195-7, 200-1, 203-4, 208, 210, 215, 283, 318, 363-4
Councils 97-8, 102, 200-2, 210, 213, 260-1, 337, 363
Coup 30, 45, 51, 55, 63, 318, 331-3, 340
CPS 268-9
Credit 43, 84-5, 313

425

Crime   129-30, 135, 139, 256-8, 268
  Property   256, 258

D

Dangers   138, 140, 175, 182, 199, 210-11, 330-1
Delegates   58, 167, 177-80, 183-5, 191, 365
Deputy Prime Minister   55, 75, 77, 147, 169, 238, 249, 284, 314, 320, 333, 335-7, 339-40, 360-2, 365
Deregulation   63, 65, 69
Direction   6, 133, 272, 284, 288, 348, 358
Dividend   256-7
  Citizen's   256-9

E

Economy   68-9, 74, 117, 130, 234, 295
Elections   24-5, 32, 35-8, 59-60, 67-70, 95-9, 104-6, 153, 204-5, 301-3, 315-16, 321-2, 324-6, 337-9, 352-4
  Consecutive   24, 43, 60, 233
  General   34-6, 39-40, 55-8, 67, 71, 77-80, 108-9, 113-14, 202-5, 239-40, 305, 316-17, 319-20, 325-7, 362-3
  Next   104, 113, 248, 305, 308-9, 312, 314, 316, 320, 339-40, 350, 360, 366
  Proportional system of   99-100, 112, 315
Electoral pacts   306-7, 314, 365

Electoral performance   25, 225, 318
Electoral reform   5, 26, 33, 77, 104, 114, 118-20, 183, 310
Electoral system   24-6, 30, 100, 106, 109-14, 117-19, 207
Electorate   28, 33, 43, 84-5, 108, 119-20, 235, 245, 260, 270, 289-90, 326, 339
Electors   15, 29, 34, 36, 38, 43, 62, 99-100, 105, 111, 113, 115-16, 188, 197, 307
Employers   15-16
Employment   130, 136, 139
Energy   130, 137-8, 277-8, 302, 358
Engagement   164, 170-2, 281, 359
  Smart   169-70
European Elections   57, 207, 221, 320, 328
European Parliament   114, 207-8, 221, 328, 359
European Union   57, 138, 220-1, 350-1

F

Factionalism   294, 297
Factions   276, 294, 296-7, 300-3
Families   65, 82, 89, 96, 129, 135-6, 145, 149, 253
Family norms   135-6
Farron, Tim   147, 179, 184-5, 212
Fast Reaction Early Decision (FRED)   75
Fortunes, liberal movement's   24
Freedom   13-14, 32, 82, 84, 125, 128, 130, 165, 168, 181, 248, 253-

Index

4, 267-8, 281, 336
Economic 232, 295
Personal 232

G

George, Lloyd 17, 25, 30, 254
GLA (Greater London Authority) 154, 202, 305
Government 3-4, 79-80, 84-7, 89-91, 96-7, 142, 185-7, 209, 223-7, 233-4, 321-3, 343-5, 350-4, 356-8, 360-1
  Liberal 25, 266
  Radical majority Liberal Democrat 355
  Stable 72, 122, 351
Government Art Collection 81, 85
Government benches 72, 323
Government policy 85, 150
Greater London Authority (GLA) 154, 202, 305
Group 3, 12, 46-7, 58, 96, 128, 132-3, 139, 149, 156, 164, 247-8, 261, 267, 295-7
  Community 260-1
Growth 38-9, 43, 55, 60, 170, 187, 204, 206, 215, 225, 297, 303, 337, 339, 343

H

Hodgson 26, 101
Hollow Men 177, 179, 181, 183, 185, 187, 189, 191
Homosexuality 165, 269
Hughes, Simon 49-50, 58, 131 154, 285, 327

Huhne, Chris 50, 52, 117, 126, 137, 145-6, 208, 212, 233, 243-4, 255, 277, 281, 298, 304
Hung Parliament 4, 72, 112, 199

I

Image 35, 39, 43, 155, 168, 192, 218, 225, 229-39, 241-5, 248, 251-2, 263, 356-7, 359-60
  Assertive Lib Dem 234
  Consistent 226-7, 250
  Liberal 232, 310
  Party's 140, 225, 229, 234, 237, 244, 277
Income 150, 254-5, 257, 346
Income tax 18, 80, 83, 150, 187, 254-5
Independence 159, 223, 248-9, 334, 360, 366
Intervention 20, 40, 175, 262, 295, 320, 347
Interventionist 295-6, 299-300
Investment 20, 72, 82, 84, 187, 203-6, 351

J

Journalists 48, 141, 144, 146, 179, 231

K

Kennedy, Charles 29, 38-52, 88, 207, 240, 243, 291, 333
Kennedy's performance 41-2
Kennedy's resignation 48-9, 52
Kingston Hospital 241-2
Kinnock, Neil 34

Kramer, Susan   129, 138, 153-5, 179

L
Labour   24-8, 34, 36, 38-40, 42-3, 55-6, 73, 89-91, 95-101, 107-10, 199-201, 230-3, 304-7, 317, 321-30
Labour and Liberal Democrat   28, 105
Labour candidate selection   153
Labour-Conservative partnership   325
Labour government   34, 168, 219, 309, 344
  Incumbent   43
Labour leaders   336
labour market   21, 137
Labour Minister   65, 83, 109
Labour MPs   91, 95, 108, 116, 178
Labour no-confidence motion   324-5
Labour parties   30, 113, 183, 301, 365
Labour Party   16, 56, 61, 96, 116, 118, 232, 268
Labour plus Liberal vote   25
Labour support   100, 210, 305
Labourite agenda   295, 300
Labour's vote   100, 152
Land   11-12, 14-18, 22, 26, 39, 56, 148, 165, 255, 257
Land grab   11-12, 14, 18
Law   3, 13, 20, 89, 144, 163, 165, 167, 266-8, 270-2
Laws, David   74, 127-30, 133, 136-7, 142-5, 147, 150, 208, 233, 264-5, 273, 297, 299

Leader   6-7, 37, 39, 45-6, 48-9, 51-2, 66-7, 275-7, 288-94, 302-4, 315-21, 334-7, 339-41, 348-9, 360-3
  First Liberal   198
  New   318, 322, 328, 338, 360
  New Lib Dem   322
  Next   310-11, 364
  Next Lib Dem   293, 326
Leader's role   50, 336, 357
Leader's speeches   179, 282
Leadership   6-8, 36-8, 51-2, 120-3, 146-8, 150-1, 154-6, 247-50, 275-7, 279-81, 287-95, 297-301, 303-14, 318-22, 327-30
  Current   7, 207, 211, 238, 276, 290, 292-3, 305, 308-9, 356, 367-8
Leadership candidates   50, 290, 310
  Prospective   290, 303
Leadership election   47, 50, 52, 126, 132, 156, 244, 277, 302-3, 310, 318, 322, 331, 335, 337
  Next   50, 293-4, 296, 302, 310-12, 318
Leadership election campaign   316
Leadership style   50-1
Leadership team   128, 275, 360-1
Left-leaning candidate   294
Left-leaning vote   25, 190, 304, 306, 312, 325-6, 330, 339
Letter   46-7, 300
Lib Dem and Conservative candidates   327

Index

Lib Dem Cabinet 140, 208, 233
Lib Dem coalition 327
Lib Dem coalition partners 89, 362
Lib Dem Deputy Prime Minister 122, 321, 335
Lib Dem election campaign leader Lord Razzall 239
Lib Dem leadership 203, 285, 299
Lib Dem leadership candidates 326
Lib Dem leadership election 121
Lib Dem line 56, 86
Lib Dem majority government 321
Lib Dem membership 282
Lib Dem MPs 47, 60, 87, 199, 285, 306, 311, 317, 329
Lib Dem support 305, 326, 339
Lib Dem-Tory coalition, new 325
Lib Dems 32-44, 55-60, 69-72, 82-91, 95-104, 109-14, 116-20, 143-7, 199-203, 220-4, 284-7, 304-8, 322-7, 329-31, 335-9
  Deal-breaking 323, 325
  Local elections 55
  Vote 111, 361
Lib-Lab coalition 75, 308
Liberal agenda 8, 129-30, 148, 210, 245
Liberal and Conservative approaches 23
Liberal approach 129, 234
Liberal base 249-50
Liberal counterpoint, defined 297
Liberal country 167

Liberal democracy 167, 174, 202
Liberal Democrat constitution 336, 364
Liberal Democrat election performance 337
Liberal Democrat image 239
Liberal Democrat initiatives 222
Liberal Democrat leadership 72, 285, 297
Liberal Democrat leadership election 294
Liberal Democrat MPs 39, 71, 73, 88, 131, 200, 207-8, 210, 306, 320, 329
Liberal Democrat opposition 87, 174
Liberal Democrat Parliamentary performance 200
Liberal Democrat policy 168, 236
Liberal Democrat selection 153
Liberal Democrat support 84, 112
Liberal Democrats 3-5, 39-43, 68-72, 74-7, 82-91, 108-14, 116-23, 152-7, 203-11, 218-26, 238-43, 258-63, 304-12, 342-5, 356-65
  General election 86
  Voting 26, 111, 365
Liberal movement 22-4, 26, 28-30, 69, 99, 107-8, 148, 160, 166, 168, 173, 196, 211, 257, 294
  Traditional 142, 166, 171
Liberal party 3, 17, 28, 31, 187, 198, 201, 212
Liberal values 43, 141, 169-71, 174
Liberal Vision 233, 296-7, 301-2, 356

429

Liberalism 21, 25, 29, 31-2, 71, 106-7, 126-7, 140, 150-1, 160, 170-1, 174-5, 254, 259-60, 287-8
  Modern 12, 14
  Traditional 163, 278-9
Liberals 5, 15-17, 20-7, 30-1, 43, 60, 63, 77, 106-8, 110-11, 135-6, 173-4, 208, 212-13, 231
  Traditional 21, 26, 184
Liberals in Parliament and Local Government 15
Libertarian 126, 175, 180, 252, 268, 278-9, 287, 295-7, 299-300
Local authorities 23, 98, 141, 201, 206-8, 260-1, 269
Local elections 57, 96, 102-3, 116, 122-3, 150, 189, 199-200, 207, 215, 237, 294, 304-5, 319, 366
Local government 15, 36, 153, 200, 202, 208-10, 215, 236, 357, 359
Local government base 37, 39, 203, 206, 208, 212, 315, 362
Local government by-elections 96
Local government seats 200, 319
Local government strength 196, 321, 340
Lone parents 136, 139
Losses 42-3, 56, 61, 96, 103-4, 117, 125, 151-2, 188, 199-200, 209-11, 288, 290, 305, 318-20
  Net 42, 97, 99, 101

M

Majority, simple 107, 109, 115, 325
Majority government 321, 330
Manifesto 32-3, 35, 80, 249-50, 289, 347
Marshall 127-8, 130, 133, 139, 144
MCB (see Muslim council of Britain)
Media 30-1, 39-40, 56, 61, 66, 69, 72, 111, 117, 144, 167, 176, 244, 273, 350-1
  National 156, 344-5
Membership 27, 32, 45, 47, 49, 53, 89, 126, 140-1, 143, 147, 151, 156, 179, 310
Ministers 46, 82, 131, 157, 178, 208, 213, 235-6, 248, 273, 323, 331, 350, 353-4, 357
Money 82, 111, 156, 201, 204-5, 253-4, 263, 272, 343
Motion 167, 212, 324, 330
  No-confidence 324-5
Muscular Christianity 161-2, 166-7, 169, 171, 174-5, 262
Muscular liberalism 19, 128, 150, 157, 159-76, 210, 236, 238, 259, 261, 280, 286, 297, 312, 354
Muscular Liberalism 161, 163, 165, 167, 169, 171, 173, 175
Muslim Council of Britain 164
Muslims 163, 165, 167

N

National Liberal Club 173, 342
National Liberals 72, 315
Negative campaigning 52, 239, 241-5, 252, 349, 359
Negotiations 5, 72-4, 114

Index

New Labour 27, 153, 162
Next general election 6-7, 44, 96, 101, 120, 160, 189, 203, 289, 315-19, 333, 337-40, 350, 352-3, 367
Non-interventionist 295-7, 299-300
Non-Orange Bookers 57, 131, 208
Nuclear Power 137

O

Offenders 135, 258
Orange Book 45-6, 49-52, 58-9, 126-9, 130-4, 137-40, 142-6, 150-1, 154-7, 162, 207-8, 257, 63, 276-80, 291-2, 297-300, 302-3, 331-2
Orange Book and Britain 58, 131-2, 233
Orange Book faction 126, 280
Orange Book leadership 57, 70, 139, 148, 155, 174, 281, 294, 298-9, 303, 306, 333
Orange Book Liberal Democrats 162
Orange Book volumes 131, 139, 141
Orange Booker 46, 132, 226, 303, 332
Orange Bookers 4, 6-7, 58-9, 79, 88, 131-3, 139-40, 142-3, 147-50, 155-7, 207-9, 226-7, 233-4, 276-81, 297-300
Organisation 7, 32, 77, 157, 164, 171, 202, 204, 214-15, 245, 275-6, 292, 315, 356, 359-62
Osborne, George 65 69, 74, 162, 240-1

P

Paddick, Brian 153-5, 157
Parents 19, 76, 82, 136-7, 147
Parliament 3, 12-15, 36-7, 40-1, 50-1, 56, 58, 63, 76-7, 87, 105-7, 206-8, 210-11, 276-7, 309-11
Parliamentary seats 6, 46, 108, 153, 200, 202, 208, 242, 319, 328, 358
Partnership 26, 90, 151, 251, 260, 285, 287, 304-5, 314, 317, 322, 337, 339
Party leaders 34, 67, 133, 208, 286, 294, 306, 314, 335, 338
Party members 48-9, 152, 180, 342
Performance 34, 50, 67-8, 72, 79, 82, 95, 99, 101, 143, 185, 203, 207, 225, 292-3
Personal liberties 258, 264-5, 270
Personality 127, 229-32, 234, 236-7, 239, 359-60
Pledge 87-9, 149-50, 188, 240, 250, 259, 288-9, 299
Policies 21, 23, 86-7, 148-50, 168, 218, 221-4, 235-7, 247-55, 257-61, 265-7, 269-73, 298-9, 359-60, 365-6
  Drug 270
  Individual 140, 237, 358
  Liberal 166, 299
  Social 169, 233, 252, 297, 299, 303
Policy agenda 238, 247, 273, 276, 360
Policymaking 58, 249-50, 252, 343

Political movements 106, 234
Polls 5, 47, 56-7, 68, 70, 96-7, 99, 101-2, 117, 120-1, 123, 126, 178-9, 325, 328-9
Population 14, 17, 39, 85, 188, 254-5, 259, 261
Poverty 19, 21, 27, 52, 187, 254-5, 358, 363
Power 3-4, 12-15, 24, 29, 75-7, 112-14, 131, 139-40, 209-10, 213-14, 249-50, 276, 303-4, 334, 362-3
Precept 204, 206
President 75, 179, 181, 184-5, 209, 278, 362
Prime Minister 19, 34-5, 60-2, 67, 72, 77-9, 85, 163, 169, 232, 238-9, 260, 283, 324, 332-3
   Roles of Deputy 314, 320, 327, 360, 362, 365
Prohibition 251, 264, 271-2, 297

Q

Quadrants 295, 299-300
   Right 296-7, 299-300

R

Reclaiming Liberalism 4, 126, 129, 174
Referendum 5, 76-7, 81, 104, 112, 115-17, 119-20, 125, 151, 177, 185, 209, 289, 334
Regulation 64-5
Representation, parliamentary 37, 39, 42, 70, 363
Resign 47, 314, 316-17, 321, 323, 333, 340

Resignation 30, 51, 66, 95, 99, 141, 146, 293, 317, 321, 323, 326, 332-3, 337
Reversals 3-4, 44, 89, 95, 200, 353, 355
Risk 1, 19, 59, 64, 111-12, 119, 132, 168, 214, 234-5, 243, 247-8, 251-2, 258, 333
Roles 38, 131, 144, 153-4, 165, 171, 180-1, 189, 201, 213, 230, 276-7, 333, 335-8, 357

S

Scenarios 143, 262, 264, 309, 313, 315-16, 319, 322-3, 326, 328, 330, 332, 334-5, 340
   Unlikely 307, 326
Schools 19-20, 65, 76, 82, 84, 134, 164
Scotland 51, 99, 104, 223, 329, 334
Scottish Nationalist Party see SNP
Scottish Parliament 99-100, 102, 223, 237
Scrapping Government Offices 81, 84
Seats 6-7, 36-9, 42-4, 55-7, 60-1, 70-2, 95-102, 108-10, 112-14, 199, 204-7, 209-12, 307-8, 319-20, 329
   By-election 205
   Constituency 100, 319
   Individual Lib Dem-held 102
   Local authority 284, 363-4
   Lost 71, 104, 343
   New 70, 98, 352
   Target 70, 199, 215

Index

Services 24, 197, 207, 209, 242, 256, 283
  Financial 64-5
Sheffield 34, 102, 104, 200
Signatories 46
Smith, John 36
SNP (Scottish Nationalist Party) 99-100, 108, 223, 225, 236, 334
Social Liberal Forum 296-7, 300-2, 304
Society 15, 17, 20, 22-3, 26, 76, 141, 149, 164-5, 187, 218, 220, 230, 251, 253
  Liberal 128, 170, 187, 250, 264-5, 270
Speech 14, 17, 22, 40, 77, 82, 147, 150, 160, 168-9, 173-4, 179-80, 184-5, 188, 265
  Free 167, 169, 175
Split 17, 47, 74, 190, 309, 314, 327, 333, 337-9, 360, 367
State 13, 20, 27, 32, 43, 59, 65, 80, 129, 135, 256-7, 264-5, 269-70, 272, 295
Steel, David 285
Student movement 87-8
Succession 292, 294, 312-13, 327
Succession Scenarios 305-6, 313, 315, 317, 319, 321, 323, 325, 327, 329, 331, 333, 335, 337, 339
Summit 1-3, 5, 195, 350, 367-8
Swinson, Jo 130-1

T

Tax rate 148, 181
Tax threshold 80, 83, 85, 148, 150
Taxes 18, 21, 69, 76, 138, 182, 219, 223, 249, 254-5, 257, 263, 298, 345
  Top rate of 22, 219, 254
Tenure 39, 42, 48, 50, 61, 71, 101, 337, 340
Thatcher, Margaret 22, 28, 62-3, 72, 237
Thinking
  Conservative 20, 142, 160
  Liberal 16, 160, 261, 270
Tories 21, 23-5, 34-6, 42-4, 85-6, 96-9, 173-4, 183, 190-1, 220-1, 304-7, 321-7, 329-31, 334, 336-9
Tory-Lib Dem coalition 306, 317, 322
Tuffrey, Mike 154-5
Tuition fees 73-4, 88, 117, 184, 236, 250, 259, 279, 288-90, 311

U

U-turn 64-5, 87, 147, 188, 236, 250, 288, 290, 309, 311
UK Independence Party see UKIP
UKIP (UK Independence Party) 91, 175, 210, 221, 328

V

VAT 74, 86-7, 138-9
Violence 88, 167-8, 170, 172, 174
Violent extremism 169-70, 172
Violent extremists 170-1
Vision 70, 172, 212, 215, 217-18, 251, 287, 350, 357-8, 361
Voters, former Lib Dem 221, 327
Votes 24-5, 36, 55, 62-3, 69-71,

86-91, 98-101, 106-9, 111-16, 152-3, 210-12, 305-6, 310-12, 330-1, 334
Real 95-6, 101-2
Tactical Labour 305-6
Total 107
Wasted 111-12

W

Wales 88, 99-100, 104, 116, 327-9
Wealth 18, 22, 141, 253, 255, 257
Wealthy 14-15, 17, 219, 223, 254
Webb Steve, 129, 135-7, 139, 346
Welfare state 15, 18, 256, 353
Welsh Assembly 100, 102, 225, 319
Wind-Cowie, Max 162-4, 166
Winner 68, 107, 115, 155
Winning 7, 26, 37, 66, 71, 102, 106, 109, 152-3, 155, 189, 205-6, 215, 260, 358
World 3, 56, 63, 83, 146, 161-2, 177, 191, 248, 260, 262, 290, 323, 347